DIVINE UTTERANCES

DIVINE UTTERANCES

THE PERFORMANCE OF AFRO-CUBAN SANTERÍA

KATHERINE J. HAGEDORN

SMITHSONIAN INSTITUTION PRESS
Washington and London

COPY EDITOR: Gregory McNamee
PRODUCTION EDITOR: Duke Johns
DESIGNER: Amber Frid-Jimenez

Library of Congress Cataloging-in-Publication Data
Hagedorn, Katherine J.
Divine utterances : the performance of Afro-Cuban Santería /
Katherine J. Hagedorn.
p.   cm.
Includes bibliographical references (p.) and index.
Discography: p.
Filmography: p.
ISBN 1-56098-922-X (alk. paper)—
ISBN 1-56098-947-5 (pbk. : alk. paper)
1. Santería music—History and criticism.   2. Blacks—Cuba—
Music—History and criticism.   I. Title.
ML3565 .H34   2001
781.7′96—dc21   2001020698

British Library Cataloguing-in-Publication Data available

Manufactured in the United States of America
08 07 06 05 04 03 02 01   5 4 3 2 1

For my parents, and for Peter, with love

CONTENTS

FIGURES

RECORDED TRACKS

The following recorded musical examples, mentioned in order in the text, are included on the CD accompanying this book.

TRACK 1. Lázaro Ros sings "Bara su ayo" for Eleguá **49**
Source: Conjunto Folklórico Nacional de Cuba, *Música Yoruba* (1996), Bembé CD 2010-2; used with kind permission.

TRACK 2. Felipe Alfonso sings "Aye le o" for Changó **51**
Source: Conjunto Folklórico Nacional de Cuba, *Música Yoruba* (1996), Bembé CD 2010-2; used with kind permission.

TRACK 3. Zenaida Armenteros sings "Yemayá Asesú" for Yemayá **53**
Source: Conjunto Folklórico Nacional de Cuba, *Música Yoruba* (1996), Bembé CD 2010-2; used with kind permission.

TRACK 4. Lázaro Ros and Zenaida Armenteros sing songs for Oyá **54**
Source: Conjunto Folklórico Nacional de Cuba, *Música Yoruba* (1996), Bembé CD 2010-2; used with kind permission.

TRACK 5. Alberto's group sings for Eleguá **74**
Source: Alberto Villarreal and his group, featuring Alberto Villarreal, Maykel Villarreal, May Villarreal, Ramiro Pedroso, and friends and neighbors. Recorded with permission for scholarly use in December 1999 in Santos Suárez, Cuba, by Katherine Hagedorn; engineered by Joseph Brennan.

and neighbors. Recorded with permission for scholarly use in December 1999 in Santos Suárez, Cuba, by Katherine Hagedorn; engineered by Joseph Brennan.

TRACK 17. Alberto's group performs a Havana-style rhythmic invocation for Ogún **125**

Source: Alberto Villarreal and his group, featuring Alberto Villarreal, Maykel Villarreal, May Villarreal, Ramiro Pedroso, and friends and neighbors. Recorded with permission for scholarly use in December 1999 in Santos Suárez, Cuba, by Katherine Hagedorn; engineered by Joseph Brennan.

TRACK 18. Alberto's group performs a Havana-style rhythmic invocation for Ochosi **125**

Source: Alberto Villarreal and his group, featuring Alberto Villarreal, Maykel Villarreal, May Villarreal, Ramiro Pedroso, and friends and neighbors. Recorded with permission for scholarly use in December 1999 in Santos Suárez, Cuba, by Katherine Hagedorn; engineered by Joseph Brennan.

TRACK 19. Francisco's group performs a Matanzas-style invocation for Ogún **125**

Source: Francisco Aguabella and his group, featuring Francisco Aguabella, Lázaro Galarraga, Joe Addington, Lealon Martínez, Skip Burnett, and others. Recorded with permission for scholarly use in September 2000 in Pasadena, California, by Joseph Brennan; engineered by Joseph Brennan.

TRACK 20. Francisco's group performs a Matanzas-style invocation for Ochosi **125**

Source: Francisco Aguabella and his group, featuring Francisco Aguabella, Lázaro Galarraga, Joe Addington, Lealon Martínez, Skip Burnett, and others. Recorded with permission for scholarly use in September 2000 in Pasadena, California, by Joseph Brennan; engineered by Joseph Brennan.

ACKNOWLEDGMENTS

I am grateful for the support and inspiration I have received from my family, friends, teachers, colleagues, and a great many institutions during the researching and writing of this book. I thank five people, whose fieldwork and writing I admire most, for their critical and essential comments on various drafts of the book: Theodore Levin for his valuable observations and keen editorial suggestions; Michelle Kisliuk for her sharp and timely insights about the book as a whole, and particularly about chapter 4; David H. Brown for his detailed and well-documented comments throughout the manuscript, which improved the book immensely; and Raúl Fernández and Michael Mason, who read three drafts of the manuscript, commenting diligently and thoughtfully on each, thereby helping move the book toward completion. I also benefited from Peter Manuel's thoughtful and detailed critique of the manuscript in its early stages. I am grateful to Joseph Brennan for helping me use Finale to notate my musical transcription, and for helping me to transform my field recordings into an earworthy compact disc.

I thank Pomona College for providing a year of academic leave (the Steele Leave) in 1998–1999, during which I wrote the first draft of the book. I am also grateful to Pomona College for awarding me three additional travel grants, after I finished my dissertation in 1995, for research in Cuba in summer 1997, winter 1999, and winter 2000. I sincerely appreciate the invitation to present a paper at the University of Miami's annual conference on religion in Cuba, which helped facilitate another field trip to Cuba in fall 1998.

I am very grateful to Scott Mahler—acquisitions editor at the Smithsonian Institution Press, descendant of Gustav, and accomplished musician in his own right—for his unfailing encouragement of my work. I am also grateful to Gregory McNamee, whose sensitive and deft copy editing has greatly clarified the manuscript, as well as to managing editor Duke Johns for expertly guiding the book through the long publication process. Cuban intellectual extraordinaire Raul Fernández supported the book and many other related projects with his insightful suggestions and continual good humor from beginning to end. Ernesto Pichardo Plá, Michael A. Mason, and David H. Brown are brilliant scholar-practitioners who are renovating the face of Afro-Cuban religious studies, and I have benefited greatly from their friendship and guidance.

To Alberto Villarreal Peñalver, Zoraida García, and their children May and Maykel I owe perhaps the largest debt of gratitude. If not for Alberto and Zoraida, much of this book could not have been written. Alberto was my first *batá* instructor, a patient teacher in all ways, and my main contact in the Conjunto Folklórico Nacional de Cuba. Zoraida, Alberto's wife, became my friend and confidante, my *oyugbona,* and my *madrina.* I thank them for their generous friendship, integrity, and constancy.

I thank Francisco Aguabella for being my drum teacher these past five years, providing me with the unique opportunity to learn *batá* and other Afro-Cuban drumming styles from an undisputed master drummer. Through these lessons, I have learned how to be patient with others as well as with myself, how to overcome difficulties, and how to learn.

Some of the ideas for the book arose from my doctoral dissertation, which I began in 1989 and completed in 1995. The five years that succeeded the completion of my dissertation built on my initial years of fieldwork in important ways, and I wish to thank the individuals and organizations who made this preliminary research possible. The Center for Cuban Studies provided the vehicle for my first research trip to Cuba in 1989 and has been an invaluable source of help and information ever since. An arts grant from the Antonio Cirino Fellowhip program in 1990 encouraged me to focus on the ideas of source and variation in performance. A well-timed research grant from the Ford Foundation in 1991 allowed me to establish invaluable relationships with teachers, friends, and colleagues in Havana. A generous travel grant from Pomona College in 1994 provided me the opportunity to confirm my field information and renew my contacts in Havana after a two-year absence.

My intellectual and emotional debts to friends and teachers in the United States and in Cuba are enormous. In the United States, I thank all my teachers at Tufts University, The Johns Hopkins University, and Brown University. In particular, I thank David Maxwell, Wayne Smith, and Carlos Moore for their timely encouragement of my research. I offer special thanks to all of my teachers at Brown University, especially Carol Babiracki, Judit Frigyesi, Michelle Kisliuk, Jeff Titon, William Beeman, and Andrew Schloss, all of whom helped shape my initial fieldwork and research interests.

In Cuba, I thank current and former members of the Conjunto Folklórico Nacional de Cuba, the Cuban Academy of Sciences, the Centro para la Investigación del Desarrollo de la Música Cubana (CIDMUC), the Museo Nacional de la Música Cubana, and the managers and employees of the *casas estudiantíles*. I thank Rogelio Martínez Furé for granting me two substantive interviews and for sharing his considerable knowledge of Cuba's African-based performance traditions. I am continually grateful to Rafael L. López Valdés for sharing his encyclopedic knowledge of Cuba's African origins so generously, and I thank him and his family for their invaluable friendship and hospitality. I am grateful to María Teresa Linares and her late husband Argeliers León for opening their home to me in 1990, and I thank María Teresa and her family for their enduring friendship in the years following our first meeting. I thank Ramiro Guerra, Carlos Aldama Pérez, and Lázaro Ros for their valuable insights about the early days of the Conjunto Folklórico. I am grateful to Leonardo Acosta and his wife Margarita for their longstanding intellectual and social companionship.

I offer sincere thanks to the members of the U.S. Interests Section in Cuba who were living in Havana from 1989 through 1994. In particular, I thank Alan and Beverly Flanigan, Dianne and Jim Basso, Lisa Bobbie Schreiber Hughes, Nancy Jackson, and Allen and Haruko Greenberg, all of whom befriended me, fed me, comforted me, and sheltered me at crucial moments in my research.

In addition to the friends I made as a direct result of my research in Havana, I also made friends outside of my research, and those friendships have become invaluable to me. Orlando Rivero Valdés and Elba Capote have been especially generous, supportive, and good-humored in their friendship and made Havana feel like home.

Special friends and family members who were not always directly related to the writing process, but who kept me emotionally and intellectually present and balanced, include Barry Altschul, Elliott Bloom, Flora Bloom, Lisa Bloom, Sam Borinsky, Kenneth Bowman, Steven Cornelius, Phyllis Cunningham, Esme, Nancy Page Fernández, Thomas Flaherty, Cynthia Fogg, the members of Gamelan Sekar Jaya, Martha Hagedorn-Krass, Nora Howard, Beth Jenner, Chris Krass, Jenifer Krass, Loca, Mardi Louiselle, Bernie Lubell, Ellen Maly, Fulgencio Marín,

Nicholas Stauffer Mason, Lydia Matthews, Justin Mongosso, William Peterson, Roddey Reid, Patricia Repar, Robert Riddell, Julia Simon, Steven Simon, Barbara Stauffer, Wayne Vitale, Margaret Waller, and Sarah Willner.

As should be evident by now, I have been the lucky beneficiary of both intellectual and emotional guidance during the writing of this book, and I believe that the best parts of this work are due in large part to this marvelously supportive network of friends, family, and colleagues. Writing this book has deepened my interest in Afro-Cuban folkloric and religious performance, and has pointed me toward additional areas of research that I hope to pursue in the future.

Finally, I offer heartfelt and ongoing gratitude to Peter Bloom for his enduring love, unwavering support, critical eye, and unflagging sense of humor during the long and arduous process of thinking, writing, reviewing, editing, and revising. I remain deeply grateful to my parents, Fred B. Hagedorn and Grace A. Hagedorn, without whose love and support I could not have begun to build the mountain. *Maferefun gbogbo oricha. Echu odara, moyuba o! Yalorde Ochún, mo dupe o!*

INTRODUCTION

Rhythms of desire, rhythms of renewal: It is the rhythm, that dense, beckoning texture that fills the spaces of my emptiness, never the same way twice. The *batá* drums make a fat, heavy sound, like raindrops on roof tiles; the wooden *claves* arrive with a sudden, insistent crack, a clean break through a window. The dense pops of the three *batá* drums nudge me playfully: Sassy *itótele* talks back to bossy *iyá*, even as little *okónkolo* worries, *ki ha, ki ha, ki ha*—and soon my skin, ears, mouth, and hands respond to the rhythmic calls: *"Ago Eleguá abukenke"*—make way for Eleguá, make way ...

DRUMSTRUCK

When I was in my second year of graduate school at Brown University, in 1988, trudging back and forth between class and my grimy two-room apartment, fighting the dull wind and cold rain of Providence, Rhode Island, I saw a poster for a group called Orlando "Puntilla" de los Ríos y Nueva Generación. They advertised themselves as an Afro-Cuban folkloric ensemble from New York, and they were to perform in October—a cold, gray month; I was already interested because of the heat and color the poster promised. The enlarged photo of the group was dominated by reds and yellows, the colors of fire. Puntilla was playing a two-headed drum across his knees, moving his hands in an orange blur, while dancers extended their legs and arms in an arc, dressed in crimson and gold outfits, their pointy crowns perched precariously atop their heads. Warmth, percussive sound, color—I longed to be near these dancing, outrageously dressed people, and to hear that drum.

The concert was held in the unlikely venue of the staid Alumni Hall at Brown University, on a stage meant for concert bands and school choirs. Putty-colored folding chairs were set up sixty deep and thirty across in the large space below the stage. By 7:45, the room was jam-packed with people, and the concert hadn't started yet. Had these people already heard of Puntilla and his new generation? Or, like me, were they simply starved for color, light, and sound? At about 8:15 three drummers walked on stage, followed by two dancers. From the moment the drummers struck their instruments, I was stunned. Each delicate stroke seemed to hit my solar plexus, and I was immediately embarrassed lest anyone guess how intimately I was experiencing the sound. I could not breathe normally, because the sounds produced by the hands of the drummers on the six drum heads were tickling my internal organs. I remained glued to my seat, barely moving, for the first part of the concert. At intermission, released from the spell, I got up and walked outside in the cold, grateful that I could once again breathe normally and move my limbs. I did not experience the second half of the concert as intensely as the first, and I don't remember much about it. But I do know that the first part of that concert compelled me to find out as much as I could about Afro-Cuban folkloric ensembles, how folkloric music might be related to religious music, the role of the mesmerizing double-headed batá drums, and how I could travel to Cuba to hear more.

After some difficult negotiations, I secured a ticket, and in July 1989, after waiting in line with about sixty other people at the unmarked gate of Miami International Airport, I boarded an early morning charter flight to José Martí International Airport in Havana. In the eleven years since, I have gone to Havana once every year or two. This fact surprises me, because I often feel as though I am still in the early 1990s, not yet done with my dissertation; still enduring the lean years of the *período especial económico* with my friends; taking lessons with master *batá* drummer Alberto Villarreal; going to drumming ceremonies for the first time; not yet "knowing" about Cuba. When I went that first time, all I really knew about Cuba, deep down in the pit of my stomach, was that I needed to hear the sound of its *batá* drums. I needed to feel tickled and then paralyzed again by those tender pops and deep strokes, to process this singular acoustic message.

But I could never recreate fully the sensations of that first time. Even when I heard the *batá* drums in religious contexts (instead of in the ubiquitous folkloric ensemble),[1] I could not simply sit down in a folding chair and let myself be taken by them. As I moved through the crowds of religious practitioners and onlookers, I would occasionally feel the twitch of a rib, the light convulsing of a stomach muscle. But never again was I fully paralyzed by the music. I began to know too much, to listen too carefully. (Why is he playing Ochosi's rhythm for Ogún? Why did she switch to the *"Ide were were nita Ochún"* song so soon?) But every now and then, when I'm not aware, I feel the beginnings of willful paralysis, the drum strokes like tiny feet dancing on my solar plexus, my body caught in a shower of rhythmic raindrops—and it happens for a few seconds, that ecstatic convergence of body and sound.

LEARNING THE SACRED OUTSIDE-IN

This book explores the encoding of the sacred in Afro-Cuban performance. As such, it deals with the complex interrelationship between race and religion in Cuba, and with the political and aesthetic issues that inform that relationship. The Conjunto Folklórico Nacional de Cuba (CFNC), Cuba's premier folkloric performance troupe, serves as a case study—what ethnographer Renato Rosaldo calls a "busy intersection" (Rosaldo 1989)—for examining how constructions of race, the politics of prerevolutionary and postrevolutionary Cuba, and contemporary practices of Santería and folklore have defined the possibilities for Afro-Cuban performance in Cuba.

The book is also, in large part, the result of my own gradual understanding of the sacred in Afro-Cuban performance. When I began my fieldwork, I learned that the *batá* drums as well as their language—those pops, strokes, and hisses—were crucial in effecting *oricha* possession in Santería religious performances. It was somewhat later that I learned that the *batá* drums usually did not speak unless spoken to (by a lead prayer-singer, or *akpwón*), except in the small private drum ceremony (the instrumental *oru seco,* without song) that precedes every *toque de santo* (Santería drumming ceremony). And, later still, I learned that women were deeply discouraged from playing the *batá* drums in religious contexts.

It was during my first field trip to Cuba that I began learning about Santería performance "outside in." That is, I learned about the folkloric versions of the songs, rhythms, and dances of Santería before I understood the religious context from which these performance traditions emerged. My preliminary hypothesis was reached even before I began my fieldwork in Cuba: the music of Santería, whether in its folkloric or religious context, was sacred. But then I had to go back through its interlocutors to trace this apparently ubiquitous sacredness. The process, like most retracings, was slow.

I began studying with the Conjunto Folklórico, which, like Puntilla's group, was a folkloric ensemble that devoted itself primarily to performing the repertoire of Cuba's African-based religions in a nonreligious context. During the first several years of my intermittent fieldwork (three months during one year, two months during another, and then a four-month bonanza thanks to an unexpectedly successful request for a scientific visa), I attended all but three performances of the Conjunto Folklórico that took place during those months. During the summer of 1992, I signed up for the Conjunto Folklórico's prestigious FolkCuba workshop, a two-week intensive course aimed at teaching non-Cubans the rudiments of Afro-Cuban music and dance, including *rumba* songs, rhythms, and dances; Santería songs, rhythms, and dances; and more popular dances, such as Cuban *salsa* and *casino*. As I immersed myself in the group's performances, I was gradually able to situate the sounds of the *batá* drums in Cuba within the larger context of rehearsed singing and dancing, and within Cuba's nationalized, historically grounded notion of "folklore."

"Folklore" in Cuba has referred primarily to the religious performance traditions of those people of African heritage who were brought to the island during almost four centuries of the Atlantic slave trade, and secondarily to the apparently secular performance traditions of Cuba's communities of African heritage. What we might think of as the "folk music" of Cuba's nonblack population has been named *música campesina* (peasant music, or farmers' music) by those who have studied it,[2] evoking the politically expedient rural (re)construction of folk traditions so familiar to scholars of nineteenth-century European nationalism (see, e.g., Dorson 1972; Hobsbawm and Ranger 1983; see also Wilcken 1991).

In Havana, at least from the late nineteenth century to the present, the concept of "Cuban folklore" has been simultaneously racialized and disempowered—racialized because it has come to refer almost exclusively to the religious performance traditions of Cubans of African heritage, and disempowered because those religious traditions were categorized by nonpractitioners not as divinely potent modes of communication between deities and mortals, but rather as "folk traditions," objectified and reconstructed without consideration for their contemporary religious context. As I attended and participated in the rehearsals and performances of the Conjunto Folklórico, I learned about the postrevolutionary genesis of the group in 1962, and about those founding members who had been investigating and reconstructing Afro-Cuban religious performance long before the 1959 revolution.

I began interviewing some of the surviving founders of the Conjunto Folklórico, many of whom were now in their seventies and eighties, as well as some of the troupe's current administrators and performers. The earliest performers of the troupe were called "informant performers" because they contributed not only their performative skills to the ensemble but also the religious "source material" that made the staged representations of these ceremonies possible. I found out about the revolutionary context of the group's establishment, the mandate of the ensemble, and the historical precedents for the group (such as the public staging of *batá* drumming in 1936 and 1937 by the prolific and ubiquitous Cuban scholar Fernando Ortíz, the grandfather of the Conjunto Folklórico), as well as past and present principles of rehearsal and staging. In 1992, my third year of fieldwork, I began taking *batá* drumming lessons from Alberto Villarreal, the lead percussionist of the Folklórico and a well-respected ceremonial drummer. With Alberto, I began attending more *toques de santo,* and I gradually increased my own involvement in Santería.

The year after I began my drum lessons with Alberto, I completed the first step of initiation into Santería by receiving the *collares* (ritual necklaces) from my *padrino* (godfather) in Washington, D.C. The following year, I received the *guerreros* (the four warrior deities of Santería), a ritual marker that signifies a deepening commitment to the practice of Santería and is commonly considered to be the second step of initiation. In 1997, several years after having received the *guerreros,* I received Ochún (my patron *oricha*), an intermediary step that sometimes obviates initiation into the priesthood of Santería, known as making *ocha* or making *santo.* Several previous divinations in 1993, 1994, and 1997 had suggested that I might have to make *santo;* after I received Ochún, I requested another divination, which, to my dismay, informed me that I would definitely have to do so. No longer willing to postpone the inevitable, in September 1998, at the beginning of a year-long sabbatical, I became initiated into Santería as a priestess of Ochún. My wide-angle lens of folkloric performance had suddenly zoomed in to the close-up focus of personally experienced religious performance.[3]

I was not a spontaneous enthusiast who became initiated after having listened once to a *toque* (typically held in honor of the "birthday" of an *oricha*). Rather, while a long parade of colleagues (in folklore, art history, sociology, religious studies, dance ethnography, and theater) became initiated into Santería, I hung back, my interest tempered with caution, shying away for several years from what appeared to be my religious calling. When I finally became initiated in 1998, it was after several years of indecision, nine years of study, and much trepidation. I came to study the folkloric renditions of these religious traditions first, and only later the religious traditions that inspired them. It has been through the lens of folkloric performances that I have framed *lo religioso,* the religious, and now it is through the lens of religious performance that I frame *lo folklórico,* the folk-loric.

These dual perspectives have clarified for me the interplay between religious and folkloric Afro-Cuban performance. Both involve and invoke aspects of the sa-cred. What is sacred in Afro-Cuban performance is the connection of utterances—created and received, gestural and musical—to constructs of the divine. This relationship is determined by intent, which in turn is negotiated among all the participants in the performance, whether they are the audience members and mu-sicians at a folkloric performance or the ritual assistants and priests at a religious ceremony. Sacred and secular inform each other, use each other, and in fact in-habit the same sphere of sacred intent. It is this sphere of sacred intent that moti-vates this book's central inquiry.

PERFORMING SANTERÍA: RELIGIOUS FOLKLORE, TOURISM, AND SCHOLARSHIP

The performative sequence at the beginning of chapter 3—from mimetic moon-walk to possession performance—distills this primary theme into its most fo-cused manifestation: the blurred boundaries of what folkloric and ceremonial percussionist Alberto would call his "work" and his "religion"; the worlds that Afro-Cuban religious performance creates and inhabits in postrevolutionary Cuba. The book explores the power of Afro-Cuban religious performance in its various guises: why, for example, folkloric or touristic representations of religious ceremonies can cause certain audience members to go into trance as readily as their religious counterparts; how Afro-Cuban sacred performance (in religious and folkloric contexts) is used to resolve some of the difficulties of daily life in Cuba; and why both religious and folkloric performance are vying for the top po-sition as the major draw for Cuba's burgeoning tourist trade. Cuba's African-based religious performance traditions now represent not only spiritual power but also, increasingly, social and economic power. Folkloric into religious, sacred into popular—the contexts of Afro-Cuban performance blend and blur, igniting "folklore," entrancing tourists, enriching practitioners.[4]

In Cuba, the compelling dramas and possibilities of Santería's ceremonies have inspired an increase in the number of initiations of priests and priestesses, as well as a concurrent and concomitant increase in tourist revenue as a result of the renaissance in religious practice. Outside of Cuba, in places such as the United States, Mexico, and Venezuela, Santería is gradually taking its place alongside the many so-called New Age religions based on recontextualized Native American rituals. Yet Santería, with its emphasis on blood sacrifice to feed emotionally volatile anthropomorphic deities, stands apart. Most of its adherents consider their devotion to the religion a lifelong commitment, requiring the daily, heavy responsibility of participating in and defending their religious practices. The norms of Santería practice in Cuba determine in large part what happens in Santería outside of Cuba, for practitioners are continually moving across geopolitical borders, despite the recent tragedies of the *balseros* ("boat people"), the decades-long embargo and concomitant absurdities of the Helms-Burton Act, the travesty of Elián González, and the limited possibilities of the United States' millennial gesture of "opening" (baseball games and educational exchange programs) toward Cuba.

Postrevolutionary Cuban Santería has had its most public appraisal in the form of a folkloric, aestheticized version of itself, performed by the Conjunto Folklórico Nacional de Cuba. The state-sponsored troupe was founded in 1962, a few years after the 1959 revolution, and seemed to map the future of Afro-Cuban performance in Cuba. It began presenting folkloric performances of Afro-Cuban religious rituals, based on the renditions provided by older religious practitioners who were initially considered informants, and who later became performers with the troupe. Although the CFNC also presented highly stylized versions of other Cuban performance traditions—such as the *rumba* and the *comparsa*—it was best known for its spectacular renditions of Afro-Cuban religious rituals, specifically, the songs and dances of Santería.

For the next two decades, *grupos folklóricos,* led by the flagship Conjunto Folklórico, seemed to define most of the public possibilities of Afro-Cuban religious performance in Cuba. In 1989, however, the political and economic infrastructures of the former Soviet Union collapsed, and by the end of 1990 Russian support for the Cuban economy had all but vanished, ushering in Cuba's *período especial económico.* The disappointing sugar harvest could not pay Cuba's debts, and the revived cigar market, though growing, was not likely to balance Cuba's massive trade deficit. Cuba's nascent pharmaceutical industry had been dependent on Soviet support, and it offered no promise of becoming a viable source of future income. Tourism seemed to be the only industry that could consistently satisfy the requirements of a struggling Cuba: it was self-sustaining, it relied on Cuba's most abundant natural resources (sun, beaches, tropical climate, easily romanticized culture, warm and humorous people), and there was a long historical precedent for it (R. Schwartz 1997). Even as the crisis of the special economic period wanes, tourism promises to play an important role in Cuba's future.

In his book *Cuba y el turismo,* Alberto Pozo Fernández points out that until 1990 about 85 percent of Cuba's foreign trade was with the former socialist countries of Eastern Europe (Pozo Fernández 1993:5), and that a quick solution to replenish this income was essential to prevent Cuba from disintegrating economically. In 1989, he adds, tourism had already brought in US$260 million to Cuba, and in the early 1990s key members of the Cuban Central Committee agreed that tourism was to be a primary focus of the post-Soviet Cuban economy. In 1991, the tourist industry brought in US$400 million, and in 1992 Cuba earned approximately US$600 million from tourism (Pozo Fernández 1993:2). The goal for 1995 earnings from tourism was US$1 billion, although no statistics were available to confirm the goal at the time of this writing. These figures are important because they show both definitive and potential growth in income in an area that can be controlled mainly by Cuban planning efforts; specifically, by emphasizing certain types of tourism. According to Pozo Fernández, tourism related to health, conventions, outdoor recreation, and culture remain Cuba's most viable options for increasing tourist revenues. Pozo Fernández specifically mentions the Conjunto Folklórico as one of the cultural institutions that constitutes a big draw for Cuba's tourist industry (1993:135). His argument is that the CFNC has reached a high level of cultural development, which helps to set Cuba apart from other comparable Caribbean tourist destinations.

Because the Conjunto Folklórico is seen to represent a pinnacle of cultural development, other folkloric and touristic forms of Afro-Cuban religious performance benefit from tourism as well. Since the mid-1980s, Afro-Cuban floor shows have become ubiquitous in most Cuban tourist hotels. Performative themes range from the anthropomorphic dramatization of a few of the major deities of Santería, a brief dance narrative of the *rumba guaguancó,* to a Tropicana-like cabaret extravaganza that refers to several African-based religious traditions simultaneously, through the choreographed use of sequined, color-coded costumes and shiny facsimiles of ritual objects (e.g., a small hatchet, a fan, a fly whisk), all wrapped in colored foil or adorned with streamers. Some of the more serious folkloric ensembles that sprang up in Cuba during the 1970s and 1980s, such as Grupo AfroCuba de Matanzas, have complained that these floor shows trivialize the importance of the Afro-Cuban contribution to Cuba's national cultural heritage. But those same groups acknowledge that the floor shows probably account in part for the recent increase in their own audiences, and for the growing popularity of Afro-Cuban culture throughout the rest of the country, as well as beyond its borders.

In addition, because practitioners of Afro-Cuban religions were persecuted for most of the history of the prerevolutionary Cuban Republic, the Castro government's recent attempts to reach out to the leaders of these religions have been met with guarded enthusiasm. Indeed, during the early years of the revolution, according to recent interviews with older practitioners of Santería and Palo Monte, it was common for black Cubans on their way to religious ceremonies to be stopped by the local police, verbally and physically harassed, and then "liberated" of the birds, foodstuffs, and ritual objects they carried with them (see Fernández Robaina 1997). This harassment continued well into the 1980s, despite the various government-sponsored research projects focusing on the performance and material culture of African-based religious traditions in Cuba, all of which relied on contemporaneous fieldwork. Beginning in the early 1990s, several high-ranking and well-respected priests of Ifá, Santería, and Palo Monte became involved with government-sponsored tours to Cuba for foreigners who want to become initiated into Santería. These tours, called Ochaturs and *santurismo*[5] by Cubans who perceive the many layers of irony in a Marxist government's sponsoring religious initiations, represent the culmination of the "folkloricization" of Afro-Cuban religious traditions. Despite its early history of persecuting practitioners of Santería and other African-based religions under the auspices of its policy of scientific atheism, the Castro regime has chosen to support selectively some of Cuba's African-based religious traditions, legalizing certain practitioners and mainstreaming these religions and their adherents into the tourist trade. The folkloricization of Afro-Cuban religious traditions describes a historicized process in which an inward-directed, noncommodified religious tradition becomes outward-directed, commodified, staged, and secularized.[6]

But this is not meant to imply that Santería itself is not already commodified, in the broadest sense of the word. The rituals and necessities of Santería exist within economies of scale; everything in Santería costs money, more or less, depending on the wealth of the ritual practitioner(s) in charge, and depending on the perceived wealth of those for whom the ceremony is performed. An initiation, to use the example of a more expensive ritual, typically costs between US$2,000 and US$3,000 in Cuba for a foreigner, though considerably less for a Cuban national (roughly 10,000 pesos, or US$500, at the current exchange rate of approximately twenty pesos to the dollar).[7] Through the Ochatur system, initiation packages may cost about US$7,000 (or more, depending on the fame and scruples of the Santero, or Santería priest), including airfare, food, lodging before and after the ceremony, and a cut for one of several tourism offices.[8] The economies of exchange of this religion seem to fit comfortably within the larger economic framework of the tourist trade.

THE CONTEXT OF THIS WORK

It is precisely tourism that both reveals and obscures Cuba's performative essence. Tourism takes many forms: the many illegal and legal visits to the island enacted by curious Americans; the sex-tourism embraced by some European businessmen; the avid consumption of books about Santería (now a mainstay in many urban bookstores); the overflowing attendance at any event featuring Cuban music. Accounts of Cuban culture, Cuban music, and Afro-Cuban religions abound in the popular press, as do stories of everyday life in Cuba, along with dire warnings about Cuba's economic and political situation. In the United States during just the last few years, nationwide tours of such popular Cuban bands as Buena Vista Social Club and Irakere have sold out weeks in advance, and in April 1999 the Afro-Cuban All Stars appeared on *A Prairie Home Companion,* the gently satirical barometer of mainstream middle America. The overwhelming success of both groups as well as of Wim Wenders's film *Buena Vista Social Club* has allowed individual band members to sign with major international record labels. The peculiarly American fascination with those parts of the world that are politically and economically off-limits has made Cuban cultural products something of a cult in the United States.

Since the early years of the revolution and culminating with the decade of the 1990s, Afro-Cuban religions such as Santería have been catapulted from the target of both persecution and prosecution to the focus of national pride and the destination of foreign tourism, and with that dramatic shift has come a burgeoning interest in the music and dance of these religious traditions. This book does not attempt to reveal the many details of Afro-Cuban religious practices; many other authors (see, e.g., Ortíz 1951, 1952, 1965; Cabrera 1986b; Gonzalez-Wippler 1973; Thompson 1983; Murphy 1988) have attempted this complex task long before I first visited the island in 1989, and several recent studies expand considerably on the work accomplished by Ortíz, Cabrera, Thompson, and their intellectual progeny (see especially D. Brown 2001; M. Mason forthcoming). Nor does my work offer a complete catalog of Cuban music. There are numerous sources on Cuban popular music in English (see Blum 1978; Crook 1982; Gerard and Sheller 1989; Manuel 1987, 1991; Robbins 1989; Moore 1997) and in Spanish (see Acosta 1983; Díaz Ayala 1981; Galan 1983; Linares 1989; León 1984; Orovio 1981), a few sources on Afro-Cuban religious music in English (see Cornelius 1989; Friedman 1982; Manuel 1991; Marks 1974), and many more in Spanish (see Acosta 1982; Alén 1986; Carpentier 1988; Casanova Oliva 1988; León 1964; Ortíz 1951, 1952–1955, 1965, 1973b; Vinueza 1986). The concept of Afro-Cuban folklore has been well laid out by Ortíz (1951), León (1961), and, more recently, by Martínez Furé (1979) and Guerra (1989). Peter Manuel (1991) provides a useful and balanced view of the relationship between that folklore and Marxism, although the events of the 1990s brought on a radical shift in that relationship, so that it now bears reexamination. The work of Béhague (1988) and Anderson (1982) on the relationship between tourism and traditional music in Brazil and Haiti challenges the definition of "folklore," as does Wilcken's (1991, 1998) long-term study of staged Haitian folklore in New York City.

My work draws on all of those areas of scholarship, but focuses mainly on the performative area between and including *lo religioso* and *lo folklórico* in Cuba.[9] It is the interplay between the two performative spheres that has led to the profusion and increased importance of *grupos folklóricos*. These folkloric troupes, which perform the songs and dances of African-based Cuban religions, represent another step in the centuries-long decontextualization of Afro-Cuban religious belief, and in a sense they have paved the way for the government-sponsored religious tourism that occurs today. There is a centuries-long continuum between the persecution of Afro-Cuban religious traditions such as Santería, Palo Monte, and Abakwá throughout the nineteenth century and the public performances of Afro-Cuban religious songs and dances sponsored by Fernando Ortíz starting in the 1930s to the seminars taught by Ortíz in the 1940s and 1950s, and thence to the establishment of the Conjunto Folklórico in 1962, culminating with the Ochatur/*santurismo* phenomenon in the 1990s.

The transformation of divine utterances—in this case, how a religious tradition, with all its attendant performative expressions, moves toward (and away from) theatrical presentation—is the focus of this work. Other scholars who have noted the dramatization of Afro-Cuban performance traditions in Cuba have labeled this process *folklorization* (see, for example, C. Moore 1988a). But this term is not wholly appropriate, given that the African-based Cuban religions in question already were considered "folklore" by many Cuban scholars, including Fernando Ortíz, since the beginning of the last century (Ortíz 1951, 1965; Martínez Furé 1979; Guerra 1989). In an effort to demonstrate that these religious rituals are not once-removed from the classification of religion (in which case they might be called folklore instead of religion), but twice-removed when they are performed on stage by the Conjunto Folklórico, I have used the term *folkloricization*: that is, the process of making a folk tradition folkloric.

SPIRALING KNOWLEDGE

I have incorporated nonlinear motion into the narrative structure of the book, starting from the outside, spiraling inward, and emerging outward once again at the end. The book begins in the present, but by chapter 6 we will have arrived at the end of the nineteenth century, examining the sociopolitical factors that contributed to the immediate success and enduring legacy of Fernando Ortíz's *Hampa afrocubana: Los negros brujos* (1906), the work that set the stage for a broad assimilation of Social Darwinist views regarding Afro-Cuban performance traditions, or "folklore." Chapter 7 brings us back to the present with a discussion of the politics and economics of folklore and religion in Cuba at the end of the twentieth century. My goal is to give the reader a sense of the way that I assimilated my experiences in Cuba, learning from specific people at specific times and in specific places, and thus to provide a grounded, situated context in which to consider my work. I take my cue from my teachers and colleagues during my years at Brown University—specifically Michelle Kisliuk, Carol Babiracki, and Jeff Titon—whose writings perform the essential work of situating the fieldworker in the field (Barz and Cooley 1997), and from Lila Abu-Lughod (1990, 1993), whose defense and use of a narrative of personal specificity (writing against culture within ethnographies of the particular) has informed and inspired this work.[10]

Chapter 1, "Notes on Fieldwork: Dreaming Ogún," provides the backdrop for my fieldwork, describing the surveillance that pervades everyday life in Havana and introducing the threat of violence that surveillance implies. Chapter 2, "El Espectáculo: Invitation to the Dance," describes the main *orichas* of the Afro-Cuban religious tradition of Santería through their portrayal in a Conjunto Folklórico folkloric performance and suggests the idea that a "competent" audience (one familiar with the religious traditions that inform these dramatizations) is necessary to appreciate fully the roots and significance of the Conjunto's performances. Chapter 3, "Embodying the Sacred in Afro-Cuban Performance: Negotiating the Rules of Engagement," provides a focused description of the two main events at a *toque de santo* in a suburb of Havana and uses this vignette to explore the overlapping rules of engagement in Afro-Cuban religious performance. Chapter 4, "Blurring the Boundaries: Merging Sacred and Profane," examines the interplay between sacred and secular intent and analyzes the summoning of the sacred in secular settings, building on the idea of the competent audience.

Chapter 5, "The Birth of the Conjunto Folklórico," recalls the beginning of Cuba's first national folkloric troupe and points to the interlocking hot-button issues of racial discrimination, maligned religious practice, and culture clash. Chapter 6, "Sacred Crimes: Criminalizing the Sacred in Historical Perspective," traces these issues back to the waning years of the Atlantic slave trade in Cuba and suggests that the early twentieth-century criminalization of Afro-Cuban religious practices (particularly evident in Fernando Ortíz's early writings) was a form of decontextualization that paved the way for the folkloric performances of the 1930s, and finally the Conjunto Folklórico of the 1960s. Chapter 7, *"Resolver* and Religious Tourism in Cuba," continues this line of thought, bringing us back to the present with an analysis of the relationship between the renaissance of Santería and tourism, framed by my own initiation into Santería.

NOTES

1. *Batá* drums are a central component of the polytheistic Afro-Cuban religious tradition popularly known as Santería. They help religious practitioners communicate with deities known as *orichas* because they are able to speak to them "in their own language" (the tonal, liturgical language called Lucumí). Afro-Cuban folkloric ensembles often play songs and rhythms taken from the Santería liturgy, though in folkloric performances these musical utterances are not intended to communicate with the *orichas.*

2. See especially Linares (1989) and León (1984) for thorough and useful "native" studies on Cuba's *música campesina.* See Díaz Ayala (1981) and Galán (1983) for encyclopedic approaches to the subject published outside of Cuba. I emphasize the difference between works published inside Cuba and those published outside the island because since the 1959 revolution, two trends have adversely affected scholarship on Cuban music: first, the restrictions by both the Cuban and the U.S. governments affecting scholars wanting to travel to and from the island to do primary research; and second, the occasional censuring by the Cuban government of cultural analyses perceived to be counterrevolutionary. Manuel (1991) provides an excellent balance of sources published in Cuba as well as outside of it.

3. During the same period I began studying *batá* drums with Francisco Aguabella in Los Angeles. His insights about and knowledge of Afro-Cuban religious and folkloric performance will be the subject of another book. He has graciously contributed recordings of some of his performances to the CD accompanying this book.

4. Dean MacCannell's pioneering work *The Tourist* (MacCannell 1999) would seem to be especially relevant here. But MacCannell deals mainly with the experience of the tourist, rather than with the goals and contexts of those who help construct the tourist experience. What is fascinating about folkloric and religious performance in Santería is the continuum or shared space between "touristic" and "authentic"—the participating of religious practitioners in making their religious tradition public spectacle, or, in MacCannell's terms, a "sight." Jeff Titon's (1999) work on tourism and authenticity among Old Regular Baptists comes closer to discussing the issues that are most relevant to this study.

5. Santería is also known as the *Regla de Ocha* (the Rule of Ocha). *Ocha* is a truncation of *oricha* (deity); hence, Ochatur means "*oricha* tourism." Noted Cuban folklorist Rogelio Martínez Furé has referred to a similar phenomenon as *santurismo,* from Santería and *turismo* (Knauer 1999).

6. By "outward-directed" I mean that the staged performance is directed toward people outside of the community of practitioners of African-based religious traditions in Cuba. "Inward-directed" implies that the purpose of the performance is for those members inside the group of religious practitioners. The two forms of performance are not necessarily mutually exclusive, but identifying the main targeted audience of each performance type clarifies other important differences in the function and interpretation of these genres.

7. The cost of a priestly initiation into Santería can vary considerably for Cuban nationals. One Havana-based Santero told me that he had initiated one of his godchildren into the priesthood of Santería in 1992 for 2,500 pesos, or roughly US$125. This was at the trough of the special economic period, which probably accounts for some of the drastic difference in price.

8. It is useful to note here that a similar initiation would likely cost between $15,000 and $20,000 in the United States. For some U.S. nationals, choosing to become initiated into Santería in Cuba is partly an economic decision.

9. There has been little scholarly attention devoted to the general topic of Cuban *grupos folklóricos* or to the CFNC. There are two Cuban books written specifically on Afro-Cuban folklore, Ramiro Guerra's *Teatralización del folklore* (1989) and Rogelio Martínez Furé's *Diálogos Imaginarios* (1979), but Guerra's book is a technical guide to making theater out of ritual with scant mention of the history or theoretical underpinnings of the concept, and Martínez Furé's book is an exploration of the idea of Afro-Cuban folklore without specific reference to how he stages this folklore in the Conjunto Folklórico. Another book, by José Millet and Rafael Brea, temptingly entitled *Grupos Folklóricos de Santiago de Cuba* (1989), provides the reader with a description of some of the performance groups in Cuba's easternmost province, but it offers no analysis as to their origins or creative inspiration. Yvonne Daniel's (1995) ethnography of the *rumba,* which focuses on *rumba* performances of the Conjunto Folklórico,

provides a useful comparison in terms of performance genre and time period. Although all these books are valuable, they underscore the lack of a conceptual link between the source and the application of "folklore" in staged performances of Afro-Cuban religious traditions.

10. See also Okely and Callaway (1992) for important essays on the integral relationship between anthropology and autobiography.

The night after I received the *guerreros* in Washington, D.C., I fell into a fitful sleep and began to dream: I am alone in the house where I grew up. It is evening, and I am waiting for my mother to return. She is late. I am sitting in the rec room, which leads out into the kitchen at the back of the house, facing the woods. The house abuts this forest, separated only by a small yard and a tiny creek a few feet wide. I look out through the windows into the woods. I am nervous. The television is on but I do not look at it. I feel as if I am being watched. I am afraid. I hear noises, as if someone is walking around inside the house. I move silently through the downstairs, locking doors and windows, cautiously peering outside, afraid of what I might see. I come into the kitchen just as someone pulls a ladder up through a skylight—a skylight that was not part of the kitchen when I was growing up. I see the blond wood of the bottom three rungs pulling away from me. I am cold, motionless with fear: Someone else has been in the house.

My mother finally comes home, not at all contrite. I am anxious as I relate the incident to her. I tell her she must call the police. She is calm, and tells me she doesn't feel comfortable bothering the police at this late hour. I plead with her, and she finally calls them, but instead of reporting what I described, she has a friendly exchange with a couple of the police officers and asks whether they would mind coming over to look around the yard. I look down through the kitchen windows that face the woods—and I see Ogún, the intruder. He is squatting in the bushes, eating dirt and gravel. He looks back at me with a blank face, expressionless as he chews the earth. He is well-muscled, almost heavy, black and bearded, dressed only in a filthy loincloth hung with small pouches and his beaded ritual *collar* of green and black worn diagonally over his shoulder. We stare at each other for a few suspended seconds, and I become angry. I am outraged that he has intruded, and I wish to punish him for it. I yell to my mother, "Look! There he is!" But he is already gone from the window, moving toward the woods.

The police finally arrive, and my mother chats amiably with the officer in charge, who treats me like a young child, although I am over thirty. "What seems to be the problem here, young lady?" The officers are all dressed like forest rangers in khaki short-sleeved shirts and chinos and, inexplicably, are wearing penny-loafers. I tell them to go after Ogún, who has moved quickly into the woods. But the police officer and his crew run slowly, daintily, stopping to figure out the best way to jump over the tiny creek without soiling their uniforms. Ogún, who moves effortlessly and swiftly, is far beyond them. He turns once to look back, marking me.

I

NOTES ON FIELDWORK
Dreaming Ogún

AFFECTIVE FIELDWORK
AND A SPLINTERED IDENTITY

When I started my fieldwork in Cuba in 1989, I hoped to become one of only about a hundred U.S. scholars who were able to visit Cuba each year to do their research. At that time, because travel to Cuba from the United States was so difficult, many people chose to go there on study tours sponsored by such organizations as the Center for Cuban Studies in New York or Global Exchange Programs in San Francisco. During the early 1990s, with the tighter enforcement of the U.S. economic embargo against Cuba and the rippling effects of the collapse of the former Soviet Union and its primarily Eastern European economic partners, the types and number of U.S. scholars allowed to work in Cuba increased somewhat, albeit according to byzantine regulations. If you applied to the U.S. Treasury Department for an academic visa to do research in Cuba (which had to be supported by an outline of your research plan, proposed budget, curriculum vitae, and a list of possible future publications) and at the same time applied to the Cuban Interests Section in Washington, D.C., for either a scientific visa or a tourist visa (supported either by a research plan or a complete itinerary of hotels and/or pensions, as well as curriculum vitae and mother's maiden name), and if both of those applications were approved by the appropriate government offices in time for your departure, then you might actually get to Havana (or Santiago, or Cienfuegos, or Trinidad) for a few weeks or, in special cases, a few months to do your fieldwork.

This cumbersome system began to change in the mid-1990s, just after dollars were declared legal tender in Cuba in 1993 and during the most publicized of the *balsero* (the name given to a Cuban who used a small wooden boat, or *balsa,* to flee to the Florida coastline) incidents of 1994 and 1995. The Cuban government intensified its efforts to attract tourist dollars at the same time that the U.S. Treasury Department enforced its $150 per diem limit on U.S. citizens traveling in Cuba. The Cuban government would grant mostly tourist visas, even to scholars, and the U.S. Treasury Department would issue permits only to seven categories of travelers, including relatives of Cubans, Cuban nationals, photojournalists, reporters from major news agencies, and professional scholars (U.S. citizens were not allowed to travel to Cuba for the purposes of tourism). In 1998 some of the regulations restricting the travel of U.S. citizens to Cuba were relaxed, so that sports teams, cultural groups, scholars, religious associations, and nongovernmental organizations could travel more easily between the two countries. During a recent field trip in December 1999, I met more Americans in Havana than ever before— an impression corroborated by the recent reinstatement of several charter flights from Miami to the island, and by the much-anticipated initiation of flights between New York and Havana in November 1999. In spring 2000 the first-ever Los Angeles–Havana flight was inaugurated, to the delight of many California residents. The trials and tribulations of Elián González notwithstanding, travel to and from Cuba seems easier now, perhaps a portent of increased exchange and cooperation between the two countries.

This chapter examines some of the changes in U.S.-Cuban relations in general and in Cuba in particular within the framework of my field experiences. I began my fieldwork at a time when the special economic period had just begun, when the possession of dollars was illegal in Cuba, and when food, toiletries, gas, electricity, and water were all scarce. Many people in Cuba attribute the worst years of the special economic period not to the collapse of the former Soviet Union and its Eastern European trade partners, but to the double whammy of this collapse combined with the ongoing U.S. economic embargo against Cuba. Everything that happened in Cuba seemed to occur in relation to and in spite of this sudden privation. My friend was able to make it to her choir rehearsal in spite of the fact that, due to the gasoline shortage, buses that once ran every hour were now running only once a day. My drum teacher was able to celebrate his *cumpleaños de santo,* the yearly party marking his initiation into Santería, even though he had no way of buying the cakes and pastries required for such an event. My neighbors had their weekly Sunday dinner with relatives despite the fact that there was no meat, no bread, and no salad, just beans and rice.

Writing about my fieldwork in Cuba evokes this continued struggle to come to terms with these especially Cuban relationships, and with the barrage of peculiarly Cuban information that infiltrated my consciousness and subtly reshaped my practice of everyday life. I remember arguing with an American colleague whom I met on a 1991 field trip about the effect of our trips to Cuba. She felt that we affected the lives of our Cuban friends and colleagues much more deeply than they affected ours, and that we could not possibly understand the ephemeral miracle of our arrival and the enduring devastation of our departure. Several days after this discussion, her Cuban friend commented that our infrequent visits—held at the Hotel Presidente bar; along the Malecón, the oceanside drive that runs from historic Old Havana to tony Miramar, passing such landmarks as the U.S. Interests Section and the elegant Hotel Nacional along the way; or in his apartment for *"un cafecito o un roncito"*[1]—were indeed "like paradise" for him because they were an escape from the recent hardships of everyday life in Cuba. When I said "I know" or "I understand" in response to his comments, my colleague sharply remarked that I couldn't possibly understand because I, unlike her friend, could leave Cuba. My ability to leave—and in that precise sense, my state of being perpetually outside the Cuban community—proved to be a trenchant metaphor for my identity as a researcher in Cuba.

Initially, I was interested in the performances of the Conjunto Folklórico Nacional de Cuba as a marker for postrevolutionary Cuban identity. Because so much of the CFNC's repertoire is based on Cuba's religious traditions of African origin, I began to learn about the tense exchange between religious and folkloric performance, and about the political implications of each category. What I would call Afro-Cuban religious performance, such as the ritual drumming ceremonies of Santería *(toques de santo)* or the initiation ceremonies of Abakwá *(plantes),*[2] provided much material for anthropological study for Cuban scholars throughout the twentieth century, and especially after late 1936, when Fernando Ortíz founded the Sociedad de Estudios Afrocubanos.[3] In fact, Ortíz and his intellectual progeny (most notably Argeliers León and Rogelio Martínez Furé), who went on to found the Teatro Nacional in 1959 and the Conjunto Folklórico in 1962, had been calling these religious traditions "folklore" since the early 1900s. Yet the term *folklore* simultaneously robs these traditions of their religious legitimacy and begins the work of decontextualizing the songs and dances from their sacred evocative purpose. In twentieth-century Cuba, the term *folklore Afro-Cubano* (Afro-Cuban folklore) has come to eclipse the potential divinity of Afro-Cuban performance, focusing mainly on isolated and decontextualized songs and dances originally meant to evoke specific deities, but now dramatized and choreographed to evoke audience applause. This process of "folkloricization" has its roots in the Cuban slave trade, and it has not been examined publicly by Cuban scholars or performers, perhaps because a close examination might reveal extant remnants of a racism long declared eradicated.

At first, my questions linking the possibility of racism with "folkloricization" were denied or ignored by performers in the Conjunto Folklórico. But gradually some of the performers in the troupe began to share similar thoughts with me. Often I was granted trust and information precisely because I was outside of the "folklore" community. To many of the people with whom I worked, I was exotic because I came from a place often vilified but rarely seen by people who still live in Cuba, and the perception of my home country was even stranger because most of the Cubans I met had relatives or friends in the United States. In fact, the various ways in which I did not fit in made me into a sort of catalyst. My presence injected a polarizing energy into otherwise stable situations: at *casas de santo* (the houses of Santeras and Santeros, which are dedicated to serving the needs of religious practitioners of Santería) people either admired or condemned my efforts to play the male-identified *batá* drums of Santería; in interviews, my American citizenship aroused either shy curiosity or deep suspicion; at social gatherings, people were either intrigued or alarmed by my close relationships with black Cubans (specifically, my drum teacher and his family, as well as a dear friend whom I met in 1990); and my attempts to learn about such African-based religions as Santería and Palo Monte without becoming immediately initiated into their congregations were either accepted graciously or rejected out of hand by Santeros and Santeras.

My initial attempts to learn more about the Conjunto Folklórico by studying some of the drumming traditions performed by the troupe were met with rejection by the group's lead percussionist. Although there were some female folkloric *batá* drummers in Cuba at that time and there was even a commercial female *batá* ensemble (Obbini Batá),[4] the drum culture in Cuba remained pervasively macho, especially in the sacred circles of the *batá* drums of Santería. There are specific injunctions in the African-based religion of Santería against women playing *batá* drums because of the fear that their reproductive powers in general and their menstrual blood in particular will weaken the *añá* (sacred inner power) of the drum. My drum teacher, Alberto Villarreal, ultimately assigned more significance to "foreign" than to "female," and agreed to teach me *batá* drumming with the proviso that I never play the *batá* drums in a ritual context, a condition I continue to honor.

Although many Cuban women play the *güiro* (gourd scraper), the *shekere* (gourd rattle), and the *claves* (wooden sticks) in the ever-increasing number of

Cuban popular and folkloric groups, few play the *batá* drums. None of the *grupos folklóricos* whose performances I attended employed women drummers. In the early 1990s, with only a handful of exceptions, the few women who learn to play *batá* in Cuba were usually foreigners—an all-female Japanese salsa band called Chica Boom; Shana, the Indonesian wife of Pino Noya, both of whom are well-known conga players based in Amsterdam; a few women from England, France, and Italy; a female dancer of Cuban descent from Boston; an accomplished female percussionist from Texas; and myself. Within the past few years, more women have become interested in learning Cuban-style *batá* drumming.[5] Since 1995, I have met accomplished women *batá* drummers from Havana, Matanzas (just east of Havana), Philadelphia, New York, Houston, Los Angeles, and San Francisco. Matanzas-based singer and drummer Amelia Pedroso formed the first all-women Afro-Cuban folkloric ensemble, including *batá* drummers, singers, and dancers. The group is called Ibbu Okún, a Cuban Lucumí name, which, in a press release from 1995, was translated as "the river and the ocean"—a reference to two female water *orichas,* Ochún and Yemayá, respectively.[6] According to Elizabeth Sayre, there are now at least four folkloric women's ensembles that feature *batá* in Cuba: Obbini Batá and Ibbu Okún in Havana, Obini Aberíkula in Matanzas, and Obini Irawó in Santiago (Sayre 2000:13). Obini Aberíkula can be translated as "women of the unconsecrated drums," and Obini Irawó can be understood to mean "women of the rainbow" or "women of the shooting star." Obbini Batá simply means "women of the *batá*."[7]

Another challenging part of my identity as a foreign woman was my U.S. citizenship. Although some U.S. citizens do go to Cuba, their presence in Cuba is typically short-lived, innocuous, and touristic. They are usually shepherded around Havana, Matanzas, or Santiago de Cuba for two or three weeks by solicitous and knowledgeable Cubatur guides (the Cuban and much more appealing versions of the former Soviet Intourist guides). The goals of these tours are very specific: learning more about Cuban filmmaking, Cuban health care, Cuban environmental policy, Afrocubanismo in Cuban literature, women's rights in Cuba, and so on. There have been very few American researchers who choose (and who are given permission) to do research for a period longer than a month in Cuba. Those who successfully navigate the maze of letters of invitation, special scholarly visas from the Cuban government, a permit from the U.S. Treasury Department, and the pressure to pay for one's stay at least one month in advance of arriving in the country are viewed with a mixture of suspicion and awe by Cubans. Some of my Cuban friends thought at one time or another that I was a spy for the U.S. State Department, an impression both incorrect and absurd. (Their impressions were balanced by my own brief periods of intense paranoia, however, when I thought that at least half of my friends and colleagues were reporting on my activities to the Cuban Ministry of the Interior, which also turned out to be an incorrect assessment.) As a result of this initial mutual suspicion, first meetings were often very strained, and I felt even more keenly than usual the need to prove myself to be not only harmless but also worthy of trust and friendship.

This need to prove myself was often thwarted from the start, however, by my readily apparent white northern European ancestry. Although there is a wide range of skin, eye, and hair color in Cuba, the majority of the population has dark eyes and hair, and skin that ranges from a pale olive to a dark brown. Some nonofficial estimates peg Cuba's black and *mulato* population at 62 percent (1985 figures in Brenner et al. 1989:537), but other estimates of Cuba's population of African origin range between 70 and 75 percent (1983 figures in C. Moore 1988a:362).[8] My straight brown hair, freckled white skin, and light blue eyes made it impossible for me to blend in. Many Cubans thought I was German or Dutch at first, some thought I was French or Spanish, and one or two thought I was Canadian. This aspect of my identity proved most problematic in working with the religious practitioners and the members of the *grupos folklóricos,* many of whom consider themselves "Afro-Cubanos," and some of whom have not yet come to fill the economic and political roles that revolutionary Cuba has projected for them. Although the burgeoning interest in Cuba during the 1960s in doing ethnographic fieldwork on Cuba's African-based traditions did spawn some black Cuban ethnographers, most of the research in this area was done (and is still done) by white Cubans about black Cubans. The research, in most cases, has been useful and interesting, and many strong friendships have resulted from the ongoing field contact. But there remains a sense, implied by Alberto Villarreal, my first drum teacher, during various conversations from 1992 to the present, that the traditions and the people themselves who are featured in this research are inevitably objectified, plugged into some greater political agenda that has little bearing on their lives or beliefs. It was this research, with its roots in the ethnographic work of Fernando Ortíz in the 1930s and 1940s, that inspired the "authentic presentations" of the Teatro Nacional in the early 1960s, and, soon thereafter, the "flashy spectacles" of the Conjunto Folklórico.[9]

Typically, the focus of these research projects has been the richly varied traditions of Cuba's African-based religions—usually Santería (practiced mostly in the northwestern provinces of Havana and Matanzas, and derived from the *oricha* or deity worship of the Yoruba peoples of Nigeria), Palo Monte (found throughout Cuba, and derived from the belief systems of the Bantu-speaking people of the

Congo Basin), Arará (concentrated in Matanzas province, derived from the religious practices of the E<u>w</u>e and Fon peoples of present-day Ghana, Benin, and Togo), and Abakwá (now mostly in the northwestern port cities of Cuba, and derived from the practices of the secret male societies of the Efik-Ibibio people east of the Niger River delta).[10] The practitioners of these religions, harassed and persecuted for several centuries, suddenly found themselves to be among the most popular representatives of Cuba's postrevolutionary identity. As Fidel Castro proclaimed during the January 1966 conference of the Organization for the Solidarity of the Peoples of Africa, Asia, and Latin America (OSPAAAL), Cuba was in fact an "overseas African country" (C. Moore 1988a:251), an image both modified and strengthened by Castro's 1975 assertion that Cubans "are a Latin-African people" (C. Moore 1988a:1).[11] By the 1980s, "Afro-Cuban cults" had become quite fashionable among foreign Cubaphiles (mostly musicians and scholars), who began to visit Cuba for the express purpose of becoming initiated into the most popular of these religions, Santería—and who perhaps unwittingly planted the seed for the recently popular tour packages featuring "Afro-Cuban" culture.

According to some of the religious practitioners with whom I worked, one of the most puzzling aspects of my identity was why I did not become initiated immediately into the religion. I was cautiously welcomed because I knew something about Santería, yet I did not belong to a ritually related community in either the United States or Cuba. As a result of this paradox, I was located somewhere in between the planeloads of foreign Cubaphiles who arrived each year to become initiated and the small group of mostly white Cuban researchers who are not religious practitioners (at least not publicly). Although my initial lack of clear commitment to the religion prevented me from learning certain ritual details, eventually I was able to conduct useful interviews about the relationship between religious performance traditions and their folkloric representations by focusing on *lo folklórico* to find out more about *lo religioso*.

These aspects of my identity—my whiteness, femaleness, and many layers of foreignness—allowed me to contract the many services offered by Havana's tourist hotels (renting a bicycle, buying a sandwich, sending telegrams and faxes, calling the United States, buying good rum for my Cuban friends and colleagues) and, perhaps most important, in my automatic admission into the *diplomercado* and *diplotienda*[12] in the still-elegant Miramar section of the city of Havana. The *diplomercado* (a huge air-conditioned building separated into gleaming aisles stocked with the brands and flavors of canned and fresh food that were difficult to find elsewhere in Havana, as well as some housewares and appliances), to my knowledge, was the only supermarket operating in Havana during the early 1990s.

It was ostensibly for the exclusive use of diplomatic personnel and their families, but with the right attitude and connections, nondiplomats and even Cubans were allowed entry. On most days, with my valid non-Cuban passport, my researcher's visa, and an attitude of entitlement, not only could I enter the *diplomercado,* but I could also bring a Cuban friend (only one Cuban was permitted per adult foreigner). Although it was possible in this way for Cubans who were not *diplomercado* employees to enter this almost mythical place, many of my friends preferred not to because of the nauseatingly sharp contrast between the cornucopia of the foreigners' *diplomercado* and the barrenness of the Cuban ration stands. I made two or three trips per week to the *diplomercado* for the various families and individuals that I came to care for, knowing that I could not possibly do enough and always feeling like I should do more. When one friend finally did accompany me into the market in 1992, he became so dizzy and nauseated from the combined shock of seeing copious amounts of food and knowing that none of this food was readily available to Cubans that he left the store and collapsed on the steps outside, his head in his hands.

"RUNNING WATER AND OTHER CONVENIENCES": THE STRATIFICATION OF CUBAN SOCIETY

All of my living arrangements in Havana demonstrated a complex social stratification that seemed to be determined by the special economic period. The places in which I stayed during my field trips—several tourist hotels, two large houses for foreign students, two houses of U.S. Foreign Service employees who were on leave, a *pensión* for researchers, and finally the apartment of a friend (the aunt of a friend of an American colleague)—revealed this stratification in ways that directly affected the terms and conditions of my fieldwork. The key to this stratification seemed to reside simultaneously outside and within Cuba. The stratification was outside Cuba in that the main characteristic of the top stratum was foreignness, and inside Cuba in that the most meaningful aspect of this same foreignness was foreign tourism within Cuba. As a Spanish colleague explained in 1992, "In Cuba there are only two types of people: *cubanos* and *extranjeros;* that is, those who pay in pesos, and those who pay in dollars." It gradually became clear to me that a hierarchy of privilege had grown up around the newly conceptualized tourist industry, at the top of which were foreign tourists (simply called *extranjeros,* the literal translation of which is "foreigners," but which is understood to mean "tourists"), and at the bottom of which were Cubans who had no hope of coming into contact with foreign tourists, much less of ever working in the much-coveted tourist industry. In the middle were Cubans with limited access to dollars, either through family connections in other countries or through their employment in one of the branches of the tourist industry (waiting tables at a tourist hotel, becoming a bartender, leading tour groups, driving a tourist taxi, and so on).

During my preliminary field trip of three weeks in July 1989, which was sponsored by the New York–based Center for Cuban Studies, I stayed with the rest of my research group at the Hotel Presidente, an elegant pink-brick twelve-story hotel built during the early part of the twentieth century, located in the fashionable Vedado section of Havana. A favorite establishment of the Center for Cuban Studies for many years, the hotel was often booked for participants in its research trips. The spacious lobby of the hotel, furnished with heavy antiques of exotic dark woods from Europe and Asia and overstuffed pinstriped sofas, spoke to the conspicuous elegance of prerevolutionary Cuba. The floor, counters, and columns were marble, and Persian rugs described the discrete sitting areas near the lobby bar and the back entrance to the pool patio. Enormous, complexly configured chandeliers hung from the gilt-edged ceilings, lighting the lobby at all hours.

There was the familiar hustle and bustle of determined and confused tourists in this hotel, but none of the tourists were Cuban. In fact, the only Cubans who were allowed to enter the hotel unaccompanied by *extranjeros* were the hotel employees. All other Cubans, if found unaccompanied in the lobby or in any other part of the hotel, were told to leave. One might wonder, as I did, how the hotel lobby guards were able to distinguish Cubans from other nationalities. The main clue, it seems, was skin color. If an unaccompanied person of color attempted to enter the hotel or was seen meandering around the lobby, she or he was immediately interrogated and had to present a valid passport or *carné de identidad* (Cuban internal passport). This criterion became clear to me as I watched the lobby guards stop the African American members of our research trip at the hotel door, while the white members came and left the hotel freely.

A Cuban friend of mine, whose skin color was not as dark as that of some of his compatriots, occasionally was able to circumvent this system of "Cuban apartheid" by dressing the part of a Mexican tourist, sporting a pastel polo shirt, jeans, designer sunglasses, and AeroMexicana flight bag. This disguise allowed him to sit on the veranda of the hotel or in the lobby for an hour or so, until one of his friends came to meet him or until he was expelled by one of the lobby guards. The concept of "Cuban apartheid" has been explored in various Cuban media, including the popular film *Mujer Transparente* (Transparent Woman, 1991) and Carlos Varela's hit song "Tropicollage." Journalist Tom Miller, watching *Mujer Transparente* at the Yara Theatre in downtown Havana, was astonished at the audience's openly angry recognition of a scene in which tourism apartheid takes place (Miller 1992:66). The lyrics of "Tropicollage" deal with the same theme:

> If you go to a hotel
> And you're not a foreigner
> They treat you differently.
> That is already happening here,
> And I want to change it.
> And whoever denies this fact
> Carries Tropicollage in his head.[13]

The second main criterion in determining Cuban nationality within a hotel setting is the U.S. dollar. Tourist hotels are generally "dollar hotels," which means that their services can be contracted only for dollars; no pesos are allowed. Until 1993, it was illegal for Cubans to possess dollars, which effectively obviated Cuban use of the tourist hotels, with the exception of specially arranged Cuban honeymoon weekends, for which sections of certain tourist hotels were set aside during the slow season (summer and fall).[14] There are, of course, Cuban hotels, which typically do not allow tourists and accept only pesos. However, these hotels "often lack running water and other conveniences" (McManus 1989:15).

The convenience of running water, however, is only one of the many reasons why Cubans might want access to the tourist hotels. First, these hotels exist on Cuban soil, in some of its most interesting and beautiful areas: the architecturally stunning Old Havana (La Habana Vieja), the long oceanfront stretch of the Malecón that runs from Old Havana to Miramar, the charming and unassuming beaches of La Habana del Este, and the internationally frequented and highly developed beaches of Varadero in neighboring Matanzas province. Second, all of these hotels have bars, restaurants, and stores, ranging from the rambling resort-style luxury of the Habana Libre Hotel (the Havana Hilton in prerevolutionary days) to the dingy, cramped rooms of the neighboring Hotel Colina. Regardless of the quality of the hotel, the pull of food, drink, and clothing has proven increasingly overwhelming for residents of Havana. Their own domestic supply of these goods, rationed since October 1990 during the first phase of the economic special period, has dwindled rapidly.

The withdrawal, starting in 1990, of the massive subsidies provided by the former Soviet Union quickly turned tropical Cuba into an economic desert island. This withdrawal of aid, as I remarked earlier, has been devastating because of the continuation of the thirty-year U.S. economic embargo against Cuba. Finally, the very thought of transient foreigners having access to some of the most beautiful and delectable treasures of Cuba, while Cuba's own citizens can only peer through the windows, is humiliating and enraging. In fact, so enraged were several thousand Havana residents by this imbalance that they rioted during the first week of August 1994, looting "dollar shops" and smashing hotel windows with rocks and rubble along the Malecón, singling out for particular damage two of the most famous tourist hotels, the Riviera and the Deauville, where I was staying for a few nights before moving to the Casa de Científicos.

A simplified, official explanation for this denial of access relies on the broad concept of revolutionary struggle, which, in this case, implies the moral superiority of a people who not only can forgo the luxuries of life (Havana Club rum, dinner at the elegant Hotel Nacional), but who can forgo them while watching potential enemies of the revolution (tourists from capitalist countries) consume these luxuries at will.[15] This explanation pivots on the notion of sacrifice for the future: the Cuban people must be willing, theoretically, to sacrifice some material luxuries in the short term so that the basic goal of the revolution, the achievement of an egalitarian socialist state, may triumph in the long run.[16]

The problem with the large-scale conceptualization of revolutionary struggle, however, is that it does not take into consideration the vastly differing levels of commitment among the individuals who make up the whole. The centralized political system of Cuban socialism seems to require relentless sacrifice, a requirement communicated in its most public and severe form by the ubiquitous billboards proclaiming *"¡Socialismo o muerte!"* (Socialism or death!). In this way, Cuba's population is treated as a monolithic entity, which might be interpreted as Comandante Castro's definition of an egalitarian society.[17] But the potentially disastrous results of this generalization were pointed out to me by a waiter, Argelio Malagón, whom I met on my second field trip. Although he was trained as an architect, at that time he was working at the Hotel Colina, where I stayed during my October 1990 visit. He commented during an interview a roughly year later (December 12, 1991) that the system of foreign tourism created a culture of self-hatred among Cubans. "We don't trust each other," he continued, "and although we may help each other, it is with duplicity, because we never know where that person stands. In Cuba, economics determine politics."[18]

Staying in hotels for my first two field trips threw this culture of self-hatred into sharp relief. As I and other well-fed foreigners sat down to our simple but

tasty morning or evening meals in the hotel dining room, I wondered whether the
skinny young waiters ever pilfered a roll or pineapple or something bigger from
the hotel kitchen. Once I asked another waiter whether the staff was allowed to
eat any food from the hotel kitchen. His face became tight and drained of color:
"Miss, if I or anyone else from the waitstaff eats food from the hotel kitchen, it is
called stealing and we are immediately fired. This is a good job, and I do not want
to be fired from it." When I reported this conversation in general and anonymous
terms to Argelio, he laughed: "What a coward. Of course it's stealing, but almost
everyone does it. Why else do you think highly educated people want to work in
hotels? I wasn't trained to be a waiter, you know. I'm an architect. And the waiter
over there was trained as a translator. But the pay is better here. There are more
opportunities for food."[19]

Cubans who work in the tourist hotels, then, are able to benefit covertly from
the system by participating in it. But Cubans who are not hotel employees also try
to benefit from the system by actions as suspect as attempting to trade pesos for
dollars on hotel premises or the simple and often innocent act of temporarily es-
caping the noonday sun by waiting in an air-conditioned hotel lobby. Such events
provoke the self-hatred to which Argelio referred, because the Cubans who work
in the tourist hotels must throw out the Cuban "loiterers" or *jineteros* (black marketeers) in order to keep their jobs and thus maintain their privileges. Although
the main stratification is between Cubans and foreigners, as a result of the potential privilege associated with the tourist industry, Cubans become stratified once
again into those who work in (and collude with) the tourist industry and those
who do not.

OGÚN REVISITED

During my third field trip, I lived in a foreign student house from November 1991
through January 1992. Here, the terms of contact between Cubans and foreigners
were simultaneously less restricted and more observed than they were in the
tourist hotels. Most of the foreign student houses were located in Miramar, the
section of Havana that boasts *"las flores caídas de quinta avenida"*[20] (the fallen flowers of Fifth Avenue) and the residences of many embassies and their staff. Many
of Miramar's private houses—large sprawling stucco structures built in the first
half of the twentieth century, with whimsical references to art deco and neoclas-
sical architecture—were nationalized by the Cuban government in the 1960s and
converted into museums, offices, and foreign student houses, or were rented or
sold to foreign governments. A typical foreign student house is two stories high,

with a large anteroom, living area, kitchen, dining room, and bathroom on the ground floor and three or four bedrooms on the top floor, each with private or adjoining bathrooms. Each bedroom has a few narrow cots, designed to accommodate slim students. I shared a room with a Swiss woman for the first few weeks after I arrived, during which time we were to sleep in one student house but eat in another in an effort to conserve resources, according to the housing supervisor.

Each student house employs several women, typically between the ages of forty-five and sixty, who cook, clean, and generally take care of the house. These women also serve as filters to prevent certain Cubans considered unfit for foreign sensibilities from bothering the foreign students. As in the tourist hotel, the main criterion for exclusion from foreign company seems to be dark skin color, with a secondary emphasis on general appearance; the cleaner and more up-to-date the clothing and hair, the more likely the audience with the foreign student. Such "filters" were not completely inappropriate, considering the increasingly persistent *jineteros* on the streets of Havana. But most of us had friends whose skin colors ranged in hue from, as one friend put it, "the outside of the coconut to the inside of the coconut."

One of the house guardians told me early in my stay that a good friend of mine (whose skin color tended toward that of the outside of the coconut) was "dangerous" for me, and that clearly she was visiting me only because she wanted something material from me—money, clothing, food, tapes, and so on. I was surprised by this woman's erroneous impression of my friend. I later discussed this exchange in general terms with my friend, and she laughed and responded, "Oh, she must have seen the flies around my head." I was stupefied by this remark. "The flies—you know, black people in Cuba attract more flies than white people, I don't know why. But she must have seen the flies and thought I had to provide for them." There was another awkward silence, in which I clearly did not get the joke. Then my friend burst out laughing and, between gasps of laughter, said, "I was only joking. You know how people are here. Who knows what these women think? Actually, you're the one they should be wary of, since you're the one who's studying that witchcraft *(brujería)* stuff. My family gave that up long ago."

In fact, my *brujería* studies prompted derisive laughter from most of the Cuban university students with whom I socialized. The fact that I was studying a topic (however tangentially) that had long been regarded as superstition by Cuba's ruling classes caused many of my friends to convulse with giggles, even as I explained the topic's specific connection to the Conjunto Folklórico and to Cuba's *grupos folklóricos* in general. Most of these students were studying law or medicine, and none had any background in folklore or ethnomusicology. All, however, had come into contact with foreign students before, mostly from Spain and Switzerland, and were thus aware of the wide range of thesis and dissertation topics selected by European graduate students. Several students remarked that my topic seemed strange because it dealt with sociology, demographics, history, comparative religions, and other appropriately "serious" topics, yet it was called "ethnomusicology," which to them sounded like the fine arts, and would seem to have nothing to do with *brujería*.

In general, with the exception of the aforementioned friend, the Cuban university students (most of whom were white and well-groomed) were not only allowed practically unlimited visiting time with the foreign students, they were occasionally allowed up into our rooms, a practice harshly discouraged by the supervisor of all the house guardians. It was after a particularly long-winded rebuke that I began to wonder how the supervisor found out about the activities of the house, inasmuch as the supervisor's office was about two miles away, in a different part of town. The guardians explained that because foreigners lived here, the house was watched by several families living nearby. Being a watcher was considered a lucrative, if distasteful, job. One family of watchers lived across the street, another lived next door, and a third family lived in back of the house. On the other side of the house was an empty building under construction, but had it been occupied, it would have contained watchers, too. The problem, said the guardians, was that we foreign students were always leaving windows and doors open, so the watchers could not only see what we were doing, but they could also hear our voices. Cubans, added the guardians, would never be so careless, especially in these times of increased *vigilancia* (vigilance). The guardians also stressed that, as far as they were concerned, we could do whatever we wished while living in the house because we were "nice young people," but we should always take care to close our doors and windows so that the watchers would have nothing substantive to report.

Because of the watchers, several of my Cuban colleagues refused to tarry in the sitting room of the student house for more than a few minutes at a time. They knew the arrangement and even the location of the watchers' houses before I got a chance to explain them myself. "You know, of course, that I can't speak freely in this house," said Rafael L. López Valdés, a well-regarded researcher at the Cuban Academy of Sciences and the director of the Cuban Ethnographic Atlas project, before he and his family moved to Puerto Rico in 1993. As a result, I conducted all of my interviews outside of my temporary residence, typically at my colleagues' homes or places of work. According to López Valdés, it would be much harder for the "supervisory organs of observation" to follow me all over Havana than to listen to the reports of the watchers. Even the interviews conducted in the homes of colleagues were occasionally cut short by the unexpected arrival of a nosy neighbor, referred to as *el elefante* (the elephant) for his enormous ears and long memory.

This feeling of being watched and overheard by a force greater than the sum of its parts was pervasive in Cuba, confirmed in part by the ubiquitous Comités para la Defensa de la Revolución (Committees for the Defense of the Revolution, abbreviated and popularly known as CDR), which were organized on almost every city block. Several of my colleagues compared Cuba's internal control to the force called "Big Brother" in George Orwell's novel *1984*. As in many socialist countries, however, the feeling of being observed does not always correspond to the reality of the observation. The entire country would have to have been in the service of the Ministry of the Interior (known as MININT) for the observation of its citizens to be as thorough as was commonly believed. In fact, it is this spontaneous need for self-control (for fear of reprisal) among its citizens, rather than the obligation to back up the feeling with a fully inclusive network of watchers, that is the goal of a totalitarian state. Due to the simple occasional unreliability of humans, watchers cannot observe all targets constantly and with unwavering attention. However, if one decides to rely on the occasional unreliability of these watchers, sooner or later the arbitrary pendulum of this pervasive observation network swings back, hitting its target unexpectedly.

The occasional unreliability of the watchers became painfully apparent to me on the Friday night before Christmas 1991, as I walked the three-quarters of a mile from the Hotel Neptuno (where I had tried unsuccessfully to call my home in the United States) back to the foreign student house. I was traumatized by what happened on my way home, and I found it therapeutic to record the events in my field notebook soon after the event (December 20, 1991), an edited version of which appears here:

> As I walked briskly from the hotel, I saw a dark figure slowly trudging up the beach road that leads to Tercera (Third Avenue). I instinctively crossed the street to the well-lit sidewalk next to the closed *diplomercado*. As I passed the *guardia* station between the *diplomercado* and the Soviet embassy, I heard footsteps behind me; I looked and saw it was the same figure who had been trudging up the beach road; now he was walking faster. I walked at a slightly quicker pace, and listened with quiet terror as the

speed of his footsteps also increased. As I turned in to the dark street that led to my house, I heard him running after me.

Angry and panicked, I tried to think of ways to scare him off, and decided to march abruptly toward him, as if to fight him. As I did so, however, he lunged forward, gasping at me and reaching for me with his left hand; with the other hand he was busy masturbating himself. I ducked his lunge and pushed him away, and then pivoted back toward the Soviet embassy. I tried to run, but as I pivoted I tore my calf muscles, taut from tension, and a bolt of pain seared my left leg like lightning.

Halfway down the block I stopped, my calf swollen, my heart beating in my throat. I limped forward to the *guardia* station, but there was no one in it. I collapsed on the curb under a street light and began to sob, my leg stretched out in front of me like a throbbing baseball bat, my stomach convulsing. After about five minutes the *guardia* returned to his post.

> *"¿Algo te pasó?"* (Did something happen to you?)
> *"Sí."* [Sob.]
> *"No llore. No llore. No llore."* (Don't cry.)
> *"¿Era negro?"* (Was he black?)
> *"No."*
> *"¿Era negro?"*
> *"No, era blanco."* (No, he was white.)
> *"¿No era negro? ¿Cierto?"* (He wasn't black? Are you sure?)

That my assailant was not black seemed impossible to the *guardia*. I gave a full description of the man: tall, white, black hair with well-trimmed beard and moustache, dressed in black, wearing a trenchcoat, and shoes with noisy heels—boots, perhaps— in his mid-thirties. The second *guardia* listened to my description, and sped away on his bicycle, only to return about five minutes later. *"No hay nadie,"* he said. (There's no one around.)

The first *guardia* kept asking me, *"¿Te hizo algo? ¿Te hizo algo?"* (Did he do anything to you?) But to me it sounded like *"¿Te suelgo? ¿Te suelgo?"*—so I responded, *"No entiendo la palabra suelgo"* (I don't understand the word *suelgo*),[21] which confused the *guardia*. Finally I understood his question and said that no, my assailant hadn't "done" anything to me, but that he had tried to. The *guardia* was clearly put off—what was the big deal if "nothing" had happened?

The *guardia* tapped my shoulder and said that the excitement was over, so I should go home. I explained to him again that I couldn't go home because I couldn't walk, and he motioned to the second *guardia* to take me home on the back of his bike. This was no small feat, for I probably weighed more than the *guardia* and my balance was offset by my now immense leg. I continued to cry on the back of the bike, despite the *guardia*'s exhortations to stop, and was relieved when we reached my house. The *guardia* was gone before I got to the door.

This incident is forever emblazoned in my memory because it provides so many contextual clues about my fieldwork in Cuba. According to several friends who work in the U.S. Interests Section and in other embassies and consulates in Cuba, the *guardia* stations around embassies should be occupied at all times. This should have been especially true for the Soviet embassy because of the close relationship between Cuba and the former Soviet embassy and because of the huge Soviet presence in Cuba even in 1991–1992, after the Soviet withdrawal had begun. Why was the *guardia* station unmanned? Where was the *guardia*? Why was he missing at the precise moment I was attacked? These questions loom larger here than they might had the attack occurred in New York City or Los Angeles precisely because Cuba prides itself on its low level of crime. "Havana is completely safe now [since the revolution]; women walk alone at night all the time and nothing happens to them," said both Cuban and foreign acquaintances during each one of my field trips. Cuba (and Havana in particular) is considered to be so safe precisely because of the pervasive *vigilancia* provided by militia and the police. But on a quiet night, what is to prevent a *guardia* from slipping away for fifteen minutes to see his girlfriend, to get a drink of water, to relieve himself? The image of *vigilancia* is more pervasive than its reality, and the tall white man with black hair and a beard took advantage of the discrepancy.

The implied racism in the comments of the *guardia* (*¿Era negro? ¿No era negro? ¿Cierto?*) is stunning in its clarity. The *guardias* assumed that my assailant was black, regardless of my description of him as white: black men, not white men, attack white women. The definition by the *guardias* of the incident itself was also disturbing: according to their calculation, nothing had happened. For the *guardias,* the attack was a failed attempt at rape, and the emphasis was placed on the failure rather than the attempt. For me, the attempt overshadowed the failure because it represented what might happen, regardless of the accepted and reiterated rhetoric about the safety of Cuba. In fact, the attempt was so important that it made me consider leaving Cuba because I no longer felt safe there as a lone female researcher. The system of *vigilancia* seemed to have broken down; was it really a coincidence that I was the one who felt the consequences? As I think about the incident now, I remember seeing something glinting in the streetlight from the inside of my attacker's trenchcoat, but I cannot transform the refracted light into an object—was it a key? a knife?

These images come back to me every time I strain the calf muscles of my left leg. It is as if the locus of the pain triggers the details of its origin. When I finally discussed this incident with my *padrino,* he interpreted it in terms of my relationship with Ogún. The details of the event—my being followed by a bearded man, the importance of the *guardia,* the noninvasive nature of the attack, and my fleeing—all pointed toward a "message" from Ogún. Within the framework of Santería I am a daughter of Ochún, thus it is my fate to be followed by the spirit of Ogún (in corporeal as well as spiritual form). According to the *patakíes*[22] (origin myths about the deities of Santería), after Ogún exiles himself from the world because he has tried to rape his mother, Ochún is the only *oricha* who is able to coax him out of the forest to interact with humans again. It is significant that these markers of Ogún in my life (the dream at the beginning of this chapter, the attempted rape, and other more recent incidents that involved being stalked) do not cause me great physical injury. In my dream I was not harmed, in the December 1991 incident I was not raped, and in the more recent stalking incidents, physical injury, though threatened, never occurred. The idea of these messages, according to Cuban religious practitioners with whom I spoke in August 1994, is that I must not only acknowledge Ogún's presence, but I must also accept it as part of my life. Ogún's energy in this case does not necessarily represent physical danger, but rather the threat of it. Ochún's energy represents the acceptance of the threat of danger without fear, which then results in the balancing of Ogún's energy with her own. (In the *patakíes,* Ochún is able to accept the threat of danger from Ogún and interact with him only because she knows that she will not be harmed.) Ogún is protector and violator, both *guardia* and stalker.

By the end of my third field trip I had gotten used to the feeling of being observed; indeed, I came to expect it. Under the tutelage of my colleagues, I learned to take the proper precautions when our interviews headed into the potentially sensitive topics of racism, religious freedom, and the commercialization of folk traditions. These precautions consisted of closing doors and windows when speaking about any aspect of Cuban politics, censoring myself when speaking to people who strongly supported certain actions (such as the execution of General Arnaldo Ochoa, a hero of the revolution, and his colleagues in July 1989 for drug trafficking) that I found repugnant, and generally trying to calibrate my own openness and trust to match the level of political awareness and dedication to the revolution of the people whom I was interviewing. I became so used to living and working in a controlled society that on my fourth field trip, from June through September 1992, I opted for the riskiest (also the cheapest and most comfortable) living situation, one that would surely provoke the highest and most intrusive level of surveillance.

This living situation also entailed housesitting for U.S. Interest Section staff, but the time period was for six weeks rather than one week, with an option to stay on once the staff member returned. In addition, while my previous housesitting engagement was for someone who worked for the Budget and Finance Office (technically under the purview of the General Accounting Office rather than the State Department, and thus slightly less suspect in the eyes of the Cuban government), this time I was housesitting for the secretary of the head of the U.S. Interest Section, a position that not only was directly supervised by the State Department, but was also considered sensitive because of the potential access to the section's head. I was told by the U.S. Interest Section security staff that the phone was most certainly tapped, and that there were watchers on all sides of the house. The house itself was about ten blocks closer to downtown Havana than where I had lived during my previous field trip, although it was still in suburban Miramar. Like many of the single-family diplomatic homes in this area, all of its rooms were on the ground floor, and all the common rooms had large picture windows or sliding glass doors that opened to the outside. The floors were made of polished granite, so bare feet made hardly a sound while heeled shoes sounded like an advancing army. The three bedrooms were on one side of the house, while the kitchen, living room, dining room, and foyer were on the other. Like most of the diplomatic houses, it was surrounded by a heavy black wrought-iron gate and its front windows were partially covered by avocado trees and leafy green shrubs.

One morning, as I went into the kitchen to prepare my morning coffee, I saw that the nearly full garbage can had been dumped all over the kitchen floor and that an entire set of Mickey Mouse measuring cups (the woman who usually lived in the house was a collector of Disney memorabilia) had been taken from the cabinet and placed upside down on the counter in a row. I notified the security staff of the U.S. Interest Section of this nocturnal visit and was informed that such things often happened and that I was being told again, innocuously but directly, that my actions were being observed by the Cuban Ministry of the Interior. At other times during my stay in this house, I found the toilet seat up (as if a man had been using the bathroom, or, to be charitable, cleaning my toilet for me), the television or radio turned on (when I had not used either one), or several books moved from one room to another.

This obvious surveillance caused many of my Cuban friends to feel uncomfortable, and they chose not to visit with me in the house. A few, however, seemed to have no problem with the observation and entered the house at will. The articulation by my friends and colleagues of their decisions to enter or not to enter my house revealed yet another type of stratification, which was based on professional distinction. A prominent musicologist and her extended family had no problem visiting me at the house and sharing a meal with me. A well-known ethnologist and his family also came to the house several times and shared meals with me. And after about a month of lessons, my drum teacher (the *responsable* or supervisor of the percussion section of the Conjunto Folklórico) and his family also came to my house and shared a meal with me. A translator of medical articles, however, would not come anywhere near my house, and a university law student whose father had been in the Cuban foreign service would stay only for very short periods of time, rarely saying a word. When I asked my friends and colleagues to elaborate on their decisions to enter the house, however, the explanation of professional distinction soon became connected to the metacategory of foreignness. One colleague remarked, "I'm a respected ethnologist. I deal with foreigners all the time. I have nothing to worry about as long as we don't talk about La Barba."[23]

Another colleague noted that as a leading musicologist it was her duty to help out people from all over the world who were interested in Cuban music, whether they came from the United States, Venezuela, or the Soviet Union, and that the study of music knows no political boundaries. The fact that these people had already had extensive contact with foreigners somehow made them less suspect, and therefore allowed them a limited freedom from fear of reprisal in this otherwise threatening situation. Those people who were not distinguished enough in their careers to have maintained professional contact with foreigners were denied the privilege of interacting with a potentially threatening foreigner without fear, and as a result most of those people chose not to interact with me in the house at all; that is, they spontaneously policed themselves.

During later field trips in 1994, 1997, and 1998, I stayed at a *pensión* for Cuban and foreign researchers (Casa de Científicos), and at a friend's apartment. These housing arrangements shared an important aspect: there was always a *guardia*. In the *pensión*, located in a beautiful section of Habana Vieja, the *guardia* was an old man who sat at the front desk, night and day, and who switched shifts with another old man. Both were relatively humorless and took their jobs seriously, writing down when people arrived or departed and taking note of telephone calls we received or made. In my friend's apartment, located in the Vedado section of Havana near the Puente de Hierro (Iron Bridge), the *guardias* were the owner of the apartment and her next-door neighbor. But over the course of my visits to Cuba throughout the 1990s, the methodology and outcome of being a *guardia* seem to have shifted, as has my approximation of that work. Initially, I felt that I was in opposition to my *guardias*, chafing at being policed. But by my 1997 and 1998 field trips, both in the company of my *padrino*, I was on friendly terms with the *guardias*, and we developed rituals of exchange, which underscored our independence from one another (both of us had resources to share, and jobs to do), as well as the possibility of friendship. During a field trip in 1999, I was back in a hotel again (the Hotel Flamingo in Vedado), wanting to experience the results of the boom in hotel construction for tourists.

FIELDING RELATIONSHIPS IN HAVANA

My relationships with friends and colleagues in the field evolved dramatically during the decade that I traveled to and from Havana. During the first two years, I fell victim to constantly shifting expectations, laboring under the wearisome burden of determining duplicity, or even triplicity. Who is telling the truth? Who has more than one truth to tell? Will she show up for the interview? Will the performance take place? Every encounter became a complex and bewildering process. My interpersonal confusion was intensified by the sometimes soporific, sometimes frenzied nature of Havana itself. Havana's tourist hotels gave off intermittent signals that the city was modern, industrialized, and tourist-friendly. Yet next door to a tourist hotel, the phones were not working; throughout the city there was a gas shortage; and everywhere Cubans were waiting in line for their daily *pancito* (a small bread roll). The daily eight-hour *apagones* (electrical blackouts), severe gas shortages, and twice-daily water shutoffs all but crippled parts of the city for much of the day during particularly difficult months. Yet the tourist industry remained unaffected. Havana seemed to represent a unique mixture of large-scale Soviet-style industrialization and small-scale Third World inefficiency, swinging from one extreme to the other so quickly and arbitrarily that appointments were uncertain, phone calls were a matter of luck, and attempts at photocopying were surreal.[24]

This pervasive sense of surveillance, combined with the underlying arbitrariness of public services, affected my participation in field relationships in several ways. The two seemingly contradictory forces often served to heighten my sense of separateness in Havana. The burdensome knowledge that various branches of the U.S. government might be observing me did not shape my adolescence, nor did I suffer the disorienting effects of the long-term unpredictability of public services. In comparison to the worldview of some of my Cuban colleagues, my own perspective was essentially benign, having been informed by relative personal freedom, stable and middle-class socioeconomic origins, and a reliable public infrastructure. This separateness often energized me, and allowed me to keep my frustration from overwhelming me when Rogelio Martínez Furé, the artistic director of the Conjunto Folklórico, didn't show up for an interview planned a month in advance due to his busy schedule because his bus never came; or when the entire *diplomercado* closed for the day just as I got there because the analog display on one of the cash registers was blinking; or when it took half an hour to place a call to María Teresa Linares, a former director of the Conjunto Folklórico and noted musicologist, because each time the call seemed to go through, her number connected to a different household. I existed in this confusing microcosm only for a few months at a time, returning to the more familiar confusions and prejudices of the United States at the end of each field trip.

My separateness and the accompanying illusory sense of control produced another reaction, that of responsibility for all my friends and colleagues who seemed to suffer as a result of this perceived surveillance and chaos. Because I did live most of my life apart from this other world, and because I presumed that I had the emotional resources to combat the massive inertia that seemed to affect many of my Cuban friends at least once a day, I took it upon myself to help them. I never showed up for an appointment empty-handed. To my drum teacher Alberto Villarreal and his family I would bring cooking oil, rice, chicken, tomato paste, pasta, chocolate, cookies, vitamins, aspirin—whatever they might have mentioned they needed during the previous visit that I could fit in my backpack for the next time.

To Rafael L. López Valdés (former ethnographer for the Cuban Academy of Sciences and advisor during my initial research) and his family I would bring rice, onions, garlic, avocados, beans, wine, cigarettes, rum, powdered milk—whatever they asked for that I could provide. Certainly these offerings could be interpreted as payment for interviews and lessons (Alberto, for example, would not accept money), but they were also a means of redressing a perceived imbalance in our lives as a whole. I had dollars, and so was relatively well-off in Cuba, even though this elevated socioeconomic status did not translate equitably to my life in the United States, where I was an indebted and impoverished graduate student. In a sense, these offerings assuaged some deep sense of guilt, simultaneously allowing me to acknowledge the absurdity of Cuba's economic situation (where the national currency is the peso, but most goods and services are bought and sold in dollars) and my limited ability to redress it, while continuing to interact with my colleagues.

A dual sense of responsibility and guilt has pursued me since I returned from Cuba in 1994, which was intensified during my trips there in 1997 and 1998. Even the act of writing letters to friends in Havana has carried with it a tremendous burden, because I feel that I should send money—not necessarily because I have extra money to send, but simply because I inevitably have more money than do my friends, and they probably need it more than I do. I write to Alberto a few times a year and enclose money whenever I know that the letter will be hand-delivered by a friend. I used to write to the López Valdés family several times a year and occasionally would send money, but lost touch with them for about a year after they moved to Puerto Rico in 1993. Their lives changed drastically, and I found it difficult to keep up with their many changes of address, jobs, and phone numbers, especially while I struggled to manage the same sort of instability in my own life.

As I distill and assimilate my fieldwork experiences in Cuba, Ogún is omnipresent. He lurks in the spirit of the *guardias,* he stalks me as he must have stalked his mother Yemú, he breaks into my house as he did in my prophetic dream. And I, like Ochún, seem to evoke his presence, sometimes taunting him, sometimes soothing him, always in sight. While Cuban tourist agencies and many a practitioner of Santería assert that it is Cuba's laughing and merciful patron saint Ochún and her flashy, powerful husband Changó that best represent the ethos of present-day Cuba,[25] my mind is drawn to Ogún—watcher, protector, violator, he who knows no boundaries.

NOTES

1. Diminutive word endings—as in *cafecito* (a cup of coffee), *roncito* (a shot of rum), and *poquitico* or *poquitín* (a little bit), where the root words are *cafe, ron,* and *poco*—are very common in Cuban Spanish, making mundane objects seem delicate, even graceful.

2. Although commonly used to refer to Abakwá initiations, *plante* is also the term for Abakwá ceremonies in general.

3. The establishment of the Sociedad de Estudios Afrocubanos was announced in the first volume of its journal (1937) by Fernando Ortíz, in the form of an open letter dated December 26, 1936. In it Ortíz asserts, "Blacks and whites must get to know and recognize each other in a reciprocal fashion in Cuba; and must come to feel jointly responsible for the historical force that they integrate. . . . The Society of Afrocuban Studies, which has just now been born, aspires to be an instrument for this examination and this union" (Ortíz 1937:5).

4. According to an elder Santero and former drummer in the Conjunto Folklórico, the name Obbini Batá means "women of the *batá*" in Cuban Lucumí.

5. Few women learn to play Nigerian Yoruba-style *batá* drums. Debra Klein, who learned Nigerian Yoruba-style *batá,* wrote a dissertation (2000) on modern *batá* performance.

6. Significantly, a Washington, D.C.-based Santero who is well-schooled in Yoruba translates this name as "depths of the ocean." This difference in translations underscores

the difficulty in securing a static, solitary meaning for any given phrase in Cuban Lucumí.

7. See Elizabeth Sayre's thoughtful and concise article on the subject of women *batá* drummers in *CBMR Digest* (2000), which was written in response to Andrea Pryor's interview with a woman *batá* drummer from Santiago, Cuba, also in *CBMR Digest* (1999). I explore the taboos associated with women playing *batá* drums in greater detail in chapter 3.

8. Figuring out Cuba's racial demographics has been the frustrating task of many scholars for the past thirty years. The most recent prerevolutionary census was completed in 1953, citing the black and *mulato* population to be 26.9 percent of the total (Casal 1979:15). The official figures for the next official Cuban census of 1970 were somehow lost, but Casal estimates that the "non-whites" would have comprised 40 percent of the total population by 1970. The last official Cuban census was completed in 1981, and cites 33.9 percent as the figure comprising Cuban blacks and *mulatos,* but its figures remain suspect by most non-Cuban scholars. For a wide range of demographic estimates, see Blutstein et al. 1971; Dzidzienyo and Casal 1979; del Aguila 1984; C. Moore 1988a; and Brenner et al. 1989. For a critical discussion of the statistical indexes for the Cuban population census and other demographic surveys, see C. Moore 1988a:357–365.

9. The terms in quotation marks are my translations of *actuaciones auténticas* and *espectáculos llamativos,* both of which Argeliers León used in an interview (October 18, 1990) to describe the differences between the presentations of the Teatro Nacional and those of the Conjunto Folklórico, respectively.

10. These definitions of derivation for Cuba's African-based traditions come from the much-repeated text that is read aloud at Conjunto Folklórico performances, which is based on research done by members of the Conjunto Folklórico and members of the Cuban Academy of Sciences.

11. For a detailed and current treatment of Cuba's historical and racial ties to Africa, see C. Moore 1988a:251–356. See Brock and Cunningham 1991 for a critical review of Moore's book. See Casal 1989 for a comparison of the socioeconomic position of Cuban blacks before and after the 1959 Cuban revolution. See Booth 1976 and Domínguez 1976 for a discussion of race relations in Cuba from 1959 to the mid-1970s. See Clytus 1970 for a personal account of how a black man fared in "red Cuba."

12. *Diplomercado* is a conjunction of *diplo* (from *diplomático,* or diplomat) and *mercado* (market, for canned goods, fresh produce, dairy, meats, etc.); *diplotienda* is a conjunction of *diplo* and *tienda* (store, for items one might purchase in a combination department-variety store).

13. The term *Cuban apartheid,* harsh though it may sound, has been adopted by Cuban and non-Cuban intellectuals alike. One of its most famous purported uses was by Carlos Varela, a Cuban singer-songwriter who spearheaded the nascent Novísima Trova (Newest Song) movement in Cuba. The Novísima Trova movement is a critical reac-

tion to the wholly prorevolutionary songs of the Nueva Trova (New Song) movement, started by now internationally famous singer-songwriters Silvio Rodríguez and
Pablo Milanés in the 1970s. Varela, though temporarily censured by the Cuban government for his critical views (most readily apparent in his popular songs "Guillermo
Tell" (William Tell) and "Tropicollage" (a play on the brand name of the cola available
for tourists and not Cubans, Tropicola), has now been rehabilitated because he has
toned down his criticism.

14. This policy changed due to the dire economic straits in which Cuba found itself. Com-
mander-in-chief Castro announced in July 1993 that Cubans could possess limited
amounts of dollars. Cubans can now stay in those hotels and shop in those stores
from which they were formerly excluded. As if to redress the imbalance, however,
there is now a new class of stores in Havana open only to embassy staff and other foreigners.

15. The idea of individual sacrifice for a common political goal (that of the revolution)
can be traced directly to the rhetoric of the Bolshevik revolution of October 1917 (see
Hosking 1985; Medin 1990). The specific application of that ideal to the Cuban situation is found throughout Castro's speeches, from that of December 2, 1961, in which
he declares his adherence to Marxism-Leninism (see Taber 1983:53), to various
speeches (March 26, 1962; September 2, 1970; November 15, 1973; December 17, 1980;
April 16, 1981; April 4, 1982) throughout the next two decades of the revolution (see
Taber 1983). The rhetoric about personal Cuban sacrifice in the face of foreign tourist
excess has been heavily emphasized since the announcement of the so-called *período
especial económico* (special economic period), which began in the fall of 1990 with the
withdrawal of Soviet economic support, and which has not ended yet.

16. The effects of the Soviet withdrawal were felt most strongly in the areas of food and
transportation, as the former Soviet Union had provided grain, oil, and machinery to
Cuba at a tremendous discount in exchange for sugar. Robert Pastor, in his 1983 analysis of the structure of the Cuban-Soviet relationship, noted Cuba's growing economic
dependence on its former patron: "The economic relationship between Cuba and the
Soviet Union has evolved from a few project agreements in the early 1960s, to membership in COMECON in 1972, to two five-year economic plans (1976–1980 and 1981–
1985), which further integrated Cuba into the Soviet economic system. From 1960 to
1979, Cuba received the equivalent of $16.6 billion in aid from the Soviet Union. . . .
The overall level of aid has quadrupled since 1974, partly in compensation for new
Cuban activities in the world and partly because the world price of sugar has declined
and that of oil has risen much more rapidly than Soviet prices" (Pastor in Brenner et
al. 1989:301). For extended discussions of the economic aspects of the former Cuban-
Soviet relationship, see Blasier and Mesa-Lago 1979, especially the chapters "COME-
CON in Cuban Development" (pp. 169–198) and "Sugar and Petroleum in Cuba-
Soviet Terms of Trade" (pp. 273–296). For specific trade statistics, see Brenner et al.
1989:537–545.

17. Again, see Taber 1983, as well as more recent speeches (1990–1995) of Castro reprinted in the daily newspaper *Granma* and in the monthly magazine *Bohemia*. Castro gives several speeches per week, so sources for this ideology are plentiful. With every speech come stronger exhortations to struggle harder with fewer resources, to fight against Yankee imperialism, to eschew luxury, and to support the state's effort to use foreign tourism to offset the deep economic misery caused by the Soviet withdrawal.

18. By summer 1992, Argelio had obtained a travel visa to visit the Netherlands, where he is now a permanent resident.

19. Interview with Argelio, October 7, 1990. Andrés Oppenheimer, in his prematurely titled book *Castro's Final Hour* (1992), identifies this phenomenon as "a worker's aristocracy," with tourist hotels acting as "a magnet for university graduates in economics, psychology, history and other professions" (Oppenheimer 1992:293).

20. This quotation is taken from the lyrics of a song by Silvio Rodríguez and refers to the prostitutes who traverse the long and lucrative stretch of Miramar's Fifth Avenue, also known as Havana's embassy row.

21. Many of the younger *guardias* come from Oriente, the easternmost province of Cuba. They leave their homes to serve in Havana because of the steady pay (in the early 1990s, the central and eastern provinces were hit harder by the *período especial económico* than the western part of the island), and because of the occasional enmity and competition between the two main cities, Havana in the west and Santiago in the east. It is unlikely that a Santiaguero will show favoritism toward a Habanero, and thus more likely that Cuban justice will be served. The Oriente accent is distinct from the Havana accent, and, in my distressed state, I could not understand the flattened vowels of the *guardia*.

22. Also called *patakín* (singular), and *patakínes* (plural). The most common spelling seems to be *pataki*; see, for example, García Cortez (1980). See J. Mason (1992) and Aróstegui Bolívar (1990) for characterizations of the *orichas* and their corresponding *patakíes*.

23. La Barba ("the beard") is but one of many names used by Cubans to refer to Fidel Castro. Other popular names include Papá ("daddy"), El Barbudo ("the bearded one"), and El Señor ("the man," or, ironically, "the Lord").

24. Although the tourist industry (including tourist hotels, tourist restaurants, tour buses, and rental car companies for tourists only) functioned fairly well, domestic services were unreliable. Dialing the same number three times from a local phone booth would connect me with three different households, none of which I had intended to call. Taking the local bus from one part of the city to another often entailed a three-hour wait, and then a half-hour ride known by Havana wits as the "bus surf," during which people were packed so tightly into the *guaguas* (buses) that if one person belched, everyone's stomach on the bus was forced to ripple in diaphragmatic sympathy—a specifically Cuban version of "the wave." Because of the paper shortage in Cuba, I supplied my own paper for photocopying. I would leave the hard-won origi-

nals and some blank paper with a clerk at the back of one of the few small *empresas* (firms) with photocopy machines. The following day a different clerk would tell me they were all "lost." Although these circumstances are common in many parts of the world, what is striking in Havana is the vast gulf between the lives of most Cubans and the lives of foreign tourists.

25. That Ochún and Changó are the patron saints of Cuba is common knowledge in Cuba. Every Cuban to whom I spoke, when the subject came up, mentioned both Changó and Ochún as patron saints of Cuba and as embodying some particularly Cuban ethos. Published sources repeating this assertion are manifold, and include Bolívar Aróstegui 1990, 1994; J. Mason 1992; and Cabrera 1980 (1974).

2

EL ESPECTÁCULO
Invitation to the Dance

The next day I told my *padrino* about the dream, and he told me about Ogún and the other *guerrero orichas*. Ogún is the second of the four warrior *orichas* in Santería (the first is Eleguá, the third is Ochosi, and the fourth is Osun). The hardest of workers, Ogún performed the physical labor that created the world. His compatriots, with whom he eats and lives, are possessed of equally impressive talents. Eleguá the trickster opens the road of possibilities with his forked stick, Ochosi the magician hunter fells his prey with his bow and arrow, and Osun the crippled healer soothes and protects with his herbal remedies. Especially in the province of Havana, the warrior *orichas* have taken on great importance in Santería. To receive *los guerreros* in Cuban Santería is to gain strong spiritual protection.

THE ORICHAS ARE COMING TO TOWN

On July 15, 1989, two days after we had arrived from Miami, several of us Americans were sitting in the bar on the tenth floor of the Hotel Presidente, on Calzada and Avenue G in the Vedado section of Havana. We had been gathered there by Sandra Levinson, our tour organizer and the director of the New York–based Center for Cuban Studies, for an informal briefing about Americans in Cuba. Buying pesos for dollars on the black market is illegal in Cuba, we were warned. Conchita would be our tour guide on any bus trips, Sandra reminded us, adding that we should not miss the Rumba Saturday show of the Conjunto Folklórico down the street, on the corner of Calzada and Fourth Street.

Four of us from a group of fifteen—Michael, Philip, Nora, and I—walked to the show venue from the hotel. The name of our three-week tour was "African Roots of Cuban Culture," general enough to encompass a broad range of interests. Michael, a calm, heavy-set African American from New Jersey, was studying Cuban *batá* drumming. Philip, tall, thin, intense, also African American, was a

44

young academic from Hartwick College in New York. His goal was to prove that the existence of *cabildos* (the fraternal mutual-aid associations of freed slaves) in the late nineteenth century was evidence of early black nationalism in Cuba. Nora, a tall, Anglo-American, graceful painter from New York City, wanted to learn more about the country that inspired such powerful nostalgia in her friends and colleagues. I, a nervous, Anglo-American, second-year graduate student in ethnomusicology at Brown University, had been riveted by the Providence performance of Afro-Cuban *batá* drummer Orlando "Puntilla" de los Ríos and his *grupo folklórico* a few months before. The sounds of the *batá* drums had penetrated my solar plexus, and I needed to hear more.

Perhaps the graceful Ochún is said to be Cuba's patron saint because of the improbably elegant dance Cubans do as they walk in the midday heat. Without slouching or slumping, they move with the ease of rustling green leaves, stirred by an invisible breeze. The wet, sizzling air transforms pastel buildings into Daliesque visions. Faces melt. Even the sounds of cars and the laughter of children become wavy, distorted by the heat.

Nora and I walked together, behind Michael and Philip. We walked in the shade when we could, but the heat pursued us. The ten blocks to the performance seemed like thirty. We moved slowly.

Eh mi amor, que linda eres. ¿Alemana? ¿Francesa? ¿Española?
(Hi, beautiful. How lovely you are. German? French? Spanish?)

Words seemed to fly at us from every side street, from hidden mouths.

¿Pero de dónde son? Veinte por uno, seguro. ¿Canadienses? ¿Holandeses?
(Where are you from? Twenty [pesos] to the dollar. Canadian? Dutch?)

We giggled softly as the liquid brown eyes of a child followed us briefly.

¡Compañera! Dáme chicle, chicle. Dáme pluma, pluma.
(Friend, give me some gum. Give me a pen.)

Trudging onward, we tried to appear oblivious to the attentive echoes.

"*Un peso . . . gracias,*" said the woman behind the iron-barred cement half-walls at Calzada and Fourth Street. The attractive young couple in front of us paid one peso each. "*Un dólar,*" said the woman behind bars to me. "*¿Un peso?*" I asked, hopefully. "*Un dólar. Un dólar.*" She waited, bored with the challenge. The four of us paid a dollar each, feeling vaguely marked. We laughed uncomfortably and searched for a place to sit. It was two o'clock in the afternoon on a Saturday, the sun was still high, and the leafy concrete patio was hardly shaded. The only shady spots (to the right of the entrance) were occupied by older people. The chairs were set up four deep to form a square-legged U facing the performance area. There were roughly two hundred seats, most of them filled. The only ones that weren't filled were the white wrought-iron cafe chairs facing the sun, on the right side of the U. These, we were informed, were reserved for tourists. (*"Son turistas?"* [Are you tourists?] *"No, pero—."* [No, but . . .] *"Pues no se puede . . ."* [Then you can't . . .] *"OK, OK, somos turistas."* [OK, OK, we're tourists.] *"Bueno, pues."* [All right, then.]) Most of the other members of the audience were sitting on plastic blue lawn chairs, which seemed much more comfortable. Only the "tourists" were made to sit in the baroquely attractive yet searingly hot white grille chairs. We obediently became tourists—a fact we were reluctant to admit, not least because U.S. law deems it illegal for Americans to be tourists in Cuba—relieved at least to be sitting down.

The drumming had none of the "cool fire" often associated with West African drumming traditions. Robert Farris Thompson has written of the "aesthetic of the cool" in West African performance (Thompson 1966; see also Chernoff 1979). His work attempts to reify an intangible sense of rhythmic intent, in which, for example, a bell pattern for fast *agbeko,* played only on the top pitch of the two-belled *gankogui,* "rides on top of" the rest of the instruments, contributing to the sense that the entire endeavor is somehow effortless, or "cool." In this particular Cuban performance, the drumming did not seem the least bit cool. Rather, it seemed as though the tempo of the piece and the interlocking patterns themselves were being pushed to some barely conscious limit, increasing the rhythmic tension, literally heating it up, the whole ensemble energized with the heat of the sun-baked concrete. The rhythms ambushed the audience, and after a while a familiar bell pattern emerged from the mix, a pattern commonly associated with West African *agbeko* performance:[1]

$$[\ | \ . \ | \ . \ | \ | \ . \ | \ . \ | \ . \ | \ ] (\text{etc.})^2$$

The monotony and velocity with which the pattern was played seemed to challenge the hearers' rhythmic equilibrium. In keeping with the heat of the performance, the bell was played even faster than it is usually played during fast *agbeko* (*agbeko* has three sections—slow, middle, and fast, and the fast bell pattern tends to stay on the top bell of the *gankogui*), but there were no Ewe drums supporting the bell. Rather, the artistic director of the group said, there were Yuka drums, which come from Bantu-speaking peoples of the Congo basin,[3] and which bear some resemblance to Ewe drums in that they are peg drums but are cylindrical rather than barrel-shaped[4] (see fig. 2.1). Another bell pattern soon emerged, rhythmically related to, but also opposing, the *agbeko* bell pattern:

$$[\ | \ \cdot \ | \ | \ \cdot \ | \ | \ \cdot \ ] \, (\text{etc.})^5$$

The supporting drums were roughly four and a half feet tall and were played with both sticks and hands, sometimes on the wooden sides of the drums to the rhythm of the bell pattern, and sometimes on the drum heads to a straight 4/4 accompaniment of the bell pattern:

$$[\ | \ \cdot \ | \ \cdot \ ] [\ | \ \cdot \ | \ \cdot \ ] [\ | \ \cdot \ | \ \cdot \ ] [\ | \ \cdot \ | \ \cdot \ ] (\text{etc.})$$

or

$$[\ | \ | \ \cdot \cdot \ ] [\ | \ | \ | \ \cdot \cdot \ ] [\ | \ | \ | \ \cdot \cdot \ ] [\ | \ | \ | \ \cdot \cdot \ ] (\text{etc.})$$

The only drum pattern on which the drummers seemed to elaborate or improvise was based on the following, more complex rhythmic pattern:

$$[\ | \ \cdot \cdot \ | \ \cdot \cdot \ | \ \cdot \cdot \ | \ \cdot \ | \ | \ | \ \cdot \ ]$$

Before the music began, Rogelio Martínez Furé, the artistic director of the group, spoke of *ritmos congos* and *influencias bantu,* the African-based performance traditions that had been passed down from the Bantu-speaking *negros de nación* (African-born Cuban slaves who spoke their native languages) to *bozal*-speaking *criollos* (slaves born in Cuba of African parents who spoke a mix of African languages and Spanish), and then to Spanish-speaking *cubanos* (slaves born in Cuba of *criollo* or Cuban parents). The most common media for this oral transmission were the religious rituals of Palo Monte, the Cuban name for Afro-Cuban religious practices derived from Bantu-speaking people of west-central and south-central Africa. The movements of the dancers represented the dances of the *palenques,* the secret encampments to which fugitive or runaway slaves fled to gain strength along their journey. The dancers were dressed plainly: white pants frayed at mid-calf length for the men with a blue or red kerchief tied around the neck, and white knee-length skirts for the women with a white blouse and a blue, yellow, or red head scarf. Their movements seemed violent and jerky; they jumped and ran, jumped and ran, occasionally kicking outward, as if in self-defense— their bodies narrating the escape of slaves from their masters.

This performance sequence represented a central mandate of the Conjunto Folklórico since its founding in 1962: the dramatization of Cuba's African-based performance traditions and histories to enlighten and delight audiences from

Figure 2.1. E*we* drums. (Pomona College collection)

Cuba and abroad. Founded a few years after the 1959 Cuban revolution, this state-sponsored group began its institutional life by presenting "folkloric" perform-ances of Afro-Cuban "religious" rituals, based on the renditions provided by older religious practitioners, many of whom became performers with the troupe. Al-though the Conjunto Folklórico also presents other Cuban performance tradi-tions—such as the *rumba,* the *contradanza,* and the *comparsa*—it is best known for its spectacular renditions of Afro-Cuban religious rituals, specifically, the *oricha* songs and dances of Santería.

INTRODUCTION TO THE ORICHAS

During the *palenque* performance, one hundred more spectators had squeezed into the audience space. Nora, Philip, Michael, and I moved to a standing position in the shade. The shade, under an awning to the right of the performance area, defined a space where Cubans and tourists mixed. Bombarded with questions about our nationalities, our linguistic capabilities, our personal lives, and our financial situations in an endless press of bodies—old and young, heavy and lean, dark and light, male and female—we smiled and looked away, too confused to answer.

In the meantime, the male musicians, all dressed in white, had emerged with another set of drums: three wooden, double-headed, intricately bound, hourglass-shaped drums—*batá* drums. A male vocalist sang into the microphone: *"Bara 'su ayo, omo yalawana mama keni irawo, eh eh."* After his opening line, the large drum *(iyá)*, whose two heads were tuned to the lowest tones, played complex calls to the medium drum *(itótele)* and the small drum *(okónkolo)*. *Itótele* and *okónkolo* responded with short, high-pitched, interlocking patterns. As the lead singer continued the praise song—*"O Bara wa yo, eke echu odara, omo yalawana mama keni irawo e"*—a dancer burst forward from the back of the performance space. She moved with little spurts of energy, running first to the right, then to the left, scanning the audience as if to find a playmate. Her striped red and black shirt and loose red pants were frayed, with a wide-brimmed straw hat to match, giving her the appearance of a playful peasant farmer. As she danced, a cluster of mostly female white-clad singers crowded around a microphone offstage, with the lead singer standing slightly apart from them. After the lead singer completed his praise song, the singers repeated two verses, standing close together behind the wrought-iron gates that separated the patio from the rehearsal building.

☺ LISTEN TO TRACK 1: Lázaro Ros singing for Eleguá in the Conjunto Folklórico.

> *Bara 'su ayo omo yalawana*
> Vital force Esu has arrived; child who divides the road.
> (Vital force who far and wide appears; child that separates, splits and divides the road.)

> *Mama keni iyawo e*
> May you not close the initiate's rightful path.[6]
> (May you not cut the initiate's mat of goodness.)

> *O Bara wa yo*
> Vital force who appears to us.
> (Vital force who comes to deliver.)

Eke e esu odara omo yalawana
Esu the mischievous one who is also good, child who divides the road.
(Forked Stick, Esù, performer of wonders, child that separates, splits and
divides the road.)

 Mama keni iyawo e
May you not close the initiate's righful path.
(May you not cut the initiate's mat of goodness.)[7]

After several trips back and forth across the patio, during which she removed a
pair of sunglasses from a hapless European spectator and placed a Cuban ob-
server's baseball cap on her head, she took a deep bow and stood to one side of
the patio. The audience tittered and clapped as she cast mischievous glances at the
now squinting European spectator and hatless Cuban. Smiling, sunglasses and
baseball cap in tow, she put her hands on her hips in a gesture of victory. This
dancer represented Eleguá, the first of the warrior deities of Santería, guardian of
the crossroads, the first *oricha* to be consulted before speaking with the other
orichas.

After the drumming for Eleguá stopped, the lead singer began again with a
powerful, arpeggiated call, and the second dancer emerged to a rhythmic pattern
that seemed much sharper and simpler than the first. Dressed in a faded purple
loincloth covered by a straw skirt, he carried a large flat-bladed knife, which he
seemed to use to cut through some imaginary brush in a repeated motion. The
unlit cigar in his mouth occasionally drooped and caught the string of green and
black beads draped diagonally over his shoulder as he repeated his cutting motion
with every step. As he stepped menacingly around the performance space, the
white-clad lead singer began the praise song.

Mariwo ye ye ye, mariwo ye ye ye
Palm fronds swirling, palm fronds swirling

Ogun alagba de o
Ogún the honored one arrives.[8]

The chorus sang back the same words, but with a countermelody. Glaring at the
audience as he moved toward the right side of the patio, the dancer took his place
purposefully next to "Eleguá," still holding his knife in his right hand. The *creyente*
(religious adherents) section applauded enthusiastically, while the tourists and *aficionados* were already looking toward the wings for the next performer. This

Figure 2.2. Gerardo Villarreal dancing for Changó, 1986. (© David Brown, all rights reserved)

dancer was Ogún, the second of the Santería warrior deities, friend of Eleguá, *oricha* of weapons and war, he whose force makes things work, perpetrator of atrocious crimes and sufferer of harsh, self-imposed penalties.

Once again the drumming stopped briefly. Then, after the singer's call, it resumed with an explosion that sounded as if six drums were playing at once. The third dancer jumped suddenly into the center of the performance space, propelled there by an invisible force. He wore a brocade vest, shiny red pants, and a small red and white crown . His pants were also cut off at mid-calf, but the hems were gathered and finished, giving him a more polished appearance. His movements were sudden and powerful and consisted mostly of thrusting his fists upward into the air, one after the other, and then bringing them down with a sudden force to his crotch. He kicked and twirled with the controlled energy of a martial artist, keeping his crown on his head all the while. The lead singer urged on the chorus (see fig. 2.2).

⊙ LISTEN TO TRACK 2: Felipe Alfonso singing "Aye le o" foxr Changó.

> *Ayé le o, ayé le o*
> Spirits plague this world, spirits plague this world.
> (The world is cruel, the world is cruel.)[9]

> *Okoro ima, okoro wa*
> The *oricha* is thunder, our *oricha*.
> (The deep calabash [gourd] is not seen, the deep calabash is searched for.)

> *Ayé le o oba ko wa o*
> Spirits plague this world, our king is strong.
> (The world is cruel, the king who flashes is searched for.)[10]

The chorus responded with same words and melody. This dancer's performance lasted longer than the previous two, and at the end of it he grabbed his crotch one more time and strutted over to the other two dancers. Several *aficionado* members of the audience stood up and yelled "*¡Que viva Changó!*" as he surveyed the audience approvingly, legs apart, arms crossed.[11]

The fourth dancer came into the performance space gracefully and calmly after being "called" by the lead vocalist, and as the drums beat a clearly discernible polyrhythmic pattern to which she swayed, moving her long skirts back and forth. Her long dress was royal blue and had puffy sleeves, a scoop neck, and a white petticoat underneath, and she wore a white cloth wrapped around her head. The sleeves, neckline, and hem bore a wavy white trim that echoed the undulating

Figure 2.3. Mercedes Riscart of the Conjunto Folklórico posing as Yemayá, 1987. © Roberto Salas for Ediciones ARTEX S.A.).

motion of her dance and of the chorus. The lead singer began the praise song, which the chorus repeated (see fig. 2.3).

♻ LISTEN TO TRACK 3: Zenaida Armenteros singing "Yemayá Asesu" in the Conjunto Folklórico.

> *Yemayá asesu, asesu Yemayá*
> Yemayá is the gush of the spring, the gush of the spring is Yemayá

Yemayá olodo, olodo Yemayá.
Yemayá is the owner of rivers, the owner of rivers is Yemayá.[12]

Her motions became frenetic as she responded to the quickening rhythms of the drums. She took a few syncopated steps to the right, spun rapidly clockwise, and then repeated those steps to the left before spinning counterclockwise, bending down low and billowing her skirts with each rotation. At the end of her dance she slowed down again and performed a deep curtsy, befitting the dignity of Yemayá, deity of maternity and the sea. As she took her place next to the other three dancers, several tourists cheered and whistled.

The fifth dancer moved onstage amid short bursts of sound, then swayed wildly back and forth, waving a short whisk broom. She spun around with more vigor than did the previous dancer and seemed to slap the air with her multicolored skirts, circling her dance space with the whisk broom all the while. Her dress and matching crown were striped with the colors of the rainbow, and she was bedecked with bracelets and earrings. Her dance communicated a violent energy similar to that of the second and third dancer, and with each arc of the whisk broom, she seemed to gather more energy. The lead singer's voice was plaintive as she called the chorus to respond. The chorus swayed back and forth as they repeated the song, without benefit of drums (see fig. 2.4).

🔊 LISTEN TO TRACK 4: Lázaro Ros and Zenaida Armenteros singing for Oyá in the Conjunto Folklórico.

> *Ayiloda ya o ku o*
> We greet you, Oyá, long life to you.
> (The Revolver who twists to create, mother, long life to you.)[13]
>
> *Olo omo 'de eke eyo ayaba.*
> We thank you, crowned daughter who faces war, beloved Queen.
> (The Owner of Children arrives, shout for joy, we turn off to meet her.)[14]

After the proud dancer finished her fierce performance, she strode over to the other dancers, whisk broom in one hand, the other hand perched on her hip. The audience clapped solemnly for Oyá, female warrior and guardian of the cemetery.

The last dancer moved onto the patio slowly after being summoned by the lead singer, and then waited, motionless, while the drums played a sweet, slow introduction. Then she put her hand up to her ear as if she had just heard them, and

Figure 2.4. Margarita Ugarte dancing for Oyá, 1986. (© David Brown, all rights reserved)

started to dance with a gentle swaying motion. Her full-skirted dress, bright yellow like her turban, had short puffy sleeves and a gathered waist. And like the preceding dancer, she also wore many bracelets and earrings. Her dance was gentle and close to the ground, and the chorus swayed gently with her.

> *Imbe imbe ma yeye*
> May you always be, Great Mother Ochún.
> (May you always be, Mother.)
>
> *Imbe imbe l'oro'de.*
> May you always be, Mother of the sacred tradition.
> (May you always be, Mother of Brass, Mother of Tradition.)
>
> *Imbe imbe ma yeye*
> May you always be, Great Mother Ochún.
> (May you always be, Mother.)
>
> *Imbe imbe l'oro'de.*
> May you always be, Mother of the sacred tradition.
> (May you always be, Mother of Brass, Mother of Tradition.)[15]

She repeated two movements: walking slowly while pushing the air on either side of her to the back with both hands, in movements of five; and lightly sloughing something off her torso with both hands, in movements of three. One woman in the *creyente* section, dressed in yellow, had her eyes closed and was singing along with the chorus, swaying back and forth. She stopped dancing in much the same way as she began, coming to a slow, graceful halt as she reached her fellow dancers. This last dancer represented Ochún, deity of rivers and romantic love, the patron saint of Cuba.

The entire audience was silent, collectively entranced, breathing as if one being. A few of the older people began to rock back and forth in their seats as the dancers moved, propelled by the *batá* rhythms. An electric charge seemed to pass through the audience, connecting us to the performance onstage. When the drumming finally stopped and the dancers took their final bows, the spell was broken, and the audience began moving and talking as before, playfully goading each other to participate in the *rumba* open to the audience that ended the performance (hence the name of the performances, Sábados de la Rumba, or Rumba Saturdays).

PRESENT TENSE: PAST MEETS FUTURE

The performance seemed to exist somewhere between religious ritual and night-club floor show, although not necessarily along a linear plane. The sequence and texture of the performance was similar to a series of well-timed, predictable *oricha* possessions. The *orichas* were "beckoned" through singing and drumming, so that they would "possess" the dancers, making them literally "dance the *orichas*." Even the order of their appearance was in keeping with the general order in which the *orichas* could be saluted during a ceremony: Eleguá is always first; followed by the rest of the warrior *orichas* (in this case represented by Ogún); then comes King Changó, who is usually followed by the major female deities, Oyá, Yemayá, and Ochún. Although Obatalá (the *oricha* most associated with the intellect, purity, and wisdom), Ochosi (a hunter-warrior *oricha* who lives with Ogún in the forest), Babalú-Ayé (a powerful deity associated with infectious diseases, especially ones that manifest on the skin), and several other well-known *orichas* were left out of this folkloric sequence, the effect of the performance was powerfully evocative: sacred sounds and gestures performed by divinely coded beings.

Steven Cornelius, in his work on Santería drummings in New York City (1989), has noted that the *batá* drumming patterns (and, I would add, the praise songs) embody "divine potential" or *aché,* that which moves us in and through the world. The sounds of sacred *batá* drums are capable of bridging the gap between heaven and earth. Similarly, Margaret Drewal, describing dancing for Ogún in Yorubaland and Brazil (1997), has extended this Yoruba concept of *aché* to include divine movement, that is, the dance of the *orichas*. The *orichas* are said to love singing, dancing, and the sound of the *batá* drums, especially when it is in their honor. Thus, even the folkloric performance of possession, with its particular focus on music and dance, can be said to embody as well as invoke the relationship between the human and the divine.

My first exposure to Cuba's African-based religious practices was the folkloric rendition of them presented by the Conjunto Folklórico, and the poetics of the performance were overwhelming. The reactions of the rest of the audience ranged from delight to light entrancement and mesmerization. Did the source of this performative power originate in the religious antecedents of the performance? Or was the strong performer-audience communication mostly a result of the high energy level of the *espectáculo*? How important was a "competent" audience for creating this power? In his work on sociolinguistic performance, William Labov has pointed out that Chomsky's (1965) "competence-performance" dichotomy is a revivification of de Saussure's (1906–1911) *langue/parole* opposition

(1983), which predates modern performance theory by sixty years. Labov asserts that "competence" *(langue)* is "the abstract knowledge of the rules of language," whereas "performance" *(parole)* is "the selection and execution of these rules" (Labov 1972:186).

In these folkloric performances, then, one can understand "competence" as the abstract knowledge of the religious "rules" or structures of Santería and other Afro-Cuban religious traditions that inform the performances of the Conjunto Folklórico. Following this logic, "performance" can be understood as the choreographed, staged events themselves, which come into being as a direct result of the "selection and execution" of certain (but not all) rules of religious performance. Each sector of the audience has a different level of knowledge of these rules or structures that govern the performance, and, as a result of these distinct "performative competencies," interacts differently with the performers of the Conjunto Folklórico.

Since that first performance in July 1989, I have attended approximately twenty events *(actuaciones)* of the Conjunto Folklórico, many of them Sábados de la Rumba.[16] The Conjunto Folklórico's repertoire, however, includes more than the narrative dances of Cuba's African heritage. The troupe is also known for its representations of Cuba's European performance traditions, such as the Cuban *contradanza* and the *habanera,* both of which were popular salon dances in Cuba during the nineteenth century. During the month of Cuban *carnaval* (July), the Conjunto Folklórico incorporates choreographed renditions of rowdy Cuban *carnaval comparsas* or musical processions. And on some Rumba Saturdays, more than half of the performance is filled with the dramatic re-creations of the religious songs and dances of Santería and other African-based Cuban religions, the renditions of which swell audiences even during the course of a single performance.

Indeed, comprehending the responses of the Conjunto Folklórico's audience is crucial to understanding the interplay between the African-based religious traditions and the secularized, commodified context in which they are performed. My belief that the audience holds the key to understanding the negotiation and perpetuation of meaning in the Conjunto Folklórico's performances has shaped my critical engagement with its work. Because the audience at a Conjunto Folklórico event is typically composed of at least four distinct groups, what is communicated between the performers and the audience is by no means monolithic. Each sector of the audience—young foreign tourists *(extranjeros),* older Cuban religious practitioners *(creyentes),* young Cuban black marketeers *(jineteros),* and the young dancers and singers hoping to perform with the troupe *(aficionados)*— lends its own particular dynamic to the performance.[17]

Figure 2.5. Spanish participant in a Sábado de la Rumba, 1990.

During the first performance I attended in 1989, most obvious among the audience members were the European and Canadian tourists or *extranjeros,* some of whom had come to Cuba in order to participate in a Conjunto Folklórico performance workshop called "FolkCuba" held twice a year (in January and in July). They made up perhaps fifty members of the audience and could be clearly picked out by their lighter skin, hair, and eyes, their fine cotton clothing, and their expensive audiovisual recording devices. They sat mostly on the right leg of the square-legged U-shaped seating arrangement and heartily cheered on their friends (also foreigners) who were performing for the first (and probably last) time with the Conjunto Folklórico (see fig. 2.5).

The center part of the U was filled with Cubans, mostly the very old and the very young, with some family members in between. These Cubans appeared to be somewhat poorer than the young urban sophisticates frequently seen on the streets near Fourth and Calzada. These people occasionally wore ill-fitting clothing—tattered blouses or skirts, rubber or plastic thong sandals that had seen better days. They were also sartorially set apart by their neck and wrist adornments: *collares* (ritual necklaces) and *idés* (ritual bracelets), the brightly colored beads of each representing their patron saints or *orichas.* These were the *creyente* members of the audience who sang along with the performers, moving as Ochún swayed, tapping their feet to Ogún's fierce stomp, laughing at Eleguá's playful antics (see fig. 2.6).

On the left leg of the U, nattily attired in horn-rimmed wire-framed glasses, tight-fitting jeans, several pounds of gold jewelry, colorful short-sleeved print shirts, and exotically patterned braids, fidgeted Havana's young *jineteros,* the fast-growing sector of the population dedicated to making a profit on the black market, mostly by selling pesos (real and counterfeit) for dollars.[18] Their best customers were tourists, who assumed that they needed plenty of Cuba's supposed national currency while they were in Cuba, and who frequently were found at performances of the Conjunto Folklórico. The *jineteros* clearly enjoyed the performance and often used the free-for-all *rumba* at the end of the performance to target a potential deal (a two-minute rumba with a charming *jinetero* or *jinetera* could make the prospect of changing money less risky, or at least more fun).

And scattered in between, usually squeezed into the front rows of the audience, were the *aficionados,* the hopeful young singers, dancers, and instrumentalists with their sights set on joining the troupe one day. Watching the performers closely, and sometimes moving in concert with them, the *aficionados* try to memorize as much of the Conjunto Folklórico's repertoire as possible by the time they get a chance to audition for the troupe.

Figure 2.6. Part of the *creyente* section of the audience for a Sábado de la Rumba, 1990.

Although all four groups were born out of Cuba's past, at this moment in Cuba's history, the *creyentes,* the *jineteros,* and the *extranjeros* and *aficionados* now seem especially representative of Cuba's past, present, and future, respectively. The *creyentes,* many of whom are old, and most of whom would not have felt comfortable wearing their *collares* and *idés* outside their *barrios* even ten years ago, represent Cuba's past. They are living links to the early twentieth-century Cuba of Fernando Ortíz, when the African-based religious traditions of Havana and Matanzas provinces were first dubbed "folklore" by the intellectual elite, and when the high priests of these religious traditions were called *brujos* (witches) by many Catholic Cubans. The *creyentes* are descended from the African slaves of the past four centuries, who relied on their *orichas* and *ngangas*[19] for survival, and who withstood the repression and prohibition of their religious practices for more than sixteen generations.

The *jineteros,* mostly in their twenties and thirties, represent the trenchant contradictions of Cuba's present. They are not necessarily godless, but they do not support the same mixture of fear and reverence toward the unknown that their prerevolutionary parents and grandparents maintained. In the scientific atheism of socialism, everything is knowable, so religion has no place in a socialist society unless its "mystery" can be deconstructed and then put to some material use.[20] At the moment, the *jineteros* have reconstructed and reinterpreted these religions as a tourist attraction (with the help of the Conjunto Folklórico), and *extranjeros* mean hard currency and material goods for the black market. Although all black market activity is illegal in Cuba (especially changing pesos for dollars), I have yet to see a uniformed policeman mingle with the audience at a Conjunto Folklórico performance to enforce the law.

These *extranjeros,* with their open hearts and open purses, represent an important component of Cuba's immediate future. They come from lands of plenty, in comparison, and many believe in economic equality, the much repeated ideal of Cuban socialism. They are charmed by the sweet sensuality of daily Cuban life and fascinated by the raw exoticism of Cuba's African heritage. They come as a byproduct of Cuba's recent joint ventures with Spain, Italy, France, and Germany in hotels, restaurants, and travel agencies. They have hard currency, and they spend it in Cuba. Occasionally they fall in love with Cubans, whom they marry and take out of the country (for which privilege the non-Cuban must pay roughly US$2,000;[21] compared to the cost of a purely Cuban marriage—approximately 45 pesos—international marriages are far more expensive). And occasionally they become initiated into one of the African-based religious traditions (sometimes after seeing a performance of the Conjunto Folklórico, or, more likely, after falling in love with a religious practitioner), which costs about US$4,000. The *afi-cionados,* with their dreams of artistic fame, and perhaps the chance to go on tour with the Conjunto Folklórico, are part of Cuba's future as well. They are linked to the *extranjeros,* in that what fuels their hope to be involved with the organization is often the chance to escape from the frequent grimness of quotidian Cuban life, to become permanent tourists in another land.

Each of these sectors brings to the performance its own energy and expectations, and thus shapes the dynamic of the performance. The *creyentes,* themselves religious practitioners, give back the spontaneous energy of sacred ritual to the performers through their extant knowledge of the original performance (the religious ceremony) on which the folkloric rendition is based. They translate the drumming and dancing that takes place in the spacious and leafy atmosphere of the Conjunto Folklórico's tiled patio into a memory of a *toque* in someone's *solar,* a typically crowded religious celebration in a one-room apartment, and their energy often ignites the troupe's performances. The *viejos* and the *ancianas* (old men and old women) are always called on or volunteer when audience participation is needed, and they provide the magic that might otherwise be missing from the performance. The old people are often relatives or friends of the early informant-performers of the Conjunto Folklórico, and occasionally they themselves have been sources of information about Cuba's African-based religions for CFNC performances.

The *jineteros,* with their well-developed sense of the value of a peso, bring to the performance their high expectations of a thoroughly entertaining *espectáculo.* They raise the stakes of performance. They are easily bored and are just as likely to strike up a conversation and potential deal with a tourist as to watch the performance. So the performance must become a show, the "authenticity" of which is constantly balanced with a Tropicana-like style, according to the estimated attention span of the audience. Whereas Yemayá might be dressed in royal blue cotton in a *casa de santo* in Regla, a port town across the bay from the city of Havana, for the Conjunto Folklórico she wears a blue sateen gown and a gauzy tulle cape, with silver sequins adorning the white trim of her dress. And if the *batá* rhythms for Changó are played in Guanabacoa[22] with a fast and complex energy only after lining out the initial chant, at a performance of the Conjunto Folklórico they are played even faster, forcing the dancer's gestures beyond *macho.*

The *extranjeros,* with their private histories of being audience members in the concert halls of London, Berlin, and Paris, and at the theaters of Montreal, Barcelona, Stockholm, and New York, bring to the performance the expectation of professionalism and the promise of hard currency. The Conjunto Folklórico, which is always interested in touring outside Cuba, is, above all, a professional troupe. Despite the informal performance space, the performance itself is formal and flawless: the barefoot dancers move with uncommon grace and strength; the drummers play with the relaxed power of life-long musicians; and the singers are well-rehearsed, on key, and usually well-miked. Whenever the troupe is introduced, their numerous European tours are mentioned in the next sentence. Indeed, because European participants have provided many of the students and most of the hard currency for the FolkCuba workshop since its establishment in 1985, the European tourists in the audience are always thanked profusely and invited to participate in next year's FolkCuba. And, like all non-Cubans, tourists pay in dollars to see the performance, while Cubans pay in pesos. The *aficionados,* seated in the front rows, place themselves near the *extranjeros,* yet also close to the *creyentes.* They closely follow the performances, memorizing gestures, songs, and rhythms, hoping to be chosen as new members during the next season's auditions.

On that first field trip in 1989, I saw myself as part *extranjera* and part *investigadora* (part foreign tourist and part researcher) and dutifully sat with the other foreign tourists at the early performances of the Conjunto Folklórico. As my fieldwork progressed, however, I began to evolve into other categories, realizing the inevitably permeable nature of these constructs. During my classes at the FolkCuba workshop, my performative intent leaned toward that of an *aficionada,* as I excitedly memorized the rhythmic phrases and dance steps of "the *orichas.*" In my attempts to navigate Cuba's byzantine three-tiered economic system of the early 1990s (one currency, pesos, for Cubans in nontourist industries; another, the *B-especial,* for Cubans in the tourist industry; and yet another, dollars or other hard currency, for foreigners), I made friends with more than a few *jineteros,* whose exchange rates varied by as much as forty pesos to the dollar. And finally, during the most recent years of my fieldwork, I have found myself sitting with the *creyentes,* singing along with the performers and swaying back and forth as Yemayá and Ochún come out to dance.

When I returned from my first trip to Cuba in July 1989, my impulse was to write that Afro-Cuban religious practitioners were being disempowered by the recontextualization and commercialization of their religious traditions. The performances of the Conjunto Folklórico seemed symptomatic of a larger policy: diluting the demographic base of Afro-Cuban religious practitioners by bombarding them with secular theatrical performances derived from their own religious traditions. One reason the policy of defanging the sacred while empowering the secular was so successful, I reasoned, was that the Cuban government knew exactly who would comprise the audience, and how each sector of the audience would function. The *creyentes* would soak up the exposure of their until recently repressed religious practices, and might even take home the overlay of the new secular context. The *jineteros* would trade Cuban pesos for tourist dollars, which was illegal until July 1993, bringing more hard currency into the Cuban economy. And the tourists would flock to the shows, the international appeal of which had already been proven on the Conjunto's first few European and African tours in the 1960s. I was so convinced of this that I presented a conference paper (Hagedorn 1992) on my hypothesis soon after I returned from one of my early field trips. What was missing from my initial analysis, however, was a more nuanced understanding of how deeply related the Conjunto Folklórico performances were to religious ceremonies.

THEATER AND RITUAL AND THE "FOLKLORICIZATION" PROCESS

Richard Schechner neatly framed the issue of "folkloricizing" religious performance in his 1990 interview with Valencia, the ritual leader of the Yaqui Indians of New Pascua, Arizona, when he asked Valencia about the Mexican Ballet Folklórico's rendition of the Yaqui Deer Dance:

VALENCIA: The people that brought this Mexican company together were practicing the various cultural dances in many parts of Mexico—anyone can learn the dance, and they did. So they brought out a very broad imitation of the deer dance.

QUESTION: How did that make the Yaquis who saw it, and who knew how to dance the deer, feel?

VALENCIA: Very, very discouraged. In fact, one of the young men that became a deer dancer was in training at that time for the military and he saw the dance in Mexico. He was very discouraged and he said: "You know, they are just making fools of the Yaquis." I told him, don't look at it that way. Look at it as a play. There's nothing religious about it, nothing Indian about it. It is for the non-Indian population. It's not a Yaqui performance.

QUESTION: Are things different in the Folklorico from the dance we saw yesterday?

VALENCIA: Everything is different. The deer head is different, the gait is different. It doesn't harm us, it frustrates us. So our people stopped doing it. It's frustrating to have somebody else say, "I'm doing a Yaqui thing," when

the Yaquis know that it is not. . . . If a hundred songs were recorded, and a
hundred songs were sold, I think that we would not use them anymore.
It's not the condition of "freshness." You have to be a Yaqui, or at least an
Indian, to understand how the mysteries of that song—the words, the
purpose of it, the spiritual purpose of it—to understand that the spiritual
benefits of the song are withdrawn if the song is commercialized.
(Schechner 1985:5)

In the case of the Mexican Ballet Folklorico's adaptation of the Yaqui Deer
Dance, the meanings are not only many, but they are also valued quite differently.
For the Yaqui, according to Valencia, the Deer Dance loses its spiritual benefits
when performed by people who are not Yaqui, who are not part of the spiritual
community, who have no basis for understanding the sacred origins of the performance. In fact, the folkloric performance becomes not only secular in this case,
but also offensive to the people who originated it. In the case of the Conjunto
Folklórico, in contrast, there seems to be little offense taken by the religious practitioners whose utterances are being borrowed and reshaped. It would seem likely
that such offense is avoided precisely because the religious practitioners themselves have taken part and continue to take part in the process of borrowing and
reshaping the religious material; that is, the rendering is impelled both by the
community of religious practitioners and by the secular, state-run institution. In
that way, the *creyentes,* especially the drummers, are able to maintain some control over the way in which their religious traditions are portrayed in a secular
context. Perhaps it is this control that allows the surface layer of meaning (perceived by those "incompetent" audience members who have no knowledge of the
religious rules that inform the performance) to be constructed without affecting
the deeper, religious core of meaning, which is accessible to "competent" audience members.

The phenomenon of presenting "ritual as theater as ritual" seems central to
understanding the dynamic between the performers and the audience, and certainly is not limited to Cuba. The Ceremonials of the Tewa Pueblo Indians, thoroughly documented by Jill Drayson Sweet (1983), provide an important parallel to
the performances of the Conjunto Folklórico. Tewa Ceremonials are commercial
performances based on village ritual events, designed to attract a non-Tewa (tourist)
audience. Like the performances of the Conjunto Folklórico, the Tewa Ceremonials "have not replaced Tewa village dramatic events; rather they have developed
as a separate kind of phenomenon" (Sweet 1983:253). According to Sweet, because
the Tewa have not permitted these Ceremonials to affect their ritual events, the

"desired experiential state of the ritual performer can still be achieved at a Ceremonial performance" (ibid.), thus supporting Schechner's (1985) suggestion that aspects of sacred and theatrical performance may overlap, and that in some cases, the theatricalized performance may refer to its sacred origins as a sort of climax. But there is an important difference between the Tewa Ceremonials and the Conjunto Folklórico performances that cut short the analogy. In the case of the Ceremonials, the Tewa themselves effected and limited the transformation from ritual to theater. In the case of the Conjunto Folklórico, however, the full transformation came not from the religious practitioners themselves, but from the artistic directors, folklorists, and choreographers of the group, who were in some sense accountable to the broader cultural policies of the Cuban government.

Then how can one classify, much less analyze, the Conjunto Folklórico's performances? Victor Turner's concept of the "ritual-theatre continuum" (1982),[23] which emphasizes not static categories but flexible continua, proves useful in locating the performative event. The idea that ritual and theater are located along the same continuum facilitates the task of differentiating between them in a performative context, but does not allow for the circular and overlapping motion that the ritual-theater-ritual pattern seems to imply. My own idea focuses not so much on a ritual-theater continuum per se, but on the overlapping and occasional cohabitation of sacred and secular, folk and folkloric within the same performative sphere.

My preliminary research suggested that the Conjunto Folklórico and other *grupos folklóricos* were recontextualizing the African-based religious traditions (already classified as folk traditions by Fernando Ortíz in the early 1900s) of black Cubans in their performances. These ritual traditions were recontextualized in order to satisfy more fully their new revolutionary function: the uplifting, informing, and dignifying entertainment of the Cuban people. As a result, some of the most religiously significant aspects of these traditions (such as the sacrifice of certain birds and four-legged animals) were excised from these representations, thus further removing these performances from the realm of daily life. They no longer represented ritual practice; rather, they communicated a beautiful and powerful world, located far away from the deeply embedded beliefs and long-standing faith that might have motivated the sacrifice of a goat or the *oricha* possession of a *creyente*.

Yet these representations still employ the powerful communicative aspects of the ritual folk traditions: the songs, the dances, and the drumming. These folkloric performances, as they are called, thus suggested the transformation from folk to folkloric, a process of "folkoricization," in which the religious practice that has been classified as a folk tradition is reinterpreted and recontextualized as a staged and commodified folkloric performance (one that we might call secular), and yet still draws upon the communicative inspiration of its folk (read "religious") roots. The divine utterances of religious performance (which are sacred, noncommercial, nonstaged, and directed inward) are translated, much like an obscure language, into a more broadly understood "lingua folklorica," the language of folkloric performance, which is secularized, staged, commodified, and directed outward, toward the audience. But when these directions overlap, and when the abstract sacred rules and their possible execution in performance are bartered between audience and performers, the relationship between sacred and secular becomes even more compelling.[24]

What is exchanged between religious and folkloric events is the intent and consequent energy of the performance. An Afro-Cuban performance that is intended to be secular will create the rehearsed, controlled, predictable energy that is common to traditional theater. An Afro-Cuban performance that is intended to be sacred will run on unrehearsed, unmediated, spontaneous energy, relying more on audience participation. Schechner (1985:10–11) refers to this type of spontaneous energy when he writes that "in all kinds of performances a certain definite threshold is crossed . . . if it isn't, the performance fails." He locates the crossing of this threshold in the intensity of audience response: "No theater performance functions detached from its audience. . . . Spectators are very aware of the moment when a performance takes off. . . . The performers have touched or moved the audience, and some kind of collaboration, collective special theatrical life, is born." This "collective special theatrical life" is the goal of most folkloric performances, yet to achieve it, folkloric performers must rely on the spontaneous creative energies of religious "body memories"—the evocation of a powerful praise song by an *akpwón*, an overwhelming gesture witnessed in an *oricha* possession, a fluid *toque* for Yemayá. Quite literally, the folkloric performers go back to the roots of the Conjunto Folklórico with each show, when the informant-performers first performed their embodied memories of *oricha* possessions.[25]

In the same way that there is proper *oricha* etiquette at a *toque de santo*, so, too, are there rules of engagement for folkloric performances. In order to understand how one participates in a folkloric performance, we must turn our attention to audience-performer interaction, specifically, the idea of a competent audience (Labov 1972). The more the audience knows about the origins of the musical and gestural articulations of folkloric performance (i.e., the more competent it is), the more likely it is that the audience will interpret the performance as having sacred as well as secular intent. Directly related to this is the idea of the polyvalence of a performance—the meanings of the performances of the Conjunto Folklórico depend on the backgrounds and expectations of the audience, and how these diverse experiential memories are communicated and understood by the performers. The idea of the audience in the Conjunto Folklórico's performances (and the relative lack thereof in religious performance, where most, if not all, who are present participate in an active way) is crucial to understanding the interpretive interplay between the religious antecedents of many of the Conjunto's pieces and the secularized, commodified context in which they are performed.

NOTES

1. The *agbeko* bell pattern, so called because of its association with the *atsiagbeko* war dance of the Ewe people of Ghana, can be found in many parts of West Africa. It was fully and permanently transplanted to Cuba during the slave trade. A. M. Jones has called it the most important pattern throughout Africa: "In fact both its ubiquity and its typically African form qualifies it to be called the African 'Signature tune'" (Jones 1959:210). John Miller Chernoff (1979) provides an excellent sociocultural analysis of the importance of this pattern in West African life, and both David Locke (1982) and James Koetting (1970) explore ways to transcribe the performance of an *agbeko* ensemble. Locke (1982:220) provides a good transcription of a slow *agbeko* ensemble.

2. In this and following transcriptions of percussive patterns, "|" means sound and "." means equally timed rest. "[ ]" indicates one cycle of the pattern.

3. According to Fernando Ortíz (1952), it is likely that the ancestors of the Yuka drums of Cuba originated in present-day Angola. For good photographs of these Yuka drums, see Ortíz 1952–1955, vol. 4, pp. 182–193).

4. Ewe drums, like *batá* drums, are considered a family. The lead drum, *atsimewu,* is considered the father of the ensemble. *Kidi,* the largest supporting drum, is the big sister, while *totodzi* and *kroboto* are the twin brothers. *Kagan,* the smallest drum, is the baby boy.

5. This is also a common bell pattern in the Ewe performance of *adjogbo* (the name of the dance and the bell pattern), according to Michelle Kisliuk (personal communication, September 1994).

6. Song texts for the *orichas* in this chapter are transliterations of what I heard at a Conjunto Folklórico performance in July 1989. I have translated these texts hesitantly, relying on L. Cabrera (1986a), M. Mason (personal communications, 1995–2000), and J. Mason (1992) for a deeper sense of their meanings. My translations are above J. Mason's translations (1992), which appear in parentheses. The song text is understood by the Cuban singers to be Yoruba but is missing the diacritical markings (and thus the pronunciation cues) typically found in transliterations of that language. Yoruba is

tonal and occasionally nasal, but in its liturgical Cuban setting it loses most of its tonality and nasality. On the rare occasion that these song texts are reproduced in print in Cuba (see Ortíz 1951, 1965, 1973; Chao Carbonero 1982), they are "Cubanized" and have none of the diacritical markings found in Yoruba dictionaries or in other Yoruba texts (for example, see African Language Institute 1991; see also Drewal 1992 and Matory 1994). Rather, they incorporate occasional accents, tildes, and umlauts, diacritical markings already found in Cuban Spanish. The mix of Yoruba root words with Cuban inflections and diacritical markings creates Cuban Lucumí, the liturgical language used by practitioners of Santería in Cuba. As a result of these many evolutions, there is a tremendous variety of transliterations and translations of Lucumí texts. I have chosen to transliterate these song texts in the Cuban fashion; that is, with only diacritical markings that are found in Cuban Spanish. For a more orthographically complete version of these song texts, see J. Mason 1992. I explore the possibilities and pitfalls of translating Cuban Lucumí praise song texts in more detail in chapter 4.

7. J. Mason here translates *irawo* as "initiate," though my experience is that *iyawó* is more properly understood as "initiate." Further, *irawo* has been translated elsewhere (Cabrera 1986a:169) as "rainbow," "star," and "comet." M. Mason (personal communication, 2000) notes that *odara* means "good"; Cabrera writes that *odara* also means "clean" (1986a:233), though J. Mason (1992) and Bolívar (1994) understand *odara* as referring to wonders.

8. L. Cabrera, J. Mason, M. Mason, and I all seem to agree that this translation is accurate.

9. My translations are above J. Mason's translations (1992), which appear in parentheses. Cabrera (1986a:71–72) lists six meanings for *ayé*: "devil or spirit from another world"; "witch"; "oars"; "an elongated shell, different from the cowrie shell"; "money"; "world."

10. Concepts of "thunder" and "strength" seem appropriate for Changó, inasmuch as he is the *oricha* associated with thunder, lightning, bravery in battle, and strength in leadership.

11. Although every history of the Yoruba peoples of Nigeria mentions Changó (usually spelled Shango or Sango in non-Cuban texts) as an important Yoruba king (referred to variously as the third king, the fourth king, and one of the early kings of the Yoruba people), there seems to be no idea—no speculation, even—about when he lived. Smith (1969:14) relates that on the basis of glottochronological evidence, the Yoruba language is between five thousand and six thousand years old. However, written evidence of the reigns of kings or the wars that they fought is lacking until the early sixteenth century, and historians of the Yoruba assume that the reigns of Oranyan, his son Shango, and the other divine progeny of Ife (sacred mythical city of the Yoruba) and Oyo had already passed into the realm of legend. See Smith (1969:3–56) for an interesting discussion of myth and historicity in Yoruba lore. See Thompson (1983) for a discussion of the necessary connection between kings and *orichas* in Yoruba thought,

with special reference to Shangó (1983:84–85). See Johnson (1969) for a history of the Yoruba. See Apter (1992:13–34) for a critique of Johnson and an interesting discussion about contradictory oral narratives in the representation of Yoruba political hierarchies. In general, it seems that Changó's importance lies not in whether or when he really lived, but in what he has come to represent in Yoruba and Cuban religious traditions: a fiery, strong, tempestuous leader, capable of meting out swift and terrible justice to his children.

12. Yemayá Asesu is one of the *caminos* (roads or avatars) of Yemayá. Olodó, however, is often associated with Ochún, as in "Olodó omí," which refers to a child of Ochún. One explanation for this may be that Yemayá and Ochún are closely related in the pantheon of Santería (Cabrera 1974). In fact, there are some *caminos* in which Yemayá and Ochún are very similar, such as Yemayá Akuará and Ochún Akuaró, where they live in the same waters, between the river and the sea.

13. My translations appear above J. Mason's translations (1992), which appear in parentheses. Cabrera (1986a:72, 252) writes that *Ayiloda* refers to act of lifting oneself up to utter a greeting, as occurs during and after the *moforibale* (ritual greeting in Santería). She also notes that *okuo* is one possible response to such a greeting. In this context, J. Mason's "long life to you" for *okuo* seems more appropriate for a divine being than Cabrera's "good day."

14. Cabrera (1986a:255) gives "thank you" as the meaning for *oló* and "to go" as the meaning for *olo*. She also gives "face" for *eké* and "lie," "jealousy," "bracelet," and "table" for *eke* (p. 105). Calling Oyá a queen who faces war seems to make sense, inasmuch as she is the only female warrior deity, known for fighting alongside her husband, Changó, when he was king of Oyó. Although other female *orichas* have roads or avatars that are warriorlike, such as Yemayá Okuti, Oyá is the only female *oricha* whose primary association is with doing battle as bravely as the men in her life, Changó and Ogún.

15. My translations are above J. Mason's translations (1992), which appear in parentheses. Cabrera (1986a:323) cites *mbe* as the verb for "to be" and gives five meanings for *yeye,* most of which seem directly related to Ochún: "good, delicious, plentiful"; "smooth"; "plums"; "mother Oshún"; and "yellow." Cabrera's definitions of *oro* are also numerous, and include "sacred," "month," "mass," "religious ceremony," "word," "the songs and drum rhythms that honor each *orisha*," "tomorrow," and "*orisha*" (1986a:275).

16. See Daniel (1995) for a thorough ethnography of Cuban *rumba*, which focuses on the Conjunto Folklórico Nacional de Cuba as the main vehicle through which the *rumba* was popularized and nationalized.

17. These "sectors" can be loosely related to MacCannell's "social structural differentiation" (1999:11), which includes differences in socioeconomic class, race, ethnicity, lifestyle, age, and other factors.

18. The black-market (unofficial, of course) exchange rate as of August 1994 was roughly 100 Cuban pesos for one U.S. dollar. In the early 1960s, the exchange rate was still roughly one peso for one dollar, and there was no viable Cuban black market for U.S.

dollars. During the 1980s, the Cuban black market for dollars exploded onto the tourist scene, locating itself mostly in Havana and in outlying beach resort areas, such as Varadero. In July 1989, the black-market exchange rate was twenty-five Cuban pesos for one U.S. dollar, and the rate rose by roughly fifteen Cuban pesos each year until 1997, when it stabilized at between twenty and twenty-five Cuban pesos to the dollar.

19. *Orichas* are deities in Yoruba-influenced Santería; *ngangas* are deities in Congo-influenced Palo Monte.

20. See Kirk (1989) and Castro (1987) for recent official statements about the status of organized religion in Cuba. See also the interview excerpt with Rafael L. López Valdés in chapter 3 and excerpts of interviews with María Teresa Linares and Argeliers León in chapter 5.

21. My source for this is "Para su matrimonio en Cuba" (For your marriage in Cuba), published by the Consultoría Jurídica Internacional (International Legal Bureau) in 1994. The cost of two international marriage licenses (one for each partner in the marriage, inasmuch as it is possible that both partners may not be in the same country at the same time) is US$525; the presence of a notary to witness the marriage outside of the offices of the International Legal Bureau is US$100 (notarization outside the bureau's legal offices is optional); the processing of all necessary certificates of birth, divorce, and death costs US$100 each; the invitation to live outside of Cuba with one's spouse costs US$120; and the issuance of the new passport to enable a Cuban to live outside of Cuba costs US$100. All told, a marriage ceremony held at the International Legal Bureau's office would require at the very least US$525 (licenses) + US$200 (two birth certificates) + US$120 (living outside of Cuba with one's spouse) + US$100 (new passport) 5 US$945.

22. Guanabacoa is a small town east of the city of Havana. It is home to Alberto's mother, *akpwón* and founding member of the Conjunto Folklórico Lázaro Ros, and many other religious practitioners and performers.

23. Turner's work is particularly interesting here because his starting point is that ritual itself is all-important (see Turner 1969), the key to any given society or culture. He extends this definition to theater as he constructs the performance continuum, along which both ritual and theater are located.

24. See the collected papers of the International Council for Traditional Music on the impact of tourism on traditional and sacred music: "There is a danger of trivializing something meaningful and important. . . . There is a spiritual danger in people's accepting a fee for something they do freely, and which they view, not as self-created art, but as a psychic force channeled through themselves" (1988:20).

25. Several CFNC members explained to me that to dance in the manner of one's head *oricha* in a nonreligious context is dangerous to the initiate and disrespectful to the *oricha*. In the early days of the Conjunto Folklórico, it is most likely that the informant-performers were embodying the memories of *oricha* possessions initiated by *orichas* other than the ones who owned their respective heads.

3

EMBODYING THE SACRED IN
AFRO-CUBAN PERFORMANCE
Negotiating the Rules of Engagement

Intrigued by Ogún's presence and encouraged by my *padrino,* I found the following *pataki* (origin story): Ogún, *oricha* of iron and war, son of Obatalá and Yemu, compatriot of Eleguá, Ochosi, and Osun, lives in the woods. He is represented by an iron cauldron filled with metal implements. His energy is hot, like the iron forge, and he needs the coolness of water to calm him. He is the spirit of all who work with iron implements and all who live by brute force. His force is the force of the blood, and of all who die by him die violently. He is the soldier, the teamster, the blacksmith, the policeman. He knows no boundaries. Ogún loved his mother, Yemú, so much that he began to desire her. He would possess her, but for the vigilance of his friend and brother, Eleguá. One day, overwhelmed by his own lust and desire, he attempted to rape his mother but was surprised in the act by his father, Obatalá. Before Obatalá could punish him—indeed, before Obatalá could utter a word—Ogún cursed himself. He exiled himself to the forest, vowing to do nothing but serve the *orichas* for the rest of his days. He worked tirelessly, but with much bitterness, causing tragedy and misery in the world.

DANCING ELEGUÁ:
EMBODYING THE SACRED

In mid-July 1997, Alberto Villarreal, my drum teacher in Havana, invited me to attend a *toque de santo* in Santos Suárez, a suburb of Havana. The *toque* was in honor of Eleguá, trickster deity and warrior of the crossroads, and was to be held in one of the large, high-ceilinged stucco houses that dominate Santos Suárez's neighborhoods. Many of these houses were built in the early part of the twentieth century, their original owners long gone in the mass postrevolutionary exodus of the 1960s. Alberto and his family moved into a house in Santos Suárez in the mid-1970s, a mile away from the house where the *toque* was to be held. Alberto, his wife

Zoraida, and I went to the *toque* together. Alberto's group had arrived earlier to eat lunch and prepare their instruments.

When we arrived, three of Alberto's drummers had already started to play. The lead singer, Jesús, sang persuasively, and the drummers responded to his calls, but nobody danced. *"Ago Eleguá o bu kenke, Ago Eleguá o bu kenke, Ago Eleguá o bu kenke, Ago Eleguá o bu kenke"* (make way for Eleguá, who is abusive and small).

✪ LISTEN TO TRACK 5: Alberto's group sings for Eleguá.

People milled about the large front room of the house, murmuring softly, neither singing nor dancing. They washed themselves in *osain* (a mixture of water and cooling, cleansing herbs) before entering the house, saluted the modest altar to the *santos* in the next room, and then stood quietly, whispering to each other and looking around. The dancing firelight of the three white candles bounced off the mangos and avocados piled in baskets on either side of the red-bordered altar. Half-calabashes filled with brightly wrapped candies and coins glittered in front of the nose-cone-shaped Eleguá and the *soperas* (porcelain soup tureens) of the rest of the major *santos*. The cowrie-shell eyes and mouth of the small cement Eleguá looked a bit menacing, slanted eyes and grim smile emerging from what looked like the top of a solid gray sombrero. After half an hour had passed, a thin young man moved in front of the drummers and lead singer and began "dancing Eleguá"—performing the leaning, off-balance cross steps associated with the mischievous deity, a few to the left, a few to the right, while miming vaudevillian gestures with an imaginary cane (Eleguá's *garabato,* or crooked stick, with which he is said to "open the road").

The young man's movements were exaggerated and showy but well executed. The young man then broke into various dance moves from other genres such as disco and hip-hop. By this time, the fifty guests had stepped back, making room for the solo dancer, but the drummers and lead singer were exchanging dark looks and glaring at the young man. Finally, Alberto stopped playing and shooed the young man away. "It's an insult—he doesn't have *santo,* and he's not possessed, and he shouldn't be dancing that way. The Santeros and Santeras haven't even danced yet. This is not a disco." Zoraida leaned over to me and whispered that the dancer was from a local folkloric ensemble and was likely planning to audition for the CFNC in the coming months. The young man, chagrined, left the room, and the crowd became hushed and still after this mild spectacle.

What had just happened? Because the room had become crowded, I remained plastered against a side wall for most of this performance, and I did not immediately understand that this bold dancer had committed an offense. Instead, I had been transfixed by his confident manner and radiant movements: the moonwalk, the triple-twirls, the half-splits (direct from Michael Jackson's "Thriller" music video). I wondered how they became transformed, translated, and transported to this place of worship, as an offering in front of the sacred *batá* drums for Eleguá, the trickster warrior. Were the dancer's movements deliberate translations from the repertoire of our human trickster, Michael Jackson—who is multiracialized, multigendered, and multitalented—to the arena of the divine trickster Eleguá— who is red on one side and black on the other (to keep his enemies guessing as to his "color"),[1] male and female,[2] and the purveyor of both divine and mundane possibilities? The young dancer's evocation of Michael Jackson for the Mischievous One—with all of its "magic" and skill and newness—seemed a raucous gift, divine in its very profanity. For did he not offer himself up to the musicians (thus to the *orichas*) with a fullness of heart?

TOQUE DE SANTO: EVOKING THE ORICHAS

A *toque de santo* is the main public religious performance of Santería, the popular name of the polytheistic religious tradition that grew from African and European roots during the four long centuries of the slave trade in Cuba. *Toque* refers to the verb *tocar* (to play) and to the specific noun *toque* (rhythm), as well as to the general noun *toque,* meaning the event itself; *santo* refers to the deities (called *santos* or *orichas*) who are evoked by the *toques*.[3] Although the performance of Santería includes other ceremonies involving music and dance (such as festive *bembés* and *güiro* ensembles), *toques de santo* require the use of the sacred *batá* drums, and are thus considered the most divinely powerful of all the religious ceremonies of Santería.

The origins of the *toque de santo* lie in the Atlantic slave trade. Cuba imported the bulk of its slaves during the nineteenth century (see Scott 1985; Helg 1995; Luciano Franco 1980). Most of the Africans captured and sold into slavery who were landed in Cuba came from a curved corridor of present-day West Africa stretching from Guinea down to Angola, and a significant plurality of these came from Nigeria, Benin, Ghana, Togo, and Cameroon (Lachatañeré 1961; Davidson 1980; Klein 1986). These African regions share some formal characteristics in their polytheistic religious traditions, which, under the chaotic and brutal conditions of slavery in Cuba, gradually developed by the end of the nineteenth century into what became known as Santería.[4] One of the most powerful similarities among the many West African polytheistic traditions thrown together in Cuba during the nineteenth century was the evocation of deities through the performance of specific praise songs, drum rhythms, and gestures. *Toques de santo* can be interpreted as a distillation of more than a century of diverse, divine performative intent.

In present-day Cuban Santería, *toques de santo* are ritual drummings, typically held as offerings to appease *orichas* or *santos*. These drumming ceremonies may also be offered to the *santos* to change the objective circumstances of one's life. For example, a divinatory reading may require that a *toque* be given to heal a leading priest in the community (D. Brown 1996:118); or an initiate may choose to celebrate her *cumpleaños de santo* (the day of "rebirth" into the Santería religion) by holding a *toque* for her "parent" deity. Each of us, according to the theology of Santería, is born to a particular *santo,* and just as our *santos* care for us, so must we care for them. Attending to one's *santo* often involves holding drumming ceremonies, in which the songs and dances of that particular *santo* are highlighted. In general, *toques de santo* can reestablish equilibrium in both religious and social life through a carefully orchestrated series of rhythms, songs, and dances.[5]

Although the deities of Santería may communicate with humans through divination, prayers, and dreams, they relish the communicative power afforded them through music and dance. Each *santo* or *oricha* "owns" certain melodic gestures, rhythms, dance movements, and praise songs, as well as specific colors, numbers, animals, foods, and natural phenomena. They respond readily to songs and dances that incorporate these associative representations—such as, in the case of the salt-water deity Yemayá (whose name is said to mean "Mother of Fishes" in Cuban Lucumí), a dance that imitates the undulations of the waves, or a song that evokes the power of the sea and its creatures. The main goal of these rhythms, songs, and dances is to summon (or goad) the *santos* to earth, so that the deities may soothe those who are grieving, heal those who are sick, rebuke those who have acted unwisely, bless those who appear to be deserving, and set the tone for the next few weeks or months in the community. For a *toque de santo* to be successful, however, each participant must know how to behave, how to engage correctly the divine potential of the ceremony.

What are the "rules of engagement" at a *toque de santo?* How does one know when to dance (or sing, or become possessed) and how? Are there different ways of participating in Afro-Cuban religious and folkloric events, and, if so, how does one discriminate between them? Why, for example, didn't the moonwalker's antics elicit whoops of pleasure from the onlookers? I wanted to clap for him, but perhaps that was part of the problem. His performance was highly self-conscious, and seemed to have little to do with "bringing down the *santo.*" His gestures, rather than referring to the attributes of an *oricha,* were ultimately self-referential; he proved that he, unlike many Cubans, had access to Michael Jackson videos, and that he had the skill to mimic precisely the moves of this gender-bending, color-coded American performer. But the musicians were not impressed.

The rules of engagement in religious and folkloric performance seem to shift in accordance with the goal or intent of the event, and with the expectations of the religious practitioners. In a *toque de santo,* for example, the aim of the ceremony is to summon one or more *orichas* to earth, so that the deities may address the needs the community through specific blessings, healings, and advice. In this case, the "rules of engagement" for each participant at a religious event are determined by socioreligious desire and necessity. In the events presented by the Conjunto Folklórico Nacional de Cuba, by contrast, the goal of a performance is primarily aesthetic excellence—the perfect (or near-perfect) execution of dance steps, percussive rhythms, song phrases, and gestures of a *toque de santo* in accordance with norms established by "folkloric" schools of performance. In the CFNC, then, the "rules" of participating are determined by one's ability to maintain a uniform standard of performance of specific rehearsed musical and physical gestures. Yet the genres of "religious Afro-Cuban performance" and "'folkloric' Afro-Cuban performance" inform each other, "use" each other, and at times even inhabit the same sphere of sacred intent (see chapter 4 for an extended discussion).

This sphere of sacred intent is most often constructed by resurrecting the memory of the sacred in both folkloric and religious performance. And in both types of performance, the memory of the sacred is translated through the body. The body is where "sacred" and "secular" meet, where the boundaries are blurred, and it is this liminal space that is both powerful and disruptive because it calls into question the performative categories implied by the terms "sacred" and "secular" and forces the participants to renegotiate their respective "rules of engagement." The young dancer called forth the body memories of his dance teacher's sacred performance of Eleguá, and then transformed them into an inspired secular celebration for that same deity, his improvisational dance causing discomfort and ultimately expulsion.

ELEGUÁ OPENS THE ROAD

Eventually, a few people began dancing again, away from the drums, with restrained movements as the *akpwón* (lead singer) and drummers resumed calling for Eleguá. I swayed uneasily, close to the wall, painfully aware of my bright purple waist pack and faded jeans amid the sea of lacy white skirts. A lanky, sad-looking, middle-aged man occasionally danced in front of the drums, moving listlessly, lethargically. His dance steps belonged to Eleguá, but he executed them without enthusiasm, without continuity. Stopping, looking sadly at the drummers and singer, then jerking into motion again, he moved from side to side, as if pulled by marionette strings. All at once he would move away, shake his head as if to rid himself of a net or web descending over his face, and then stop again. At one point he crouched in the corner of the room, near the drummers, and began to cry, looking around furtively at the other guests. He seemed weak and depleted, out of place.

Suddenly the *akpwón* began directing his songs toward this man, and the drummers intensified their responses, playing loudly and quickly, playing onto him. The tension in the room became palpable, full of unpredictable energy. The man held his head, shaking it, his upper body bobbing up and down; he seemed to want to escape—from what? From the music? From the people? From some unknowable pounding in his head? The *akpwón* began gesticulating, punctuating his words with an accusatory finger pointed in the man's face, palms open in supplication at the man's hips, bending toward the man and stomping at the end of each phrase, pursuing the man in a tight arc in front of the drums.

An electric current passed through the man. He became live, in the same way that a wire becomes live when electricity passes through it—taut, uplifted, energized, his eyes big and bright, with no trace of sadness. He looked as though someone had possessed his body from the inside and was now using his eyes as windows, lighting them up like candles. He greeted the *akpwón,* saluted the drummers and their drums, *okónkolo, itótele,* and then *iyá* (the drum who is a child, the drum who follows, and the mother drum, respectively),[6] and then began greeting some of the Santeros and Santeras, occasionally passing his hands over and alongside their heads, eyes burning all the while. Alberto said, *"Llegó Eleguá"* (Eleguá has come), and the drummers nodded their heads, sweaty and half-smiling. Eleguá looked around at the gathered celebrants mischievously, purposefully, trying to catch someone's eye. I wanted to look at him but did not want him to look at me. He looked away, I looked; he looked at me, I looked away. He moved toward my area, and I half-turned away, not ready for the encounter.

He was led by the owner of the house and a Santera to a back room, and I breathed again. There was a break in the drumming while Eleguá was helped out of his "street clothes" and into clothes made especially for him. Alberto shook his head at Zoraida and motioned to her to wait outside on the porch when he saw her swaying back and forth, her eyes rolling back, half-smiling, shivering slightly. I went outside with Zoraida, happy to escape the heat. "Why did Alberto make you wait outside?" I asked. "He doesn't want me to catch the *santo.*" Perhaps catching the *santo,* like catching a cold, seemed ultimately unavoidable in Alberto's worldview. "Why not?" I asked. "It's too much," she answered, "and he can't help me because he's drumming. He can't throw down his drum in the middle of a *toque* and make sure I'm all right." I looked through the open door and noticed that Eleguá had returned. Zoraida did not want to go back inside while Eleguá was on the loose, so I entered the house again on my own, careful to keep close to the back wall, mindful of the threat and promise of *oricha* possession.

Eleguá had emerged wearing a red pair of shorts cut off below the knees with black trim, and a matching shirt with an open collar and short sleeves.[7] The shirt and shorts were covered with Cuban and American paper money, mostly one- and five-dollar bills, that had been pinned to the outfit. He wore no hat, but borrowed the drummers' baseball caps and other people's hats at the beginning of his visit. He began talking to various guests, especially Santeros and Santeras, in a high-pitched voice, in a mixture of what seemed to be Cuban Spanish and Lucumí, the liturgical Yoruba language associated with *oricha* worship. The celebrants dropped to the ground to salute him, and some pinned more money to his outfit or put coins into his hands. He would occasionally call out commands to the musicians, who would respond by playing the requested tune. We danced cautiously, gradually joining in to sing the chorus.

At one point Eleguá gestured for all the Santeros and Santeras to dance in a circle, clockwise, in front of the musicians. He rounded up all those dressed in white and wearing *collares* (a set of five ritual beaded necklaces signifying the first stage of initiation into Santería) and pushed them in front of the drummers.[8] He walked around the outside of the dancing circle, counterclockwise, looking the dancers up and down, raising his eyebrows, staring hard at the faces of one or two, whose eyes remained cast downward. Soon afterward he shooed all the Santeros to the back of the room and concentrated only on the Santeras, leering and gesticulating at them as they continued dancing in a circle. He squatted on his heels, near the musicians, and at times appeared to be looking up the white dresses of the Santeras, while he smiled and blinked with pleasure, rubbing his hands together. One Santera, shy and plump, who had been trying to remain inconspicuous by standing and swaying toward the back of the room with the other guests, refused to look at Eleguá, keeping her head down and her torso turned away. On noticing this, Eleguá immediately sought her out and gestured toward her to dance with the other Santeras, finally making her dance alone, in front of the drums.

As she danced, apparently embarrassed and uncomfortable, Eleguá crouched down again, looking up her layers of white skirts and leering at her thighs. For a moment he rolled onto the floor for a better view, grinning and blinking. She tried to ease herself back to the corner away from the drums, but each time she tried, Eleguá would stand in her way, forcing her to stay in the middle, in front of the drums. He finally stood up, half-dancing with her, moving in close to her face, and forced her to look into his eyes. The moment she made eye contact with him, a shudder ran through her body, and she held her head. She tried again to go back to the corner, but this time Eleguá grabbed her by the shoulders and brought her face close to his. Her body went rigid, as if shocked, and then she fell away from him, holding her head, staggering from side to side, her torso rocking back and forth. Her eyes rolled back in her head, and each time she came close to Eleguá in her staggered dance, she shuddered again, shocked by the electric current of possession. After about ten more minutes of this interaction, Eleguá allowed himself to be led to the back room again, where he gave private consultations to the owners of the house and to other ranking Santeros and Santeras. The shy Santera eventually moved to the back corner of the room, eyes half-closed, still swaying and shuddering, not yet free of Eleguá's gift.

SACRED KNOWLEDGE AND COMPETENT ENGAGEMENT

Protectors of Cuba's African heritage and representatives of its future, ritual musicians hold the key to an analysis of the *toque,* and control the first stage of engagement. Alberto is the lead drummer in this group of ritual musicians. In addition to being a much-in-demand *batá* drummer for *toques de santo,* he is also the head percussionist in the CFNC. He and his group, consisting of two lead singers and five *batá* drummers (three "regular" drummers and two "relief" drummers), have been playing together for almost ten years and usually play several *toques* a week. Most of the members of his group also play *batá* drums in the CFNC, as well as *conga* drums, *shekeres,* or *güiros* (two names for the beaded gourd rattles featured in a *güiro* ensemble), *claves* (two wooden sticks that provide a syncopated rhythmic "backbone"), *agogos* (metal bells), and other percussive instruments (see fig. 3.1).

Although *shekeres, agogos, claves,* and even *conga* drums may be used in other Santería ceremonies, the three double-headed *batá* drums are the most effective instruments for evoking the *orichas* during a *toque.*[9] They are second in importance only to the personalized praise songs that flatter and taunt the *orichas.* It is the drummers' job to respond to the calls invoked by the lead singer, or *akpwón,* during the ceremony. These praise songs and *batá* rhythms are meant to bring the *oricha* to earth, so that it may speak through the body of a possessed devotee.

Figure 3.1. Alberto Villarreal and members of his group at Alberto's house, listening to a recording of themselves performing the *oru cantado,* 1999.

The July 1997 *toque* was a birthday celebration for Eleguá, and the primary goal was to bring him to earth so that he might share his sacred knowledge.

Eleguá, the first of the warrior *orichas,* and guardian of the crossroads, is a trickster deity, who is often associated with mischievous behavior and the arbitrariness of fate. He is first and last in the sequential evocation of the Santería pantheon of *orichas,* and he opens (or closes) the path of communication between humans and the rest of the *orichas.* Eleguá speaks first in Santería, providing a framework for the messages of the other *orichas.* Within the cosmology of Santería, everyone is "born to" a particular *oricha,* which means that everyone has access to the privileges and responsibilities of *oricha* worship, whether or not we choose to actualize the potential of that divine relationship. The *oricha* to whom one is born is known as one's "head" *oricha,* which relationship is confirmed through divination and consecrated during a seven-day initiation process known as "making *santo.*"[10] Children of a particular *oricha* are said to possess some of the qualities of that *oricha.* For example, a child of Eleguá might be both mischievous and able to make things happen quickly (opening roads right and left). Eleguá is the head *oricha* of Alberto, which may be another reason why Alberto and his group were asked to play.

The *akpwón* and drummers are responsible for keeping the *toque* going, keeping its energy flowing at a high level so that the *oricha* will "come down." Yet this task cannot be accomplished by the musicians alone. They need the help of the other members of the community to effect a successful *toque*.[11] It is the collective energy of a *toque* that brings down an *oricha,* not simply the efforts of the musicians, even though it is the musicians' responsibility to engage the attendees. This is usually a big job (what if people are tired? hungry? anxious?), so the musicians depend mostly on priests and priestesses of Santería (Santeros and Santeras, respectively) to help lead the singing and dancing. These Santeros and Santeras have attended many *toques de santo* and know how to lead the choral responses and the dancing. They are as invested in "bringing down the *santo*" as the musicians are, and understand the power and meaning of the songs and dances initiated by the musicians. The Santeros and Santeras, unlike uninitiated *creyentes,* are fully competent participants, and it is precisely this competence that sharpens the focus of sacred intent at a *toque*.[12]

As a result, the ranking priests and priestesses of Santería determine the second stage of engagement at a *toque*. The musicians are responsible for establishing the connection between heaven and earth, but Santeros and Santeras are responsible for directing it, and passing on the benefits of this divine intervention to their *ahijados,* or godchildren. Dancing alone or first in front of the drums is considered a privilege in Santería, usually reserved for those priests and priestesses who have the most years in the religion, those who are oldest in *santo*. They are assumed to have witnessed and experienced enough *oricha* dances to be able to perform them correctly; that is, to do justice to the divine motions (see M. Drewal 1997) as well as to the divine rhythms that inspire them (see Cornelius 1989). As Drewal notes, the dances of the *orichas,* if performed well, help create divine energy, or *aché,* thus strengthening the connection between heaven and earth. If one dances poorly or inappropriately in front of the drums, the insult to the *orichas* becomes greater, precisely because of the missed opportunity to dance well.[13]

Dancing alone in front of the drums also implies self-importance, but if that importance is derived from any place other than the hierarchy of the Santería clergy, it is not valid in a *toque*. The young moonwalker, though technically adept, was not "important" within the religion; that is, he didn't have *santo,* and he wasn't possessed by an *oricha*. He should not have danced at all, much less alone, until much later in the ceremony. Of course, some Santeros and Santeras have toes that twinkle, and others have feet of lead. But those priests and priestesses who cannot dance well do not dance alone in front of the drums (unless they are required to do so for liturgical reasons).[14] Rather, they will hang back, following their colleagues in *santo* who can translate the tricky *batá* rhythms into Eleguá's crooked step, Ogún's syncopated chopping motion, or Yemayá's sudden swirling.

The "harm," then, in dancing the moonwalk in front of drums intended for Eleguá was that Eleguá did not "choose" this man as a dancer; that is, he did not possess him or "make" him do the moonwalk. If the ranking priests and priestesses of Santería and the ritual musicians had been convinced that the young dancer had been possessed, then Michael Jackson's moonwalk would not have been a problem. Rather, it might have become incorporated into other *oricha* possession dances. As it was, however, the young man seemed merely to be showing off. His movements lacked sacred intent, and, moreover, he was quite possibly preventing other people at the ceremony from "catching the spirit" by diverting attention from the task at hand, which was bringing down Eleguá. Communal religious intent was thus temporarily thwarted, diffused, and redirected toward inappropriate, albeit ingenious, folkloric spectacle.

TOQUE ETIQUETTE AND SACRED INTENT

Engaging appropriately in a *toque de santo,* then, requires the competent use of sacred knowledge. The evocative performance of the moonwalker suggests that not only did the young man not know the "rules" of a *toque de santo,* but neither did the owners of the house. What does this relative lack of sacred knowledge mean for the life of this religious performance tradition? How is *toque* etiquette transferred, and by whom?

Toque etiquette varies widely from *casa templo* (house of worship) to *casa templo,* but what is much less variable is the philosophy that informs the rules of etiquette for each particular "house." "Tradition" might vary from house to house on the same block, from city to city, and from country to country, but what keeps religious practice unified is the overriding theology that invents it, and the *santo* families that are created and enlarged each time a new *creyente* is initiated into the religion. The young man, a product of the Cuban revolution and enrolled in one of the *aficionado* schools of folkloric performance, was likely not a *creyente,* and so would have no immediate reason to know the performative rules of a *toque de santo.* As Alberto has stated on many occasions, the younger members of folkloric groups are much more likely to interpret the songs and dances that are based on Afro-Cuban religious traditions as "art," all but dismissing their religious content and antecedents. The moonwalker was focusing on the aesthetic excellence of his gestures, not on the function of those gestures for a religious ceremony. One begins to understand how sacred intent is communicated through the varied talents and expressions of human devotees, without much regard for the uniformity of tone or gesture. The younger dancer was a more accomplished dancer than the older one; his gestures were cleaner, longer, better defined—but they lacked sacred intent, and thus were of secondary importance.[15] The smaller, lackluster steps of the older man gradually gained sacred potential, which manifested itself as *oricha* possession, and which was ultimately of more value to the religious practitioners at the *toque* than the stylized, witty dance of the young man.

As for the owners of the house, they were told by their Santero (perhaps during their initiation) that they needed to have a *tambor* for Eleguá each year, according to a divinatory reading. Obedient *creyentes,* they did as they were told, and to good effect. But fulfilling one's religious obligations according to the steps outlined by a religious elder is distinct from acceding to these requirements with a full understanding of the theological framework that informs them. If the presiding Santero had been in the front room when the moonwalker had assumed center stage, doubtless he would have removed the dancer. But, barring that, the dancer performed his technically adept moves in the presence of the owners of the house (who did not understand that such dancing was considered an affront rather than a celebration) until the musicians—several Santeros and a Babalawo (an Ifá high priest) among them, and thus themselves ranking religious officiants—told him to stop.[16]

After the young man left the *toque,* the atmosphere of the house became calmer, and the energy of the musicians was again directed toward bringing down Eleguá. In fact, one could argue that the spiritual "balance" of the ceremony was restored by the "true" arrival of Eleguá, even though his mischievous antics threatened to disrupt the ceremony once again. It is precisely because these two performative sequences provoked such different reactions at the same *toque* that they invite comparison. A call-and-response pattern emerges between secular and sacred, in which the second, possessed dancer, supported by the musicians, seemed to redress the mistakes of the first. Unlike the folkloric dancer, the dancer possessed by Eleguá greeted the musicians and the drums, thanking them for bringing him to earth—underlining the "*oricha* etiquette" that the first dancer lacked. Additionally, the possessed dancer made all the Santeros and Santeras dance in a circle in front of the drums, a "modeling" of appropriate ritual behavior omitted by the first dancer. And the possessed dancer did not simply dance like Eleguá, he acted like Eleguá: he grabbed all the hats he could find and stuck them on his head, playing up Eleguá's childlike mischief; and he looked up the skirts of the Santeras and leered at them, displaying Eleguá's often lascivious sexual appetites. But he also zeroed in on the most unlikely candidate for possession (a fearful, newly made Santera), thus proving his capacity to "force open the road" for those who seem unwilling to travel it, and for whom such a journey might prove dangerous. In this way, Eleguá could be interpreted as "acting out," showing, in effect, the same sort of unbridled bravado as the folkloric dancer; but this time in the realm of the divine.

No longer demonstrating appropriate ritual behavior, but rather indulging in competitive behavior, Eleguá "took" the reticent Santera, just because he could. Unsuspecting and unwilling, when possessed, she could not even dance, but rather staggered about, not able to shoulder the burden of possession fully. And although one could include Eleguá's behavior within a larger portfolio of mischievous "Eleguá" scenarios, this particular case seemed to be a deliberate flexing of divine muscles, designed to show the participants who was boss. At first glance, the "taking" of the shy Santera did not seem to achieve social equilibrium—that is, Eleguá could not speak through her because she was not an experienced vessel, nor could he dance through her because she was too unsteady. What this act did accomplish, however, was to remind the participants of the unpredictability and power of true *oricha* possession. In this way, the attention of the participants was redirected toward the goal of the ceremony, the bringing to earth of an *oricha,* with all of its unpredictable and overwhelming potential.

"EL FOLKLORE" AND *"LA RELIGIÓN":* ENGAGING ALBERTO

According to Alberto, many Cuban ritual musicians are also involved in folkloric performance, either through the Conjunto Folklórico or through smaller local ensembles. As a result, the task of differentiating between religious and folkloric intent is constant. Alberto, lead drummer of the Conjunto Folklórico and respected *olú batá,* works hard to maintain the difference between *"el folklore"* and *"la religión."* For those who are initiated into Santería, the possibility of insulting an *oricha* is real and daunting. If, for example, Alberto had allowed the moon-walker to continue sliding and writhing in front of the drums until he danced himself out, the communal energy necessary for bringing down the *santo* would have been so scattered and unfocused that Eleguá might never have arrived. And if Eleguá had never arrived, much of the blame for his absence would have fallen on the musicians, inasmuch as they are responsible for "bridging the gap between heaven and earth" (Cornelius 1989). If such a failure were to happen several times on Alberto's watch, he and his group would no longer be asked to play at *toques,* for his ability to bridge the gap—an important form of *aché*—would be assumed to be weak or dysfunctional. Such a judgment would deprive him and his group not only of money but also, and more importantly, of ritual status in the community. For this reason, Alberto and other "dual" musicians keep the two genres separate in an attempt to protect and promote the divine possibilities of sacred intent, while continuing to serve the political and economic interests that benefit from the dramatization of these ceremonies.

In one of the two formal interviews he consented to give during my lessons with him (conducted on August 11 and September 1, 1992), Alberto stated that the drummers were the "essence" of the Conjunto Folklórico. Given the primary importance of singers in *toques de santo* as well as in folkloric performances, I asked Alberto why he chose drummers over singers as the essential group. He explained that the *batá* drum is the central symbol of the religion,[17] and the religion is the heart of the CFNC, so the drummers—those who communicate the religion by playing the drums—are the emotional center of the troupe. The drummers determine the experience of the musical performance, and they, perhaps more than any of the other performers, negotiate the many boundaries between sacred and secular. According to Alberto, of the three main types of performers in the current Conjunto Folklórico—drummers, dancers, and singers—only the drummers are all *creyentes*, mostly in Santería, but also in Palo Monte, Abakwá, and Arará.[18]

AV: At the heart of the Conjunto are the religious people. When the Conjunto was first founded, there were a lot of things that were hard to endure, like the pay, like too much work. But the way in which it came about, with each one of us providing our own instruments because the Conjunto didn't have instruments—basically, the Conjunto was formed by religious people, who were the ones who made religion into art by their strength, their abilities, their instruments, their clothing. These *batá* drums [the unconsecrated ones with which Alberto taught me], for example, were made by a member of the Conjunto Folklórico Nacional. They're the oldest drums in the Conjunto Folklórico, and they're mine. They used to belong to Jesús Pérez, the *responsable* of percussion when the Conjunto first started.[19] He brought some of his instruments, and José Castillo also contributed some of his instruments. Emilio O'Farrill, who is still alive, I think, and now lives in Guanabacoa, he was a founder of the Conjunto, and he brought to it his knowledge of Palo [Palo Monte], because he's a Palero [priest of Palo Monte]. Oriol Bustamante, also a Palero, brought his knowledge of Palo to the group, as well. All of this is just to say that the Conjunto was born of that which is religious, it was born of the religion. We [the drummers] were capable of bringing the religion to art.

Drummers are different than the rest of the performers. There are 109 members in the Folklorico, and ten are drummers. We're the core. But we're always treated like dirt—like savages. There's always been a split between the dancers and the drummers. All the drummers come from humble backgrounds. We learned our music on the streets. We didn't go to any fancy school [*aficionado* schools]. We're *macho,* and so we have to be treated a little differently. Sometimes people forget that. But the drummers are the center of the group. Without the drummers, there'd be no rhythm, and without rhythm, there's nothing.

Although he had been playing *batá* drums "on the streets"[20] since he was ten years old, Alberto began working with the Conjunto Folklórico in 1971 as a dancer when he was in his twenties. From 1971 to 1973 he studied dancing and drumming at the training school run by the Conjunto Folklórico. Because of his religio-musical training, he knew many of the ritual *batá* drumming patterns before he entered the CFNC training school, but he did not know the rules and regulations of playing *batá* drums for the choreographed, theatrical performances of the troupe. In 1974 he went on his first tour with the group, during which he danced and played *batá* drums. In 1978 Alberto "graduated to percussion," meaning that he then became regarded as a full-time percussionist for the group rather than as part dancer and part apprentice drummer. His brother Gerardo Villarreal began performing as a dancer with the Conjunto in 1980 and still dances for the troupe. Alberto has played solely percussion for the group since 1978. He has been the *responsable* or head percussionist for almost fifteen years, before which he was the *suplente* or second-in-command for several years.

Alberto, Gerardo, and their siblings were raised mainly by their mother, a renowned Santera, in Guanabacoa, a neighborhood southeast of downtown Havana known for the fervent beliefs of its *creyentes* (Cabrera 1954). One of Alberto's brothers became a Babalawo, and now lives a few blocks from the house where they grew up. Not surprisingly, Guanabacoa is the home of many of the Conjunto Folklórico's drummers, past and present. Highly regarded by fellow drummers and directors alike, Alberto is a hard-working family man. He and his wife Zoraida have two sons, May and Maykel, both of whom are drummers like their father. Maykel, born in 1977, has been playing *okónkolo* (the smallest of the *batá* drums) at *toques* with his father since the mid-1990s and has started playing *itótele* (the middle drum). May, born in 1980, plays *okónkolo* for Alberto's group and occasionally tries *itótele*. Alberto is a full-time drummer, often teaching private *folklórico* lessons in the morning, working at the CFNC until late afternoon, and then drumming for several more hours at a *toque* until late at night. Alberto, Zoraida, and May all made *santo* in the 1990s; Maykel made *santo* in July 2000. Alberto was sworn to the *batá* drums years ago. Maykel completed the same ceremony in 1999, and May became *jurado* (sworn to the drums) in December 2000. Alberto's religious and musical community begins with his family and extends outward into his work world.

Both my interviews and my lessons with Alberto were hard won. Initially, I approached Alberto to continue teaching me *batá* lessons privately after the CFNC FolkCuba group sessions ended in early July 1992. The double-headed hand-drumming had been difficult for me, and I had not done particularly well during the first few days of class. By the end of the three-week workshop, I felt I had made good progress, and I wanted to learn more. On three different occasions Alberto had said no to my request, but my fourth attempt brought the affirmative response I had hoped for.

This procession of rejections was largely the result of a series of consultations Alberto had requested with his Babalawo and his *oricha,* Eleguá. Three times I asked for lessons, and three times the answer after these consultations was no. Another factor that may have played a role in Alberto's initial rejections was his feeling that I lacked the ability to play *batá* well. (He did not admit this lack of faith in my abilities until well into the second month of our private lessons, when it became clear that I was not immune to good teaching.) The fourth time I asked, however, both his Babalawo and his *oricha* said yes, provided that I would pay no money to him for the lessons. This stipulation seemed odd to me at the time, for two reasons: U.S. dollars helped to ease the daily economic stress of *la lucha,* and most artists who taught foreign students required them to pay for their lessons in dollars. Despite my consternation and confusion, Alberto insisted that I not pay him in money. For this reason, in exchange for my lessons I gave Alberto and his family various food products, batteries, tapes, cigarettes, rum, soap, a fan, small household items (detergent, sponges, and so on), and finally a bicycle. After several years, and multiple conversations with Alberto and his Babalawo, I found out that Alberto had not accepted money for the lessons in order to protect himself. Through divination, Eleguá had talked at that time of possible malice directed toward Alberto, and had specified that the malice would likely come through money. As a result, Alberto was counseled by his Babalawo to accept not money, but rather products in exchange for his teaching services.

Most of my discussions with Alberto occurred between and sometimes during our drum lessons. Several times Alberto expressed to me his discomfort with the act of "just talking": "I'm not a talker; I'm a thinker. I don't like to talk." When I asked him why he finally decided to grant me a couple of interviews, he said that it was his responsibility to protect me as well as to teach me, and that I had to learn how to listen to him. I understood why it was now his task to teach me, as Eleguá and his Babalawo had advised him, but I did not understand why he had taken on the dual responsibility of protecting me and helping me "learn how to listen to him." When I asked Alberto about this responsibility, his explanation began with a personal reference to the *orichas*. Alberto told me that he was a son of Eleguá. Because I am a daughter of Ochún, he explained, it was his responsibility to protect me because Eleguá protects Ochún. Because I was not yet fully "in the religion," however, he also had to see to it that I did not misstep or cause injury to myself or others through my ignorance. Therefore, I had to learn how to listen to him, which often meant learning to be patient when he did not answer my questions directly or respond to my requests.

ENGENDERING *BATÁ*

According to Alberto, he agreed to teach me *batá* drumming not only because his *padrino* and his *santo* finally said yes, but also because I am not a Cuban woman. Cuban women, he said, are *atrevida* (impudent, bold, brash), which, in the context of *batá* drumming, means that they will try to play the *batá* drums in a religious context, despite the deeply held conviction that female ceremonial *batá* drummers are anathema to Santería. The feeling among the male *creyente* drummers of the Conjunto Folklórico during the first two decades of its existence was that no woman—no matter her origin or nationality—should be allowed play the sacred *batá* drums. In the 1980s, at least within Alberto's community, *batá* drummers allowed that perhaps one could teach Cuban women to play the *batá* drums in certain secular circumstances, but that one should not teach more than a few. Those few women who learned were forbidden from playing the drums in sacred contexts. The FolkCuba workshops (for non-Cubans only, aimed at attracting tourism) began in 1986, at which time Mario Jáuregui, a lead drummer in the CFNC, began teaching non-Cuban women *batá* drumming. Alberto and his drumming colleagues held out until 1989, at which time they, too, were persuaded to teach *batá* drumming to Cuban and non-Cuban women. "At first we [drummers in the CFNC] didn't really understand why we had to do it, it wasn't clear. But after Mario did it, we started to think about it, and we've all taught women at one time or another since 1989."

The Cuban women who were taught *batá*, according to Alberto, did prove to be *atrevida*—heady, perhaps, with the newly elasticized boundaries of their liberation. The first thing they wanted to do once they learned how to play *batá* drums was to play in religious ceremonies. Finally, it was decided within the CFNC that it would be safest if Cuban *batá* drummers taught only foreign women, particularly those from Europe and North America, because *anglo-sajona* women were far less likely to trespass into the religion with their newfound *batá* skills and likely would confine themselves to playing in secular *batá* groups. When I questioned Alberto more closely about why he had finally agreed to teach me, Alberto confirmed this attitude. He said that it was clear that I was not *atrevida*, that I was not going to embarrass him, a factor second in importance only to obtaining the permission of his *santo* (Eleguá) and his Babalawo.

I commenced my lessons with Alberto two days after he finally agreed to teach me. Before we began playing, I asked him a few questions about the relationship between Santería and its folkloric representation in the Conjunto Folklórico. He answered my questions as long as they referred to the motions my hands made on the drums, but evaded or ignored questions about the potentially religious context of the music. This drama replayed itself each day for a week. We got along quite well when I concentrated only on the sounds I was making with the drums, but he regarded me with frustration and suspicion when I asked about the religious function of these sounds. Even though from the beginning of our lessons I had expressed my interest in the performance tradition as a whole, Alberto still seemed to find some of my questions inappropriate. Only when I shared with him my own experiences of the religion and promised not to play *batá* drums in a ritual context was he more relaxed about answering questions of a religious nature. However, because I was not initiated into Santería at the time, Alberto would never reveal anything more than general ideas about the religion.

Our lessons typically would start with Alberto teaching me the *okónkolo* (the smallest and highest-pitched of the *batá* drums, with the easiest, most repetitive part) line to a *toque* for a particular *oricha*. After playing the *okónkolo* part several times for me on his *iyá* (the largest and lowest-pitched of the drums, with the most complex lines and infinite possibilities for variation), he would motion for me to mimic the line on the *okónkolo*. Once I had mastered the *okónkolo* part, he would begin teaching me the *itótele* part to this *toque* (*itótele* being the medium-pitched middle drum, with lines that mostly correspond to the *iyá's* calls and improvisations), also playing it on the *iyá* first for me before I played it on the *itótele*. Finally, he would get to the *iyá* part, inevitably the most complex of the three, and learning a line for *iyá* occasionally would take more than an hour. As he played *iyá*, he would often sing the praise song that evoked the rhythmic call we were working on (see fig. 3.2).

☻ LISTEN TO TRACK 6: Alberto's group singing and playing for Ogún.

Once Alberto felt that I had mastered the parts, he would draft someone else in the house (May or Maykel, or a neighbor or fellow Conjunto drummer who happened to be visiting) to play the third drum. The third drum usually would be *itótele* or *okónkolo,* as Alberto would require that I play the *iyá* part, especially if one of his compatriots from the Conjunto was visiting. I was never sure why he pushed me to play *iyá* in front of his colleagues. I felt uncomfortable around his colleagues during these impromptu exams because they often smiled or giggled through my admittedly amateur renditions of *toques.* Twice during these public performances I felt secure in my playing of the *iyá* part: once during a rhythm for Ogún and once during a rhythm for Eleguá. My occasional nervousness and feelings of inadequacy notwithstanding, many of our most interesting conversations about religion and folkloric performance took place during these lessons.

According to Alberto, some of my questions could not be answered until I "got the religion," and others could never be answered simply because of my gender. The main question that could never be answered because of my gender had to do with the sacred communicative potential of the *batá* drums, known as *añá.*[21] The *añá,* often characterized as an avatar or "road" of the female deity Ochún (which makes *añá* a deity unto itself),[22] is the sacred inner substance of the drum that provides the divine power of its voice. That Ochún, whose brass bells *(cha-woro)* are affixed to the rims of the drums, is associated with the *añá* of the *batá* drum (which are usually associated with the macho Changó) is not surprising, for she is the only female *oricha* who is able to communicate with all the other *orichas* at all times—even Ogún at his most intransigent. She represents both desirability and promiscuity; she evokes passion and then responds enthusiastically—as gregarious in her social world as the drums are broadly expressive in their ritual world.

Despite this female aspect of *añá,* according to Alberto, women should not even talk about *añá. Añá* is seldom discussed in general; even initiated *batá* drummers rarely talk about it. Alberto barely mentioned it by name, preferring to refer to it by its definition, "the sacred inner power of the *batá* drum." During one of our September 1992 lessons, Alberto told a story about the Cuban all-female *batá* group, Obbini Batá (women of the *batá*). He said that they once made the mistake of asking the forgiveness of the *añá* during a performance at an Italian restaurant in Old Havana.[23] They thus incurred the wrath of the entire male *batá* drumming community in Havana. According to Alberto, "there is no need to talk about it, much less ask its forgiveness—they just should have played and not talked about it." Speaking the name of *añá* was tantamount to knowing about it, and knowing about this sacred inner power of the drum perhaps came too close to using it.

Religious practitioners maintain that the *añá* of the *ilu batá* or consecrated drums will be destroyed if a menstruating woman touches the drums. This taboo,

Figure 3.2. Transcription of song for Ogún.

Notes: The two drum heads of the *iyá* have the lowest tuning, the heads of the *itótele* are tuned slightly higher, and the heads of the *okónkolo* are tuned the highest of the three kinds of drums.

Each drum staff has a high note and a low note. The high note represents the pitch of the *chachá* (smaller drum head); the low note represents the pitch of the *boca* (larger drum head). The *iyá's* part is placed on the higher drum staff, even though its pitches are the lowest of the three, because its part leads the other two drums, and because it responds most immediately to the vocal line.

Whenever the *chachá* is struck alone, the hand playing the *boca* should always be pressing on, but not striking, the *boca*. There are several different ways of striking the *batá* heads: an open stroke, a closed (muffled) stroke, and a time-keeping tap. In this strong *toque* for Ogún, however, almost all of the strokes are open, with the exception of the time-keeping taps of the *iyá*. Regular note heads signify open strokes, and other note heads (*) signify time-keeping taps.

This transcription represents an ideal and compressed conversation between *iyá* and *itótele*, one in which all three drummers are paying close attention to each other and to the *akpwón*. The vocal line is based on several performances by members of the Conjunto Folklórico, who based their renditions on recordings by Merceditas Valdés.

Figure 3.2. (continued)

Figure 3.2. *(continued)*

Figure 3.2. *(continued)*

according to Alberto, extends to nonmenstruating women, too. In fact, some drummers are convinced that if women play consecrated *batá* drums, the women will become infertile (Sandra Dillard, personal communication). Other drummers believe that if women play the drums, the *fardela* (brownish paste placed in the center of the *batá* drum heads to tune them) will "jump off" as a sign that the drums are no longer sacred. Some drummers, according to Francisco Aguabella, believe that because *añá* is associated with the female deity Ochún, and because Ochún thoroughly enjoys the company of men, it is much more likely that the message of the drums will be delivered and heard if men are the messengers. The taboos surrounding women playing consecrated *batá* drums seem to focus on women's reproductive powers—that these powers are so strong that they can suddenly deprive the *batá* drum of its sacred potential, or, in contrast, that the sacred power of the consecrated *batá* drum is so strong that it can deprive women of their reproductive capabilities.

One theory about the relationship between menstruating women and *batá*-playing taboos evinced to me recently by a Miami-based Santero is that because Ochún "owns" the sacred potential of the *batá* drum, and because Ochún helps women to give birth, when women have their periods, it means they will not give birth that month, and that saddens or angers Ochún, so, as punishment, she deprives the player of the consecrated *batá* drum (the menstruating woman) of the power to communicate with the *orichas* through the drum rhythms. Elizabeth Sayre, herself an accomplished *batá* drummer, has compiled several more explanations for why women are prohibited from playing consecrated *batá* drums: playing consecrated *batá* drums is considered a ritual cleansing, and because women already cleanse themselves through menstruation, *batá* drumming is superfluous for them; although the spirit of *añá* may be female, the owner of the *batá* drums is the macho *oricha* Changó, and women cannot "enact the masculinity appropriate to this situation";[24] and women's menstrual blood may be mistaken for an offering to *añá* (Sayre 2000:12).[25]

My sense is that playing *batá* drums for several hours during a ceremony is truly punishing work that requires tremendous stamina, specifically in the upper body. Most women do not develop the muscles in their shoulders, back, arms, and wrists necessary to play these drums for the long stretches at a time required of ceremonial drummers. In addition, it takes tremendous focus not to be carried away (and ultimately possessed) by the power of this music; even people who consider themselves well fortified in body and mind can become possessed by *orichas*. Male *batá* drummers are routinely prohibited from playing if they show signs of becoming possessed by an *oricha*. Because *oricha* possession itself can be seen as a gendered dynamic involving submission to a greater power (the two verbs most commonly used for possession, *montar* and *coger*, are also used in the context of sexual intercourse), the projection of feminine qualities onto the possessed person and masculine qualities onto the *oricha* is understandable. However, during the past few years several women have become interested in playing *batá* drums at Santería ceremonies, and thus have begun to develop the necessary psychological stamina and physical endurance. At the time of this writing, there were at least a few women in major cities in the United States who were actually playing *batá* drums at religious ceremonies, although, to my knowledge, their drums were not consecrated.[26] As male *batá* drummers teach an increasing number of female students, and as the music of Santería continues to gain widespread popularity, the future of this taboo resides in an ongoing process of negotiation between musicians and religious practitioners.

PERFORMING THE REGLA DE OCHA

In order to be a good drummer in the Conjunto Folklórico, according to Alberto, one not only must have the religion, one must respect its rules. When I asked Alberto who decided the content of the Conjunto Folklórico's performances, he responded that there were different departments that could influence the decision—such as research, management, percussion, chorus, dance, the board of directors—but that ultimately Rogelio Martínez Furé, the *asesor* or artistic advisor to the group, made the final decision. Immediately afterward, however, Alberto began talking about the new dancers (those who had attended the *aficionado* schools) who did not appreciate the religious basis of the folkloric *toques,* and how these young people considered the Conjunto Folklórico's performances to be art, without any religious aspect.

> KH: I wanted to learn more about who decides what to include in your programs. Do you make these decisions, or [Rogelio Martínez] Furé, or Teresita Gonzalez—or who decides?
>
> AV: There are different departments in the Folklórico. There is the research department, headed by Rogelio Martínez Furé; there is the management department, which is Teresa [González, the former director of the CFNC]; there is the percussion department. There's a department that is called the artistic board. Furé makes the final decision. . . . But there's folklore that carries religion, and folklore that doesn't carry religion. The *rumba,* for example, doesn't carry religion. The Conjunto presents two types of folk-

lore, so religious questions don't pop up all the time. . . . When there are discrepancies, normally everyone comes to some sort of agreement after a meeting of the management board. But sometimes, if, for example, the choreographer wants a *toque* to go really fast, like the recording on the cassette [of the Conjunto Folklórico]—a *toque* for Ochún, to show off the dancers—I'll say no. You can't rush Ochún, she has to start sweet and slow [*dulce, suavecito, despacito*]. If the choreographer persists, I'll keep saying no, and I'll refuse to play. The rest of the percussionists will side with me, and there will be kind of a strike [*huelga*]. When all is said and done, the choreographer, or whoever it might be, has to come to an agreement with the wishes of the percussionists about religious issues. . . . There are many people, dancers in particular, who are new, and who don't appreciate the folkloric *toques* as something that came out of the religion. On the contrary, these young people think about the pieces in the Conjunto as real "art," without the religious aspect. It's a problem, because you cannot separate art from religion in this case.

Alberto sees his religion not only as something beyond compromise, but also as a source of power and authority in the aesthetic skirmishes that he and his colleagues may face on a daily basis. His religion informs and is inseparable from his work. When I asked Alberto about the connection between his religion and his work, however, he said there was none. "My job is over here [right hand], and my religion is over here [left hand]. This [his job] has nothing to do with this [his religion]. We don't tell the secrets of our religion in the Folklórico. That would be impossible—because then it wouldn't be my job, it would be my religion."

Alberto sees himself, and *creyente* drummers in general, as true representatives of the religion. In this sense, he acts as a preserver of his religious tradition, although he claims that his work and his religion are totally separate. He is an absentee guardian of the authenticity of the folkloric renditions of his religion, which is to say that he does not allow his religious persona to participate actively in the folkloric performances, but the passive knowledge of what that religious persona would require during a religious ceremony is allowed to remain, and it safeguards the remnants of the performance's spiritual dignity. He dissuades the troupe from playing just the *toque* (drumming without singing) or the *baile* (drumming for a particular *oricha* dance) for Yemayá, when, in a real ceremony, the musicians would play the *toque*, the *canto* (drumming with singing), and the *baile*, and he may see it as "the very least" that he can do, perhaps deliberately so. In the same way that he guards the authenticity of the folkloric renditions of his reli-

Figure 3.3. Alberto Villarreal and his drums at the Conjunto Folklórico (conga drum in foreground; commercially made *batá* drums in background), 1994.

gion, he also guards the secrets, so that the partial version he gives is absolutely authentic, compromising neither the integrity of the folkloric performance nor the sanctity of its religious antecedent (see fig. 3.3).

Early in my fieldwork (October 17, 1990) I asked Havana-based Babalawo Hermes Valera Ramírez whether there were any differences between "real" ritual music and "folkloric" ritual music. He said of course there were differences; that was the whole point. In the "real" music, according to Hermes, the drums are sacred *(consagrados, sagrados, bautizados)* and thus have power; in the "folkloric" music, however, sacred drums are not used, so the music does not have sacred power. The drums, whether they have been blessed or not, may look the same, but their "abilities" would be different.[27] Hermes continued by saying that everything about the two musics could be "the same"—*toques, cantos, bailes*—but because one set of drums is sacred and the other is not, the sacred set of drums will be able to call the *orichas,* while the music of the *tambores judíos* (literally, Jewish drums, meaning nonsacred *batá* drums, which therefore do not possess *añá*) will remain on earth, unable to communicate with the *orichas.*[28]

The drummers in the Conjunto Folklórico are the main actors in the negotiation process between sacred and secular aspects of performance. They, unlike other sections of the troupe, are all *creyentes,* and typically perform outside of the CFNC in sacred performance contexts. Thus, their assimilation of and distinction between sacred and secular performance contexts is essential to how and what the troupe performs. How religion is "brought" to art seems to revolve around the paradoxical and elusive questions regarding the differences and separations between the two. Although Alberto seems to contradict himself on this subject, his definitions of religion, secrets, work, and art may be flexible. Later on in this conversation he noted that, in theory at least, people could become possessed listening to a *tambor judío* as well as a *tambor de fundamento,* because all the *toques* (in this case, rhythms) are genuine. And yet, he explained soon thereafter, "We [the drummers] have one way of playing for a nonreligious *toque* [celebration] and another way of playing for a religious *toque.* There are parts that we simply don't play in a Folklórico performance: the secret parts."

The "secret parts" Alberto refers to are the drum calls performed during the *oru seco,* or the "dry sequence," which means that the drum rhythms are unaccompanied by song. The *oru seco* is performed at the beginning of every *toque de santo.* It is an essential performative tool because this series of rhythms speaks to the *orichas* "in their own language," letting them know that a ceremony is about to begin—alerting them to the possibilities of communicating with their human adherents. Because tape recording and videotaping are prohibited during *toques de santo,* I was not able to record Alberto's playing at a religious drumming to compare it Folklórico drumming. From listening carefully to various religious *toques* in December 2000, December 1999, September 1998, July 1997, August 1994, and August 1992, and several others in December 1990–January 1991 and October 1990, I have come to believe that the difference between religious drumming and folkloric drumming is determined largely by intent, which is integrally linked to the context of the performance, and that the context then helps determines the intent's aesthetic manifestation. The essence of "folkloricization" seems to be the transformation of this deeply evocative ritual language into the moral equivalent of soundbites.

Yet religion and *espectáculo,* "sacred" and "secular" do inform each other and do overlap, which is what makes their articulated distinction so compelling. According to Alberto and his group, the musicians use the same *batá* rhythms and songs in folkloric performances as they do in *toques de santo.* What differs is the intent of the performance, and the relative competence of the participants. The intent of a *toque de santo* is to bring down the *oricha,* an intent realized with the help of competent, ritually savvy participants. The intent of a folkloric performance is not to bring down the *santo,* but rather to provide a mimetic representation thereof (Taussig 1993), and the relative competence of the audience is less important. The efficacy of a *toque* depends on bringing down the *santo,* which in turn depends on the ability of the *batá* drummers, because the arrival of the *santo* signals the ceremony's success. The appearance of Eleguá (or Yemayá, or Ogún, or Changó), regardless of their actions, balances the community, because it provides material reassurance to the participants that the *orichas* do inhabit their world— that they are witness to the vicissitudes of their children's lives. Eleguá's surprise taking of the shy Santera provided irrefutable evidence of his presence.

Both the young moonwalker and the older dancer who became possessed by Eleguá dance at the crossroads of Cuba's performative potential. Rap, rock, jazz, funk, pop, punk—all of these music and dance forms make their way into Havana's households from the United States and elsewhere. Yet there are tacit rules governing both Afro-Cuban folkloric and religious performance that shelter indigenous genres from a steady onslaught of cross-breeding. It is as though Afro-Cuban folkloric and religious performance are the lifeblood of the country's expressive culture, and, as such, must be protected and must remain intact. The microcosmic performance of Afro-Cuban folklore and religion informs the macrocosmic context of Cuba in the world, overlapping and superimposing various rules of engagement.

NOTES

1. A parable regarding Eleguá describes his face (and sometimes his cap) being painted red on one side and black on the other, to keep his enemies fighting among themselves about what color he is. See, for example, Thompson (1983:19) and Cosentino (1987). This parable likely comes from the *odu* (*diloggún* divination sign) 8-8, in which two inseparable friends part because of an argument about the color of Eleguá's clothing (see Valdés Garriz 1995:33, 64).

2. Eleguá, who is also known as Esu Eleguá (or simply Esu), is highly yet ambiguously sexed, so much so that he is represented as both male and female. "Esu is not restricted to human distinctions of gender; he is at once both male and female. Although his masculinity is depicted as visually and graphically overwhelming, his equally expressive femininity renders his enormous sexuality ambiguous, contrary, and genderless. Figuratively, Esu is female when he is positive, attentive, conforming,

predictable, and gentle. He is male when he is negative, inattentive, nonconforming, unpredictable, and ruthless" (J. Mason 1992:54–55; see also J. Mason 1985:16–18).

3. A *toque de santo* may also be called a *tambor,* a literal translation of which is "drum." When *tambor* refers to a Santería ceremony, however, it is understood as a "drumming." The term *tambor* may subsume *toque de santo, bembé, güiro,* and *güemilere* (all names for a Santería party honoring an *oricha*), which makes it a more general referent. I use the term *toque de santo* throughout this chapter because I am referring to this specific drumming ceremony within Santería performance.

4. See D. Brown (1989, 2001) and Palmié (1995) for insightful and viable hypotheses regarding cultural transfer and the evolution of Afro-Cuban religious traditions.

5. Michael Marcuzzi calls this process the *tratado* in Santería *toques de santo*—"the essential musical form used to organize musical choices based on previously successful, trance-inducing patterns" (Marcuzzi 1996:6).

6. For an *oricha* to salute the *batá* drums upon arrival is quite common. The order in which Eleguá saluted them, however, is unusual. Typically, both *orichas* and humans salute the drums in order of relative importance, which is determined by several factors: the status of the *orichas* associated with the particular *batá* drums, the status of the *batá* drums within the ensemble, and the owner of *añá* (the sacred inner substance of the *batá* drums). Yemayá is associated with the *iyá;* because Yemayá is Changó's elder (and, according to some *patakíes,* Changó's mother), because the *iyá* leads the *batá* ensemble, and because the *iyá* has *añá, iyá* is typically saluted first. Changó is associated with the *okónkolo,* the smallest drum; because Changó "owns" *batá* drums in general, and because he is an important *oricha, okónkolo* is typically saluted second. Ochún is associated with *itótele;* because Ochún is the youngest *oricha,* and thus has less status than her elders Changó and Yemayá, *itótele* is typically saluted last. However, there are variations: drummers and children of Changó may salute *okónkolo,* the smallest drum, first, because *okónkolo* is associated with Changó, "owner" of the *batá* drums; alternatively, some people salute the drums in order of size: *iyá* (largest), *itótele* (medium), and *okónkolo* (smallest). That Eleguá saluted *okónkolo* first may signal several things: that he was intent on upending some of the more predictable behaviors associated with *toques de santo;* that he wanted to honor the smallest drum as a way of honoring Changó, the *oricha* most associated with the *batá* drums; that he may have forgotten or disregarded drum salutation etiquette; or that he may have particularly enjoyed *okónkolo*'s playing during his *toque* (*okónkolo* normally maintains a steady rhythm, such as *"ki ha, ki ha, ki ha,"* during most *toques,* but in Eleguá's *toque* known as "Latopa," *okónkolo*'s part includes many interesting variations).

7. Red and black, two very powerful colors in Yoruba cosmology, belong to the unpredictable Eleguá. "Red is dangerous. It is too hot. Yorubas run away from red; they fear it. . . . Black is another beautiful color that people fear, or run from. Those two colors have power and they are able to swallow up other colors" (M. Drewal 1992:147). See also M. Drewal (1992:150, 178, 209) and Galembo (1993, esp. pp. 49–95).

8. These color-coded beaded necklaces represent the five "major" *orichas:* Red and black beads for Eleguá, white for Obatalá, blue and clear for Yemayá, red and white for Changó, and yellow for Ochún. If a practitioner becomes fully initiated into Santería, these necklaces will be restrung with more elaborate color patterns, as they will need to refer to specific avatars or "roads" of each *oricha*. For example, Obatalá Ayagunna, a warrior path of Obatalá, typically takes a pattern of sixteen white beads with eight red beads.

9. During a *bembé* or *güemilere,* for example, *conga* drums and other percussive instruments may be used to celebrate and perhaps even evoke certain *orichas* (see Cornelius 1989:73–101, 345).

10. Making *santo,* which refers to the process of becoming initiated into Santería, is also called making *ocha* (*ocha* is a truncated form of *oricha,* or deity), *el asiento* (the "seating" or "enthroning" of an *oricha*), and *kariocha* (putting *ocha* [*oricha*] into one's head). I prefer "making *santo*" because *"santo"* refers directly to the popular name by which the religious tradition is known (Santería), and the gerund suggests the lengthy process of preparation and realization involved in the final event. See chapter 7 for a personally contextualized representation of making *santo,* and see M. Mason (1997) for a detailed description and analysis of the initiation process in Santería.

11. At a drumming in San Francisco, California, in January 1999, the *akpwón,* who was visiting from Havana, reprimanded the attendees, yelling at us to "Sing! Sing!" He added, "If you don't sing with us, we can't finish the *toque*. I don't care what you sing. If you don't know the words, sing blah blah blah, but just sing!" In San Francisco, it is much less likely for the adherents to know the Yoruba words to particular songs of the Santería liturgy than it is for *creyentes* (believers) in Havana to do so. Knowing what he was up against, the Havana-based *akpwón* was asking for vocal energy of any kind from the Anglo worshippers. Despite our weak voices and slurred diction, the *akpwón* and the drummers eventually finished the *toque,* which in this case meant facilitating two *oricha* possessions, helping the host Santera complete her ritual obligations, and ending the ceremony before nightfall.

12. Friedman (1982:252–282) discusses to the continual negotiation of power between the Santero who sponsors the *toque de santo,* and the lead *batalero* who is contracted by the Santero to play at the *toque*. He notes that the agendas of the head Santero and the lead *batalero* may not be the same (the Santero's reasons for holding the toque often focus on the needs of humans; the *batalero*'s reasons for participating in the *toque* depend more directly on pleasing the *orichas*), which difference may lead to "moral gaps" in the performance of the *toque*. These "moral gaps," explains Friedman, are often bridged by religious "mysticism," the employment of language, dress, and behavior that only the drummers and the Santeros will be able to understand, thus creating common ground between the Santero and the *olu batá* (lead *batá* drummer), and thus allowing the successful completion of the *toque*.

13. In September 1999, during my first *cumpleaños de santo,* I was presented to the *batá*

drums, one of the final components in the process of priestly initiation into Santería. Because my head (and thus my head *oricha*) was to be introduced to the sacred *batá* drums during this event, great emphasis was placed on my ability to dance correctly in front of these sacred entities. Two ritual assistants helped me rehearse the dance steps of Ochún, my head *oricha,* after which I was told to watch a young Santera who was "a really good dancer," so that I could mimic her steps and not embarrass myself or the *orichas* during this important ceremony.

14. Occasionally a Santero or Santera needs to dance in front of the drums as an *ebbó,* or offering, to the *orichas.* The need for this offering may be revealed during the course of the Santero's initiation into Santería or during an additional divinatory reading. In either case, for that particular priest or priestess, dancing appropriately in front of the drums is considered a powerful offering that elicits great blessings.

15. At the exhibit of Haitian Vodou, which opened at the UCLA Fowler Museum in 1996 and was at the New York Museum of Natural History through early January 1999, on display were thousands of items from *vodou* altars. Tucked in between the many objects for the mischievous Gede spirits and the beautiful and powerful Ezili *lwa* (deities) were various representations of Bosou, *lwa* of the forest, a magical bull who is typically rendered with three horns. In a couple of small altar paintings, however, Bosou only had two horns. I asked the two Haitian artists manning the crafts table at this exhibit why some Bosous had only two horns, when Bosou is "supposed" to have three. They said that the details of the *lwa* (as rendered by religious artists) don't matter as much as the feeling behind the work and the reasons for making it. "Bosou is Bosou, and he knows he is Bosou whether the artist calls to him with two horns or with three."

16. The relationship between Babalawos and Santeros (and Santeras) is both intimate and fraught with tension. The Ifá divination system, in which Babalawos are high priests, is central to certain practices within Santería, such as specific initiation ceremonies (although even this is subject to variation, depending on the *casa templo*). Yet Santeros and Santeras also use other means of divination (coconut pieces, for example) in their ceremonies. The *oricha* of Ifá divination, Orúnmila (also called Orula), is an important *oricha* in the Santería pantheon, yet Ifá also exists as a divination system and religious tradition separate from Santería. When one is initiated into the priesthood of Santería, it is customary to receive one's *ebbó de entrada* ("entrance offering," a divination ceremony that precedes the seven-day *asiento,* which alerts the initiate and her *padrino* or *madrina* to potential difficulties—spiritual, material, and mortal) from a priest who has been trained in Ifá. Also during the *asiento,* Babalawos often perform the *matanzas,* or the ritual sacrifice of animals. Yet priests of Ifá are not necessary for the success of these events, and most other Santería ceremonies can be accomplished without the presence of Babalawos. Indeed, Santeros and Santeras read cowrie shells as well as coconut pieces in their divination practices, so some religious practitioners have argued

that Babalawos are superfluous to Santería practice. Nonetheless, Ifá-trained priests are present at some Santería ceremonies, and many practitioners of Santería in Havana are both Santeros and Babalawos. See D. Brown (2001) for a useful discussion of the symbiotic and troubled relationship between Ifá and Santería. See Bascom's work for a thorough explanation of the Ifá divination system in Cuba (1952) and in Nigeria (1969a, 1980). See Valdés Garriz (1995) for an excellent analysis of *diloggún* divination, which is closely related to Ifá divination. See Epega and Neimark (1995) for a recent English translation of and commentary on Nigerian Ifá texts.

17. According to Alberto, when he talks about "the religion" in the context of the CFNC, he is referring to two entities, one specific and one general. The first referent is Santería, his "home religion." The second referent is the group of African-based religions practiced in Cuba from which many of the Conjunto Folklórico's performances are derived—which would include Santería, Palo Monte, Arará, and Abakwá.

18. Arará is sometimes considered a branch of Santería (Lachatañeré 1939; Ortíz 1952; Moreno 1988), although its origins in the Ewe-Fon region of Ghana, Togo, Benin, and Nigeria make its musical and material culture distinct from that of the Yoruba. For example, Arará drums look more like Ewe drums than like Yoruba drums, and the structure of Arará religious music, though dying out in Cuba (the last Arará *casa templo* is in Matanzas, the province just east of Havana) sounds more like that of contemporary religious singing and drumming from Togo and Benin than like that of Yoruba-based *cantos* and *toques.*

19. Jesús Pérez also bequeathed to Alberto his consecrated set of *batá* drums, the *tambores de fundamento.* These drums, covered with intricately beaded cloths of blue and white, yellow and white, and red and white, for Yemayá's *iyá,* Ochún's *itótele,* and Changó's *okónkolo,* respectively, are played only at religious ceremonies.

20. "On the streets" in this case means at *toques de santo.* Alberto often uses the expression "to play in the streets" when he refers to going to someone's house to play for a *toque* or a *bembé.*

21. *Ayán, anyá,* and *anyé* are alternative spellings of *añá.*

22. See J. Mason (1992) and Bolívar Aróstegui (1990) for narrative sketches of Ochún and other major *orichas* within the Santería pantheon.

23. Obbini Batá performed twice weekly at the Don Giovanni restaurant (which served Italian food, mostly for tourists) in Old Havana during most of 1992, and also appeared at a performance in honor of deceased 1940s crooner and mambo king Benny Moré at the Karl Marx Theatre in Miramar during the summer of 1992.

24. This assertion seems contradictory, as there are numerous Santería priestesses of Changó and female initiates who often get possessed by Changó, during which time they are very likely to enact Changó's masculinity.

25. This last explanation is particularly interesting because one of the stated reasons for animal sacrifice in Santería is that it is an acceptable substitute for human sacrifice.

According to this reasoning, dripping one's own blood (menstrual or not) by mistake on the consecrated drums, stones, or other material objects that represent an *oricha* could create an unfortunate precedent for the future.

26. In addition, there is growing interest among a few British female *batá* drummers in playing for Santería ceremonies, and there are rumors circulating in several Internet chat rooms that Cuban women are interested in playing *batá* drums for Santería ceremonies outside of Cuba. (Afrocubaweb.com is the main source for both of these statements. Of the many websites that carry information about Cuba's African heritage, Afrocubaweb.com is the most reliable and most visited website for information regarding Afro-Cuban religious and folkloric events, tours, and trends.)

27. The commercially available metal-rimmed drums from such music stores as Latin Percussion, for example, would never be used for ritual purposes. The very materials used to construct these commercial drums preclude their use in religious rituals: the *batá* drums are said to belong to Changó, the *oricha* of thunder and virility, whose ritual manifestation is usually represented by wooden implements, such as a hatchet, small drums, and a lidded container. Changó's rival, Ogún, is the god of war and iron, and his implements—including a cauldron, chains, and railroad ties—are always made out of metal (usually iron). Changó and Ogún are enemies, so to affix Ogún's iron onto Changó's wooden drums is tantamount to blasphemy; the enmity between the two gods would preclude a clear message sent by the drums to *orún* (heaven) and might even anger Changó or Ogún or both. Only wooden drums, made out of a single log, are ritually acceptable.

28. It is likely that nonsacred drums are called *tambores judíos* in this case because of Spanish Catholicism's prevalent formal and historically anti-Semitic influence in Santería. In *Nuevo Catauro de Cubanismos* (1985:307), at the end of an entry defining *judío* primarily as a common Cuban bird with black plumage, known as a *judío* because of its call *("hu-i-o")*, Fernando Ortíz writes that, in the language of *"los negros brujos"* of Cuba, *judío* means "that which is bad." An additional meaning of *judío,* as cited in Esteban Pichardo's *Diccionario provincial y casi razonado de vozes y frases cubanas* (1875:362), is "unreligious and impious," which supports the hypothesis that playing unconsecrated drums may be considered impious and even sacrilegious.

4

BLURRING THE BOUNDARIES
Merging Sacred and Profane

The *pataki* ended with Ochún coaxing Ogún out of the forest: Ogún's shame sent him
deep into the woods, and although several *orichas*, including his mother, tried to coax
him out, Ogún hid from them, pressing deeper and deeper into the forest. He ate leaves
and berries and the animals he killed with his metal implements, as well as soil from the
forest floor. After many other *orichas* had tried and failed to find Ogún, Ochún, the goddess of the rivers and of romantic love, set about to soothe Ogún's bitterness in order to
save the world from destruction. Dressed in the yellow of the sun and carrying a jar of
honey, she made her way to a clearing where a river ran through the forest. Sensing that
Ogún was near, she began to bathe herself, singing softly and laughing. As she turned
around she saw him staring at her, expressionless. She moved toward him, dancing, and
kissed him, offering him honey. After this encounter with sweetness, Ogún continued
working, without bitterness, and the world became tranquil. And so it is that Ochún is
the only one who can bring Ogún out of the forest: From bitterness comes sweetness.

SUMMONING THE SACRED IN A PROFANE WORLD
Yeye Ochún

At a winter 1991 Conjunto Folklórico performance in Havana at the Teatro
Mella, I witnessed an older woman in the audience become possessed by her
oricha during a rendition of a praise song for Ochún, deity of rivers and romantic
love: *"Omi, Omi Yeye, Omi Yeye ma sara wa o."* (Water, Mother's water, yes, we are
satisfied with Great Mother's water.[1]) The woman stood up abruptly in her seat,
shivered violently for half a minute, threw her head back and forth with her eyes
closed, and then started sing-shouting to the performers on stage: *"Yeye Ochún!
Ma yeye Ochún!"* (Mother Ochún! Great Mother Ochún!) She swayed back and
forth with her arms held slightly out, as if she were wearing a full skirt. After a

few minutes of this, two Cuban theater ushers arrived and picked her up, at which point she became rigid, then limp. They carried her out of the auditorium.

Although the audience immediately surrounding this woman (including myself) seemed mildly surprised, after she was taken out of the theater, people settled back into their seats to watch the show—which was, on some ur-level, designed to provoke just such a response of *oricha* possession, for, as the directors, singers, and drummers of the Conjunto Folklórico often assert, the Afro-Cuban songs and rhythms of their folkloric shows are "authentic." And yet the appropriate surface response to this folkloric performance was in fact a form of passive consumption; an aural and visual absorption of the sounds and gestures of the performance without actually letting in, letting on, or letting out sacred significance.

Less than a year after this experience, I arranged an interview with Alberto Villarreal, lead percussionist of the Conjunto Folklórico and my drum teacher at the time. After asking him about the repertoire of the ensemble (see chapter 2), I told him what I had witnessed at the performance. At first he denied that such a thing was possible, but then he admitted that inappropriate possessions had occurred at other times during the ensemble's performances. He maintained that because the *batá* rhythms were "real," it was always possible that people could become mounted by their *orichas* in a theater, but that they should not—because the theater is a public, rather than a sacred, place. Alberto's use of the terms "public" and "sacred" *(público* and *sagrado)* could be understood within the context of Mircea Eliade's "hierophany," that is, "the manifestation of the sacred in some ordinary object [or place]" (Eliade 1959:11). The woman who became possessed was evoking the religious antecedents of the performance from their folkloric trappings, and her possession was in fact a sacred manifestation in an ordinary, profane place.

Alberto asserted that this woman had shown a lack of respect toward her *oricha* to become possessed during a staged performance. *("Es una falta de respeto al oricha, pasarlo en un escenario.")* If the intent of the performance had been sacred, which would have entailed the use of consecrated drums (*ilu batá* or *tambores de fundamento,* which possess *añá*) then its sacred manifestation would have become clear, making the very same auditorium or house or patch of earth that was once "public" and "ordinary" now "sacred." Eliade's "hierophany" is of importance here because it provides a useful conceptual structure for understanding the potential fluidity of the relationship between sacred and secular performance. The intent of the winter 1991 CFNC performance was secular, making the performance space secular, too. Thus, according to Alberto, the woman who became possessed during this secular performance insulted not only her *oricha* but also the musicians, who determine the rules of engagement (i.e., appropriate times and venues) for communicating with the *orichas*.

Alberto's idea of "disrespecting" one's *oricha* implies that the subject of the possession has some measure of control over the experience. If one can control whether one becomes possessed in a public or a sacred place, this invites the possibility of controlling one's possession experience altogether. Practitioners who remember starting to become possessed have told me that their experience of *oricha* possession was oriented toward "letting it happen to you, letting it enter you" *(dejarlo pasarte, dejarlo entrarte);* allowing oneself to become fully possessed by a spirit or deity is actually quite difficult. Because *oricha* possession requires giving up one's consciousness to the *oricha,* a typical response is to fight against relinquishing the familiar—that is, one's own consciousness. Learning how to become possessed is a process that usually takes years of practice, during which time one develops a repertoire of "body memories" of both failed and successful possessions.[2] Including the possibility of *oricha* possession within the parameters of daily lived experience (for example, seeing *oricha* possessions as a child, and thus considering them one of the many possibilities of everyday life) makes the possession process easier to imagine, and thus easier to embody.

Que Viva Changó

The late Ramiro Guerra, former choreographer for the Conjunto Folklórico and a renowned performer of contemporary dance, told me the story of how, in the 1970s, one of the troupe's dancers, Santiago Alfonso, became possessed by his *oricha* while he was in his dressing room before a performance. According to Ramiro, Santiago (who later also became a choreographer for the CFNC and then moved on to choreograph for the Tropicana nightclub and El Caribe club in the Hotel Habana Libre) was crouching like an animal on his hands and feet, shouting "nonsense syllables." Ramiro walked into the dressing room, enraged at Santiago because he was late for the initial call for performers to be on stage, and ordered him to get dressed and ready. Santiago did not respond to Ramiro, because he was possessed by Changó, his head *oricha.* After several more attempts to communicate with Santiago, Ramiro finally decided to meet the *oricha* on its own terms. Switching modes, he said, "Changó, if you care enough about your son Santiago, you will let him go now, because if you don't, he will lose his job. You decide." A minute later, Santiago was dressed, cleaned up, and on stage.

Santiago, a self-described *creyente,* or believer, had access to the same body memory for his possession performance in the dressing room as he did for his possession performance on stage. The movements are the same, but the intent is different. One is tempted to theorize as to why Santiago allowed himself to become possessed in his dressing room right before a show—perhaps he didn't feel like working that day? Perhaps he was annoyed with Ramiro? Ramiro did not mention any singing or drumming happening in the background that might have prompted such a possession, although such sonic stimuli cannot be ruled out (a full "run-through" would often precede a performance, according to Ramiro).

It is important to note that, whatever prompted the possession performance, Ramiro chose to take this apparently divine manifestation at face value. Ramiro was not a practitioner of any of the African-based religions, although he often articulated his respect for them. He directed his frustration not toward Santiago but toward Changó, and he got the desired results. One wonders whether Santiago was consc(ient)iously playing the role of Changó, listening to Ramiro only because Ramiro had accepted him in that role. If Ramiro had immediately addressed his rage to Santiago, perhaps Santiago might have started throwing chairs at Ramiro and jumping on tables in his incarnation as Changó.

Ramiro might have been so flexible in his modes of interaction because he consciously trained himself to participate in the world of Afro-Cuban folklore. Although his background was in modern dance, he retooled himself for his work in folklore, studying the movements of African-based religious dance in the Conjunto Folklórico's *aficionado* school along with some of the neophytes. He, like many other choreographers, was overwhelmed by the beauty of the unrehearsed, unchoreographed performances in the 1960s. The renditions by the early informant/performers of possession performances were precisely what informed his and other choreographers' work. In the early days of the CFNC, the categories of sacred and profane were fused intentionally, the boundaries deliberately blurred; religious performance was invoked in secular settings as part of the process of shaping the "raw religious material" into theater.

Ogún Mariwó

In 1990 members of the Conjunto Folklórico recreated a series of possession performances for a movie about Santería in Cuba. Made by Cuban filmmaker Gloria Rolando, *Oggún* (1992) was meant to highlight the qualities of that warrior *oricha* through the life of the former lead singer in the Conjunto Folklórico, Lázaro Ros, a "son" of Ogún (alt. Oggún) in Santería. Many of the performers in the film have experienced religious possession and so have a body memory of it. The cast of characters is similar to the early informant/performers of the Conjunto Folklórico, who lived the experience of Santería and other religions of African origin for decades before they joined the troupe, and whose secularized performances for the CFNC relied on an intricate network of sacred emotional and physical memories that neophytes and nonbelievers lack.

At first, the rhythms of the *batá* drums, the songs, and the dances for this videotaped possession performance are indistinguishable from the rhythms, songs, and dances of a "real" *oricha* possession. (Audio, video, or photo documentation of a ceremony is considered offensive, if not sacrilegious, and rarely happens,[3] which underscores the nonreligious nature of the possession performance that Rolando videotaped.) But precisely because the performances sound the same, because the space between sacred and secular is inaudible, understanding the terms of where and how the sound gets produced might be more important than what is heard. The intent of the possession performance gains primacy over the performance itself, but because of a shared corpus of body memories of possession, some aspect of the sacred is recalled. Clearly, in the case of the feigned possession, the intent is not to bring down the deity—that is, the intent is *not* to get possessed, but rather to mimic possession so expertly that the experience *seems* real on film. But the success of the staged possession performance relies almost completely on those bodies who have been possessed, so the boundaries between "source" and "derivation" become blurred and even irrelevant. The summoning up of the sacred origins of this filmed possession performance is essential to the film's communicative power; indeed, someone unfamiliar with the circumstances of the film might consider the possession sequence "real."

In an article about her work, Rolando notes that the most vital and difficult scenes during the making of *Oggún* were those of the *tambor*:

> The structure of the documentary rests on the interview with Lázaro Ros, the scenes of recreations of the *patakís,* and the best moments of the *tambor* to Oggún filmed on Sunday, September 2, 1990. These images were the first to be recorded. The songs and the dances filmed in the colonial patio of Old Havana represent what is known as *tambor (añá* in Lucumí). A *tambor* is offered to an *orisha* in thanks or as a way of overcoming certain difficulties in life. The *tambor* is celebrated in houses with the doors open, and anyone who behaves respectfully may enter. Only the initiates have the right to dance before the sacred *tambores batá* (drums). In my opinion, this was the most difficult task for the crew (including the editing). Moreover, that atmosphere could not be repeated. (Rolando in Lindsay 1996:261)

Rolando's use of the term "documentary" and her assertion that the performance and editing of the *tambor* scene was "the most difficult" for the crew allude once more to the challenge of maintaining the balance between "real" ritual and "staged" spectacle in the dramatization of religious practices. The atmosphere of the *tambor* could not be repeated precisely because the cast was heading toward the spontaneity of religious expression, and away from the predictability of rehearsed, staged spectacle.

James Peacock (1990) suggests that the difference between sacred and secular performance lies precisely in the predictability afforded by rehearsal. He notes that one of the main differences between the two performative acts is that secular performance requires rehearsals of the same materials or, in my terms, units of performance; a rehearsal of form, if you will. Extending his idea, I would assert that sacred performance, though it may occur with predictability, is also a rehearsal, but of a different nature. Sacred performance involves the rehearsal of function rather than form, and the units of performance, though they may be identifiable, need not provide the event with the same predictability or surface structure as a performance of secular intent. Although the success of a secular performance might rely on the perfectly executed repetition of a series of units of performance, the efficacy of Afro-Cuban religious practice resides in the repetition of function—which includes songs, praise names, prayers, rhythms, and gestures—all of which will be effective because of the intent and context of the repetition, not necessarily because of the aesthetic value of the repetitive act itself.

Mama Lola and Ezili Dantò

This idea of rehearsing function rather than form can be connected to many other sacred traditions of the West African diaspora, chief among them those religions that share Cuba's Yoruba and Dahomey roots. In the spring of 1996 I attended the opening events of the African Vodou exhibit at UCLA's Fowler Museum (which traveled throughout the country and opened at the Museum of Natural History in New York in late 1998). I was especially interested in this exhibit because Haitian Vodou and Cuban Santería share important theological traits and deity names from their common origins in southwest Nigeria and Benin. I was teaching a seminar on African performance traditions that semester and decided to take my students to the exhibit. One of the events at the UCLA opening was a lecture/discussion led by Karen Brown, author of numerous articles and a book on Haitian Vodou in Brooklyn called *Mama Lola: A Vodou Priestess in Brooklyn* (1991), and the Manbo (Vodou priestess) herself, Mama Lola, born Marie Thérèse Alourdes Macena Margaux Kowalski, and also known as Alourdes Margaux.

Alourdes was accompanied into the auditorium beneath the Fowler by her daughter Maggie and Karen Brown. After providing a brief narrative about her religious practice, she began to answer the audience's many questions. One woman yelled out cheerfully, "Sing us a song, Mama Lola! Sing us a song!" Karen and Alourdes looked confused, and the woman clarified her request: "I hear you're a good singer. Sing us one of your songs." Alourdes responded, "You mean to the *lwa*?" The woman nodded, and then several other people joined in the request, yelling out the names of various female *lwa* (deities of Vodou), such as Ezili Freda, Ezili Dantò, and Lasyrenn.

Alourdes thought for a moment, and then began to sing a song to Ezili Dantò, her "mother" in Vodou. Within fifteen seconds of beginning her song, she began to manifest many of the signs of possession in Haitian Vodou: her body shook, her eyes rolled back in her head and then closed as she convulsed, and she began shouting angry orders at the audience, her eyes now wide open and blazing fiercely. The audience gasped collectively and murmured its concern. Karen and Maggie both tried to calm the spirit by holding Alourdes taut, and Maggie tried to get the spirit to leave her mother's body by talking to it and holding her mother's head. Finally, Alourdes went limp and was led to a chair at the edge of the stage to rest. No one spoke about the errant possession within the public space of the auditorium after Alourdes had recovered. "What happened?" she asked in a bewildered voice after she came back to human consciousness. Her daughter responded to her in a voice the audience could not hear, perhaps informing her that Ezili Dantò had come down to tell this UCLA audience what was what.

According to Karen Brown, most of the songs to Ezili Dantò evoke her intense and sudden power. She is one of the water deities, but she is also known as a Petwo or "hot" deity, associated with a fierce protection of her children and occasional outbursts of violence. Even the very beginning of a song Mama Lola sings every time she evokes Ezili Dantò marks the violence and the suffering of this deity (K. Brown 1991:232–233):

> *Di ye!*
> *Set kou'd kouto, set kou'd ponya.*
> *Prete'm terinn-nan, m'al vomi san ye.*
> *Set kou'd kouto, set kou'd ponya.*
> *Prete'm terinn-nan, m'al vomi san ye.*
>
> Say hey!
> Seven stabs of the knife, seven stabs of the sword.

Hand me that basin, I'm going to vomit blood.
Seven stabs of the knife, seven stabs of the sword.
Hand me that basin, I'm going to vomit blood.[4]

The Fowler auditorium is a prime example of the "profane" space Eliade refers to in his discussion of "hierophany." Why would Mama Lola allow herself to become possessed in such an unlikely forum? Why would Ezili Dantò choose to arrive in such an unfamiliar space? Mama Lola might have become nervous before an audience of strangers at UCLA, which might have brought on Mama Lola's "inappropriate" possession—but she has been performing for large groups of people for many years, so why become nervous now?

My hypothesis is that sometimes the song, with its particular melodic contours, syllabic rhythms, and emotional content, potentially brings on possession for Mama Lola no matter where she performs it. This theory is connected to the idea of performative intent; that is, if Mama Lola's main experience of singing songs to Ezili Dantò is to bring her to earth (i.e., to evoke the possession of her body by Ezili Dantò), then the most familiar performative intent (perhaps the only intent) associated with that song is spirit possession, and the song likely cannot be sung any other way by Mama Lola. In other words, she cannot sing it with the intent to please a group of academics at UCLA, nor can she sing it with the intent to impress people with her vocal abilities; function pervades and indeed overwhelms form in this case.

What is interesting about Mama Lola's background, and what ties her experiences to those of the Conjunto Folklórico, is that she performed for several years, from the age of fifteen, in Haiti's Troupe Folklorique Nationale, Haiti's national folkloric ensemble, in the early 1950s (K. Brown 1991:237). Founded in 1949, the troupe's repertoire included songs and dances from Haiti's Rada and Petwo Vodou traditions, and thus likely included songs to Ezili Dantò. One must also keep in mind that Alourdes was "chosen" to serve the lwa from the age of seven (K. Brown 1991:224–225), so she was differentiating between folklorique and lwa performance contexts at least in her teens. If such a differentiation is possible between "work" and "religion," as Alberto would say, why did Alourdes not choose to distinguish between the two contexts at UCLA? Or, more specifically, why was the "religious" context allowed to overtake the "work" context, even for a few minutes?

Karen Brown provides an interesting hypothesis for this transformative transgression in her discussion of the trauma many Haitians experienced on leaving (needing to leave, being forced to leave) Haiti. She describes the U.S. Immigration and Naturalization Services refugee facilities for unaccompanied minors during the Haitian "boat people" crisis of the mid-1980s. Alone and frightened in this apparently hostile and foreign facility, some of the Haitian children had turned to the *lwa* for help and had been possessed by their spirits. This alarmed the staff at the refugee facility, and one of them called on Karen for advice. She brought Mama Lola to the facility to counsel the children and concluded that there was a parallel between the behavior of these newly arrived Haitian children in the United States and the behavior of the newly arrived slaves in Haiti:

> When the elders, the priests, the institutions, the musical instruments, the images, the altars, and the sacred objects are absent, where do you turn for spiritual aid? In an African-based religion, possession seems an obvious answer. In Yorubaland and Dahomey, two of the areas of origin for Haiti's [and Cuba's] slave population, most possession-performances were formulaic affairs with more or less predictable words and gestures. In the New World, however, in that early time when the body and the voice were the slaves' principal mnemonic devices, possession could well have received much greater emphasis, and possession-performances could have quickly become much more extemporaneous and expressive. In other words, cut loose from their African base and institutional moorings, the spirits may well have burst into flower. Times of crisis are often times of high creativity. (K. Brown 1991:253)

Following this suggestion, then, might one hypothesize a "crisis" in Afro-Cuban religious practice that leads to possession performances in profane or at least inappropriate spaces?[5] One could argue that in Cuba, the state-sponsored folkloricization of the Afro-Cuban religious traditions imparts some of the shock. Seeing one's religious tradition stripped of its theological moorings for the purposes of theatrical staging, mostly for people who have little sense of its origins or its meaning, might prove traumatic. Or one could take the explanation back even farther, and plant the trauma in the double-barreled effect of having been persecuted for one's religious beliefs for most of one's life, and then seeing some of the trappings of those beliefs put on state-sponsored display, mainly for the amusement and entertainment of nonbelievers. The first public decree that actively repressed these African-based religions was issued by the Spanish colonial government in 1842, entitled the "Reglamento de Esclavos" (rules for slaves), which proclaimed that Spanish slaveholders must instruct the slaves "in the basic principles of the Roman Catholic Apostolic Religion" to the exclusion of all other religions (Kirk 1989:17). Although all Cuban governments from that time until the fall of Fulgencio Batista in 1958 have suppressed the practice of Afro-Cuban religious traditions with some consistency, by far the most organized and articulated policy of repression came from the early revolutionary government itself. At the very least, the radical shift in the Cuban state's interpretation and use of Afro-Cuban religious traditions such as Santería is deeply confusing, if not traumatic.

Paradoxically, this sense of trauma and displacement effects two complementary yet contradictory impulses: it is precisely this trauma that is being managed in the determination of and adherence to the rules of engagement in religious and folkloric performance, yet it is also this trauma that permits a sort of improvisatory foray from the sacred into the secular, and back again. The summoning and consequent performance of the sacred in a profane environment can be construed as the ultimate improvisation, the ultimate risk, the ultimate search for help in a world gone mad—when the divine inspiration of spontaneous creation is gently tossed into the audience, like a gift, in the hopes that it will be received by a kindred and wise spirit, someone who understands the origins of the gesture: a sacred convergence of utterance and reception.

THE CORPOREAL TRANSLATION OF MEMORY

The constant combination of these divine utterances—singing, drumming, dancing, and praising—is the source of Afro-Cuban performative power. The repeated articulation of sacred names and phrases through singing, drumming, and dancing enhances the potentiality of a deity, encouraging it to exist through a collective rehearsal of its name or attributes.[6] Margaret Drewal, in her incisive article "Dancing for Ogún in Yorubaland and in Brazil" (1997), notes that words become not only semantic referents but also sensorial triggers. Drewal's examples include the phrase *"Ke ge, ke ge, ke ge"*—meant to invoke Ogún, but also meant to evoke Ogún's violence by imitating the sound of a lopped-off head rolling down a hill. The plosive-velar power of pronouncing *"ke ge"* matches its semantic referent, and is reinforced by a lurching dance, in which each foot lands heavily, accompanied by swinging the arm on the same side.

Whether or not one understands the Yoruba language, this performance world creates a sense of heaviness, of explosive power (as in the plosive-velar combination of *ke ge*), and of latent violence. Although such a strong case cannot be made for every last divine utterance, the words of Yoruba praise songs often communicate as much through the clicks, hisses, and pops of their required pronunciation as they do through their semantic meanings. The very sounds of these words, and the way that one feels as one's body (lungs, larynx, throat, mouth, teeth, facial mask) produces these sounds, often evoke some central attribute of the deity to whom they refer. And one's arms and legs, as they lurch from side to side for Ogún or for Eleguá, or sway and circle gracefully for Yemayá or Ochún, retrieve and communicate an essential corporeal message about the nature of divinity in Santería, whether or not one is a *creyente.*

This utterative power is located at the center of the sensorial experience that is translated from sacred to secular. It is the memory of the utterance, whether vocal or gestural, that moves fluidly from religious to profane, radiating outward to imbue a secular folkloric performance with possible sacredness. And the experience of translating the sacred into the secular—and back again—is mediated through the body. In fact, the primary goal of a mimetic folkloric performance seems to be the resurrection of potential (if not actual) sacredness during the circumscribed length of the staged performance. The dancers, singers, and drummers labor to recreate a bit of the magic that exists in a *"real" toque de santo,* complete with competent audience and willing mediums, yet without the religious belief system and familiar history that would typically inform it. But the performers cannot control the effects of their divinely inspired utterances on the audience. This re-created magic often evokes spirit possession among the faithful, even when the context and the intent of the performance is apparently secular.[7]

IMPROVISATION: TRANSLATING *ACHÉ* FROM SACRED TO SECULAR

During the past ten years of intermittent fieldwork, I have been an attentive audience member and participant in many *toques de santo* (most of them in Havana) and in folkloric performances (mostly of the Conjunto Folklórico, also in Havana). It is through a comparison of the two performance genres that I have begun to understand the interplay between religious and folkloric performance. The Conjunto Folklórico's dramatizations of the songs and dances of Santería, for example, are mimetic representations (Taussig 1993) of divine manifestations, such as possession performances. Mimesis, in this case, is achieved primarily through the performance of singing, drumming (which includes clapping and playing the *claves* here), and dancing that have their origins in religious contexts. I refer to this complex of singing, drumming, and dancing as divine utterances, in both folkloric and religious contexts, because the origins of the musical articulations and physical movements are kept in mind, and in body, in both contexts. The divinity of any given expression remains nearby, if not at the forefront of, the performance.

With each religious performance I attended, I noticed variations in the representations of the songs, rhythms, and dances of the *orichas*. Although each *oricha* owns particular songs, *batá* rhythms, and dances, each of these utterances is sub-

ject to interpretation and improvisation by the performers. As a result, for example, a song for Eleguá might vary somewhat in pitch, tempo, and melodic deco-
ration depending on who sings it, but each singer is likely to maintain a similar
melodic contour from performance to performance. And although the lead *batá*
drum *(iyá)* might call to the middle and small *batá* drums *(itótele* and *okónkolo*, respectively) with thunderous and distracting patterns for Eleguá, within this maze
of rhythms is an implied structure each player understands and responds to. The
differences in any given religious performance are spurred on by the dynamics of
the ceremony. If a practitioner is on the verge of being possessed, the lead singer
(akpwón) may switch quickly from song to song—forcing the choral respondents
to pay closer attention to each phrase (because they will soon have to answer it),
causing the drummers to adjust their corresponding rhythmic patterns, and making the dancers change their steps—in an effort to effect possession. These improvisations and variations are so frequent within the tradition that they seem to
defy transcription, and they make the task of generalizing about this variable performance practice extremely difficult for people unfamiliar with its context. The
efficacy of the tradition depends on the ability of each performer to interpret a
praise text, song, rhythm, or dance in the context of the ceremony, such that improvisation literally revivifies the performance.

✪ LISTEN TO TRACK 7: Francisco Aguabella's group performing a chant
     for Eleguá.

Bruno Nettl, in the introduction to his edited volume on improvisation, refers
to John Baily's idea that improvisation relies on the creation of "unique musical
utterances" during the act of performance (Nettl 1998:9). The creation of unique
utterances is also essential to bringing down the *santo* in a Santería ritual drumming. In religious performance, divine utterances are created from models or archetypes during moments of religious obligation and inspiration—obligation because the participants in a *toque de santo* are bound to bring down an *oricha*, and
inspiration because seeing a *creyente* begin to become possessed typically inspires
a series of creative musical and gestural utterances to complete the process. These
improvisations on the archetypes or "divine standards" enhance the *aché*, or divine potential, of the performance, and thus of the ceremony in general.

Aché is a central concept in Yoruba cosmology that has been transferred intact
to the Cuban practice of Santería. It refers to both the realized and inherent divine potential in all aspects of life, even in apparently inert objects. Although all
beings possess *aché*, people who are initiated into Santería generally gain more
aché (which, in a performative context, can be understood as the power to make

things happen), and each of their physical attributes also communicates *aché*. Therefore, an initiate's breath, hair, extremities, and all organs and body fluids are divinely potent carriers of *aché*. It follows from this that vocalized texts and songs (which emanate from the breath) as well as danced and drummed gestures (which are formed by the extremities) also possess *aché*. Because new variations and improvisations bring with them the possibility of enhancing *aché*, they are not simply desirable but necessary to galvanize the energy of a religious performance.

Of course, improvisation within Afro-Cuban religious performance, as in any performative genre, must exist within a recognizable structure. What is interesting about improvisation and variation in Afro-Cuban Santería performances is that there is a fine balance between predictable utterances (such as, for example, a well-known line in a praise song that immediately cues the chorus) and spontaneous, inspired improvisation. The acts of chanting and singing are powerful within a Santería ceremony, and they determine the course of events. The perfect combination of the "stand-by" praise songs with spontaneous praise songs "of the moment" is likely to result in *oricha* possession.

Recall the possession performance in Santos Suarez that I recounted in chapter 2: It was when the tall, lanky man started to get possessed that the *akpwón* (lead singer) focused his energy—his vocal *aché*—on the man, singing "onto" him the praises that he thought would evoke or goad Eleguá into coming down. At this point, the *akpwón* was drawing on his powerful arsenal of chants and praise songs, trying one after another until one of these utterances did the trick—from the chant, *"Ago Eleguá o bu kenke"* (Make way for Eleguá who is abusive and small), asking permission to evoke Eleguá, to the more specific reference, *"Oko okan odara"* (The virile one is good),[8] to a welcoming of the deity, *"Ago to yo ma de ka wa o"* (Make way, the chief has arrived, let us go to him).[9] All the while, the drummers were changing their rhythms depending on the *akpwón's* choices, and the chorus was trying to sing back the appropriate response, while swaying and stepping back and forth. It was a group performance, with the *akpwón* leading the improvisation.

⊕ LISTEN TO TRACK 8: Francisco's group performing songs for Eleguá.
⊕ LISTEN TO TRACK 9: Francisco's group performing a series of rhythms marking the end of the *toque de santo*.

In folkloric renditions of these events, because the *akpwón* is not focusing on bringing down an *oricha*, there is little incentive to improvise in an immediate, divinely inspired way. What happens instead is that the songs and dances are transcribed into rehearsed memory, usually becoming more static with each rendition. The role of the *akpwón* as religious mediator is no longer relevant, so the *akpwón* / lead singer becomes but a catalyst for the rehearsed responses of the chorus. Even so, a lead singer trained in a religious context as an *akpwón* will likely vary his or her folkloric rendition of a particular praise song each time he or she performs it just enough to make it sound fresh. Consider, for example, the many and varied recordings of Lázaro Ros and Merceditas Valdés, both of whom were originally trained as *akpwónes* before they began singing in folkloric contexts; or the recordings of the folkloric groups of Francisco Aguabella and Alberto Villarreal, the members of which also play for *toques de santo*.

🔊 LISTEN TO TRACK 10: Francisco's group performing "Ago Eleguá e."

🔊 LISTEN TO TRACK 11: Alberto's group performing "Eleguá Alaroye."

The folkloric renditions of Santería performances share many formal attributes with their religious counterparts, and, as a result, improvisation and variation do occur in folkloric performances, but to a lesser extent than in religious performances, and with a different intent. The intent of an improvisation in a folkloric setting cannot be to help along a possession, because (in theory) no one is being possessed. Improvisation in a folkloric setting is directed at jolting the audience and the other performers awake from the drowsy familiarity of repetitive tunes and phrases. But when a singer trained as an *akpwón* improvises in a folkloric performance, the body memory of having invoked *oricha* possession through an improvisatory performances of a praise song influences the performative intent of the moment, so that even an incompetent audience is blinded—just for a split-second—by the brightness of the utterance.

Likewise, although the *batá* drums still respond to the songs of the lead singer in a folkloric performance, the drummers usually know in advance which songs the lead singer will choose, and in which order, because of the rehearsal process. They are no longer scrambling to follow the praise songs of the lead singer as they might be in a possession performance. Their concentration is focused on beginning and ending each call in a polished way, befitting a public show for which people have paid money. The dancers are probably the most constrained in their roles, inasmuch as they no longer are primed to respond to a possible *oricha* possession but rather to perform the stylized and condensed physical tropes created by the choreographer to represent each *oricha*. The folkloric performances are about ninety minutes each (not counting intermission), and there is no time for improvisation. In a religious *toque de santo,* time might be viewed as the benevolent provider of a series of infinite possibilities, including the arrival of a deity; time as a doorway, leading outward and upward from high noon to sundown. In the folkloric performances, time is a strict matron, opening the door at 3:00 P.M.

and closing it just before 5:00 P.M.: There's no time for fooling around—we've got a show to present.

Praise Song Texts

In an interview (July 1, 1992), Rogelio Martinez Furé, the Conjunto Folklórico's current *asesor* (artistic advisor) and one of its original founders, told me that he had "shortened and changed around some of the songs of the *orichas*" (see, for example, the arrangements on the commercially available tape *Conjunto Folklórico Nacional* [latest edition, 1989], for which he claims credit as composer). According to Martínez Furé, his ability to understand Yoruba and his familiarity with these texts as a religious practitioner made him feel "free to use his sense of poetry in combining different song texts." Martínez Furé is the author of several volumes of Yoruba poetry, which he has translated into Spanish. He combines different song texts within the extant corpus of songs for particular *orichas*. He has not attached a chant for Oyá, for example, to the opening prayer for Eleguá. Rather, his sense of poetry leads him to truncate and repeat certain key phrases in the *cantos* for specific *orichas*.

In a religious context, some song texts are associated with other song texts, such as in a song for Eleguá: *"O jí mì'ni e a, Al'àdó ní'sè èsù mì'ni, Alároyé al'àdó ní'sè"* (You who wakes one up, agitates one. The owner of the medicine gourd has power. Esu agitates one. Alároyé the owner of the medicine gourd has power [J. Mason 1992:64–65]). Martínez Furé's version of the song is: *"O jí mì'ni e a, Al'adó ní'se, O jí mì'ni"* (You who wakes one up, agitates one, The owner of the medicine gourd has power. You who wakes one up). He leaves out the middle of the song text, which refers specifically to Esu (a manifestation of Eleguá) and Alaroye (a road of Eleguá), and later uses the first phrase *(O jí mì'ni e a)* as a sort of chorus. The song might be considered to be incomplete by a religious practitioner, though the retention of a key phrase for Eleguá *(O jí mì'ni)*[10] maintains the song's relevance to the deity. Although improvisatory play with song texts is relatively common in a sacred performance context, the stasis implied by the compositional process is not. Martínez Furé's truncation and "reordering" the song texts would have been well within the realm of performative possibility in a religious context. It is the maintenance of those particular sequences by means of recordings and rehearsals that removes it from a religious context, and, of course, that makes the final product polished and comforting in its predictability. (Refer back to Track 1: Lázaro Ros singing *"O jí mì'ni e a"* for Eleguá.)

It is important to note here that Martínez Furé's "poetic license" could also be considered a sacred utterance, in that he improvises with the material in the same way that a religious practitioner might in the throes of a *toque de santo*. But what is not divinely inspired or common practice in religious tradition is for these improvisations to become static entities, stuck in one particular sequence through the reification of rehearsals (rehearsing form rather than function). Indeed, what is striking about the performances of the Conjunto Folklórico is that there is surprisingly little room for improvisation, making the variations and improvisations of sacred intent that much more evident and powerful in comparison.

Another important aspect in improvisation within Afro-Cuban religious performance is the translation and transformation of liturgical Yoruba (Lucumí) into Cuban Spanish. Most Cubans do not understand Lucumí, with the exception of certain words and phrases that have seeped into the Cuban vernacular, such as *aché* and the praise names of certain *orichas* (Babalú Ayé, Ochún, Yemayá, Orúnmila, and Eleguá, for example). Many Cubans, however, know some of the praise songs associated with Santería. This specific yet partial knowledge creates potentially endless variations in the performance of the Santería liturgy: many Yoruba sounds do not exist in Cuban Spanish, and certain consonants and consonant clusters (*d* and *r, y* and *l, b* and *w, kp* and *w, gb* and *b,* for example) sound very similar, especially when one cannot see the mouth that produces them. The "foreign" sounds morph into "Cuban" sounds, and the similar-sounding consonants converge and occasionally become interchangeable, making a "source" version or "primary" meaning difficult to determine.

The Santería liturgy is rife with examples:

> "*Iya mi le odo*" (My mother's house is the river) is sung and understood as "*Iya mi le oro*" (My mother's house is tradition).

> "*O jimini e a*" (One who agitates) is performed and understood as "*Echu mini e a*" (Echu who agitates).

> "*Awa ni ye o Ogun mariwo*" (We come to honor you Ogun of the palm fronds) can be performed and understood as "*Awa ni le o Ogun mariwo*" (We come to occupy the house of Ogun of the palm fronds).

> "*Ogún wa nile, Ogún wa l'ona*" (Ogún comes to occupy the house, Ogún comes to have the road) is occasionally performed and understood as "*Ogún pa n'ilé, Ogún pa l'oná*" (Ogún kills in the house, Ogún kills on the road).[11]

Depending on who is singing the praise songs, the texts take on distinct meanings with the variation of particular consonants and syllables. In fact, it may be more apt to refer to this phenomenon as a variation rather than an improvisation, inasmuch as it is not clear that the variations created by these consonant substitutions are always deliberate or even conscious. What is more important is that this liturgical tradition is highly variable, both deliberately and inadvertently, and new meanings emerge with each spontaneous rendition, so that attempts to freeze it or standardize it move definitively away from sacred (and common) practice. In the contemporary practice of Santería, ritual efficacy resides primarily in the intent and act of repetition, not necessarily in the words that are being repeated or in their contested meanings.

Praise-Song Melodies

Melodic variations in a song text are typically the result of spontaneous and deliberate improvisation, which are usually accomplished by the lead singer. In fact, the lead singer may break into a long and personal prayer to an *oricha* within the opening verse of a song, and the drummers and other singers have to wait patiently until she finishes with her own invocation before they can respond to a more general call with which they are familiar. The choral responses to the lead singer, although they typically mimic the praise song lined out by the *akpwón,* may split into two- and three-part harmony (not necessarily Western tertian harmony), depending on the training and inspiration of the singers. If the *akpwón* likes what she hears and considers it inspiring to the *orichas,* she may elect to sing the same verse of the praise song several times, just to hear the harmonized playback. There are also liturgical reasons for this kind of repetition. For example, songs for Osain, the powerful *oricha* of healing and cleansing whose herbal remedies purify every ceremony in Santería, are typically sung twice. Within the imaginable corpus of sung variations, the texts are quite similar, and the melodic contour remains intact. What varies most are the melodic decorations, harmonic choral accompaniment, and the rhythmic phrasings of each song.

In folkloric renditions of *oricha* praise songs, a lead singer lines out or calls the first verse (or, because many songs are short, the entire song) in free meter, and the chorus responds by repeating part or all of the phrase. The lead singer may line out the song in a metered structure and at the same tempo as the chorus, or may sing at a slightly slower tempo than the chorus, with a free meter. The chorus typically responds to the lead singer's call, singing the same melodic contour, but with a regular meter and less melodic ornamentation.

Batá *Rhythms*

Determining patterns of improvisation and variation for ceremonial *batá* drumming is challenging not only because the lead drummers (those who play the *iyá*, or "mother drum") shape each call with their own style, but also because there are at least two extant drumming traditions for the ceremonies of Santería—one from Havana, and one from Matanzas, just east of Havana. Certain rhythms, rather than representing one *oricha* only, have come to be played for several *orichas*, or in some cases, for all the *orichas*. The Yakotá rhythm, which is commonly associated with Yemayá, is also played for Ochún, Obatalá, and the *eguns* (*muertos,* or ancestors). The *chachalokofún* rhythm can be played for any *oricha* as a "breakout" dance section (imagine that a *toque* is becoming too stayed, too reserved, and that the drummers want more audience participation—*chachalokofún* is the rhythm that makes people get up and dance). The Iyesá rhythm is played for Ochún (Iyesá is said to be the name of Ochún's Nigerian homeland), Eleguá, and Obatalá. And the Arará rhythm is played for Babalú Ayé, Afrekete, Ebbioso, and the Arará songs.

⊛ LISTEN TO TRACK 12: Alberto's group performs Yakota rhythms and songs for Yemayá.

⊛ LISTEN TO TRACK 13: Alberto's group performs Arará rhythms and songs for San Lázaro/Babalú Ayé.

⊛ LISTEN TO TRACK 14: Francisco's group performs songs for San Lázaro/Babalú Ayé.

⊛ LISTEN TO TRACK 15: Francisco's group performs Iyesá rhythms and songs for Ochún.

⊛ LISTEN TO TRACK 16: Alberto's group performs a song for Ochún.

Carlos Aldama Pérez, a lead *batá* drummer with the Conjunto Folklórico from its inception in 1962 until 1989, when he retired from the troupe, explains this "mixing and matching" in the following way:

> Batá rhythms used to be played only for Lucumí songs; each song had its particular
> rhythm. Yakotá used to be played only for the dead. And Iyesá was only played for
> Iyesá songs, with Iyesá drums. But what happened? Well, what happened was that we
> would have *toques* where people from Iyesá would attend, and they wouldn't know
> the *batá* rhythms, but they would know Iyesá, so we began to play Iyesá rhythms for
> them on the *batá* drums. And with the Arará, we have a particular *batá* rhythm that is
> for Yegua, but we adapted it to Arará songs, so that we could salute San Lázaro,
> Yemayá, and other *santos* with Arará songs. The Arará songs were supposed to be

played with Arará drums, but the only Arará drums were in Matanzas, because that's where all the Arará people are. So when the Matanceros [people from Matanzas] came to Havana to visit, they taught us the rhythms, and we played them on the *batá.* . . .[12]

Iyesá is from Matanzas, too. When Iyesá people came from Matanzas to visit, we had to have something to play for them, so that's how *chachalokofún* came about. *Chachalokofún* has a lot of *bembé* influence, from the Iyesá tradition. The *bembé* drums are Iyesá drums, but we play those rhythms on the *batá.* And now we play *chachalokofún* for all the *orichas.* (Interview, May 28, 1999)

The cross-pollination of rhythms between Havana and Matanzas does not always result in a new "hybridized" adaptation. Sometimes the rhythms are simply switched around. The primary calls for Ogún and Ochosi in the *oru seco,* for example, are reversed from the Havana to the Matanzas practice. This is particularly interesting because these two calls are never separated in religious performance; one rhythm leads into the next, with no break. (Usually, each *oricha* is called with a discrete set of rhythms, after which there is a pause to prepare for the next *oricha*'s rhythmic evocation.) So what happened in this case is that the inseparable rhythmic sequences became mirror images of each other, making Ogún and Ochosi rhythmically interchangeable. Carlos Aldama Pérez's explanation for why this may have happened is that the two warrior *orichas* are said to be inseparable brothers who live in the same camp in the forest. In their material manifestations (both Ogún and Ochosi are represented by sacred stones and metal tools), they eat together during Santería ceremonies (they are fed the same animals) and live together, usually in Ogún's black metal cauldron. According to Aldama Pérez, because the two *orichas* are so tightly connected, both mythologically and in their material manifestations, their rhythms mean something very similar, so reversing their order does very little to upset the spiritual balance of a *toque.*

☯ LISTEN TO TRACK 17: Alberto's group performs a Havana-style rhythmic evocation for Ogún.

☯ LISTEN TO TRACK 18: Alberto's group performs a Havana-style rhythmic evocation for Ochosi.

☯ LISTEN TO TRACK 19: Francisco's group performs a Matanzas-style invocation for Ogún.

☯ LISTEN TO TRACK 20: Francisco's group performs a Matanzas-style invocation for Ochosi.

Steven Cornelius's and John Amira's (1992) transcriptions of *batá* rhythms from a Santería community in New York (all of whom were trained in the Havana style) offer a glimpse of the possible rhythmic variations within a specific group of *batá* players. After many months of transcribing these complex rhythms, Cornelius admitted the shortcomings of representing this constantly changing performance practice in such a static manner:

> There is no single correct way to play the batá salutes. Batá drumming is an oral tradition. It lives in the performers' minds rather than on the printed page. Therefore, despite the fact that the rhythms are highly formalized, they are also undergoing constant transformation, and although every authentic performance must conform to basic traditional models, each ensemble will develop its own individual performance style and rhythmic feel. . . . In short, a study of New York tradition reveals that while there are definitely correct and incorrect ways to play the salute rhythms, to a certain extent each generation, ensemble, and individual performer will internalize and recreate the tradition in his own musical voice. Due to the above factors it is unlikely that any performance would ever conform exactly with the transcriptions in this book. . . . Therefore, the transcriptions act as paradigms. (Amira and Cornelius 1992:1–2)

In folkloric performance, most of the possibilities for improvisation and variation are no longer relevant. The performance becomes predictable, with the *batá* drummers usually coming in at the end of the lead singer's call, or at the beginning of the chorus's response. In some cases, the *batá* drums may come in earlier (at the beginning or in the middle of the lead singer's call), or later (in the middle of the chorus response), depending on the context of the performance and the staging goals of the choreographer and artistic advisor. The interplay between the drumming and the dancing is predetermined, with a particular rhythmic pattern belonging to a particular song, the combination of which corresponds to a specific dance.

Dance Movements

The gestural improvisation that takes place in a *toque de santo* is easier to describe, only because it is through identifiable gestures that *orichas* express themselves, gestural tropes that the practitioners respond to or mimic. When an *oricha* finally comes down during a *toque de santo,* the deity moves about the room, picking out adepts to bless or advise. But the manner in which that *oricha* moves is particular to the deity alone. Ochún, deity of sweet waters, for example, may "clean" people with her skirts as soon as she arrives. Changó, deity of the dance and the drum, may try to get people to dance as he struts about the room, barking out orders. Eleguá, mischievous deity of the crossroads, may steal a hat or a piece of jewelry, or demand candy or money before he will talk to any of the adepts. If a practitioner becomes possessed by one of those deities, he or she will likely mimic some of those gestural tropes.

The rest of the practitioners make way for the *orichas,* throwing themselves on the floor in obeisance (a gesture known as *moforibale*) when the *oricha* arrives, and performing a version of a two-step dance while the *akpwón* and drummers work to bring down another *santo.* If the practitioners are particularly good dancers, they may try to perform the dance steps that are associated with a particular *oricha* (for example, one of Ogún's dance steps matches precisely the rhythm of the *rumba guaguancó clave* ([| . . | . . . | . . | . | . . .], where "|" is a stroke and "." is an equally timed rest) and mimics Ogún's iconic motion of cutting through the forest. (See Barbara Browning's [1995] on divine choreography in Brazilian samba.) Folkloric dancing includes an array of these stock gestures, each of which corresponds to a particular *oricha*—such as the whipping up of the air with a whisk broom for Oyá, the darting back and forth across the stage for Eleguá, the exaggerated deafness and subsequent laughter of Ochún, and the spinning, swirling motion of Yemayá.

FOLKCUBA AND THE STANDARDIZING OF FOLKLORIC PERFORMANCE

FolkCuba, the workshop designed in the mid-1980s by the Conjunto Folklórico specifically for the purpose of teaching Afro-Cuban performance traditions to non-Cubans—that is, representing Cuba's "flag" to foreigners—was taught with hardly any reference to the religious context of the performance traditions. Regardless of Alberto Villarreal's background in Santería and in spite of Fernando Ortíz's apparent conflation of "religion" and "folklore," folklore seems to exist without religion in the context of the FolkCuba workshops. In *batá* drumming class, we learned many rhythms, but only after the program was over did I learn the specific contexts of the rhythms. In dance class, we threshed and cut through imaginary forests and occasionally fanned ourselves, but we were rarely told that those hand motions were related to the threshing of Ogún or to the fanning of Ochún. To those temporary students who had no previous background in Cuba's African-based religions, the dancing and drumming were simply random steps and random actions, set to *batá* rhythms that were pleasing, but arbitrary. To those who already had a background (*creyentes* from Puerto Rico, for example, or people who had participated in the FolkCuba program before), these dance motions and drum rhythms made more sense. In general, however, there was very little effort to contextualize this "folklore" within the religious tradition from which it originated.

Perhaps this lack of contextualization is due to the fact that, almost forty years after the troupe's establishment, the changing context of the performance no longer has much bearing on the units of the performance. That is, the basic drum patterns themselves change very little from a sacred performance to a secular performance. The songs, too, remain fairly consistent from a religious to a secular context. The dance motions, though stylized in secular representation, are still clearly recognizable and easily traced to their sacred, less formulaic antecedents. In effect, the change in context is assumed and perhaps even anticipated by the teachers. The teachers, all of whom are professional performers in the Conjunto Folklórico and all of whom are familiar with the religious antecedents of the performance, do not volunteer background information about its religious origins.

The acceptance and reproduction of these recontextualized performance traditions in the FolkCuba workshops in particular and in the Conjunto Folklórico performances in general imply that they maintain a polyvalent, many-layered significance. At the very least, they embody one set of meanings for the performers and audience members who are *creyentes,* and another set of meanings for those performers and audience members who have no experience with the religious context (see chapter 3). One can compare this polyvalence of meanings with a common performance practice in jazz, in which a jazz standard is reinterpreted and recontextualized by each performer, sometimes to such an extent that only if one knows the chord changes of the "original" version can one incorporate that knowledge into one's (re)construction of the song and its subsequent meaning. For some listeners or audience members, there is no immediate knowledge of the original jazz standard, and the current or derived version of the performance represents all the possibilities of that song. That the listener may be lacking the knowledge of the original context of the composed jazz standard does not necessarily diminish the significance of any given performance, but the addition of that knowledge would enrich the listener's experience of the performance, if only by adding another layer to the interpretive texture.[13]

In the FolkCuba workshops, there is no need to supply any context other than the workshop itself because the songs, drum patterns, and dances are constructed as aesthetically pleasing, contained packages. They are reiterated in the FolkCuba workshops and in CFNC rehearsals and concerts as a series of connected units of performance to be mastered. This emphasis on the unit of performance (the vocal timbre, the melodic phrase, the drum stroke, the dance step) rather than on an earlier, fully religious context has several effects on the performance as a whole. First, the performances become standardized, which makes them easier to understand and absorb. There is now a "right way" to dance Yemayá in the Folklórico, likely originated by Nieves Fresneda (see chapter 5), and all other ways of dancing for the goddess of the sea are wrong, or at least unfamiliar, because they do not conform to the standard. The standardization of the performance makes improvements in technique much easier to attain because there is a specific goal toward which to strive—placing the foot down gently and flatly, with heel and ball touching the floor at the same time, or speeding up the tempo of the *batá* rhythms just as Yemayá is two steps into her swirling motion, or maintaining the ascending interval of a perfect fourth rather than some microtonal variant between a major third and a perfect fourth in one of Yemayá's songs. With this standardization and precision of technique, however, comes a loss of spontaneity and a lack of variation, both of which would be crucial in a religious performance of the same material.

A second, related effect of this emphasis on the unit of performance is that the performance becomes predictable and easier to control, both in rehearsal and in concert settings. Songs for particular *orichas* are arranged one at a time, then the drums and choreography are added; thus the rhythms and songs and dances for an *oricha* become a unified body of material to be mastered, a piece to be rehearsed and occasionally dissected (for the purpose of mastering an especially difficult downward twirl or melodic contour or rhythmic transition). Conversely, mastering a unit of performance seems to have little relevance in a sacred context. Rather, one concentrates on mastering the rules of engagement with other participants to facilitate communication with the divine. The specific gesture or rhythmic pattern or melodic turn is less important than the way in which the ritual performer interacts with the divine, using musical and corporeal tools, so that in religious performance, form becomes subjugated to function.

At a *toque de santo,* one would not necessarily know the order of events, such as when a practitioner might become possessed or when the group of practitioners who are responding to the lead singer's call might inspire ten or fifteen repetitions of a certain song. The *toque* begins with the prescribed order of playing the *oru seco,* the *batá* sequence performed without singing or dancing, in which all of the major *orichas* (Eleguá is first and last) are saluted. But what happens after that depends on the people paying the drummers and on the other participants in the *toque.* If there are several good lead singers, and experienced dancers, the singing and dancing might go on for hours, with many *orichas* coming down to bless the house. If there seems to be little interest in singing or dancing, the drummers will not play for very long, and the *toque* will be short, or, in Alberto's words, *"normal"* (adequate, nothing special). The collective hope of any *toque de santo* is that the prayers, songs, rhythms, and dances will be strong enough and the energy focused enough to bring down the *santo*.

REPRESENTING THE ARCHETYPE

In light of the foregoing discussions of improvisation, variation, and standardization, it becomes clear that to transcribe exactly what occurs at any given religious performance does not give an accurate sense of the performance practice as a whole. The melodic and textual creations of the singer, the rhythmic improvisation of the *iyá* drummer, and the gestural responses of the practitioners to the arrival of an *oricha* during one ceremony, for example, cannot be captured and showcased as "the performance" with representational integrity. Even a sonically or visually vivid transcription, such as an audiotape or videotape, runs the risk of conveying a static image of a performance tradition that requires, and lives by, constant change. Yet it was through attempts at transcription that I was able to articulate an important aspect of this performance tradition. Building on Cornelius's "paradigmatic" *batá* transcriptions, I refer to the collectively constructed corpus of praise-song texts, melodies, *batá* rhythms, and physical tropes as archetypes. Variations and improvisations in each religious performance grow from these textual, melodic, rhythmic, and gestural archetypes, and in fact depend on the archetypes for their meaning.[14]

In Santería religious performance, an archetype exists as an abstract (and still variable) concept, which is concretized and articulated through performance.[15] During a *toque de santo,* this collectively constructed archetype serves to bring together the variations in the experiences of performers and practitioners, thus creating the possibility for the informed call-and-response sequences between *akpwón* and chorus, within the corps of lead dancers, and among the *iyá, itótele,* and *okónkolo,* which eventually yield the divine utterances that evoke possession. Each participant strives to hear an archetypal structure of a praise song or rhythm within the variation that is being performed, and from that particular performance, a new understanding emerges of the archetype's possibilities.

Understanding additional possibilities of an archetype brings up the question of the learning process in Santería performance. If there are so many variations and improvisatory possibilities, what exactly is taught to potential performers? How can one teach something that is constantly changing? One response is that any lead performer—whether singer, drummer, or dancer—teaches his or her perception of an archetypal structure. This archetypal structure will vary from teacher to teacher (not everyone begins the "Latopa" rhythm for Eleguá in precisely the same way, for example, even though most people recognize any number of versions as "Latopa").

In my experience, lead performers also teach improvisational possibilities, ways to think about improvising on the archetypal structure, but only after the neophyte has reached a basic level of performative competence; that is, only after the student understands the basic aural, visual, and gestural components of a given archetypal praise song, rhythm, or movement. This notion of a constantly moving target calls into question what one might call the body of material to be taught. What happens when that body does not remain constant? The implication is that what is being taught (and learned) is not necessarily a fixed repertoire of songs, patterns, dances, and the like, but rather a way of hearing and performing and conveying the structures that inform these chants, rhythms, and gestures in a unique and meaningful way.[16] What is being taught, ultimately, after the student learns to imitate the teacher's gestures, is how to perform *differently* from one's teacher.

This idea of imitation ultimately leading to (improvisatory) difference is directly connected to the notion of performative intent. One learns basic rules of performance and engagement with the other performers in order to know how to interpret and bend those appropriately. If one does not have the initial feel for a rhythm, for example, how can one improvise successfully from it? Even if the pitch sequences and rhythmic patterns that govern their articulation seem the same from one musician to another, the musician's intent (and/or talent) changes our perception of the sound production.

A specific example of this slippery (yet compelling) idea of intent has to do with the idea of "swing" in *batá* performance. In an ideal universe, every *batalero* at every ceremony will be able to make his rhythms swing.[17] It is this swing, this extra microvariation in interpretation, that propels the sound forward, and that excites a physical reaction from listeners. Playing the *batá* rhythms "straight" will still sound good; it just won't move the room. And if you don't move the room, you won't bring down the *santo*.

When I first started studying *batá* drums with Alberto Villarreal in 1991, my level of competence was so low that I was rarely able to focus on the sense of swing in the playing of other drummers and had no hope of attaining it myself. I was getting the rhythms, but I could not make them swing. Some apparently intangible feeling or ability to interact rhythmically was missing. One could argue that I was *almost* getting the rhythms, but that certain microrhythmic differences (all but indiscernible to the human ear) were making swing unattainable. One could also argue that my intent (in a broad musical sense) was so vastly different from my teacher's that I would not be able to achieve that sense of swing for quite some time. Then, of course, one must try to define all those experiences that go into creating musical intent—does it have to do with years of practice? surroundings? musical history? innate talent? reception? perception? hearing? coordination? all of these things? Or perhaps one can distill the idea of musical intent to microscopic performative details. But if those details are so microscopic, can they not be isolated and mastered, at which point, might they cease to become meaningful in and of themselves as details, and rather gain meaning from the larger category or context from which they emerge?

Now, years later, I almost always discern the intent to swing in others, and can sometimes perform it in those rare but happy incidents of unself-conscious playing. One can understand the idea of swing as the rhythmic force that is the primary element propelling one musical moment into the next, over and over again, with metrical regularity and continuity. Instead of holding a musical ensemble together or allowing harmonic or melodic phrases to guide the ensemble to the next resting place, the rhythm section relentlessly pushes the music forward, impelling a physical, gestural reaction to it—swing, in all senses of the word. But in order to swing, one has to be relaxed. And part of the ability to mediate between *orichas* and humans (which drummers must do in a *toque de santo*) rests on one's ability to relax enough to propel and be propelled by the collective impulse of the moment.

The very act of hitting the head of a drum to produce a sound appropriate to the context of a given performance (whether tutorial, folkloric, or religious) is a matter of intent and *aché*. Initially, Alberto refused to teach me because, in his words, I "played like a girl." One way of understanding that comment or evaluation is that I did not yet possess the intent or *aché* (the result of long disciplined performative experience) to transfer intent to affective or performative action at will. Because Santería drumming is a male-dominated domain, the ideology of masculine power colors the perception of who is likely to possess and develop the *aché* to make performative action conform to intent. The ceremonial *batá* drummers with whom I have worked maintain that few women (if any) will ever possess the physical strength, coordination, determination, discipline, endurance, and will to transform those qualities into religious intent.

In the same way that the *akpwón* sang onto the man starting to become possessed by Eleguá in Santos Suarez (see chapter 2), so any act of helping a possession along is also a divine utterance. One pushes the intent or *aché* of possession onto another person through sound: singing, calling out praise names, ringing a bell, playing the drums—all of these sounds assault the body, in the same way that one's "intentful" hand assaults the head of the drum to provoke possession, propelling the moment, pushing the *creyente* over the edge of consciousness and control, into a vehicle driven by the *orichas*.

NOTES

1. According to Cabrera (1986a:323), *yeye* means everything from "good," "smooth," and "delicious" to "mother Oshún" and "yellow." *Ma* means "mother," usually for an older woman (p. 205). In this case, I have taken it to mean "great mother," as in a respected female elder with many children and grandchildren.

2. Friedman (1982:274–275) has noted that "fake possessions" are often a source of strife between the *batá* drummers and the sponsoring Santero. But a "fake possession," when someone is feigning being mounted by an *oricha*, is distinct from a "failed possession," when someone is trying to let the *oricha* take control but ultimately cannot. According to Friedman, those who fake *oricha* possessions during a *toque de santo* are usually found out and are considered to have committed the ultimate disrespectful act: making a mockery of the religion.

3. Practitioners may receive permission from their *orichas*, via divination, to document certain ceremonies for educational purposes (Michael Mason, personal communication, July 2000).

4. This song refers to a murder: a man killed his female partner by stabbing her seven times. See K. Brown (1991:233–234) for a more complete history and context of the song.

5. Cros Sandoval (1979) describes Santería as a sort of mental health-care system for Cubans in exile, similar to Karen Brown's (1991) characterization of Haitian Vodou in New York City. The two religious traditions will become even more closely related after Mama Lola becomes a Santera to complement her work as a Manbo. During the past few years, many of the people who have come to seek help from Mama Lola at her Brooklyn apartment have been religious practitioners of Santería. Mama Lola is responding to the change in her religious constituency by adapting to it, fortifying the extant links between Santería and Vodou.

6. The same argument can be made for other aspects of ritual repetition in Santería, such as animal sacrifice, silent prayer, and altar-making. Michael Mason (1994) writes eloquently of the performative power of the repetitive act of bowing one's head to the ground in *moforibale*, the ritual greeting of Santería. Ysamur Flores-Peña and Roberta J. Evanchuk (1994) persuasively argue that the material objects of Santería "speak without a voice." Similarly, David Brown (1993) provides stunning visual evidence of the deeply held conviction among practitioners that the visual aspects of the

ritual objects of Santería (color, texture, sheen, and pattern) combine with and enhance spiritual practice to effect communication with the divine. Because my emphasis here is primarily on physically propelled and experienced utterances (spoken prayer, songs, percussive rhythms, and dance gestures), I leave these other important aspects of Santería ritual for my colleagues to pursue.

7. Baudrillard's theories of simulacra and simulation (Baudrillard 1994), in which the representation of the "real" becomes as compelling and desirable and consumable as—and, in fact, moreso than—the source itself, are instructive here.

8. J. Mason's version of this phrase is "The First Penis is the performer of wonders," which is a more evocative way of expressing a similar thought.

9. Certain praise songs belong only to specific avatars or *caminos* (roads) of an *oricha*, so the songs sung by the *akpwón* not only persuade the *oricha* into mounting the *creyente* but also help determine which road of that *oricha* is being manifested during possession. "Yemayá Asesu" (the *camino* of Yemayá, which refers to the gush of the spring and the cleansing flow of gutter water), and "Ochún Ikole" (the *camino* of Ochún, which refers to the stream [and vulture] carrying away offerings) are two examples of such praise songs. The various meanings of the more obscure praise songs (such as "Oko okan odara") remain the subject of debate among *akpwónes* and Santeros alike.

10. "*O jí mi'ni*" is a phrase that belongs to Esu-Eleguá, so even though Esu is not specifically mentioned in Martínez Furé's version of the song, that phrase marks the song as Eleguá's. It is also likely that *O jí* (pronounced Ochi) and *Esu* (pronounced Echu) are exchanged in praise song lyrics because they sound very similar.

11. These transliterations can be found in J. Mason (1992). They are based on the Matanzas, rather than the Havana, praise-song tradition, but Havana-based Santeros and *bataleros* who perform in both Matanzas and Havana maintain that the differences between the two praise-song (and *batá*) traditions are dwindling. (Conversation with Alberto Villarreal, July 12, 1997; conversation with Carlos Aldama Pérez, May 14, 1999.)

12. According to Carlos Aldama Pérez, the only set of consecrated Arará drums in Havana is owned by Andrés Chacón, who lives in the Marianao district of Havana. All the other consecrated sets of Arará drums are in Matanzas.

13. An obvious correlate to the sacred/secular performances and contexts of the Conjunto Folklórico would be the gamelan, kecak, and other religiously based performance traditions of Bali. As with the FolkCuba performances in Cuba, the performers of kecak in Bali, for example, may have a deep and multilayered context into which to place their experience, while many of their audience members may have little or no context for the performance at all, and so may understand the performance mostly as entertainment, as part of a tourist package.

14. Anthony Giddens (1979), in his analysis of action, structure, and conflict in society, writes that the structure of a given organization or community becomes apparent only through individual (or group) agency. Although there would seem to be similarities between Giddens's formulation and my own, the distinction resides in the fact

that in Santería religious performance, performers rely on the archetype (or structure) only for the new life that it will give each variation and improvisation. The archetype is not necessarily performed into existence, even though its structure is essential to the new rhythmic, vocal, or gestural utterance that arises from it.

15. Shawn Lindsay comments on the concretization of rhythms through performance in his essay on hand drumming: "We had learned enough to actualize the identity of gestures and sounds, and the result was uncanny. It was as if we were dancing, wrestling, fencing without visible signs of contact" (Lindsay in Jackson 1996:201).

16. I have had a similar experience learning from Ewe (Ghanaian) master drummers, whose interpretations of lead and supporting drums parts for such "standards" as *agbeko* vary just enough to confuse the neophyte. But once one understands more fully the structure of the bell pattern (which is the rhythmic backbone of this genre), for example, it is easier to comprehend the variations of the drums. Again, the point is to focus on the integral relationship between archetypal structure and discrete performances.

17. As a compliment, *bataleros* may call the performance of a certain *toque "sabroso"* ("tasty"), or they may yell out *"dále"* ("do it," "give it your all"), *"métele"* (get into it), or *"jícamo"* as a sign of encouragement during the most intense moments of the *toque,* if the drummers are working hard and the rhythms sound good (personal communications with Alberto Villarreal, September 1998, and Francisco Aguabella, August 2000). I have not heard a Cuban equivalent for the word "swing" as I use it here, although one drummer thought that *"jícamo"* came close (personal communication with Francisco Aguabella, August 2000). Charles Keil, among others, has written at length on the concept of "swing" in his essay on participatory discrepancies (1994:96–108), in which he invokes Leonard B. Meyer's (1956) discussion of "swing" as a "matter of microsyntax" (1994:104).

5

THE BIRTH OF THE CONJUNTO FOLKLÓRICO

There are *patakíes* for all the *orichas*, and they are intimately linked to the proverbs of Ifá divination. These *patakíes* are evoked consistently through the prayers, songs, and dances of religious performance, and their repetition imbues them with sacred significance. The *patakín* for Ogún and Ochún is well known among Cuban practitioners of Santería because Ochún is considered to be the patron saint of Cuba. She represents Cuba's anthropomorphized national ethos—a sweet, laughing, flirtatious *mulata* whose seductive charms help her to survive in the difficult and dangerous world. Yet Ochún, like the other major *orichas*, has many *caminos*, some of which are neither sweet nor seductive. Ochún Ibu-Kole, for example, drags herself through the river mud, is poor, and has only one dress to wear. The dress, once yellow, is now white and torn from so many wearings and washings. Ochún Ibu-Kole's messenger is the vulture (known as *aura tiñosa* in Cuban Spanish), who helps her prepare *trabajos* (spells) and is the first to eat what has been killed.

BRAVE NEW WORLD: EL TEATRO NACIONAL DE CUBA

The late Ramiro Guerra, a renowned theorist, interpreter, and choreographer of contemporary dance in Cuba, maintained a unique perspective on the Conjunto Folklórico as a former choreographer and dancer, part manager and part performer, for the troupe. He conceptualized and choreographed some of the CFNC's most famous and enduring pieces, such as Tríptico Oriental (Eastern Triptych), and was enthusiastically active in Havana's burgeoning arts scene before and after the revolution. He recalled in an interview with me (August 6, 1992):[1]

But of course, in the early days the performers had to be told: "Stop! Enough already! Change the tune!" They had no sense of theater, no sense of audience interest levels.

They were just doing what comes naturally, so to speak, and if a toque or canto for Yemayá was lasting thirty minutes or an hour, it never occurred to them to stop it. We—the choreographers, the folklorists, the dramaturges—had to shape that raw material, that raw energy into theatre. Very rewarding, but very difficult.

In his seventies at the time of our interviews and still a robust and lively thinker, Ramiro was invaluable in helping me contextualize the early years of the Conjunto Folklórico's performances. Ramiro's relationship with the early informant/performers seems to have been more flexible than that of some of the other choreographers. (Rodolfo Reyes, the first choreographer for the CFNC, left after two years, and Elena Noriega, who was both director and choreographer, left after less than a year. Both of these early choreographers found it difficult to keep their artistic goals for the troupe intact amid the constantly shifting power dynamics between the performers and the administration.) Ramiro, though not a *creyente,* was able to understand enough about the mechanisms and hierarchies of Cuba's African-based religions to communicate with the performers' religious personas, when necessary, as is illustrated by his story of how Santiago Alfonso once became possessed by the spirit of Changó while in his dressing room (see chapter 4).

Initially, according to Ramiro, when the 1959 revolution came and the new cultural organizations such as the Teatro Nacional and later the Conjunto Folklórico were established, there was a tremendous sense of excitement and relief among artists because they believed that they would no longer have to struggle to survive; the revolution was offering to subsidize them. Moreover, they were ecstatic at the thought of no longer changing their art to fit commercial demands. The Teatro Nacional, the unique institution that preceded and eventually gave birth to the Conjunto Folklórico, was a research organization, library, and performing arts venue all in one, fully funded by the new Cuban government.

The Teatro Nacional was founded in the months immediately following the January 1959 revolution by a group of revolutionary intellectuals, led by Isabel Monal, all of whom were members of the Partido Social Popular (People's Socialist Party). The Teatro Nacional consisted of five departments, each of which had become an independent institution by the mid-1960s. The department of music, directed by Carlos Fariñas, provided the beginnings of the Orquesta Sinfónica Nacional. The department of modern dance, directed by Ramiro Guerra, eventually became the Grupo de Danza Contemporánea. The department of theatre, directed by Fermín Borges, paved the way for the foundation of many small theatres in Havana throughout the 1960s. The choral department, directed by Serafin Pro,[2] became the Coro Polifónico Nacional. And the Department of Folklore, directed by Argeliers León, eventually led to the founding of the Conjunto Folklórico Nacional de Cuba and of the Institute of Ethnology and Folklore within the Cuban Academy of Sciences.[3]

As Ramiro and several other participants in the Teatro Nacional project pointed out during our interviews, the late composer and ethnomusicologist Argeliers León was a key figure in the conceptualization and utilization of Cuba's "Africanized" folklore. León was not only the director of the Teatro Nacional's Department of Folklore, he was a driving force in the perpetuation of Fernando Ortíz's research on Cuba's African-based traditions.[4] León, who died in February 1991, was the protegé of Fernando Ortíz (1881–1969), respectfully known as the "third discoverer of Cuba" because of his broad-ranging and massive scholarly oeuvre.[5] A self-described staunch supporter of the revolution's struggles against Cuba's previously classist and racist society, León saw in the Teatro Nacional an opportunity to combine his academic and artistic interests with the goals of the revolution:[6] "As a national theatre, the Teatro Nacional de Cuba endeavors to be an institution that not only mounts theatrical productions but also brings together a series of activities that contribute to the total and coordinated effort of the work-plan of the Revolution. . . . a combination of theatre, library, museum, archive, and ministry [of culture]."[7]

THE DEPARTMENT OF FOLKLORE, THE CFNC, AND THE INSTITUTE OF ETHNOLOGY AND FOLKLORE

From October 1960 through May 1961, he recalled in an interview with me (October 18, 1990), León organized a series of seminars on the interpretation, approach, and analysis of folklore: *"Enseñabamos cómo preguntar al negro sobre cosas muy íntimas, muy adentro . . . cómo formar preguntas a álguien muy diferente que nosotros . . . cómo organizar y analizar el dato"* (We were teaching how to ask the black man about very private, personal things . . . how to formulate questions for someone very different from ourselves . . . how to organize and analyze data). These "private, personal things" about which León was training his students to ask often dealt with Afro-Cuban religious practices, as is evident from the student papers from the seminars, some of which were published in the journal of the Teatro Nacional's Department of Folklore, *Actas del Folklore,* and later in the spin-off folklore journal of the Academy of Sciences, *Etnología y Folklore.*[8] León, Isaac Barreal (an ethnologist and León's friend and colleague), María Teresa Linares (a noted musicologist and León's wife), Manuel Moreno Fraginals (a well-respected historian of slavery in Cuba), and Peter Neumann (an East German anthropologist from the Dresden Museum of Ethnology) all taught sections on various aspects of Afro-Cuban culture, and also published their research in *Actas del Folklore* and later in *Etnología y Folklore*.[9] León taught fieldwork techniques, Barreal ethnology, Linares folk music, Fraginals social history, and Neumann ethnomethodology.

This seminar produced the next generation of scholars in Afro-Cuban studies in Cuba, including Rogelio Martínez Furé (current *asesor* of the Conjunto Folklórico), Rafael L. López Valdés (senior researcher and director of the Cuban Ethnographic Atlas project at the Cuban Academy of Sciences until 1993 [see López Valdés 1989]), and Miguel Barnet (a noted and prolific author who often incorporates Afro-Cuban themes into his novels). In a December 1991 interview, López Valdés described the goals of the seminar, and how these goals may have changed with the founding of the Conjunto Folklórico:

> I participated in the same seminar in which Rogelio, Miguel Barnet, and that whole
> group of people participated. And of all of the participants, I think the three of us—
> Rogelio, Miguel, and I—are the ones who continued doing this sort of work, each
> one of us in a different form: Miguel in a literary form, Rogelio in a theatrical form,
> and I in an investigative form. The rest of the seminar participants went their separate
> ways, and now are doing things that have nothing to do with this world of African in-
> fluence. At that time, the intention was the following: to give new vitality, more
> weight, and greater value to the African influences expressed through the music and
> dance used in popular culture, and to return this from the top to the people. This
> seems to me to have been Argeliers's main goal, without any of these complications
> about *"folklorización,"*[10] about reducing it to folklore, to the exotic, to something su-
> perficial—rather, it was a positive goal.

In December 1961 the Institute of Ethnology and Folklore was founded under the auspices of the Consejo de Cultura (Council of Culture), which was a branch of the Ministry of Education.[11] From the 1959 revolution until the late 1960s, when the Cuban government established a Ministry of Culture, all cultural activity was decreed and approved through the Consejo de Cultura, which was under the auspices of the Ministry of Education. In March 1962 the Cuban government decreed the foundation of the Cuban Academy of Sciences. The same decree that established the Cuban Academy of Sciences specified that the Institute of Ethnology and Folklore, originally under the purview of the Consejo de Cultura of the Ministry of Education, was now part of the separate organ of the Academy of Sciences. Also in the early months of 1962, the Conjunto Folklórico Nacional

de Cuba was founded by Rogelio Martínez Furé, an alumnus of the Teatro Nacional folklore seminar led by León, and Rodolfo Reyes Cortés, a renowned Mexican choreographer and dancer.

According to Martínez Furé (1980:3), the Conjunto Folklórico was founded in
order to "satisfy the need of the Cuban people for an institution capable of retrieving Cuba's music and dance traditions for integration into the new national
culture." León, who had directed the Department of Folklore of the Teatro Nacional, was then appointed by the Ministry of Education to be the director of the
Institute of Ethnology and Folklore of the Academy of Sciences. In a December
1991 interview, Rafael López Valdés, a researcher with the Cuban Academy of Sciences since 1962, described the intellectual impact of this institutional separation
on León's original unified vision:

> As of 1962, the two lines that had previously been joined, that is, the investigative line
> and the spectacle line, were now institutionally separated. On the one hand, the Insti-
> tution of Ethnology and Folklore was created, which was followed by the Academy
> of Sciences, and that already had an investigative character. On the other hand, there
> was the Conjunto Folklórico Nacional, which already had as its goal the mounting of
> spectacles. So during this entire period, the dancers and musicians were not *aficiona-
> dos,* that is, they had not taken dance classes and such. Rather, they were simply
> townspeople of these same religious groups [Santería, Palo Monte, Abakwá], like
> Nieves Fresneda, a Santera who was a daughter of Yemayá. So, old Santeras and
> younger people, too—Lázaro Ros, and Jesús Pérez, the famous *batá* player—all of
> these people were practitioners. Emilio O'Farrill was a practitioner of Palo Monte.
> This whole group of people was organized choreographically, and presented the
> spectacles as part of a choreographic and theatrical concept.

León's original vision was that the Teatro Nacional de Cuba in general and the
Department of Folklore in particular could become vehicles for scholarly research and public education through theatrical presentation. His own research on
West African sculpture and religion provided a link to his plans for the Teatro Nacional's Department of Folklore (see León 1961a, 1969a). By emphasizing the folklife of Cuba's African-based population in the Department of Folklore's dramatizations, he hoped to demystify the various Afro-Cuban religions, and thus to
remedy at least one aspect of Cuba's legendary racism: the ignorance and consequent fear of those Afro-Cuban religious rituals commonly referred to by white
Cubans as *brujería,* or "witchcraft."[12] Under León's direction, the Department of
Folklore had become the institutional branch of the Teatro Nacional that most

focused on Cuba's African heritage.[13] The Department of Folklore's dramatizations of Afro-Cuban religious rituals were, at the time of its foundation, the first of their kind. Not only was the Teatro Nacional de Cuba the first state-supported organization to present public performances of sacred rituals, but it was also the first to rely on informants who were themselves religious practitioners.

The sacred *batá* drums of Santería were first heard in a public, secular setting in May 1936, in an "ethnographic conference" organized and sponsored by Fernando Ortíz.[14] The highlight of the conference was a presentation on the music of Santería, which featured Pablo Roche, Aguedo Morales, and Jesús Pérez performing on *aberíkula* (unconsecrated) *batá* drums made by Roche and commissioned by Ortíz for this very purpose. León took this public presentation of formerly private and sacred religious rituals one step further by institutionalizing these performances within the scheduled programming for the Teatro Nacional. The Department of Folklore was shaped entirely by León, who used as his model the experience of his teacher, Fernando Ortíz. León, the author of several books on Cuban music and editor of a prominent journal of Cuban folklore,[15] had become a devotee[16] of Fernando Ortíz after having attended Ortíz's informal seminars in the 1930s and 1940s on Afro-Cuban culture, and paid close attention to Ortíz's ethnographic performances. In the same way that Ortíz illustrated his conferences with musical performances, León sought to bring the music of Santería, Palo Monte, and Abakwá to the public through a series of "ethnographically authentic" *espectáculos* sponsored by the Department of Folklore.

AUTHENTICITY IN PERFORMANCE

The early presentations of the Teatro Nacional's Department of Folklore and those of its successor, the Academy of Science's Institute for Ethnology and Folklore, insisted León, were authentic, and quite popular. The most remarkable of these early performances was held in 1964, and represented the performance traditions of the Abakwá, a male secret society with its roots in the all-male "Leopard societies" of the Calabar region of West Africa[17] (see the sacred drawings[18] indicating deities in figs. 5.1 and 5.2). Known in Cuba for the extreme secrecy of their initiation practices and for their alleged connection to organized crime in both prerevolutionary and postrevolutionary Cuba, most of the members of the Abakwá[19] were dockworkers in the northwestern provinces of Havana and Matanzas. León stressed the authenticity of this performance in our October 1990 interview, noting the competence and participation of the audience:

Figure 5.1. Abakwá *firma* (sacred drawing) from the
1964 program of Concierto Abakwá.

The *toques* [rhythms] were the same, the songs were the same [as they would be in a
ritual context] . . . because the public that attended understood these songs. This created a very interesting effect, which was that in the middle of a song or a presentation, there was a dialogue between the "officiant" performer and the audience members who were believers. The foreigners really liked this. And it was especially notable
in the Abakwá performances. . . . In the *plante* [Abakwá initiation ceremony], there
were blacks who participated in this performance as if it were real. . . . In fact, the
Abakwá performance at the Biblioteca Nacional was perhaps the best we ever did.
We had the river, the *diablitos* [*íremes,plante*], the whole thing. Jean-Paul Sartre was
there, and he loved it. He felt that he had seen a type of drama comparable to that of
the great Greek dramas because it established a dialogue between the audience and
the performer. It was certainly stupendous. . . . These performances that we did at
first were completely authentic; we used informants who were believers, very much
involved in the religion. . . .

According to León and Linares, the Abakwá performance generated much
interest and some criticism in the intellectual community, and it sparked a few
fistfights between those religious practitioners in the audience who felt that the
informants gave away too many secrets and those (usually family members) who
defended the informants' rights to limited fame and fortune. This performance
was held in 1964 at the Biblioteca Nacional (National Library), which had become

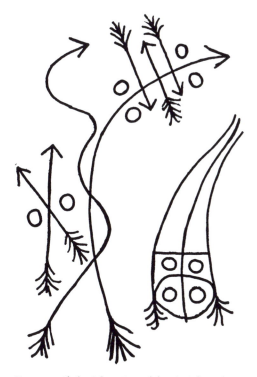

Figure 5.2. Abakwá *firma* (sacred drawing) from the
1964 program of Concierto Abakwá.

a meeting place for some of the revolution's intellectuals, including (at that time) Jean-Paul Sartre. Sartre came up to León the next day at the University of Havana and told him that the Abakwá performance had moved and impressed him deeply. Then Sartre hugged and kissed León, telling him it was the best drama he had ever seen. Unfortunately, these kisses, witnessed by other members of the Teatro Nacional, marked León as one whose work was not appropriate for the still-evolving socialist aesthetic of the revolution.[20] Soon thereafter, León was voted out of the Teatro Nacional by the other department directors. León noted that the very same people who voted him out in public came up to him in private to congratulate him on the "very fine performance" of his Grupo Abakwá.

ARGELIERS LEÓN AND MARÍA TERESA LINARES

I conducted my first in-depth interviews in Cuba with María Teresa Linares and her husband, the late Argeliers León, in October 1990. At first, both of them seemed to share in the enthusiasm of reminiscing about the early 1960s; however, later it became clear that whereas León possessed much enthusiasm for *música folklórica afrocubana* (Afro-Cuban folkloric music), Linares focused much of her attention on *música folklórica campesina* (peasant music, generally of European descent). León continued working in the area of Afro-Cuban folkloric traditions through the 1970s, during which time he traveled to Africa and published a book on African sculpture. Toward the end of the 1970s he began concentrating his efforts on contemporary composition, but he maintained enough interest in the field of Afro-Cuban studies to begin preparing an annotated edition of Fernando Ortíz's monumental work *Los instrumentos de la música afrocubana* (Instruments of Afro-Cuban Music, five volumes),[21] for several years before his death in early 1991. Linares, León's wife of more than forty years and the renowned author of numerous books and articles on Cuban music,[22] was the director of the National Museum of Music from the mid-1980s to the late 1990s. In addition to having produced the prize-winning seven-record series *Antología de la música afrocubana* (Anthology of Afro-Cuban Music), she was also one of the CFNC's early directors.

Linares and León had deeply contrasting experiences with the Teatro Nacional and the Conjunto Folklórico. I met both of them in October 1990, yet Linares had avoided telling me until summer 1992 that, as a manager of the troupe in the early 1960s, she had been the object of numerous *trabajos* (malevolent works of witchcraft or "spells"), which culminated in her being shot several times in the leg by a disgruntled Conjunto Folkórico drummer. After that event, she had severed all administrative ties to the troupe and had distanced herself from Afro-Cuban ritual music in general, while her husband had continued his research in this area. Far from being a united front, two of the most important figures in the establishment of the Conjunto Folklórico had widely disparate views about the troupe, especially about its beginnings.

During our first meeting, both of them spoke at length about their more than forty years of involvement in the study, preservation, and recreation of Cuba's African heritage. At the time of the first interview (October 4, 1990), Linares acted as the eyes and occasionally the memory of her husband. He was almost blind owing to ruptured blood vessels near the iris, and his memory for names was failing. This and subsequent interviews were held in the front room of their home, an airy, two-bedroom apartment located on the first floor of a modest two-story building in the Vedado section of Havana. Both were fervent Communists, and, in keeping with the revolutionary tenets of scientific atheism, had rejected their Catholic upbringing. Many of my questions focused on Communist, atheist

Cuba's embrace of certain aspects of the African-based religions, and the apparent contradiction therein.

> AL: The most fervent black religious believer of Obatala, the most fervent practitioner—his son is reading Marx.

> KH: Yes, and that ties in with the question I have, which is, how does Marxist theory mix with the religions—and they are religions—of these Afro-Cuban ceremonies?

> MTL: No, they don't mix. One or the other wins.

> AL: Well, one or the other prevails in the individual, in accordance with whatever that belief means to the individual at the time when that individual is living. Because, of course, as soon as the individual dies, we don't really care what he thought anymore. The interest that sociology and ethnography and the sciences in general hold for us is in finding out what people think while they are alive. Once they die, we bury them and their thoughts.

> MTL: We know of a lot of cases of very religious parents, who live in very important *casas de religión* [homes that serve as centers of Afro-Cuban religious practice], and their kids learn how to read and write in the revolutionary school, they go away to revolutionary camps and come back very politicized, believing that what their parents believe in isn't worth a thing, is backward, and belongs in the Dark Ages. . . . And so a certain type of antagonism is produced—not a violent one, as the parents continue loving their children, and as the children continue respecting their parents—but they don't respect the religion, and it's a shock.

> AL: Yes, the antagonism is very clear here, and it's happening in the present day. You can see it by penetrating even a little bit into these groups, it's very clear. By the same token, there are those people who continue to hold onto these beliefs—

> MTL: Yes, they continue to hold onto them—

> AL: And no one tries to take these beliefs away from them. They can make their ritual baths each day, say their prayers each day, sacrifice their animals. And no one interferes with them. They continue to believe. But there also exists the type of person who is now free, who no longer be-

lieves in this religion, it is no longer compulsory. These belief systems are even more compulsive than Catholicism itself. You get punished for doing certain things—don't do thus and such, for you'll be punished. Catholicism is compulsive, too, but when you're told that God will punish you, at night you can say your prayers, pray to some saint, and sleep well, knowing that that saint will protect you and that you have asked for forgiveness from God. In the African religions, that's not the case. If you do something wrong, believe me, you will pay for it in all ways. So what Marxism does is to produce a certain type of independence from these religious beliefs, such that the individual himself has control over his life.

KH: A friend of mine told me that he thinks that 90 percent of Cubans are *creyentes* in one way or another.

MTL: This is an exaggeration. It's very exaggerated.

AL: Yes.

KH: Well, he doesn't know, but he was thinking about it, and that's what he came up with.

MTL: No, 90 percent is almost the entire population—that's ridiculous.

KH: What would you say, maybe 70 percent?

MTL: No, these religions are practiced a lot today, but they are the religions of the minority.

AL: Yes, but they've expanded—

MTL: No—

AL: They've expanded considerably recently.

MTL: Just because they've expanded recently doesn't mean that they make up more than about 5 percent. It's just absurd to think that the entire population is involved—our population is very large, very heterogeneous.

KH: But as a popular religion, which doesn't require masses or anything—my friend told me that it's very fascinating and exciting, but the practitioners may not understand a lot about these religions—like in the Conjunto Folklórico they see them represented—

MTL: Oh, I see. Like a hobby. Yes, they participate in these religions like they would participate in a hobby.[23]

Understanding the vast difference of opinion regarding how many people are practitioners of Afro-Cuban religions in Cuba is essential to grasping both the importance and the elusive nature of these religions in contemporary, postrevolutionary Cuba. It is weirdly counterrevolutionary and prorevolutionary at once to be involved in these Afro-Cuban religions; counterrevolutionary because of the revolution's firmly inculcated precepts of scientific atheism, and prorevolutionary because of the potential connection with tourism and the mythical construction of all of Cuba's people as "Afro-Cubans." Comandante Fidel Castro and other government officials have made numerous statements asserting that Cubans are a "Latin-African people" (C. Moore 1988:3) and that "every Cuban has a drop of *sangre negrita* [black blood], so all Cubans are Afro-Cubans,"[24] and thus "Afro-Cuban" is redundant.[25] The importance and power of this statement resides not in its representation of a documented, empirical truth about the origins of the Cuban people, but in its representation of a growing, nationalized self-perception. Since the 1959 revolution, the Cuban national ethos has become "Africanized," catapulting one of the Western hemisphere's most racialized societies into a state of so-called reverse discrimination, in which inclusion within the generous and opaque label of Cuban sometimes requires admitting and embracing a general and occasionally mythical African heritage.

Linares's idea of religion as a "hobby" provides an important clue to understanding how Afro-Cuban religions were categorized in the Teatro Nacional's seminars and presentations. Santería, Palo Monte, Arará, and Abakwá were not regarded seriously as religions; rather, they were considered charming and exotic remnants of a prerevolutionary past, to be engaged in the bright, revolutionary present not with religious awe but with a combination of bemused interest and scholarly objectivity. Hobbies can be serious business. When I explained in this interview that I was interested specifically in the representation of Cuba's African-based traditions by the Conjunto Folklórico, León became very animated. He had studied under Fernando Ortíz in the 1940s, he explained, and remained dedicated to studying, documenting, and presenting only the *"manifestaciones puras"* of those traditions. What had sparked his interest was my question regarding the difference between the work of the CFNC and that of the Department of Folklore of the Teatro Nacional. According to León, just after the *triunfo de la Revolución*, he helped found the Department of Folklore. In 1961, under the auspices of the Department of Folklore, he published a series of journals called *Actas del Folklore* (named after the series of articles published by Fernando Ortíz called *Actas del Folklore Afro-Cubano*), which is still regarded as an important source of information about Cuba's African-based traditions. In addition to publishing the journal, the Department of Folklore conducted research on various aspects of Afro-Cuban culture, and then found people who were practitioners to present these different traditions in dramatized performances.

MANIFESTACIONES PURAS, ESPECTÁCULOS, AND AFICIONADOS

León stressed that each of his presentations in the 1960s required a different group of people (priests of Santería for the Santería performances, priests of Palo Monte for the Palo Monte performances, initiates of Abakwá for the Abakwá performances, and so on), which heightened the authenticity of his presentations. In contrast, he pointed out, the Conjunto Folklórico used the same group of people for each presentation: *"El Conjunto es un grupo fijo; nunca cambia"* (The Conjunto is a set group; it never changes).[26] Rather than learn these traditions through the life-long exposure to them that a religious upbringing might provide, the performers in the CFNC were (and still are) trained in Cuba's arts schools with concentrations in theater, dance, drumming, and singing for the sole purpose of performing with the troupe. León asserted that, because of the emphasis on entertainment rather than on accuracy of detail, the CFNC ended up putting on *espectáculos* that were much larger than life. For example, the headdress of Yemayá might be transformed from a simple blue-and-white checked bandana to an electric-blue satin cockscomb atop the head of some marvelously coiffed and rouged dancer. In addition, he noted, there is a greater use of *refranes* (refrains or short choral responses within a call-and-response format) in the songs rather than the longer improvisatory interaction that often characterizes a sacred performance, so that this overwhelming visual image is accompanied by overly simplified and formalized vocal responses.

With the founding of the CFNC, León's power over the creative mandate of presenting public performances of Afro-Cuban religious rituals waned. His original plan, which was to continue using religious practitioners as informants and as performers, was altered by the new management of the troupe, led by Rogelio Martínez Furé. The CFNC began including singers and dancers not involved in Afro-Cuban religious traditions in its theatrical presentations. Rather than use religious practitioners only for dramatizations of the Afro-Cuban religious tradition to which they belonged, the Conjunto Folklórico began using the same performers (religious practitioners or not) for all the dramatizations, whether the performances were derived from Santería, Palo Monte, Arará, or Abakwá. This use of one secular core troupe for all the dramatizations of the religious rituals eventually led to the founding of schools that would teach the dances and songs of the religious traditions out of context. Rather than learn them as a result of having been a religious practitioner, students *(aficionados)* in these schools would learn the Afro-Cuban religious songs and dances in a classroom context.[27]

According to León, the performances that resulted from students trained in *aficionado* schools maintained a delicate balance between entertainment and authenticity. They were accessible and flashy enough to attract the attention of an audience addicted to excess, who might just as likely go to a Tropicana show as to a Conjunto Folklórico performance (see chapter 4), and yet authentic and referential enough to attract an audience raised in these African-based religious traditions. What was most interesting and disturbing to León was the effect of the exaggeration and simplification on the local contingent of the Conjunto Folklórico's audience. Though these *creyentes* might be partially repelled by the exaggerated representation of their religions in the *espectáculos,* believed León, they were also intrigued and impressed enough to go back to their *casas de santo* and imitate them. This hypothesis seemed plausible enough to me, except that the religious ceremonies I attended were hosted by people who did not have enough money to buy the flashy costumes and other attributes that the Conjunto Folklórico uses in its performances. What is being imitated with increasing frequency, it turns out, are the gestural and theatrical tropes associated with each *oricha*—the stylized circular whipping motions of Oyá's whisk, the chopping motions of Ogún's *machete,* the laughter and coy deafness (signaled by cocking one's head and cupping an ear) of Ochún, the thrusting of imaginary lightning bolts into Changó's crotch—with or without the flashy material trappings of "spectacle."

It was the *aficionado* schools that marked the final breaking point between the original vision of the Department of Folklore *presentaciones* and the Conjunto Folklórico *espectáculos.* The gap between the primary goals of authenticity and entertainment had become too large. León's interest in *el folklore afrocubano* had taken root when he began studying with Fernando Ortíz in the 1940s, when simply presenting "Afro-Cuban" religious ceremonies in public was spectacle enough. When León spoke of the genesis of his own work in folklore during this interview, he became very moved. He spoke about his *"informantes,"* about the *"hombres feos, prietos, viejos"* (ugly, dark, old men) that had become part of his family, that had sat at his table with his wife and children, that were his true friends—and he began to sob. *"Perdón, es mi edad"* (Pardon me, it's my age).

To León, his work with *"los cultos negros"* meant much more than scholarship. He began working and developing friendships with his *informantes* at a time when prejudice against blacks was commonplace in Cuba. His actions were considered outrageous by some, and yet his respect for and friendship with these people were genuine and affectionate. Most of his *informantes* are long dead, which is to say that many of his best friends are now gone. The time of ground-breaking research in this particular area is also gone. His former students—Martínez Furé, López Valdés, Barnet—have gone on to do their own work. This dearth of protégés from that golden era, combined with the pain that he suffered as a self-described "nonpolitical" academician whose main interest was not in dramatic presentation but in research, may have contributed to his sense of depression and loss. *"Yo no soy político—y no sabía nada de los telones, los reflectores; lo que me interesaba eran las investigaciones"* (I'm not political—and I didn't know anything about curtains or stage lights; what interested me was research).

Much of León's early fieldwork in the 1940s and 1950s had focused on José "Trinidad" Torregrosa, a well-known Afro-Cuban drummer born in 1897 in the Cerro section of Havana who had been one of the original drummers for the Teatro Nacional and the Conjunto Folklórico productions. Torregrosa was also one of the few *batá* drum makers still practicing his art in Havana, and León had become quite close to him as a friend and informant. Torregrosa was extraordinary not only because he was a highly accomplished drum maker, but also because he maintained a self-reflexive attitude about his art and religion, as evidenced in the large scrapbook with hundreds of mementos from the last two decades of his life. On one page is a photo of a business card from anthropologist William Bascom given to Torregrosa. On another page is a newspaper photo of a "Native Chief of Rhodesia." Next to it is a newspaper clipping (in English) about African American artists in the United States. A few pages later is a note from Argeliers León to Torregrosa: "For my brother Trinidad, with the affection and fondness that you have evoked in me in such a short time." On the facing page is a program from a concert for a summer-school class taught by León in 1947, in which Torregrosa participated. Torregrosa bequeathed the scrapbook to León at his death, and León left it to his wife María Teresa Linares when he died.

I asked León whether any *grupos puros* like those formed by Torregrosa still existed in Cuba, and he responded that most of the *tumbadores* (drummers, from *tumbadora,* the lowest-pitched conga drum) in his original group had died. The second- and third-generation *tumbadores* were doing one of two things: (1) playing drums for the Conjunto Folklórico or for other folkloric groups—not because they necessarily believed in the religion, but because it was easy and steady money; or (2) forgoing the opportunity to play the drums in favor of pursuing more lucrative and social rewarding careers, such as doctors, lawyers, and engineers. *"Y esto fue una conquista de la Revolución. Los médicos negros, abogados negros, ingenieros negros, esto no existía antes de la Revolución. Esto fue un triunfo, sí"* (And this was a victory of the revolution. Black doctors, black lawyers, black engineers, such things did not exist before the revolution. This was truly a triumph).

ORIGINS OF THE CONJUNTO FOLKLÓRICO: DISSENTING VIEWS

The history of the Conjunto Folklórico and the Teatro Nacional that I have recounted thus far makes both endeavors seem to have been unqualified successes, at least from the twinned perspectives of the government's agenda and the administrators of both groups. But one of the few surviving "founding informant/performers" of the group, Lázaro Ros, gave me a much different view when I spoke with him on August 10, 1992. After much prodding, I had convinced Alberto, my drum teacher, to take me to Ros's house for an interview. A fine mist fell from the sky as Alberto and I carried our bicycles up the several flights of stairs to Ros's apartment. As we entered his apartment, the mist changed to rain and covered the earth suddenly, as if it were dumped from a great bucket. There were several young men in Ros's apartment sitting on the floor and on the couch, waiting for Ros to come out of his bedroom. Alberto and I joined them. When Ros came into the front room, he and Alberto greeted each other briefly, without the usual shoulder slaps or hugs, and went into the kitchen. I remained in the front room with the young men.

After a few moments, Ros came out of the kitchen and sat down close to me on the couch. He smelled of alcohol, sleep, and sweat. He looked quite thin for his six-foot height, and his hands were shaking. He leaned over and gave me a wet kiss on the cheek while putting his hand on my knee: "You're very sweet, very nice. What do you want?" "I want to know about the Conjunto Folklórico in the early days, and what your role was." Ros let out a barking laugh and moved in close: *"Fue una mierda. Todo una mierda. El Conjunto Folklórico fue una mierda total"* (It was shit. It was all shit. The Conjunto Folklórico was just a big piece of shit). I glanced at Alberto, who was looking out the window. The rain had stopped. Ros's vehemence about the Folklórico intrigued me, and I started to ask him a few more questions about his experiences with the troupe. He put his hand up as if to stop me, and articulated with careful though slurred diction: *"Yo no trabajo sin pago. Se venden mis discos compactos para 90 dolares en Italia, y no me pagan nada. Y Oggún, la película—nada. Y mis discos, Olorún, Síntesis, Mezcla—nada. Entonces, si tú quieres trabajar conmigo, tú debes pagarme"* (I don't work without being paid. My compact discs are sold for 90 [probably 19] dollars in Italy, and they don't pay me a thing. And *Oggún*, the film—nothing. And my records, *Olorún, Síntesis, Mezcla*—nothing. So, if you want to work with me, you'd better pay me). I had very little money with me at the time, and I told him that I would get in touch with him later in the month for a paid interview. By the time I was able to visit him again in 1994, he had gone on tour to the United States, and our paid interview never took place.

Recently, I met Ernesto Pichardo Plá, noted *obbá* and priest of Santería, as well as a long-time student of *oríate* Roque Duarte (an *oríate* is a highly trained diviner in Santería who performs and interprets the *itá* of Santería initiates). Pichardo told me that Duarte, also a renowned Santero, was among the founding inform-ant/performers of the Conjunto Folklórico. But Duarte's views of the founda-tion of the group, according to Pichardo, were wholly negative. Living in exile in Florida since the early 1960s, Duarte, along with other ex-performers of the Con-junto Folklórico, has nurtured a growing enmity toward a regime that he believes has systematically devalued and sold out his religious traditions. According to Duarte, the anthropologists hired by the Teatro Nacional's Department of Folk-lore to do research on Afro-Cuban residents of Havana during the early years of the revolution were also providing data to those members of the Central Com-mittee responsible for the *zafra* (annual sugar harvest). Any Afro-Cuban person who did not seem to be gainfully employed at the time of the "anthropological study" was considered to be a potential practitioner of an Afro-Cuban religion. The theory was that if an Afro-Cuban could survive without working in some publicly recognized revolutionary activity, then that person was likely making a living, illegally, by practicing one or more Afro-Cuban religions.

These "suspects" were then rounded up in 1961 and put on a bus headed for the countryside to help with the *zafra*. Families were split up, friends separated, and other job opportunities squelched—except for one. The detained Afro-Cubans were ultimately given a choice: work for the *zafra* or try out for the Conjunto Folklórico. Those who agreed to audition were then judged according to their abilities, and those who seemed to have little singing, dancing, or instrumental ca-pabilities were put back on the bus for the cane fields.

Joining the Conjunto Folklórico meant not only singing and dancing, but also sitting in classrooms and seminars to listen to lectures about how the revolution would benefit Afro-Cubans and how Afro-Cubans should cooperate with its goals by sharing and teaching their "folklore" (religions) in order to help this triumph occur. In a Radio Martí broadcast from Miami, Duarte called Trinidad Torregrosa and Lázaro Ros and others "traitors to the religion" (meaning Santería). They made the choice to share their knowledge of the religion for a meager-paying steady job, thus making a secret tradition essentially public, or, in Duarte's view, selling out. It should be noted that in the early 1960s Duarte was a member of the elite paramilitary group sponsored by Batista's supporters whose main goal was to create violent chaos around Castro and his followers. Duarte's political stance at the time certainly would have strengthened his objections to the revolutionary platform of the Conjunto Folklórico. Nonetheless, this alternate view of the Teatro Nacional/Conjunto Folklórico project allows for a broader interpretation of the text that follows, and puts into perspective the project as a whole. The stated goal of the project was to engage Cuba's African roots from the bottom up, but what happened instead was an imposition of this will from the top down, with little input from the Afro-Cuban "informant-performers" until the decision to form the troupe had already been made.

THE SACRED COWS

During my interview with León, he never mentioned that his wife had been director of the Conjunto Folklórico in the early 1960s. After León died unexpectedly in early 1991 of heart failure, I had several more interviews with Linares about these same topics, and she did not mention her directorship, either; I first learned of it from Rafael L. López Valdés. Only in 1992, during an interview on August 23, two years after we had first met, did Linares share her experiences as CFNC director with me. Whereas León had focused more on the institutions that were involved during the genesis of the Teatro Nacional and the Academy of Sciences, Linares focused on the individuals who staffed those institutions.

Her initial reticence in discussing her own experiences, I found out, was due to an event that occurred while she was director, which so traumatized her that in the subsequent thirty years she never returned to the group, neither as an administrator nor as a member of the audience. Her memories of and reactions to her time with the Conjunto Folklórico are much less idealized than those of León, and take into account the inevitable tensions as well as the rewarding collaborations of this "brave new world" in which blacks and whites worked side by side, receiving the same pay and ostensibly the same social status for their work. Her most vivid memories about the early days of the Conjunto Folklórico focus on its first international tour and on the incident that caused her to resign as director. Unlike León, who spoke with a certain economy and brevity, when Linares finally spoke about those turbulent times, she spoke with great emotion. The following is my translation of excerpts from this interview, along with explanatory comments:

> MTL: On this tour [the first international tour of the Conjunto Folklórico], it
> became obvious that people who came from the streets, people who had

been living at such a low level in the inner city, without a politicization or education process, could not step out of the "red" pages of the newspaper [the pages in the Havana newspapers where criminals and their crimes are listed], with all that this implies, and into the Théâtre des Nations in Paris.

KH: A very elegant, well-known place.

MTL: And with a level of culture and organization very different from what they had known here. The result of this tour was a disaster.

KH: And what year was this? 1962? 1963?

MTL: I think it was 1962 or 1963. [The troupe's first international tour was in 1964.] It was disastrous. They robbed, they committed atrocities. They swindled people—they went to Algeria, Spain, [Belgium,] and of course France, it was their first stop—they went to various places in Europe. And everywhere they committed petty crimes. And it was here that Rogelio Martínez Furé was implicated in the event that eventually caused his separation from the group. After this, the Conjunto had various managers. And every new management was confronted with disastrous disciplinary problems. Because these people are not disciplined. They are not disciplined like an artist. An artist, no matter how lively he is, has to have a series of disciplinary principles—for rehearsal, for presentation to the public, for rectitude in his own life. They would miss rehearsals because they were drunk, they would lose all memory of what happened like they were in a coma—and it was because they were drunk all the time. And these people would be living in a hotel, cooking in the room, spilling grease all over the carpet, and they got everything dirty, they burned the carpet, they cleaned their shoes on the bedspreads, and they just did dreadful things. There were complaints in all the hotels about these people. And our embassy always had to save face and pay the bill for what they did.

Linares emphasizes that many of the original members of the Conjunto Folklórico were from *las páginas rojas*, that is, criminals. The idea that black Cubans who were practitioners of African-based religions were likely to be criminals did not originate with Linares. Rather, this idea came to light in its most public form with the publication of Fernando Ortíz's first book on "Afro-Cuban" culture, published in 1906: *Hampa afro-cubana: Los negros brujos (apuntes para un estudio de etnología criminal)* (Afro-Cuban underworld: Black sorcerers—Notes for a study of criminal ethnology). Ortiz, though he wrote books about the anthropology, musicology, and history of Cuba, was a lawyer by training, and initially was interested in the African-based traditions of Cuba's black population to support his thesis that the *brujería* or "sorcery" of this sector of the population caused an increase in crime in Havana and the two surrounding provinces of Matanzas and Pinar del Río (the westernmost province of mainland Cuba). This thesis was reinforced by the mafialike practices of the Abakwá society, which exacted harsh penalties (sometimes death) for betraying any member of the brotherhood (Cabrera 1970). However, this impression was not confirmed by the practices of other African-based religions; Ortiz, in his first attempt to understand the African influence in Cuba, had seized upon its most visible manifestation, the infamy of which had already been exaggerated in the popular imagination of Havana, and had formed erroneous generalizations based on this particular group. Inaccurate as this initial assessment might have been, Ortiz was a respected scholar in Cuba and his views were absorbed and assimilated by an entire generation of Cuban scholars. (See chapter 6 for more on the historical context and evolution of Ortiz's brand of Social Darwinism.)

In this context, the "petty crimes" allegedly committed by the original members of the CFNC on their first international tour become slightly less credible, or at least exaggerated. Certainly there were breaches of good conduct and highly irresponsible behavior; it remains unclear, however, whether the entire group behaved in this way, or whether the most grievous incidents were caused by a few badly behaved individuals. Roque Duarte's observations about the troupe's foundation suggest the possibility that at least some of these performers were not in the group of their own free will and were not invested in protecting the reputation of the government that had perhaps coerced them into the group. Percussionist Carlos Aldama Pérez noted that this tour was "one big party" for him and his friends, none of whom had ever traveled outside of Cuba. "We were drinking and carrying on most of the time," remembered Aldama Pérez. "It was great." Even the troupe's current *asesor* (artistic advisor), Rogelio Martínez Furé, was temporarily dismissed from the group during that tour after committing an act of "drunken debauchery" during an all-night beach party in Spain.[28]

Linares made the point earlier in the interview that at its inception, the Conjunto Folklórico "was not a cultural institution; it was a group of Santeros." She referred to the original group of seven informants (which she remembered as six)—Nieves Fresneda, Trinidad Torregrosa, Jesús Pérez, José Oriol Bustamante, Manuela Alonso Valdés, Emilio O'Farrill y Escoto, and Lázaro Ros—as "the sacred cows." This attitude, if manifested during her tenure as director of the group, may have contributed to her traumatic separation from the group. These statements, combined with her comments about the performers' lack of "artistic" discipline and Duarte's critical comments, imply that underneath the newly varnished layer of revolutionary enthusiasm for the project were several rougher layers of mistrust and wariness, as well as a hair-trigger readiness to lose faith in the endeavor. But because the events in question happened in the early 1960s, and because Linares did not accompany the group on their first international tour, it is difficult to evaluate her portrayal of their collective character. In addition, Linares had not spoken about these incidents in decades, a silence that implies not only trauma but also a deep sense of loyalty to the goals of this revolutionary troupe.

KH: I wanted to ask you whether you thought that the disasters that were committed by these people in the hotels and in the restaurants were the result of differences between the cultures themselves, or whether they were the result of some sort of resentment, along the lines of, Oh—these people have more than I had when I was growing up, so I'm going to destroy everything—

MTL: No, no. It was a problem of formal education. It was a problem of formal education. They went to France, and they didn't like the food in the restaurants or in the hotels. They were accustomed to eating rice, and to cooking meat with lots of fat, and to cooking things the way they wanted to. So they bought a hotplate, because they were receiving pretty good pay, so they bought this hotplate and brought it to the room, and they bought the rice and the meat and cooked it according to their tastes. And if they got mud all over everything and made a mess, it didn't matter—because the same thing would have happened in their own houses. In other words, they behaved in these new places exactly as they would have in their own homes, due to the lack of formal education. And they pulled the same tricks in the stores—because they thought, well, the same thing—the stores had more of what they wanted, so they acted badly in the stores. I was told about people who walked into a department store in Belgium and opened their purses and threw in necklaces, costume jewelry, and all sorts of things, and when they left, the store employees were waiting for them.

KH: They stole everything.

MTL: Yes—but they had a TV surveillance system in the store, and so they all got caught. This was quite a scene.

KH: So—did they get thrown in jail?

MTL: No, no, no. They had to pay fines. They paid fines.

KH: Wow. And this was on the first tour.

MTL: Yes, and the second and the third. They always did it. So, there were various crises in the management of the Conjunto, and it was necessary to get a responsible and knowledgeable director. So they called on me.

KH: And this was—

MTL: This was in 1965–1966. Argeliers was in Africa [doing research] at the time. And I wrote to him and told him that I had been asked to take charge of the Conjunto Folklórico, but that I didn't want to do it. And he advised me that under no circumstances should I accept this proposal.

KH: Why not?

MTL: Why not? Because he felt that I shouldn't spend my energy on them, nor should I entangle myself with problems that I couldn't solve.

KH: Oh.

MTL: But then came the order from the president of the Academy of Sciences, who was my boss, that I had to help these people. I told him that I didn't want to accept this responsibility, and he said that it would only be temporary. And that temporarily I would spend one-half of every day at the Conjunto and the other half at the Academy of Sciences.

KH: So you had two jobs?

MTL: Two jobs. The Conjunto paid half my salary, and the Academy of Sciences paid the other half. But I didn't want to be dependent on the Academy of Sciences in any way. So I was there—I don't think I was there for longer than a year. During the first national tour that we had, I was already having problems with the group.

KH: Really? What kind?

MTL: Disciplinary problems. Multitudinous quarrels, in which they became enraged and started beating on one another and committed all sorts of atrocities. And I wasn't present at the time, because I was in the hotel. So when it came time for rehearsal, and I arrived and wanted to impose some discipline, they all told me that nothing happened. And what did they say to me? "No, I didn't see anything" or "I fainted" or "I was asleep" or "I wasn't watching" or "I wasn't there at the time"—and every last one of them denied that anything had ever happened.

Linares was, by this time, León's wife and a well-respected musicologist with a specialty in *música campesina* (folk music of the rural areas of Cuba, typically performed by whites and *mulatos*). It was most likely the combination of these two factors that culminated in Linares's selection for the directorship of the Conjunto Folklórico. That León advised her not to take the position is interesting but not surprising, since he had already voiced his disapproval of the CFNC's "exaggerated and inauthentic" performances. The "problems that Linares couldn't solve" most likely refer to the disciplinary problems already manifested by the troupe on their international and national tours, as well as the probability that some of the performers did not want to be there. León, having already worked with Torregrosa and some of the other informants on the Teatro Nacional project, perhaps knew the scope of these problems better than Linares, although not necessarily through the actions of these seven informants. Rather, the majority of the informants were priests or priestesses of their respective African-based religions, and each had *ahijados* (initiates), some of whom had come to be initiated as a way of resolving problems in their lives. As a way of helping these *ahijados* and also maintaining the loyalty of ritual kinship, these informants had arranged for some of their *ahijados* to perform in the Conjunto Folklórico.

MTL: . . . I remember one occasion when they were rehearsing a ballet that they were performing when I took charge of the Conjunto. Manuela Alonso, when she felt like it, was a better dancer than Nieves Fresneda. And she did a demonstration of how Babalú-Ayé dances when he manifests himself as *aura tiñosa* [vulture; according to Linares, a *camino* (literally, road) or avatar of Babalú-Ayé, Yoruba deity of poverty, disease, and infirmity].[29] And this woman danced as if she were *aura tiñosa* herself, in such a magisterial manner that I was taken aback. This was one of the best presentations of this dance that I had ever seen in my life. And I realized at that moment that here was a series of values that was disappearing. The salaries of these people were very low. From the very beginning they were made out to be poor people who had no culture, no education past the sixth grade, and who only knew how to dance. And so they were given very low salaries. But I thought that, in the same way that the prima ballerinas in the Ballet Nacional had good salaries, Nieves Fresneda, and this person [Manuela] Alonso—

KH: Ah ha, Manuela.

MTL: —And some other people should also have good salaries.

KH: Yes, of course.

MTL: And so I took a look at the salary scale, as it went lower and lower and lower. And some people were placed there because they were *ahijado de* Nieves [Fresneda], *ahijado de* Jesús [Pérez], *ahijado de* [José] Oriol Busta-mante, who was a big chief here. And I discovered that there was a sub-structure. The Conjunto had a structure, as did the Consejo de Cultura [Council of Culture]. And according to the structure of the Consejo de Cultura, there was to be one manager, one administrator, a series of in-formants—of which there were six—six sacred cows [actually, there were seven]—because there was Trinidad Torregrosa, Nieves Fresneda, [José] Oriol [Bustamante], [Emilio] O'Farrill—who were old people who really knew a lot, and who could carry on the traditions and teach a lot, who could do things—like Manuela [Alonso]—stop and say, No, you don't dance it that way, you dance it this way—and teach it. And these people had to have a certain level [of expertise]. So they [the Consejo de Cultura] told me that I should apply a salary scale to these people. And I looked for advisors to help me do this, and there were people from modern dance, from the Ballet Nacional, from the theatre—like set directors and other people who could help me determine things that I couldn't necessarily measure on my own.

    So I formulated a salary scale, which consisted of "A" for the inform-ants, "B" for the people who did many different things—because I was looking for productivity, and there were people who danced well in the Congo, Abakwá, and Yoruba styles, and there were people who played the *tres* and played the *son,* and there were people who did many other things. There were also people who could only do one thing.

KH: So those people [who did only one thing] weren't supposed to receive as much?

MTL: Not as good a salary. Of course. So there were some people who did not adapt very well to this salary scale. And one of those who did not adapt was also very *achuchado. Achuchado* means in a constant state of rage and hatred, against me.

KH: Oh, against you.

MTL: Yes, everyone prodded him [*le ponían electrodos*] to attack me. There were several. It was on that sort of a plane. But this guy was a really bad person. This guy was a pimp. When they would go tour, he would take a few of the girls who were in the Conjunto and exploit them, like prostitutes.

EL ACHUCHADO

As a result of the ritual network of Santeros, Santeras, and *ahijados*, there was a social structure forming within the Conjunto Folklórico that had very little to do with the administrative superstructure that was being imposed from the director's office. Linares seems to have been keenly aware of this parallel governance. What is perhaps more important here, however, is that she was also aware of the great talent possessed by some of these people and of the intense beauty of their performances. Her attempt to obtain higher salaries for them, albeit it within the hierarchical framework of a salary scale, is tangible proof of her appreciation of them as artists. What she did not appreciate were the somewhat brazen efforts of several of the less qualified musicians to gain a salary level comparable to that of the more talented and versatile performers.

The disagreement with the *músico achuchado* (enraged musician) was not the first of such confrontations. Early in her tenure, Linares suggested to Nieves Fresneda (the most sacred of the so-called sacred cows) that the CFNC present a performance of the *iyawó* ceremony of Santería (the initiation ceremony, or *asiento*, of an *ahijado*). Nieves refused, saying that she would not allow such a sacred event to be performed on stage, and added that if Linares persisted in her efforts to stage the *iyawó* ceremony, Nieves would leave the troupe and take all of her *ahijados* with her. Linares noted to herself that such a departure would cut the CFNC's membership in half, but said out loud to Nieves that there were a lot of other Nieves Fresnedas to be found in the city of Havana, and a lot of other *ahijados* who would be interested in joining the Conjunto Folklórico. The result of this standoff was a long-standing grudge between the two women. Nieves did not leave the CFNC, and the *iyawó* ceremony was never staged. Linares's confrontation with *el achuchado*, however, turned out to have more serious consequences.

MTL: . . . So, anyway, there were people like that [like the pimp]. People who had no morals. And I tried to eliminate a lot of those people who were doing damage to me within the Conjunto.

KH: Yes. By eliminate them, you mean reject them?

MTL: Demote them. Demote them. So one of those who was not demoted, who stayed in the Conjunto, wanted to be "A" level, but he couldn't be "A" level because he wasn't among the best—

KH: He wasn't "A."

MTL: He wasn't "A." He asked for a meeting with me. And everyone was alert to the fact that something was going to happen in this meeting. And everyone was expectant, waiting. So we had the meeting that morning. The labor union [*el sindicato*], the Council for Labor Justice [Consejo de Justicia Laboral] where he had filed his complaint, and I don't remember who else was there—and myself. The labor union representative was Jesús Pérez [informant and drummer for the Conjunto Folklórico], who was the *iyamba* [head officiant of Abakwá ceremonies] of an Abakwá *potencia* [group] that was functioning clandestinely within the Conjunto, and all of his Abakwás [*ahijados* of Abakwá] were there with him. The representative from the Council for Labor Justice was [José] Oriol [Bustamante] [also an informant and drummer for the CFNC], who also had all his clandestine *ahijados* there—he was the *gran mago* [high priest], the *tata nganga* [Congo term meaning priest of Palo Monte] of this group.

KH: Of what?

MTL: Of Palo [Palo Monte].

KH: Ay.

MTL: So, of what use were these official organizations, if, extraofficially, it was they [the "cult" leaders] who dominated within the Conjunto? I realized that there were two distinct social structures—

KH: And that one structure was more powerful than the other, right?

MTL: Yes—

KH: That of the men—

MTL: Yes, it was that one. There was no other law than that one [that of Abakwá, Palo Monte, etc.].

KH: Whew.

MTL: So, I explained to him very calmly that he couldn't be "A."

KH: Because he wasn't "A."

MTL: He wasn't "A." He lacked this and this and this and this and this. And I told him that he couldn't be "B," because he lacked this and this and this and this and this. I told him that he was "C," but that he could become "B" if he could overcome these things, and that he could become "A" if he overcame the other things, if he became more capable and bettered himself in every sense of the word. So they didn't say anything—the Council for Labor Justice could have challenged me; the labor union could have challenged me. But they didn't say anything, because it was demonstrated—

KH: Because you were right—

MTL: Because it was demonstrated that I was right. So they all left. And he went behind the curtains and took out the things that belonged to the Conjunto—like a costume, a pair of ballet slippers, a whole series of things. He dumped them on my desk, and just left them there, on top of my desk. He said, "Take them. I'm returning all this." I said, "Why are you returning all this?" "Because I'm leaving here." I said, "Listen, I'm going to remind you of the Yoruba proverb that says, 'Never be the first one to turn away' [Nunca aparta por la primera]." And he said, "No, I've thought this over pretty well, and I know what I'm going to do." He opened his shirt, took out a pistol, and fired a shot at my chest.

KH: At your chest?

MTL: Yes. But at the moment that I saw him take out a pistol, I started to scream. And I ducked and the shot didn't hit me, but rather hit a person who was in back of me, running, fleeing from my screams. She was running into the bathroom.

KH: Did he kill her?

MTL: No, the bullet passed through her neck and left a mark. It went through her trachea. And she lost so much blood—because when she fell it was a shock, and the blood came out like a fountain.

KH: Silvina? No—

MTL: Silvina. Silvina Fabars. Silvina Fabars had just come into the Conjunto by means of a competition. And she was a stupendous dancer and an even better singer.

KH: But no longer.

MTL: No, no—she lost her voice. So Silvina Fabars fell down, and I, completely terrified, threw myself to the ground, and hid under the desk. So Rodolfo Reyes [Mexican choreographer of the Conjunto[30]] was talking with another artist in the vestibule of the entrance to where I worked. He got up to leave, but he thought that he [the disgruntled pistol-wielding employee] was going to attack him. And when Rodolfo saw that he [the employee] was still shooting, he threw himself to the ground, and the bullet grazed both his shoulders, from one side to the other. The other man who was with him [Rodolfo Reyes] jumped out the window onto the patio outside. So everyone left me alone, and he came back to the desk and shot me there, under the desk. The bullets were fired at such close range, the mouth of the gun was so close, and the gunpowder so hot, that it burned my mouth and tongue, and I let out some horrifying screams. My chest and arms were burned, and I was screaming, screaming, screaming a lot, and all of me was burned. And I didn't get shot but one bullet here [points to left leg], and one here [continues pointing to legs], and one here, in my thigh, right here.

KH: Yes, and you still have the—

MTL: The mark [*huella*].

KH: Yes, yes—whew.

MTL: So, mentally, I was thinking that this was the most miserable and ridiculous way to have to die—and I was in fact dying, because I was very close to the end. But mentally, the rate at which your thoughts run by—I was actually counting the shots. And I counted, and it was an automatic pistol that would shoot eight bullets—

KH: And how many bullets did he shoot at you?

MTL: Six.

KH: Six.

MTL: No—seven, because he shot one at Rodolfo, but he shot the rest of them at me. [One bullet hit Silvina Fabars, which may be why Linares initially said six.]

MTL: So, anyway, he shot all of his bullets at me, and one at Rodolfo. And so I realized that there were no more bullets left in his gun, and that he might try to enlist the help of some other brute, but I gathered myself together and got up. I got out from under the desk, and I saw him on the stairs with his pistol held high. And I realized—

KH: —But everyone saw him, right?

MTL: Yes.

KH: Everyone saw it, and knew who it was, right?

MTL: Yes. Absolutely.

KH: And what was his name? Or don't you—

MTL: Miguel Valdés.

KH: Miguel Valdés. And is he still alive?

MTL: No, no. His story is very dark, very terrible. He left there running, and disappeared. So people started to come out, and they saw me lying there, injured, and they wanted to take care of me, but I said, no—take care of Fabars [Silvina].

KH: Yes. Take care of Silvina.

MTL: Yes, of Silvina.

KH: Yes.

MTL: At the time I didn't remember anybody's name—not Silvina's, not his [Miguel Valdés's], not anybody's.

KH: Because it was a tremendous trauma.

MTL: But I could, however, still pick myself up and give orders—that people should attend to Silvina and attend to Rogelio—to Rodolfo, who had a shirt just covered with blood. And I did feel the blood running down my leg and filling my shoe. But, well, I wanted to walk—but my legs refused to respond. And so I sat in an easy chair, and started to give orders. And so they finally took care of me, and took me in a paint truck—because by this time everyone on the street was talking about what had happened— to Calixto García [Hospital]. And when I got there, they took my blood pressure, and it was 80 over 120. But when the doctor asked me what happened, I didn't know what to tell him. And who hurt me? I didn't remember his name. So the man who took care of me, the *rumba* dancer named Santacruz, told the doctor his [Miguel Valdés's] name. So, they attended to me, they took X-rays, they took care of my leg, Argeliers arrived, [Isaac] Barreal arrived—

[MTL starts to cry, as does KH]

MTL: Well, when Argeliers got to the hospital, I was able to tell him, at that moment, what I thought of these people. I told him that he, and Don Fernando, and [Isaac] Barreal, and myself, and many people, had thought that all these people had been living this life of blood, sweat, and tears, living in opposition to society, because they had been very abused by society. But I determined, in that moment, that they had no chance of salvation. That they had no possibility of ever being helped.

There are multiple tragedies within this story. María Teresa Linares was critically wounded in the leg and severely traumatized. Silvina Fabars almost died as a result of the bullet wounds to her throat and ultimately lost her voice. Rodolfo Reyes was also hit by a bullet and left the troupe as a result. Miguel Valdés, who had maimed these three people, continued on his path of self-destruction and died violently several years later. And relations between the administrators and the performers became irreparably strained. As a result of this violent confrontation, Linares's thinking about the troupe reverted to reactionary racial stereotypes, broadening the already wide cultural gaps between the administrators and the performers. In fact, during the early years of the troupe, the scene that occurred between Linares and Valdés can be seen not just as predictable, but as probable. María Teresa Linares and Miguel Valdés were coming from such vastly different backgrounds and expectations that they could not possibly understand or trust one another, at least not initially.

In the few field recordings of religious ceremonies I have heard from the 1950s and 1960s, what is striking to me is that the beautiful voices singing to Ochún or Yemayá or Changó do not adhere to a Western pitch structure or "regular" rhythms or a *bel canto* singing style; rather, the beauty of the performance depends on the ability of those voices to communicate religious context and intent. Standardized, performative perfection is not the goal in religious ceremonies, yet these "founding informant/performers" were being asked to perform their religious ceremonies and then were "ranked" for these performances—not in accordance with any hierarchy they would have recognized (performative *aché*, years in the religion, godparental connections), but rather in accordance with externally determined standards governing specific units of performance: being able to sing on key and dance on cue; being able to dance, play a *shekere*, and sing at the same time; and so on. These requirements have little to do with religious performance, and yet they were being imposed upon the performers—albeit with absence of malice. This imposition of values was also evident in the public teamwork between whites and blacks (administrators and performers, respectively), in which the informant/performers were made to conform to the artistic and structural vision of the administrators.

María Teresa Linares's and Miguel Valdés's tragic experience within the Conjunto Folklórico sheds light on an important issue in the CFNC's development. Despite the best intentions and enthusiasm of the revolution, tensions caused by differences in race, class, and religious beliefs were reproduced within the Conjunto Folklórico. Not only was the relationship of Santeros and *ahijados* being replicated within the troupe, but the hierarchy of white management and black performers was also represented in microcosm. The vast majority of the early directors and administrators of the CFNC were white, like Linares, and came from upper-middle-class homes in Cuba and Mexico. The vast majority of the early informant/performers of the Conjunto Folklórico were black and came from the poorer areas of urban Havana.[31] As a result, the tensions between the two vastly different types of upbringing often exploded, usually ending in the early resignation of the director, and a few times ending in violence.

The Conjunto Folklórico went through many general directors until 1980, most of whom lasted only a year or two. This parade of directors emphasizes its early instability as an institution, the most notable cause of which would seem to be the vast cultural differences between the management and the employees. The first director, Marta Blanco, held her post from 1962 to 1964. According to Linares, she renounced the CFNC in Spain during their infamous first international tour and came back to Cuba by herself and without a job. Then came Elena Noriega, the Mexican choreographer who was said to have been driven crazy (literally) by a combination of *trabajos* (evil spells) and lack of artistic discipline on the part of the performers. Linares took over the directorship for less than a year, until sometime in 1965. Then there was a director who was not particularly well qualified in folklore or in arts management, who was ordered by the Consejo Nacional de Cultura to become the director of the Conjunto Folklórico. Apparently by this time, the CFNC's reputation preceded it, and no one wanted to direct it. This ill-qualified director lasted roughly one year.

The next director was, according to Linares, a decent person, committed to the revolution and enthusiastic about the CFNC's potential. Unfortunately, he made the mistake of coming to "take possession" of the Conjunto Folklórico on his first day of work in full military dress. The informant/performers decided to initiate their new director into their world and proceeded to take him to *fiestas de santo, plantes de* Abakwá, and so on. He became so involved in these religions and, according to Linares, eventually "compromised" himself to such an extent with one of the young female dancers that he was eventually removed from his post at the Conjunto Folklórico by the Consejo Nacional de Cultura. There may have been one or two other directors of the troupe in the 1970s, but none of the people with whom I spoke (both former and current members of the troupe) was able to remember who they were. In 1980 Teresa González[32] was appointed to direct the Conjunto Folklórico, and she held that position for almost two decades. Her longevity as director may have been facilitated by the large number of retirements and deaths of the original informant / performers in the mid-1980s and early 1990s. During the late 1990s Gonzalez suffered from health problems. In July 2000 Johannes García, a veteran dancer who has been with the troupe for more than thirty years, assumed the directorship of the CFNC.

Both the Teatro Nacional and the Conjunto Folklórico participated in shaping a nascent revolutionary aesthetic, and their founders, most notably Argeliers León, his wife María Teresa Linares, and Rogelio Martínez Furé, were motivated and inspired by the intellectual synergy that often follows radical political and social change: Cuba was going to transform itself from the corrupt, racist, and classist society of the Batista regime to a responsible, independent, just society. The revolution would provide the impetus and the possibility for racial, social, and economic equality in Cuba, and the Teatro Nacional and Conjunto Folklórico would contribute to the cause through its performances.

Understanding the backgrounds and aspirations of the original participants is key to gaining insight into the aesthetic and political development of the troupe from its inception in 1962 to the present day. Only a few of the original participants in the Teatro Nacional / Conjunto Folklórico project are still involved in the CFNC. The original participants interviewed in this chapter no longer work with the Conjunto Folklórico in any capacity. But the attempt to forge a national culture for Cuba in the early years of the revolution, in accordance with the visions of both León and Martínez Furé, was, in fact, partially successful. Certainly, Cuba's long-standing racism[33] could not be eradicated in a few short years. Nonetheless, the confrontation of African and European Cuba in a public performative environment laid the groundwork for future cooperation in other domains. The "authenticity" so valued by León is no longer so important in the Conjunto's performances. It is the dramatic force of the performance that takes precedence now, pushing the continual negotiation and construction of Cuba's identity to the forefront. But the intellectual roots of the Conjunto Folklórico and its predecessor, the Teatro Nacional, still infuse the troupe's performances. Fernando Ortíz, the so-called father of Afrocubanismo, continues to cast a long shadow over his intellectual progeny. Ortíz first recontextualized Santería by locating it within the realm of crime and then continued this process by presenting public, staged performances of the music and dance of Santería in the 1930s, outside of any liturgical context. It is by situating Ortíz within his historical context that we can best understand the beginnings of this parallel process, and perhaps comprehend the future of this continual appropriation and recontextualization of Cuba's African heritage.

NOTES

1. See Pájares Santiesteban (1993) for a detailed account of Ramiro Guerra's contribution to modern and folkloric dance in Cuba.
2. In the conclusion of his book on Afrocubanismo in the twenties and thirties in Cuba, Robin Moore (1997:222) points out that musicians and other artists were relying much more on the avant-garde than on popular culture for their inspiration in the 1940s. The influential Grupo de Renovación Musical, which included Serafin Pro (future choral director of the Teatro Nacional project), Harold Gramatges, Hilario Gonzáles, and other well-known composers, "downplayed Afro-Cuban themes."
3. See *Actas de Folklore* (1961) No. 1, and Nos. 10–12 (three volumes were combined in the last issue of the publication), respectively, in which the founding of the Department of Folklore within the Teatro Nacional and the subsequent establishment of the Institute of Ethnology and Folklore within the Academy of Sciences are announced and justified.
4. Interview with Isaac Barreal (December 1, 1991); interview with Maria Teresa Linares (December 18, 1991); interview with Rafael L. López Valdés (December 30, 1991). In these interviews, all expressed their initial excitement about the impending transformation of Cuban society and about their role in this transformation via the Teatro Nacional.
5. Christopher Columbus is said to be the first discoverer of Cuba, Alexander von Humboldt (sometimes referred to as Alejandro de Humboldt) is the second, and Don Fernando Ortíz is the third (Marinello 1989:563).
6. The primary impetus for the Cuban revolution of 1959 emerged during the early 1950s; the revolution itself is considered by many Cubans to be a process that continues to this day.
7. León in *Actas del Folklore* (1961, no. 1). At the time of the establishment of the Teatro Nacional de Cuba, there was no Cuban Ministry of Culture.
8. See especially works by the following authors in *Actas del Folklore:* Barnet (1961a, [no.

1]), Martínez Furé (1961a [no. 3]), López Valdés (1961 [no. 5]), and Pérez de la Riva (1961 [no. 5]); and by López Valdés in *Etnología y Folklore* (1966 [no. 2]).

9. See, for example, León in *Actas del Folklore* (1961b [no. 5]), Neumann in *Etnología y Folklore* (1969 [no. 7]), and León in *Etnología y Folklore* (1969 [no. 8]). Africanist Ulli Beier, a supporter of the Teatro Nacional de Cuba, also published in *Actas del Folklore* (1961a, 1961b [nos. 2 and 8]). The most prolific participant in these seminars was Rómulo Lachatañeré, author of the important works *¡Oh, Mío Yemayá!* (1938) and *Manual de Santería* (1942), who began publishing articles on the Afro-Cuban religious practices of Santería and Palo Monte in Fernando Ortíz's journal *Estudios Afrocubanos* in 1939, and who published in no fewer than seven of the ten issues of *Actas del Folklore* (1961a–g [nos. 2–8]).

10. Scholars such as C. Moore (1988) and López Valdés (1991) use the term *"folklorization"* to describe a process of exoticizing and objectifying Afro-Cuban religious traditions. As I first noted in chapter 1, my term *folkloricization* describes a process that may include exoticism and objectification, but that also involves conscious interaction between the performative source, in this case African-based religions in Cuba, and the Conjunto Folklórico's dramatic renditions thereof.

11. An announcement of the establishment of the Institute of Ethnology and Folklore appears in the final issue of *Actas del Folklore* (nos. 10–12).

12. Interview with Argeliers León (October 18, 1990); interview with Maria Teresa Linares (December 18, 1991). León and Linares both emphasized the anticipated educational effect of the Teatro's performances.

13. Other departments of the Teatro Nacional included the National Chorus, the Symphony Orchestra, the National Ballet, and the Contemporary Dance Ensemble, all of which incorporated some aspects of Afro-Cuban cultural expression into their repertoire.

14. This performance was referred to as an "ethnographic conference with a schematic exposition of the liturgical character, instruments, music, chants, and dances of the sacred music of the Yoruba negros" in the "Notas y Noticias" section of the first issue of Ortíz's journal of the Sociedad de Estudios Afrocubanos, *Estudios Afrocubanos:Revista Semestral* (I [1]:163).

15. Among León's many distinguished works, *Del canto y el tiempo* (1984), *Música folklórica cubana* (1964), *El patrimonio folklórico musical cubano* (1952), and the editorship of his monthly journal *Actas del Folklore* are the most relevant for this study.

16. Several of his former colleagues at CIDMUC (Center for the Study of the Development of Cuban Music) referred to him as having been a "brilliant" student and later colleague of Ortíz. María Teresa also emphasized her husband's intelligence and accomplishments, particularly in the realm of "Afro-Cuban folklore."

17. León was not the first to have the idea of an Abakwá performance. In 1933, three years before Ortíz's public presentation of the first "ethnographic conference" and *batá*

concert, noted Cuban musicologist Odilio Urfé featured the presentation of an entire Abakwá *cabildo* as the centerpiece of his "Primer Festival Musical Folklórico" (see Ministerio de Cultura 1982:158.)

18. In *La sociedad secreta abakuá* (1970), her book on Abakwá practices in Cuba and the United States, Lydia Cabrera calls these sacred pictographs *anaforuana*, which is an Abakwá word. However, the Cuban practitioners with whom I spoke with called these drawings *firmas*, which is the same word they use to describe the sacred drawings of other Afro-Cuban religious traditions, such as Palo Monte and Santería. Many practitioners of Abakwá are also practitioners of Santería and Palo Monte, which may explain the blanket usage of the word *firmas* to describe the sacred drawings associated with each tradition.

19. Abakwá is the name of a secret male society in Cuba derived from the secret male societies prevalent throughout West Africa (such as the Leopard society). Technically, it would not be considered an Afro-Cuban religious tradition because it is more of a men's society than a religion. However, in Cuba it has come to be grouped with Santería, Palo Monte, and Arará in folkloric performances and in museums, perhaps because its geographical origins, hierarchical social structures, and complex initiation processes are similar to those of Santería, Palo Monte, and Arará. López Valdés (1966), Deschamps Chapeaux (1967), Lydia Cabrera (1970), Isabel Castellanos (1977), Edward Mullen (1987), and Fernando Ortíz (1906, 1916, 1951, 1952, 1965, 1968, 1973) have documented the powerful influence of the Abakwá secret society in Cuba.

20. Although I asked both Argeliers León and María Teresa Linares several times why the approval of Jean-Paul Sartre might condemn the endeavor, they were not able to determine a causal relationship between the two events. Perhaps Sartre's break with the Soviet Marxists in the early 1960s represented an unacceptable political softening to certain hard-line Cubans. Sartre's accolades might then have been used as evidence against León, leading to his eventual marginalization. It is also worth noting that in 1971, renowned and outspoken Cuban poet Heberto Padilla (*Fuera del Juego*, 1968) was arrested for having committed "serious transgressions" against the revolution. European and Latin American intellectuals, among them Sartre, Mario Vargas Llosa, and Carlos Fuentes, condemned the incident as "morally repugnant" and "politically objectionable" (del Aguila 1984:140).

21. Had León finished the work before his death, a revised edition of this immense and unique work annotated by a devout follower of Ortíz would have been widely celebrated by scholars and musicians in Cuba and the United States. Steven Cornelius has noted that these particular works of Ortíz are so valued in the New York metropolitan area that they have been consistently stolen from area public libraries (Cornelius 1989:56). Several libraries and cultural institutions in the Miami and New York metropolitan areas have photocopies of this work (the photocopies themselves are sold for roughly $300 per set), but few institutions possess the original edition of the bound volumes (La Habana: Publicaciones de la Dirección de Cultura del Ministerio de Edu-

cación, 1952–1955). Occasionally one can find original editions of the work in antiquarian bookstores in Cuba and France, which now sell for roughly $500 per five-volume set. Parts of this work were recently republished in Cuba in a series of pamphlets (La Habana: Editorial Letras Cubanas, 1995–1996,), each pamphlet representing one instrument. The most recent republication (1998) of Ortíz's masterwork, from a Spanish publishing house, is in two volumes.

22. Her prolific and distinguished career has included such important scholarly staples in Cuban musicology as *La música y el pueblo* (1989) and *La música popular* (1970), along with a ground-breaking study entitled *El sucu-sucu de Isla de Pinos* (1970).

23. According to López Valdés (interview, December 3, 1991), a former pupil of Argeliers León and senior researcher in the Department of Anthropology at the Cuban Academy of Sciences, the majority of the Cuban population (90 percent) practices some sort of religion, and within that 90 percent, the majority practices a religion of African origin. In his view, "pure Catholicism" is a minority religion in Cuban society, and is practiced by a maximum of 10 percent of the population. Catholicism's influence on Cuba's religions of African origins, according to López Valdés, is exaggerated, "more formal than essential."

24. This comment was made during a lecture by López Valdés arranged for the "Afro-Cuban culture" study trip sponsored by the Center for Cuban Studies, July 1989. López Valdés, a highly regarded ethnologist from the Cuban Academy of Sciences, emigrated to Puerto Rico in 1993. For the past thirty-five years, his research has focused on the history and current practices of religions of African origin in Cuba, and on the racial composition of the Cuban population.

25. See C. Moore (1988:102). The term "Afro-Cuban" remains problematic today, although it is used with increasing frequency in the tourist industry.

26. Interview (October 18, 1990). It should be noted here that the early performances of the Conjunto Folklórico (in the 1960s) were more similar to those of the Department of Folklore than they are now. Rogelio Martínez Furé studied with Fernando Ortíz and also with Argeliers León, so his training led him initially to emphasize "authenticity" as opposed to "entertainment value." The *espectáculos* of the Conjunto Folklórico became more "entertaining" during the 1970s and 1980s.

27. Combining aspects of religious practice (from Santería and Palo Monte, for example) is not uncommon among religious practitioners in Havana (see, for instance, Lachatañeré 1961e, 1961g). See also chapter 4 for a discussion of the musical interactions and combinations resulting from Santería, Iyesá, and Arará performance. León's ideal of *manifestaciones puras* of Santería and Palo Monte, with no overlap, did not correspond to the realities of religious practice.

28. After a fifteen-year absence, he returned to the group in the late 1970s as its *asesor*, a career move officially sanctioned by then director Teresa Gonzalez in the early 1980s. (Interview with María Teresa Linares, August 23, 1992.)

29. María Teresa Linares refers to the *aura tiñosa* as a *camino* of Babalú Ayé, but other au-

thors (J. Mason 1992; Aróstegui Bolívar 1990; García Cortez 1980) write that the *aura tiñosa* is a *camino* of Ochún, and is also her messenger. Mason does note that one of Babalú Ayé's roads is the vulture, but it is called *suvinenge* (vulture child of Nenge), not *aura tiñosa*. Because so few women are initiated into Babalú-Ayé, it is more likely that Manuela Alonso danced the *aura tiñosa* of Ochún.

30. The CFNC hired several Mexican choreographers during the 1960s, including Rodolfo Reyes and Elena Noriega. Mexican choreographers may have been invited to guest-direct the Cuban Folklórico in its early years because of the hugely successful Ballet Folklórico de México, which was founded in the 1950s in response to the Mexican government's efforts to create a national culture out of the disparate performance traditions of the Mexican states (see Nájera Ramírez 1989).

31. In writing about the Troupe Folklorique Nationale of Haiti and other Haitian folkloric ensembles, Wilcken notes the same dynamic: "Many poor and working-class Haitians have played in the troupes because of their ability to drum or sing, but middle- and upper-class personnel have made the artistic decisions" (Wilcken 1998:169).

32. I tried to interview Teresa González four times during my 1991–1992 field trip to Cuba, and again during my 1994 trip, but each time she declined, citing lack of time and a busy schedule.

33. It is interesting to note that the last prerevolutionary leader of Cuba, Fulgencio Batista, appointed many people of color in provincial governments, especially in Oriente province, the easternmost part of Cuba.

6

SACRED CRIMES

Criminalizing the Sacred in Historical Perspective

> Ogún Awanile, Obatalá Ayagunna, Yemayá Asesú: How are the different *caminos* of each
> *oricha* made manifest in our daily lives? Through our ways of being in the world: how we
> walk, how we talk, how we eat; how we love, how we think, how we die. Through names,
> games, and political campaigns. Ogún Awanile stays in the forest, hunting and thinking.
> Obatalá Ayagunna fights until he can fight no more, and he will die fighting if he has to.
> Yemayá Asesú is serious and does not dance, speaking only after she eats duck. Some of
> us grow into our roads gradually, with the privilege of time; others are bound tightly to
> their roads from the beginning, their every action shouting "Ayagunna!" or "Awanile!"
> Ultimately, our *caminos* help anchor us deep in the ground, *ìjinlèe,* to our past and to our
> present, preparing us for the future.

VIVA LA REVOLUCIÓN:
ORTÍZ GETS DRAFTED

Rogelio Martínez Furé, the current *asesor* (artistic advisor) of the Conjunto Folk-lórico, is a tall, serious man, whose cowrie-shell bracelet sets off his brightly colored African wax-print shirt. A gifted student of both Argeliers León and Fernando Ortíz, his artistic vision has guided the Conjunto Folklórico for most of its institutional life, from 1962 through the mid-1960s, and then again throughout the 1980s and 1990s.[1] In a July 1992 interview, Martínez Furé stated that he considered Ortíz to be the single greatest influence on his institutional and intellectual work. In fact, Martínez Furé's well-known book *Diálogos imaginarios,* written in the mid-1970s and published in 1979, is an "imaginary dialogue" with Fernando Ortíz about the ideology and uses of "folklore." Even in the first chapter of his book, Martínez Furé promotes the idea of stimulating the transformation and development of folklore, by "cleaning up the folk":

The development of a country's folklore can be stimulated in an intelligent and scientific way. So-called *negative* folklore (superstitions, taboos without a scientific basis, idealistic concepts about supernatural forces that govern men's lives, curanderistic practices, coprophagy, xenophobia, etc.) can be eliminated little by little, while enriching and employing *positive* folklore (all that helps in the harmonic development of society, all that contributes to the reinforcement of solidarity among men, all that exalts the traditions of fighting against oppression, scientific and beneficial pharmacology, and all the artistic forms that grew up around popular religious concepts, but which possess cultural values independent of their idealistic content, which can be purified, and given a new social revolutionary function). (Martínez Furé 1979:267)

Martínez Furé's ideology about folklore establishes important links to Cuba's past and present—to his mentor's early writings, and to the application of those writings within a revolutionary cultural framework. One can trace the idea of eliminating "negative folklore" back to Ortíz's first (and infamous) book, *Hampa afro-cubana: Los negros brujos (apuntes para un estudio de etnología criminal)* [Afro-Cuban underworld: Black sorcerers—Notes for a study of criminal ethnology], published in Madrid in 1906. And one can locate the roots of recontextualizing "folklore" even farther back, in the writings of Ortíz's mentors and collaborators—Italian criminologists Cesare Lombroso and Enrico Ferri, and the Havana police force of the late nineteenth and early twentieth centuries—whose work helped criminalize the Afro-Cuban religious practices of the nineteenth and early twentieth centuries (Lombroso 1968; Ferri 1967; Roche Monteagudo 1925; Urrutía y Blanco 1882).

One cannot escape the massive influence of Fernando Ortíz in Cuba. Lauded as Cuba's foremost scientist, anthropologist, musicologist, and essayist,[2] Ortíz published more than a thousand books, articles, papers, and pamphlets in his lifetime (1881–1969) on most aspects of Afro-Cuban life in Cuba (see García-Carranza 1970). Ortíz was born in Cuba to a Cuban mother and a Spanish father. Early in his childhood, the family moved to Madrid, and, with the exception of brief stints studying law at the Universidad de la Habana, Ortíz was trained as a lawyer primarily in Madrid. In fact, he did not live in Havana full-time until 1907, at the age of twenty-six, after the publication of his first book. Although Ortíz was living in Cuba while Cuba was fighting its war of independence from Spain (a cause with which he sympathized), there is little in his background that would account for his apparently sudden and total dedication to the study of Cuba's African population. Cultural historian Edward Mullen (1987:113) provides a clear point of departure: "A lawyer by training, Ortíz became interested in African culture for what it could reveal about crime in Cuba. In his early writing he is predominantly a criminologist." In that role, Ortíz sought to pinpoint and eventually eliminate the cause of crime in Cuba, which he associated with *la mala vida cubana,* which, in turn, he located primarily in Cuba's black community.

In the first chapter of *Hampa afro-cubana: Los negros brujos,* Ortíz asserts that the best way of understanding this "evil life" is to look at the "ethnic components" of Cuban society: "whites," "blacks," and "yellows" (Ortíz discounts the Amerindian—"bronze"—component as having little or no influence on Cuban society [Ortíz 1973:10]). Each of these groups brought particular vices to Cuba, but these vices were absorbed and assimilated in different ways, such that the vices of the whites were, in the end, no different than those of whites anywhere (and thus, according to Ortíz, easily dismissed), and the vices of the yellows ultimately amounted to little more than illegal lotteries (lamentable, but also easily dismissed), but the vices of the blacks had spread throughout Cuban society, and were proving to be dangerous, enduring, and deeply rooted (1973a:19):[3]

> *La raza blanca influyó en el hampa cubana mediante los vicios europeos, modificados y agravados bajo ciertos aspectos por factores sociales hijos del ambiente. La raza negra aportó sus supersticiones, su sensualismo, su impulsividad, en fin, su psiquis africana. La raza amarilla trajo la embriaguez por el opio, sus vicios homosexuales y otras refinadas corrupciones de su secular civilización. . . . La raza negra es la que bajo muchos aspectos ha conseguido marcar característicamente la mala vida cubana, comunicándole sus supersticiones, sus organizaciones, sus lenguajes, sus danzas, etc., y son hijos legítimos suyos la brujería y el ñañiguismo, que tanto significan en el hampa de Cuba.*

(The white race influenced the Cuban underworld with its European vices, modified and aggravated in certain ways by social factors, subject to the environment. The black race brought its superstitions, its sensualism, its impulsiveness; ultimately, its African psyche. The yellow race brought the intoxication of opium, its homosexual vices, and other refined corruptions of its secular civilization. . . . It is the black race that in many respects has left its characteristic mark on the Cuban bad life, passing on [to Cuba] its superstitions, organizations, languages, dances, etc., and its legitimate sons are sorcery and ñañiguismo, which are so significant in the Cuban underworld.)

The Cuban body as a whole is sick, Ortíz tells us, and the disease can be localized in Afro-Cuban expressive culture:[4]

> *Los tipos de su mala vida han de parecerse, como los de su vida buena, pues así como la enfermedad se desarrolla según las condiciones fisiológicas del individuo en quien hace presa, así el hampa es un reflejo de la sociedad en que vegeta.* (1973a:9)

(The types of [Cuba's] bad life have seemed to be similar to those of its good life; just as
a sickness develops according to the physiological conditions of the individual on which
it preys, so is the [Cuban] underworld a reflection of the society in which it grows.)

Mullen (1987:118) points out that Ortíz's pervasive use of metaphors of disease in
this early work reflected the discourse of medical scientists such as Robert Koch
and Louis Pasteur, whose work in the late 1880s focused on the microorganism as
the locus for the origin and development of disease. Ortíz broadened this discourse of pathogeny to refer to Cuban society as a whole; his idea of a cure for *la
mala vida Cubana* was to civilize (read deafricanize) Cuba's black population—in
Martínez Furé's words, seventy years later, "to eliminate negative folklore."

THE POWER OF POSITIVIST THINKING

Ortíz's most influential mentor in the early 1900s was the Italian positivist Cesare
Lombroso, who wrote a prologue-letter for *Hampa afro-cubana: Los negros brujos,*
and, by association, Lombroso's student and colleague, Enrico Ferri. Both Lombroso and Ferri considered themselves to be criminologists, though Lombroso
was a physician who worked as an Army psychiatrist and Ferri a trial lawyer. Ortíz
spent most of the three years between 1902 and 1905 studying with Lombroso and
Ferri in Italy, absorbing and modifying their theories of criminal typologies (i.e.,
anthropological types correlated with habitual criminal conduct). Most disturbing among Lombroso's and Ferri's analyses of the criminal is the idea of the "born
criminal," an atavistic creature who reproduces "primitive" traits and habits of the
(evolutionary) past, and who can be readily identified by certain physical characteristics. Although Lombroso goes into great detail in many of his works regarding the skeletal shape, earlobes, finger length, height, and other features of the
born criminal, he sums up the typical criminal physical type so: "In general, many
criminals have outstanding ears, abundant hair, a sparse beard, enormous frontal
sinuses and jaws, a square and projecting chin, broad cheekbones, frequent gestures, in fact a type resembling the Mongolian and sometimes the Negro" (Lombroso 1968:xviii).

Prominent scientists of the 1880s and 1890s objected to Lombroso's theories
and determined that Lombroso's criminal type had no basis in biological fact,[5] and
yet Lombroso's work was considered seriously by British, French, Spanish, Italian
(and Cuban) criminologists throughout the 1880s, 1890s, and into the twentieth
century, until a few years after Lombroso's death in 1909. In the introduction to a
revised edition of Lombroso's *Crime: Its Causes and Remedies,* prominent crimi-

nologist Maurice Parmelee summarized one of the main criticisms that scientists of previous generations had directed at Lombroso's work:

> Lombroso seems to have been somewhat ignorant of biology, and especially of the theory of heredity. This is indicated, for example, by the loose way in which he uses the term, "atavism." . . . It is very evident that many of the criminal characteristics which Lombroso calls atavistic are not hereditary in their origin, but are cases of arrested development either before or after birth. (Parmelee in Lombroso 1968:xxxi)

One of Lombroso's notable examples of "atavistic" behavior was tattooing, which he seemed to believe was an "inherited habit." In Lombroso's view, tattoos, along with some of the physical characteristics mentioned above, were enough to convict a man of a crime, lack of real evidence notwithstanding. Of a man accused of robbing and murdering a rich farmer, for example, he writes:

> Upon examination I found that this man had outstanding ears, great maxillaries and cheek bones, lemurine appendix, division of the frontal bone, premature wrinkles, sinister look, nose twisted to the right—in short a physiognomy approaching the criminal type; pupils very slightly mobile . . . a large picture of a woman tattooed upon his breast, with the words, "Remembrance of Celine Laura" (his wife), and on his arm the picture of a girl. He had an epileptic aunt and an insane cousin, and investigation showed that he was a gambler and an idler. In every way then biology furnished in this case indications which joined with the other evidence, would have been enough to convict him in a country less tender towards criminals. Notwithstanding this he was acquitted. (Lombroso 1968:437)

Lombroso condemns the man because of his physical characteristics, habits, and troubled relatives (he hypothesized a continuum between "born criminals," "morally insane people," and "epileptics"). Following Lombroso's example, Ortíz seems to have taken this methodology to its logical extreme by racializing the notion of crime in Cuba, relying on the broader physical characteristics of a biological construct of race, and then locating specific vices (habits) in racial types (whites, yellows, and blacks). It is no surprise that Ortíz finds the most grievous of those vices in *la raza negra,* given the Social Darwinian roots of his training, which posited a gradual sociophysical evolution from dark races to light, and given the quickly changing nature and composition of Cuban society at the end of the nineteenth century.

The Ten Years' War (1868–1878), though it had established that Cuba's black community could mobilize itself in an insurrectionist military campaign, had not resulted in the total emancipation of Cuba's slaves. The emancipation of all

Cuban slaves was formally and practically accomplished only in 1886, by which time Cubans of African heritage were beginning to realize the possibilities of their own political power as a means of gaining civil rights. By 1902, they had organized their own political party (Partido Independiente de Color). As historian Aline Helg (1995:15) notes, from the 1870s through the 1895 War for Independence and into the twentieth century, "Afro-Cubans took advantage of the new spheres for challenges that were beginning to open and conducted their own struggle within the larger movement against the colonial power . . . using the domains in which Spanish authority was weak, such as religion and culture, to organize independently."[6]

The physical characteristics outlined by Lombroso must have been easily applied to Cuba's (colored) underclasses; what is surprising is that the Asian community was let off the hook so easily. Perhaps this is because Cuba's Asian population was much less of a presence than its black population. The 1877 Cuban census listed 199,094 people of African heritage (including mestizos) and only 47,116 Asians;[7] by 1899, the Cuban census listed 1,052, 397 *blancos;* 234,738 *negros; 270,805 mestizos;* and only 14,857 *asiáticos* (Serviat 1980:181). If there had been only 14,000 people of African heritage in Cuba in 1899, one wonders whether Ortíz would have had the motive to write *Hampa afro-cubana: Los negros brujos*. As it was, however, the growing numbers and independence of Cuba's black community "incited the white elite to make more explicit the ideology of white supremacy. . . . Social Darwinism and positivism provided the intellectual framework in which the elite reflected about race and Cubans" (Helg 1995:16). Published in 1906, *Hampa afro-cubana: Los negros brujos* was a timely and haunting reflection of white Cuban fears.[8]

Ortíz diligently followed Lombroso's methodology in locating his object of study. Lombroso spent several years studying the characteristics of criminals in Italy's jails, implicitly relying on the Italian judicial system to identify his subject. Ortíz, too, relied on the Cuban judicial system; but Ortiz, rather than visiting Cuba's jails, learned most of what he knew about "Afro-Cuban criminals" from reading *Los criminales de Cuba y D. José Trujillo* (1882), a 471-page compendium of Havana Police Captain Trujillo's more than five hundred cases spanning fifteen years, from December 1866 to December 1881.

LOS CRIMINALES DE CUBA

Published in Barcelona, *Los criminales de Cuba y D. José Trujillo* was edited and arranged by Carlos Urrutía y Blanco. The core of the book is Urrutía's collection and summary of cases that the dashing and persistent Don José Trujillo y Mona-

Figure 6.1. Oval sketch of Don José Trujillo y Mon-
agas, from frontispiece of *Los criminales de Cuba*
(c. 1881). (Courtesy of the Bancroft Library, University
of California, Berkeley)

gas dealt with during his fifteen-year tenure at the Havana Police Department (see
fig. 6.1). Each case has a number, and each number refers to a criminal (and sometimes to several). In most cases, the criminals have been sketched by an artist, so
many of the almost six hundred pages of the book contain an oval likeness of one
or two of the (mostly) men. The sketches are reminiscent of the many sketches
in Lombroso's and Ferri's works, and imply additional, if unstated, evidence against
the accused. Here is an example of one of the early entries:

> *Número 29: Moreno Benito Congo, natural de África, soltero, de 26 años, fogonero y emanci-*
> *pado, consignado a D. Eduardo Yesser. En 14 de Julio de 1867 lo detuvo Trujillo, porque a las*
> *ocho y media de la noche hirió en la espalda al moreno Justo Criollo, esclavo de D. Juan Campos.*
> *Remitió el agresor a la cárcel a disposición del Sr. Alcalde Mayor de Belén, y el paciente al Hos-*
> *pital Civil, iniciando las correspondientes diligencias sumarias, en cuya tramitación, se enfermó*
> *el Benito, y trasladado al Hospital, falleció en 24 de Mayo de 1868.* (Urrutía y Blanco 1882:35)

(Number 29: Moreno Benito Congo, born in Africa, bachelor, age 26, fireman and
emancipated, assigned to Don Eduardo Yesser. On 14 July 1867 Trujillo detained him,

because at eight-thirty at night he [Benito] inflicted a back injury on moreno Justo Criollo, slave of Don Juan Campos. Trujillo dispatched the aggressor [Benito] to the jail at the disposition of the Chief Mayor of Belén, and sent the patient [Justo] to the Civil Hospital. While Trujillo was initiating the appropriate indictment proceedings, Benito became ill. He was moved to the Hospital, and died on May 24, 1868.)

From these few sentences emerges the life—and death—of an "Afro-Cuban criminal." The backgrounds and social statuses of all the actors are evident even in their names. Moreno Benito Congo tells us his social standing, his color, and even his possible provenience. The title *moreno* is used for Benito instead of "Don,"[9] and it signifies his color, which is similar to *trigueño*,[10] or the color of dark wheat (darker than *pardo*, which is a synonym for *mulato*). Because he is referred to first by his color and only later by his first name, we know that his social standing is near the bottom of the ladder. His last name, "Congo," jumps out as a regional and ethnic marker, a detail magnified by the fact that this twenty-six-year-old bachelor was born in Africa. His parents are not listed, a poignant omission inasmuch as all of the criminals born in Cuba at least have the comfort of their parents on the next line of the police summary. (Moreno Pedro Vizcochea, also born in Africa, and also a bachelor at the time of his arrest in 1879, is listed as having "Incógnito" and "Incógnita" as his father and mother. Pedro, twenty-one years old at the time, also used the surname "Congo" while he was in prison [Urrutía y Blanco 1882:254].)

Benito was said to have injured Moreno Justo Criollo, another combination of names that speaks volumes. "Moreno" tells us that his skin color was similar to that of Benito's, and the addition of Criollo implies that Justo was born in Cuba of African parents (Pichardo 1985:191).[11] Justo (which means just or righteous one) was a slave, according to the report, whose master was Don Juan Campos. Benito was *emancipado* (found on an illegal incoming slave ship and "emancipated" by the Spanish government), though not a "free man" (he had not bought his liberty), a status made clear by the fact that he was "assigned" by the Spanish government to Don Eduardo Yesser. The act of emancipating shipboard Africans in the 1860s and 1870s offered no guarantees of financial independence or social status, and often augured ill for the unfortunate Africans.[12] The emancipated Benito was then forced to work for Don Eduardo Yesser (a surname which in English conjures up images of subjugation and obedience), probably for grueling and unpaid labor in the cane fields.

Benito harmed Justo, according to the report, yet, oddly, Benito was the one who fell ill during Trujillo's indictment proceedings, and then died ten months later. What were Trujillo's indictment proceedings? Interrogation? Threats? Beatings? It is possible that Benito became ill only from nervousness and fear during the proceedings, although that reaction in and of itself might tell us something about the reputation and perceptions of the Havana Provincial Police in the second half of the nineteenth century. Many of the reports in *Los criminales de Cuba* suggest similar circumstances of arrest and mistreatment; the dark-skinned alleged criminals were often detained or arrested by Trujillo because they looked suspicious, or because a third party accused them of indulging in "scandalous behavior." In many cases, Afro-Cuban suspects were jailed for eight months or more as a result of being charged with petty crimes such as stealing a hat or a round of cheese, or carrying a razor, and not infrequently died in prison.

Although "guilty until proven innocent" seems to have been the modus operandi for Trujillo when dealing with Afro-Cuban suspects, this attitude was often tempered by a curious paternalism. Urrutía y Blanco often notes that "Moreno X" or "Pardo Y" has changed his ways since his arrest and is now living a quiet life, or is actually a respected member of his "native" community, despite his crime. These narratives emphasize the point that any text inscribes the contemporary perspectives of its time. In this example, what seems evident is the belief in the civilizing or rehabilitating potential of incarceration, especially for Cuban blacks. Consider the following excerpt:

> *Número 74: Moreno José Teodoro Cárdenas y González, natural de la Habana, soltero, de 23 años, albañil, hijo de Juan de la Cruz y de Belén. En 18 de Diciembre de 1868 lo capturó Trujillo por hurto de una caja de vinos y lo remitió a la Real Carcel a disposición del Juzgado de Belén, que con aprobación de la Excelentísima Audiencia lo condenó a siete meses de Presidio, que cumplió el 20 de Octubre de 1869. Este individuo, además de esa condena, ha sufrido cinco más de encierros impuestos por distintos Juzgados, y ha tenido quince ingresos en la Real Carcel por cuadrillero y escandaloso, heridas, por llevar armas, faltas a los agentes de la Autoridad, reyertas, homicidios y amenazas. En la actualidad, y como lo hizo siempre, reside en el barrio de Jesús María, donde, como en los circumvecinos, es respetado y temido por los de su clase, aun entre los más valientes de ellos.*

> (Number 74: Moreno José Teodoro Cárdenas y González, born in Habana, bachelor, age 23, bricklayer, son of Juan de la Cruz and Belén. On December 18, 1868, Trujillo captured him [José Teodoro] for the theft of a case of wine and dispatched him to the Royal Prison at the disposition of the Judge of Belén, who, with the approval of the jury, condemned him to seven months in the Presidio, which he completed on October 20, 1869. This individual, in addition to this sentence, has suffered five additional jail sentences imposed by various Judges, and has been in the Royal Jail fifteen times, for being a scandalous gang member, inflicting injuries, bearing arms, committing

offenses against agents of authority, getting into fights, homicide, and threats. He is now living in the Jesús María neighborhood, as he has always done, where, in his surroundings, he is respected and feared by those of his class, even the bravest of them.)

It should be noted that José Teodoro was arrested only two months after Carlos Manuel de Céspedes's October declaration of revolt against Spanish rule, which initiated the Ten Years' War. Although initially the rebels proclaimed themselves in formal agreement with the abolition of slavery, by December 1868 they had decided that the abolition of slavery would have to follow their victory, rather than precede it. Slaves could help fight in the rebellion only with permission of their masters, according to Céspedes. Any persons fomenting slave rebellions independent of Céspedes's revolt were subject to the death penalty. As of April 1869, however, competing rebel groups on the island drew up the Reglamento de Libertos, which stated that all people on the island, regardless of color, were free, or *libertos*. When José Teodoro went into prison in December 1868, he was still a slave, but when he got out in October 1869, he might have been considered a free man (see fig. 6.2).

Urrutía y Blanco's compendium of Trujillo's cases contains important information about the attitudes of white colonial *peninsulares* and *criollos* toward Cubans of African descent on the eve of emancipation in Cuba. The excitement and chaos surrounding the impending rebellion against Spain and the unpredictable actions of more than one hundred thousand potential *libertos* led to a crackdown by the Provincial Police Force on all of Havana's inhabitants, but especially those of African heritage. Interestingly, most of the criminals in Trujillo's casebook are white, of Spanish descent. Urrutía y Blanco (1882:448) cites 533 *peninsulares ibéricos*, 475 *cubanos blancos*, 137 *cubanos de color*, 56 *extranjeros*, 62 *asiáticos*, 16 *africanos*, and 211 *"indefinidos,"* for a total of 1,490 criminals processed by Trujillo over a fifteen-year period. More than one thousand white criminals to little more than 150 criminals of African heritage is an overwhelming ratio. Yet much of the evidence to support Ortíz's thesis for *Hampa afro-cubana: Los negros brujos* that criminal behavior was an Afro-Cuban trait came from this casebook. Rather than reflect an objective truth about the color of crime, the obsession with Cuba's black population as the criminalizing infection of the country suggests that white Spaniards and white *criollos* living in Cuba at the turn of the century were deeply frightened by the prospect of a free black population and channeled this fear into imagined or highly exaggerated possibilities of theft, sexual assault, and witchcraft.

Figure 6.2. Oval sketch of José Teodoro Cárdenas
y González, from *Los criminales de Cuba* (c. 1881)
(Courtesy of the Bancroft Library, University of
California, Berkeley)

CUBA AND THE ATLANTIC SLAVE TRADE

Only the relatively recent and conscious emphasis on Cuba's African origins has
allowed its scholars to begin to come to terms with its history of annihilation and
exploitation. Walterio Carbonell's *Crítica: Como surgió la cultura nacional* (1961)
marks a turning point in the postrevolutionary Cuban understanding of the history of slavery. Carbonell suggests that the slave revolts, oral culture, and religious traditions of nineteenth-century and early twentieth-century Afro-Cubans
were the real roots of the Cuban revolution, thus implying that the legitimate suc-
cessors to the revolution were, in fact, Cuba's long-oppressed black population.
Carbonell's work was immediately banned and its author imprisoned, so threatening did the young revolutionary government find his suggestions (interview

with Carbonell, August 1992; see also Helg 1995:253, n. 22). More recent works by such respected scholars as Carlos Moore (1988) and Lourdes Casal (1977, 1989) provide a less radical view of the political role of Cuba's black population, yet have also provoked pointed rejoinders from the Cuban government and occasional censorship.

Considering that roughly 50 percent of the Cuban population was of African descent in the mid-nineteenth century (Scott 1985:7), and that interracial unions were common (though not legally binding),[13] one begins to understand the demographic and psychological depth of Cuba's Africanness, and the fear that began to overwhelm Cuba's white population by the late nineteenth century as it considered the possibilities of emancipation.

It is useful to consider Cuba's role in the Atlantic slave trade to gain a more nuanced understanding of how the prevailing attitudes about Cuba's black population at the turn of the twentieth century might have been influenced by the events of the nineteenth century. Some of the first African slaves landed on Cuban shores in 1511, and under Spanish rule, Cuba continued to import slaves until the early 1870s.[14] The indigenous Arawak and Taino peoples were annihilated by Spain's invasion and colonization of the island during the first two centuries of the slave trade. Spain then imported African, Asian, and Yucatecan laborers to "replace" the indigenous peoples who were to have worked on Cuba's sugar, tobacco, and coffee plantations. The heaviest volume of Cuba's slave trade occurred during the middle decades of the nineteenth century, in accordance with the height of Cuba's sugar production.[15] Cuba's burgeoning sugar economy in the middle decades of the nineteenth century depended on the plantation system, which in turn depended on slave labor. As a result, Cuba continued to import slaves clandestinely for several decades after its representatives had signed treaties abolishing the slave trade.

Cuba's specific role in the Atlantic slave trade can be best contextualized within the scope and depth of the atrocity as a whole. Philip Curtin's *The Atlantic Slave Trade: A Census* (1969) provided important data for estimating the total number of slaves landed alive in the Americas during the four long centuries of the Atlantic slave trade. Curtin, basing his work on an exhaustive review of shipping registers and a reevaluation of secondary sources, estimated that roughly 9.5 million slaves had been landed alive in the Americas between 1451 and 1870, with a margin of error of 20 percent (1969:88–89). Basil Davidson, in his revised version of *The African Slave Trade* (1980), uses Curtin's estimate as a starting point, but warns that Curtin's estimate is low, and thus adds Curtin's 20 percent margin of error for a more accurate assessment.[16] Davidson arrives at a figure between 11 and 12 million slaves landed alive during those four centuries, a figure considerably less than the 15–20 million generally believed to have been correct by scholars in the first half of the twentieth century (Davidson 1980:95), and more than Curtin's well-respected but somewhat conservative estimate.[17]

Cuba figures directly in the difficulty in estimating the total number of landed slaves. One of the main problems, it seems, is that although slave trade to Cuba was technically to have ended in 1820 with the instigation of the British policy of patrolling the African coast and searching ships for slaves, between 1820 and 1860 the clandestine slave trade flourished; consequently, official documents of this time period are not a reliable source for accurate estimates of initial importations and the number of slaves who arrived alive. Even taking into account the unreliability of official documents during these decades, most estimates show that roughly 250,000 slaves were landed in Cuba during this "clandestine" period (an average of roughly 9,000 per year). In *Slave Emancipation in Cuba* (1985:10), Rebecca Scott calculates that the total number of slaves imported to Cuba between 1840 and 1867 was 246,798. Both Curtin and Manuel Moreno Fraginals, Cuban author of *El ingenio* (The Sugar Mill) (1978), agree that between 1817 and 1860 roughly 450,000 slaves were landed alive. And according to Davidson (1980:91), roughly a million slaves were landed alive in Cuba between 1791 and 1840, although not all of them stayed in Cuba.[18] All of these estimates overlap the period of the theoretically illegal slave trade, and, when taken together, imply that the legal sanctions against the slave trade periodically levied by Britain against the Spanish government during the first half of the nineteenth century did very little to stem the flow of slaves to Cuba.

Britain was at the forefront of the abolition campaign, and, with the United States, succeeded in abolishing its slave trade as of 1808. France and Denmark had abolished their slave trades in the 1790s, and most of the newly formed Latin American republics had abolished their slave trades before 1820.[19] Spain and Portugal, however, remained outlaws. Indeed, although Britain signed treaties in 1815 and 1817 with Spain and Portugal, respectively, to gradually abolish the slave trade, Herbert Klein (1986:247–248) notes that "through constant prevarication," Spain and Portugal were able to continue their slave trades until well into the second half of the nineteenth century. "The Spaniards," he continues, "whose Cuban possession remained their most important colony, refused all demands for abolition, or carried out meaningless abolition decrees which did not stop the trade."[20]

The general picture that emerges here is that under Spanish rule, Cuba was one of the least conscientious countries in stemming the slave trade, and that it indeed found ways to evade the abolition laws that other European powers (under pressure from Britain) were obeying with little or no incident. Further, Cuba was one of the major importers of slaves; according to Curtin (1969:88–89), (Portuguese) Brazil, (French) Haiti, and (British) Jamaica were the only countries that imported more slaves than Cuba.[21] Cuba was also comparable to Brazil in the marked lateness of both its "abolition" of the slave trade (1868 for Cuba, 1850 for Brazil), and in the final emancipation of its slaves (1886 for Cuba, 1888 for Brazil). In short, Cuba absorbed one of the largest and longest influxes of African slaves in the New World and was reluctant to give up this most profitable endeavor, prolonging its illegal trade for several years after the law prohibiting such traffic came into effect.

FEAR AND LOATHING IN HAVANA

By the late 1880s and the early 1890s, the possibilities of emancipation were becoming clearer to all sectors of the Cuban population, with Cubans of African heritage standing to gain political, economic, and social power at the possible expense of white Cubans. The new social order created fear and confusion among Cuba's white population. Helg (1995:17–18) posits "three stereotypical images of Afro-Cubans, corresponding to three levels of fear." The first stereotype was that Cuba's black population was an organized and determined polity, full of hatred for its white "masters," which led to the fear that blacks would successfully revolt, like the Haitian blacks did in the 1790s, thus making Cuba a black republic. The second stereotype was that Afro-Cuban culture amounted to no more than "magic, witchcraft, criminality, and anthropophagy," leading to the fear that this "African barbarism," if left unchecked, would stamp out Cuba's white, Western civilization. The third stereotype was that all Afro-Cuban men were sexually rapacious, which created the fear that if these sexual savages were left to their own devices they would most certainly rape Cuba's white women, thus polluting the perceived racial purity of Cuba's ruling classes. These stereotypes and fears were easily translatable into crimes in the minds of Spanish and Cuban whites—the possession of a razor or a knife might help foment a rebellion; religious gatherings for Lucumí, Congo, or Abakwá ceremonies had to be outlawed because they were "barbarous"; and no interaction between a black male and a white female could be permitted, for such fraternization could lead to rape.

This ideology of racialized crime worked in tandem with rumors about and arrests of members of *ñáñigo* or Abakwá societies. The first *ñáñigos* in Cuba were an elite brotherhood of African-born *carabalíes* (slaves from the Calabar region of Cameroon), who were legally incorporated in Regla in 1836, under the protection of the *cabildo de nación carabalí* Apapá Epí.[22] The first *cabildos* appeared in Cuba in the mid-1500s[23] and were fraternal mutual aid societies for slaves organized and partially controlled by the Catholic Church. As Cuba's black population increased dramatically during the nineteenth century due to the increase in slave importations mainly from West Africa, so increased the visibility and membership of the *cabildos*. Immortalized by Ortíz's "La fiesta cubana del Día de Reyes" (1920) and again the subject of another essay in "Los cabildos afrocubanos" (1921), by the 1880s the festivals of the *cabildos* had become a recognizable and important aspect of public life in Havana. But the Ten Years' War and the process of emancipation in Cuba (1880–1886) had catalyzed ideologies of assimilation among Cuban whites. If Cuba's black population was to enter into white society, it would have to leave behind its most evident and visible Africanisms. The *cabildos* were eventually seen by assimilationist Cuban whites as regressive and divisive entities, forming an obstacle to black Cuba's assimilation into white Cuban society. Beginning in the late 1870s, and culminating in specific laws passed by the provincial government in 1882, 1884, and 1888, respectively, the religious activities of *cabildos* were curtailed and finally prohibited, gradually turning them into nothing more than loosely affiliated social clubs. By the late 1880s, demoralized and "deafricanized," many of them had ceased to exist (Castellanos and Castellanos 1990:250–252; Ortíz 1921:22–24).

Though the first Abakwá society made its home in a *cabildo,* there were few similarities between the two groups. Like the *cabildos,* the Abakwá *potencias* (societies) gained political and economic power during the nineteenth century, but unlike the *cabildos,* much of this ability to *resolver* (resolve problems, get things done) took shape well beyond the circumscriptions of the Catholic Church. *Cabildo de nación* Apapá Epí, in which the first *potencia* made its home, had a legal dispensation to exist, like many other *cabildos de nación* since the 1820s,[24] having paid for a governmental license for its residence (Urrutía y Blanco 1882:364), and so could not be legally dislodged without governmental decree. The second *juego* (society) of *ñáñigos* was formed with the grudging permission and eventual patronage of the Apapá society. There was some debate within the Apapá society regarding whether slaves born in Cuba *(criollos),* rather than in Africa *(africanos),* should be allowed to form or even join these *juegos.* Eventually, however, the Acabatón *juego* was formed, consisting of twenty-five *criollo* slaves from rich slave houses in Havana (Urrutía y Blanco 1882:364).

Little more than twenty-five years later, the first white *juego* (Ocobio) was formed in 1863 in the ninth district, by the *juego* Bacocó, of the second district of Havana. The members of Bacocó were punished for selling the secret of the *ñáñigo* society to white people, because, according to Trujillo's understanding, this secret should not even have been known by people of mixed race *(mestizos)*, much less white people *(blancos)*, inasmuch as white people had brought so much misery to the people of Africa. Nonetheless, *ñáñigo juegos* of *negros, mestizos,* and *blancos* sprang up all over Habana province, and by 1880, Trujillo and Urrutía reported that there were eighty-three *ñáñigo* societies in the province, five of which were white (Urrutía y Blanco 1882:370–372).

These societies demanded fierce loyalty, and their initiation rites were based on the Carabali "Leopard" societies of the Calabar region of West Africa. The response to an offense against a *ñáñigo* was certainly physical punishment, and possibly a fight to the death. The *ñáñigo* societies acted much in the same way as unions *(sindicatos),* collecting dues and making sure their members were able to work. Most of these *sindicatos ñañigueros* focused on the dock workers of Cuba's western ports, so that all loading and unloading of ships' cargo in Havana, Matanzas, and Cárdenas (just east of Matanzas) was controlled by the *ñáñigos.*[25] As early as 1839, black *ñáñigos* were arrested for congregating under Spanish colonial laws prohibiting illicit gatherings, and by 1876 the Abakwá society itself was specifically targeted in a law prohibiting its very existence (Ortíz 1921; Sosa 1982; Helg 1995; D. Brown 2001). By the end of the nineteenth century, *ñáñigos* had become fused in the popular imagination with all Afro-Cuban religious traditions and societies (see Angel Carreras 1985:78–79; Helg 1995:107; D. Brown 2001, chap. 1).

Urrutía (and Trujillo) easily came to the conclusion that crime and *ñáñigos* were positively correlated. Consider the reportage of the following case (which also includes a near-death experience, causing an apparent rejection of the wicked ways of the Cuban underworld):

> *Número 104: Moreno Enrique Horruitinier, (á) Sucumbento, natural de la Habana, soltero, cocinero, de 19 años, hijo de Luís y de Micaela. En 29 de Junio de 1874 lo capturó Trujillo por estar reclamado como miliciano prófugo y como portación de una navaja. Este individuo, cuando sólo tenía 17 años, ya pertenecía a la sociedad de "ñáñigos," y como tal y por cuadrillero, escandaloso y quimerista, fué preso en 13 de Agosto de 1872. Después, en los años de 1874 y 75 sufrió otras prisiones por heridas graves y homicidio, siendo objeto una vez de reyerta en cuestión de partidas, y de la cual salió gravemente herido. Actualmente, ha variado en su modo de ser y observa una conducta regular.* (Urrutía y Blanco 1882:116)

> (Number 104: Moreno Enrique Horruitinier, alias Sucumbento, born in Havana, bachelor, cook, age nineteen, son of Luís and Micaela. On June 29, 1874, Trujillo captured him for deserting the military and for carrying a razor. This individual, when he was

only seventeen years old, already belonged to the *ñáñigo* society. As such, and because he was a gang member as well as a scandalous and quarrelsome person, he went to prison on August 13, 1872. Afterward, during 1874 and '75, he suffered other prison sentences for inflicting serious wounds and homicide, as he was the cause of a card fight, from which he emerged gravely injured. Lately, he has changed his ways and is observing fairly good conduct.)

Because Horruitinier (Sucumbento) was a member of the *ñáñigo* society, it was no surprise to Urrutía that he had already been sent to jail in 1872. Toward the end of the book is case number 470, in which thirty-five men were arrested for participating in a *ñáñigo* meeting in 1881. (Such meetings were declared illegal in 1876 by royal decree.) Interestingly, only two of these men are listed as *pardo* or *moreno*—the rest were white, according to their titles (Don José Rodríguez Ramos, Don José López Fernández, and so on). The *juego* that was arrested was likely Ecoria Efor, in the third district, the second of five white *juegos* to be established in the province of Habana (Urrutía y Blanco 1882:369). Immediately following case number 470 is a twenty-page section that deals with the *ñáñigos* or Abakwá societies, detailing the history, evolution, and dispersion of these societies in Cuba.

It is important to note here that the attitudes of white Cubans about race were not developing in a nationalist vacuum in the 1880s and 1890s. The Spanish colonial government effectively joined forces with the U.S. occupying army during this time in an attempt to keep the island dependent on one or the other colonial master. In an attempt to weaken the multiracial independence movements of the 1890s—comprising Cubans of all hues, in accordance with the heartfelt goal of Cuban independence leader and martyr José Martí—the Spanish colonial regime intensified existing racial hatred and fear. The leaders of the independence movement, both black and white, tried to demonstrate that Spain's ulterior motive in its racial fear-mongering was to quell Cuba's chances for independence. Furthermore, the United States, then at the height of the Jim Crow period, directly exacerbated the racist sentiments of Cuba's white elite during its intervention and occupation of the island beginning in 1898 (Perez 1983). Theodore Roosevelt, a racist in his own right, led U.S. soldiers into Cuba, and, upon his return, wrote columns about the "lack of valor" of U.S. black soldiers under fire (Kaplan 1995). Moreover, the United States intervened in Cuba right after Plessy v. Ferguson, the 1896 Supreme Court case that established the "blood purity" rules in the United States, at the height of the separatist paranoia.[26] In its intervention, the United States sided with the elite racist sugar landowners and helped turn Cuba into a version of the American South. Castellanos and Castellanos (1990:294–298) note that the practice of lynching free people of color in Cuba was introduced during the U.S. occupation, likely by U.S. soldiers.

From the end of the nineteenth century through at least the first decade of the twentieth, the combination of a well-fueled racism and an obsession with *ñáñigos* led to a general trend of subsuming all Afro-Cuban religions under the rubric of *ñañiguismo,* which provides the context in which Ortíz's work was written and received.[27] The fever pitch reached its height with the murders of two white children, ten-year-old Celia and twenty-month-old Zoila, in Havana in 1904. These two murders occurred within four months of each other, and both were attributed to *brujos,* or sorcerers, despite the weak and circumstantial evidence linking either case to *brujería.* Celia was found dead with a knife in her throat (likely "resisting rape," according to the popular press), and a local, illiterate black man was identified by one witness as the suspect, although other witnesses provided quite different descriptions of the suspect's height and physique. Sebastián Fernández (known as Tin-Tán by his friends), the chosen suspect, was sentenced to death on December 4, 1904, with an execution date to be arranged in the following months. He was found hanged in his cell on April 6, 1905. (Helg notes that less than a week after Tin-Tán's death, "the policemen who had arrested him were decorated by the government" [1995:109].)

The case of La Niña Zoila stirred up even more public animosity and fear toward Cubans of African heritage, because after the infant Zoila was kidnapped her heart was removed. Her kidnapping and apparent "ritual murder" were rumored to have been connected to the *cabildo* Congo Real in Gabriel (outside of Havana), whose members were said to require her blood and heart to prevent the deaths of certain black women and children in the community. An African-born former slave, Lucumí Domingo Boucourt, who lived in the countryside at least thirty miles away from Gabriel, was arrested for the crime because he was a "well-known *brujo.*" El Negro Bocú, as he came to be called, and his alleged accomplice, Víctor Molina, were garroted in January 1906. "From the 1900s to the 1920s," notes Helg, citing a 1987 interview with Argeliers León, "white Cuban children were taught by their parents to run away at the sight of a black man carrying a bag, because he could well be a brujo ready to kidnap them" (Helg 1995:113).[28] Most of the original informant/performers of the Conjunto Folklórico were born around the turn of the century (between 1890 and 1910), and so were born into this atmosphere of fear and loathing in Havana. The *brujos* of the 1920s became the *héroes* of the 1960s.

THE EVOLUTION OF ORTÍZ'S THINKING

Ortíz cites all these cases of *"brujería,"* as well as many more he collected from the popular press of the early 1900s, in the penultimate chapter of *Hampa afro-cubana: Los negros brujos*. The book, in fact, is a curious mixture of excerpts from the local press, scientist musings, and gossipy narrative. Critical theorists Edward Mullen (1987) and Antonio Benítez Rojo (1988) observe that this mélange of narrative discourses marks Ortíz as a postmodern writer, rescuing him from the realm of positivist theorists. But if Ortíz can no longer claim membership in the Social Darwinists' club, then his role as omniscient narrator, now exposed as fragmented and multivocal, also becomes less reliable.

Ortíz's early work seems to have been in complete agreement with the popular racist notions of his compatriots. His writing not only resonated with this broadly supported ideology of racial inequality, but also propagated it. Only by locating and echoing the pulse of Cuba at the turn of the century could Ortíz begin to sound his own understanding of Cubanness. For Ortíz, the end of the 1920s marked "a rupture with criminology" (R. Moore 1994:38), as well as a rejection of his earlier, Lombroso-inspired ideology of Afro-Cuban "atavism" (see, e.g., Ortíz 1929). In May 1936, Ortíz sponsored the first ethnographic conference on the music of Santería (featuring *batá* drummers Pablo Roche, Aguedo Morales, and Jesús Pérez), and in late 1936 Ortíz founded the Sociedad de Estudios Afrocubanos, dedicated, as he wrote in the first issue of his journal *Estudios Afrocubanos*, to helping "whites and blacks know and recognize each other reciprocally in Cuba, and to feel jointly responsible for the historical force that they integrate." In 1940 he introduced his now famous metaphor for Cubanness, the *ajiaco* (a spicy, enduring stew of leftovers).

A la cazuela iba todo lo comestible. . . . Todo se cocinaba junto y todo se sazonaba con fuertes dosis de ají, las cuales encubrían todos los sinsabores bajo el excitante supremo de su picor. De esa olla se sacaba cada vez lo que entonces se quería comer; lo sobrante allí quedaba para la comida venidera. Así como ahora saboreamos en Cuba . . . dejados de una comida para la del día siguiente, así se hacía siempre con el ajiaco original. (1940b:155)

(Into the pot went anything that was edible. . . . Everything was cooked together and seasoned with strong doses of hot pepper, which covered up the duller ingredients with an exciting burning sensation. Each time they would take out from the pot what they wanted to eat; the leftovers helped constitute the next meal. And then as now we still relish in Cuba . . . the leftovers of a meal the following day, always made from the original *ajiaco*.)

The *ajiaco* definition of Cubanness can be understood at least as a metaphor for an appreciation of cultural and racial difference, if not absolute racial equality. But one is left to wonder: are the "exciting burning sensations" ignited by Afro-Cuban performance traditions? In an earlier version of the article, delivered at a conference that same year at the University of Havana, Ortíz had honed the metaphor. He characterized Cuban culture as having been produced by the "disintegration" of the *ajiaco*'s basic elements in the eternal boil of the cauldron, which elements, having been distilled to their most elemental essences, have mixed together to create their own unique character: *"mestizaje de razas, mestizaje de culturas"* (Ortíz quoted in Iznaga 1989:51).

Ortíz published his theory of "transculturation" several months later, in his well-known book *Contrapunteo cubano del tabaco y el azúcar* (1940). His neologism was mainly a response to Melville Herskovits's coining of the term *acculturation* (1938) to describe what happened to black cultural traditions in the New World during and after slavery. For Ortíz, the term implied acquiring a new culture, but it did nothing to explain the loss or transformation of the aggressed culture. The term *transculturation* was better, he believed, because it "encompassed all phases of the [cultural] parabola." Ortíz likened the transculturative process of Cuba's population of Spanish and African heritage to the copulation of two individuals: "the offspring always has something of both parents, yet it remains distinct" (Ortíz quoted in Iznaga 1989:56).

In 1942 Afro-Cuban scholar and literary activist Rómulo Lachatañeré published *Manual de santería (el sistema de cultos lucumís),* the first scholarly attempt in Cuba to understand Santería as a religious system and contextualize it in (then) contemporary Cuba. Lachatañeré was prolific and outspoken: his book *¡¡Oh Mío Yemaya!!* appeared in 1938, his four-part work on the religious system of the Lucumís appeared in 1939 in *Estudios Afrocubanos,* the *Manual* appeared in 1942, and his later work was published posthumously in most of the issues of *Actas del Folklore* (1961), after his death in 1952. Lachatañeré critiques Ortíz's early approach to Afro-Cuban studies (starting with *Hampa afro-cubana: Los negros brujos*) in the preface of *Manual de santería,* asserting that Ortíz's method of analysis was "totally inadequate for coming to a definitive solution to the discussion [on Afro-Cuban religions]"; he added that even though Ortíz had greatly modified his first approach and criterion in later publications, "there still has not appeared a single work that addresses the true nature of Afrocuban beliefs" (Latchatañeré 1995:9). Later, in the same preface, he notes the French sociologist Lucien Lévy-Bruhl's influence on Ortíz's work, using a quotation from Ortíz's "La religión en la poesía mulata," (1937b) which implies that blacks have a "paralogic mentality which does not analyze the cause of phenomena" (Lachatañeré 1995:10). Although Lachatañeré does not claim to provide the "definitive solution" to an analysis of Afro-Cuban religious traditions, his ground-breaking efforts to understand them as religious systems (not as witchcraft), and to characterize their practitioners as priests (rather than as witches), raised the intellectual bar for subsequent analyses of Afro-Cuban religions.

Perhaps as a result of Lachatañeré's criticisms, Ortíz moved more swiftly away from the scientific racism and overdetermined metaphors that had informed his earlier publications. In 1946 he finished and published the influential *El engaño de las razas,* in which he refuted most of the racist tenets of Social Darwinism he had relied on at the turn of the century. And by 1950 Ortíz was fully involved in the observation and documentation of Afro-Cuban religious performance. Although he may not always have admired the technical proficiency or aesthetic values of Afro-Cuban religious musicians and dancers (R. Moore 1994), he was able to in-still in his students a sense of the importance of these performance traditions for understanding twentieth-century Cuban identity.

Rafael L. López Valdés, a student of both Ortíz and León, noted in an inter-view with me (January 7, 1992) that even Ortíz's use of the term *afrocubano* in the early part of the twentieth century emphasized the potential importance of "black Cuba":

> The possibility of black Cuba, of Afro-Cuban influence playing a role in the forma-tion of a national Cuban culture had been negated until Ortíz emphasized this poten-tial by using the term *afrocubano.* . . . The term *afrocubano* in the 1940s played an im-portant part in emphasizing the importance of African influence in Cuba. Many important cultural figures in Cuba in the early decades of the twentieth century— including Alejo Carpentier, Amadeo Roldán, Fernando Ortíz, Nicolas Guillén—were part of the Afrocubanista movement. This movement started certainly by 1906, with the publication of Ortíz's book *Los negros brujos,* and then continued for several decades, renewed with each publication by Ortíz.

In fact, the comprehensive works of Fernando Ortíz on Afro-Cuban tradi-tions spawned a series of studies on *folklore afrocubano,* a term popularized by Ortíz himself to describe the panoply of African-based religious and secular tra-ditions in Cuba. But Ortíz's relationship to the Negritude movement that was taking shape elsewhere in the Caribbean and Francophone Africa is complex. Although he is considered by some to be the father of Afrocubanismo, he just as easily represents the deeply ingrained racism of the period.[29] Ortíz's brand of

Afrocubanismo, though focused on Cuba's population of African heritage, was not necessarily aimed at improving their lot in life. Ortíz was a white, Spanish- and Cuban-educated scholar who had a deep, if objectifying, interest in all things Afro-Cuban. Mullen (1987:115) notes that it was "remarkable" not only that *Hampa afro-cubana: Los negros brujos* became "the point of departure for an extensive exploration of 'Cubanidad' (a search for the Cuban national essence)," but that this seminal work "was written by a man who spent the better part of his early life outside of Cuba, and thus could hardly be considered 'typically' Cuban." It is also remarkable that Ortíz started his career with such a negative perspective regarding the intrinsic value of his subject.

Ortíz's scholarly interest and support did not necessarily translate into black empowerment, which was part of the point of Negritude in other countries—empowerment despite and independence from a largely white colonial intellectual superstructure. Rather, Ortíz's work and perspective allowed for further objectification and romanticization of Cuba's blacks through the continued exposure of their "positive folklore." Through his students, and their students, and other cultural leaders of the Afrocubanista movement, the process of publicizing and exposing certain aspects of Afro-Cuban religious traditions as "positive folklore" continued up to and through the Cuban revolution of 1959.

LOCATING AFRO-CUBAN FOLKLORE

Widely varying interpretations of Cuba's racial composition have fueled both prerevolutionary and postrevolutionary constructions of twentieth-century Cuban identity. Cuba's population has alternately been described as "primarily European" and "essentially Latin-African" during the same time period, with census statistics available to back up either claim.[30] Although statistics can be manipulated to support almost any agenda, what seems to be at issue here is the construction of race in Cuba, and, more specifically, the potentially vast difference in perceptions about race on the part of the census sponsor, the census taker, and the census participant. Of immediate importance here is that the conditions of nineteenth- and early twentieth-century Cuban blacks are evoked and carefully shaped first as a socioeconomic nadir from which to improve, and later as the basis for the revolution's preliminary ideas of a national Cuban culture, many of which were manifested in the Teatro Nacional and the Conjunto Folklórico, along the lines of the performative structures set up by Ortíz.

Martínez Furé's understanding of "Afro-Cuban" and "folklore" is put into daily

practice as he helps shape the *espectáculos* of the Conjunto Folklórico, and many
of those ideas were first formulated in his book:

> I decided to write a book in response to other people's reactions to Cuban popular
> traditional culture—people who called it witchcraft, primitive, etc.—but I had to write
> it within the framework of a socialist country. Let's face it, we're not in Paris, or Lon-
> don, or New York—we're in Cuba, in a socialist country. . . . But I'm not in favor of
> interpreting folklore as something that should be in museums, something that can't
> be touched, something exotic. It brings me back to Don Fernando's [Ortíz] phrase:
> *ciencia, conciencia, y paciencia* [science, conscience, and patience]—the science to ap-
> proach the study of my ethnicity, the conscience to give responses that are relevant
> to the Cuban of today, and the patience to proceed in defining myself, to determine
> who I am. I didn't come from Spain, nor did they bring me from Africa. I know that I
> am an Antillean, a Hispano-African, an African American, and a man. . . . For me, that
> which is Cuban is in a constant process of dialectical enrichment: In 1840, the *batá*
> drum was an African drum; in 1936, it was an Afro-Cuban drum; in 1992, it is a Cuban
> drum. (Interview, July 1, 1992)

Although Martínez Furé used both *Afro-Cuban* and *folklore* early in the interview and in his book, later in the interview he maintained that he rejected the use
of both terms, because the way in which they are used in Cuba now is contrary
to the way in which they were first conceived and used by Ortíz. According to
Martínez Furé, Ortíz used the term *Afro-Cuban* as a means of emphasizing Cuba's
African heritage in response to the racism that had gripped the country during
slavery, through emancipation (1886), and into the twentieth century. *Afro-Cuban*
is now considered a racist term because it implies that in Cuba there exists a white
culture and a black culture, which "is simply not true now: our culture is *mestiza*—
Afro-European."

In other words, the term *Afro-Cuban* no longer corresponds to the racial climate in Cuba, and is not only racist, but redundant, because, theoretically, all
Cubans are "Afro-Cubans." The term *folklore,* according to Martínez Furé, is not
only racist but also classist, for it refers back to prerevolutionary concepts of
"high" culture and "low" folklore, with the high, valued culture belonging almost
exclusively to the white Cubans of European heritage and the low, devalued folklore belonging almost exclusively to the black Cubans of African heritage. *Folklore,* then, like *Afro-Cuban,* is no longer a relevant term because it does not correspond to Cuba's now ostensibly raceless, classless revolutionary society.

It is useful to compare Martínez Furé's vision and critique of *folklore* (and *Afro-*

Cuban, or what Alberto calls ("black") with that of the *responsable* (head) of the CFNC percussion department, Alberto Villarreal. I asked Alberto about his understanding of the term *folklore* as it related to the work of the Conjunto Folklórico during our September 1992 interview. Alberto's vision of "folklore," like that of Fernando Ortíz, refers specifically to the religious performance traditions of Cuba's African-based population:

> We [the members of the Conjunto Folklórico] are looking for a way for folklore to be a principal source in Cuba, because really, from the point of view of art, the principal source for Cuba is the Conjunto Folklórico Nacional. . . . So every time that Cuba's folklore is to be represented in other countries, they send us [the Conjunto Folklórico]—they don't send the Ballet or the Orchestra.

> Of course, folklore has always been a little bit off to the side, which can be understood as the attempt to eliminate it by people who don't understand how the Conjunto Folklórico was founded. There have been people who have wanted to eliminate the Conjunto, too, because they said we are religious, we are black—but now they know that they can't eliminate the Conjunto. *Because no country can eliminate its folklore* [emphasis mine]. To represent a country's folklore is like representing its flag. They have finally realized this. So, for this reason, there has been more of an effort to educate foreigners than Cubans on the part of the Conjunto. Because all those foreigners who come to Cuba to learn about art come to the Conjunto Folklórico Nacional. FolkCuba is very famous, and so we ourselves, the integrators of the Conjunto, are famous because everyone who comes here from abroad comes to see us—like you.

SACRED CRIMES AND MISDEMEANORS

Ortíz's work on Afro-Cuban religious traditions from the beginning of the twentieth century racialized crime and "folklore" (which, according to Ortíz's definition, included Afro-Cuban religions), merging the two categories. In fact, Ortíz's understanding of the sociology of crime sets up the possible parameters for a "transformation" from sacred to secular. Initially he locates the sacred within the realm of the criminal with his book *Hampa afro-cubana: Los negros brujos,* and this widely read and broadly absorbed misrepresentation of Afro-Cuban religious performance allows for the absolutely elastic interpretation and recontextualization of these ritual events to the 1950s, and into the postrevolutionary era. In other words, if these ceremonies were initially viewed as crimes by the scholar who spent most of his adult life documenting them, then it is no great stretch to view them now as commercially viable tourist events. Ortíz participated actively in interpreting sacred practice as crime, and then reworking that "crime" into spectacle.[31] The criminalization of sacred practice was gradually replaced with "spectacle-iza-tion," as Ortíz began to organize public presentations of formerly private (and often prohibited) Afro-Cuban religious performance. In both ways, Afro-Cuban religious practice became decontextualized, disembodied, disempowered.

But if, as Mercedes Cros Sandoval (1979) asserts, Santería is a "mental health-care system" for the shock of exile,[32] what does it mean that sacred intent is con-fused and conflated with criminal intent? Is it simply the collision of cultural values, or is there something theologically valid about seeing crimes and misdemeanors in Santería rituals? The physicality of sympathetic magic, in which one sheds the blood of a bird instead of the blood of a human, works because the stand-in or metaphor can be disassociated from the primary source only in a limited way be-fore it loses its ritual and symbolic power: blood is blood and flesh is flesh; wine and bread won't do.

It is precisely the blood sacrifice that riles up nonpractitioners. In Hialeah, Florida, in Miami-Dade County (home to hundreds of thousands of exiled Cubans), only in 1993, after years of litigation, did the Church of the Lukumí Babalú-Ayé (an institution dedicated to the practice of Santería, led by *obbá* Ernesto Pichardo Plá) finally win its case: the Supreme Court ruled that the ani-mal sacrifice practiced in Santería was protected under the Constitution's basic freedoms of religious expression. In Cuba, even until the early 1980s, religious prac-titioners of Santería were routinely arrested on their way to initiations, their cars or trucks brimming with animals and occasionally Santeros. According to Carlos Aldama Pérez and Alberto Villarreal, the animals would be confiscated and the occupants thrown in jail for a few weeks.

During the late 1960s these religions experienced a small surge in popularity and appreciation in Cuba, partially due to the revolutionary regime's nascent pol-icy of celebrating Cuba's African heritage, manifested primarily in the Conjunto Folklórico's performances. But during the 1970s and 1980s, as a result of the Cuban government's redoubling of its efforts to enforce "scientific atheism" in Cuba (Kirk 1989; C. Moore 1988a), practitioners of these African-based religions were again actively intimidated and oppressed.[33] During the decades of the 1970s and 1980s, atheist revolutionaries maintained a consistently pejorative evaluation of practitioners of African-based religions in Cuba, which was a continuation of prerevolutionary pejorative and classist attitudes. Practicing Santería openly in Cuba during that time evoked the same type of discrimination that existed before the revolution, which meant, Rafael López Valdés told me, that the Santero or Ba-balawo would be regarded as intellectually inferior and primitive and would not be eligible for high-level government jobs because they were not "politically integrated."

An important subset of the prisoners of color who were freed and subsequently directed toward the United States in the 1980 Marielito exodus from Cuba were practitioners of Santería.[34] Although discrimination against religious practitioners through the 1980s and into the 1990s typically has taken the form of limited employment opportunities and exclusion from the Cuban Communist Party, every time a Santero or a Palero wants to hold a ceremony, he still has to ask for permission from the police, and, even now, permission is occasionally denied. Although there is no hard-and-fast rule for determining who will be able to practice Afro-Cuban religions in peace, those Santeros and Paleros who are more likely to be granted permission to hold ceremonies usually have cooperated with the Cuban government's Ochatur project: "positive" folklore for the new millennium.

NOTES

1. After helping to found the troupe in 1962, Martínez Furé was dismissed for sexually explicit public behavior in Spain during the troupe's first international tour in 1964. (During the almost forty years of the Franco regime, sexually explicit public behavior was illegal and covered a multitude of acts, from prolonged kissing to teenage groping to any public displays of homosexual affection.) Martínez Furé rejoined the group as its *asesor* in the late 1970s. (See chapter 5 for an extended analysis of the first international tour of the Conjunto Folklórico.)

2. See Mullen (1987:112) for an entertaining look at the misguided, yet not undeserved, reverence with which people who have never read Ortíz's work regard him.

3. Ortíz was likely influenced in his thinking by such nineteenth-century Social Darwinists as Auguste Comte Joseph Arthur de Gobineau, who wrote that humanity could be divided into three races: the negro race (darkest, intellectually inferior, and closest to animals), the yellow race (inclined toward apathy, mediocre thinkers, and uncreative), and the white race (rational, orderly, physically beautiful, and intellectually superior) (Gobineau 1970). López Valdés turns Ortíz's theory on its side with *Componentes africanos en el etnos cubano* (1985), which explores the many forms of African heritage most Cubans possess.

4. See Barbara Browning's *Infectious Rhythm: Metaphors of Contagion and the Spread of African Culture* (1998) for a compelling critique of a contemporary and parallel pathology of the U.S. "body."

5. See, in particular, Ferri (1967:52–124). Ferri, though a staunch supporter of his friend and mentor, devotes an entire chapter of his lengthy book to "fundamental objections to the anthropological data" of Lombroso.

6. See D. Brown (1989; 2001, chap. 2) for a full discussion of the origins and sociopolitical potential of Afro-Cuban religious organizations, or *cabildos*. See also Serviat (1980:169–176) for a list of registered *cabildos* and other black societies in Cuba.

7. See Scott (1985:90) for the results of the 1877 census. Of additional interest is the fact that in 1846 whites were a minority in Cuba, outnumbered by 47,000 free coloreds and slaves (425,767 whites to 472,985 free coloreds and slaves). By the 1862 census, the population of whites had increased to 729,957, with free coloreds, *emancipados*, slaves, Asians, and Yucatecans making up a separate total of 629,281. See Scott (1985:6–7).

8. Noted Cuban forensic pathologist Israel Castellanos pursued Ortíz's brand of Social Darwinism through 1917 (Castellanos 1914a, 1914b, 1916–1917).

9. Scott (1985:274) notes that in 1893 it became legal in Cuba for men of color to use the title Don, "though white public opinion in some areas still scoffed at such a pretension." Nonetheless, in *Los criminales de Cuba,* all white criminals were referred to as "Don," while all criminals of color were referred to as "Moreno," "Pardo," or "Negro."

10. Pichardo (1985:433, 589). According to Pichardo, social historian and linguist of the period, "Moreno *es sinónimo de* Trigueño; *pero al* Negro *tambien se dice* Moreno *para dulzificar la espresion y nunca* Trigueño; *así como* Pardo *al* Mulato. *En conjunto,* Negros y Mulatos *son la* Gente de color. *Los* Asiáticos *se enumeran oficialmente entre los* Blancos" (*Moreno* is a synonym for *trigueño,* but one also calls a Negro *moreno* [never *trigueño*] to sweeten the expression; this is like calling a Mulato *pardo.* As a whole, *negros* and *mulatos* are people of color. Asians are officially counted among the whites).

11. Pichardo (1985:191) also notes that for a white person, *Criollo* means having been born on the island of Cuba to parents of European (usually Spanish) heritage.

12. Scott (1985:70–71) writes of the plight of the *emancipados:* "They had remained a special category, their labor contracted out by the government. Because employers had so little interest in their long-term well-being, *emancipados* were in some cases treated worse than slaves."

13. See Klein (1986:254–264) and Knight (1970:85–120) for a basic idea of race relations, and, more specifically, miscegenation, in nineteenth-century Cuba.

14. See Luciano Franco (1980:320–390) for a sense of the slow process of dismantling the slave trade in Cuba. Although the slave trade was formally ended in Cuba in 1868, Luciano Franco maintains (p. 389) that Cuba continued importing a reduced number of slaves clandestinely until 1870: "*El maestro Don Fernando Ortíz nos informó que todavía en 1870, el 25 de enero, se desembarcó en Jibacoa, Jaruco (provincia de la Habana) un cargamento de 600 africanos, y que a su juicio, había sido el último llegado a Cuba en plena decadencia de la trata esclavista africana*" (Professor Don Fernando Ortíz informed us that even as late as 1870, on January 25, a shipment of 600 African slaves disembarked in Jibacoa, Jaruco [in Habana province], and that was, to his knowledge, the last shipment to arrive in Cuba, marking the complete decline of the African slave trade). In a July 1989 lecture in Havana, Rafael L. López Valdés asserted that Cuba continued to import slaves until 1873.

15. Rebecca Scott's *Slave Emancipation in Cuba* (1985:7) has useful statistics on the racial composition of the Cuban population in the middle of the nineteenth century. See also Knight (1970:86) for comparative statistics on the growth and racial composition of the Cuban population from 1840 to 1887.

16. Curtin himself revised some of his estimates in the light of new evidence from Dutch and British shipping registers in the 1970s (provided by Roger Anstey and Johannes Postma, in Engerman and Genovese 1975:3–31, 33–49; see also Curtin 1969:107–128), but concluded that the effect of these revisions on his total estimate of 9.5 million would be minor.

17. According to López Valdés, contemporary Cuban scholars consider that roughly 20 million slaves were taken from Africa during the entire Atlantic slave trade, and that the mortality rate was between 40 and 60 percent, leaving a large margin of error (4 million) for those 8 or 12 million landed alive.

18. Curtin (1969:46) cites 702,000 as the total number of slaves imported to Cuba during the entirety of the Atlantic slave trade. However, this figure seems low, given that Davidson and other scholars believe that more than a million slaves may have been landed alive on Cuban soil during a fifty-year period (1790–1840). Regardless, the number was immense. For the sake of ease of calculation and for the sake of consistency with recent Cuban estimates, I use the figure of one million to represent the total of slaves landed alive in Cuba during the Atlantic slave trade, which, by Davidson's calculations, would make Cuba's share of the trade closer to 10 percent of the total, rather than 7 percent, as Curtin (1969:88) has suggested.

19. It should be emphasized here that the abolition of the slave trade by a given country was rarely contemporaneous with the emancipation of its slaves. For example, although England abolished the slave trade in 1808, it did not end slavery until 1834. (Knight [1970:180] claims that Britain did not succeed in abolishing slavery throughout its empire until 1838.) Likewise, the French and the Danes, after having abolished the slave trade in the 1790s, did not emancipate their slaves until 1848. And although the United States abolished the trade in 1808, the Emancipation Proclamation was not enacted until 1863 (and even then applied only to states and territories in rebellion). Cuba and Brazil were the last to abolish both the slave trade and slavery. Cuba's slave trade was abolished (nominally, at least) in 1868, with final emancipation coming only in 1886. Brazil, however, held out for two more years; although its slave trade was abolished by 1850, it did not free its slaves until 1888. See Murray (1980) for a detailed historical account of the political, military, and economic forces that contributed to the century-long fight to abolish the slave trade and slavery in Cuba; see Klein (1986:243–271) for a useful summary.

20. For a detailed description of Spain's "meaningless abolition decrees," see the thoroughly useful chapter entitled "Burla y escarnio de los tratados internacionales" (The mockery and ridicule of international treaties) in Luciano Franco (1980).

21. Again, Curtin's estimates here are likely on the low side, considering that his estimate

for the total number of slaves landed alive in Cuba was 702,000, rather than the roughly one million cited by Cuban and other scholars. He estimates that Jamaica imported a total of 748,000; Haiti imported 864,000; and Brazil imported 3,647,000 during the Atlantic slave trade. If we add a margin of error of 20 percent, as Davidson did, we end up with roughly 900,000 for Jamaica; roughly 1,070,000 for Haiti; and roughly 4,200,000 for Brazil.

22. López Valdés uses Apapá Efí instead of Apapá Epí (1966:25).

23. Ortíz suggests that the *cabildos de africanos* were organizing as early as the fourteenth century in southern Spain, where they joined forces with Seville's gypsy population between the fifteenth and eighteenth centuries because of the two groups' marginal social and economic position (1973c:126–127). From Seville, according to Ortíz, these *cabildos negros* came to the New World, reproducing their organizations wherever there was a large population of Africans (p. 129).

24. See D. Brown (1989; 2001, chap. 2) for a cogent analysis of the sociopolitical function of Afro-Cuban *cabildos* of the nineteenth century.

25. See López Valdés (1966:5–26) for details about the *ñáñigo* dockworkers of Cuba's western ports.

26. Plessy *v.* Ferguson set the precedent for the "separate but equal" justification for segregation that was not overturned until almost sixty years later, with Brown *v.* Board of Education (1954). For more on Plessy *v.* Ferguson, see Plessy (1968), Lofgren (1987), and B. Thomas (1997).

27. See, for example, newspaper accounts from *La Lucha* and *El Mundo,* 1902–1905; see also Angel Carreras (1985).

28. A recent program sponsored by the Ministerio de Educación addressed this specific and pervasive image. The program was entitled "El hombre con el saco" (The man with the bag) (Michael Mason, personal communication, July 2000).

29. Le Riverend (1973), Mullen (1987), and R. Moore (1994) support this dual thesis.

30. For a detailed, recent, and controversial analysis of race in Cuba, see C. Moore (1988a), particularly appendix 2 (pp. 357–365), provocatively entitled "Is Cuba a Black or White Country?"

31. Making crime into spectacle is by no means limited to Cuba, and in fact continues to thrive in the United States. Consider two popular syndicated television shows in the United States, *Cops* and *Emergency 911,* which represent and dramatize "real-life crimes" for the titillation of millions of television viewers.

32. Consider K. Brown's thesis again (1991), cited in chapter 4, as well as Cros Sandoval's study (1979). Both Vodou and Santería can be seen as ways to deal with the trauma of exile—forced exile first from West Africa, exile within the new "homeland" of Haiti and Cuba because of governmental restrictions regarding religious practice, and then voluntary and force exile from Haiti and Cuba within the United States, where these religious practices also do not fit within white Anglo-Saxon "normative behavior."

33. The Cuban government likely redoubled its efforts to enforce "scientific atheism" in

response to criticism by the Soviet Union. This criticism was directed mostly against the Cuban Catholic church, but also had an effect on Cuba's African-based religions because of their syncretic association with Catholicism. Kirk (1989:103) observes that although the revolutionary government did not set out to destroy organized religions, "it clearly tried to inhibit and limit religious activities."

34. See D. Brown (1989:109–120). Citing sociologist Heriberto Dixon, Brown asserts that between 20 percent and 40 percent of the 125,000 Cubans who came to the United States during the Mariel exodus were of African heritage and suggests that a substantial percentage of that group were practitioners of Santería.

7

RESOLVER AND RELIGIOUS TOURISM IN CUBA

According to the cowrie shells of *diloggún* divination,[1] I am a daughter of Ochún, *oricha* of all things golden and sweet, lover of laughter and dance, she who leads Ogún the warrior out of the forest. The shells also tell me that I am a *mortera*, which is not surprising, inasmuch as Ochún is said to flirt with everyone, even Iku (Death), who is her friend and pays her respect. My *camino* is Ibu-Akuaro, Ochún of the quail, happy, hard-working, and a little crazy. Ibu-Akuaro lives where the river meets the sea and has a close relationship with Yemayá Akuara, who also lives there. Ibu-Akuaro refuses to make *trabajos*, attending instead to the infirm and lovesick. A vast constellation of ritual kinships allows my life to be influenced by deities from Yorubaland, Nigeria, via Havana, Washington, and San Francisco. My *padrino*, or godfather, also a child of Ochún, mediates these kinships through his practice as a Santero, much of which relies on a knowledge of the hundreds of *patakíes* of the *orichas*. The *patakíes* and proverbs that emerge through divination at my *itá* predict lightness and laughter, misunderstandings and disappointment, success and enlightenment, fear and envy, and above all, struggle—*la lucha*.

THE DEAD FIND PARKING IN SAN FRANCISCO

She is serene and statuesque, and her smile inspires confidence as her calm eyes look outward. Not a hair is out of place. Three men at her feet look up at her, overjoyed at their good fortune, for she has saved them. But she is not unique. There are hundreds, maybe thousands like her, varying in style and size but not in function. She is La Caridad del Cobre, patron saint of Cuba, sometimes referred to as La Cachita, also known as Ochún, the Yoruba and Santería goddess of the sweet waters (rivers) and romantic love, rescuer of the three fishermen (the three Juans) said to have been drowning in a storm off the coast of eastern Cuba when a mystical vision of La Caridad pulled them to safety. She is often found in Catholic churches, but even more frequently in cemeteries. In churches she is usually made of wood, her garments painted in gold and blue, her eyes peeking out from a recessed alcove; in cemeteries she is typically made of gray and white marble chiseled to cold, peaceful perfection, a baby in her arms and coins at her feet.

In Havana's Cementerio Cristobal Colón (Christopher Columbus cemetery), La Caridad and her myriad sisters act as anthropomorphic markers of Cuba's European and African heritage. The flowing robes, long wavy hair, and Caucasian features of Spanish Catholic Mariolatry appear on all the Caridades, and occasionally one finds a rusted railroad tie wrapped in wire or a small cloth bag with flowers and a dead chicken inside it, remnants of an otherworldly exchange, lying primly at their feet. The two cultures meet here in silence, together for all eternity. But the quiet order of the cemetery is a welcome relief from the noisy chaos of the surrounding streets. In fact, the cemetery seems like a silent city unto itself, with street names such as Calle M and Avenida 8, and with the "neighborhoods" of rich, lighter-skinned Cubans resting comfortably in their one-room mansions while the poorer, darker Cubans are squeezed into concrete boxes, one plot almost on top of the next. There are wooden coffins, recently unearthed, that lie empty along the main walkway, one with a rotting wooden leg still in it. In one section of the cemetery are hundreds of small cement boxes, each with initials and dates, each filled with one set of bones—the physical remains of a life. Near the small cement boxes is a part of the cemetery known as the "Abakwá" section, and it is there that one is most likely to find a dead chicken or dog.

Dead chickens, dogs, and flowers serve as a reminder of an aspect of Cuban life that is inevitable even after death, one that has become even more necessary since the *período especial económico* (special economic period): *la necesidad de resolver,* or the need to "resolve" things. Although the dictionary definition of the word *resolver* is "to resolve," in Cuba, survival means "resolving" things in the broadest sense of the word. *"Tengo que resolverme alimentos"* means "I have to find a way to get myself some food," to solve the omnipresent problem of food shortages. *"Hay que resolver el transporte al trabajo"* means "I have to figure out a way to get to work," that is, to work around the lack of gasoline, the flat-tired bicycles, and the few city buses that traverse their routes perhaps twice in one day. *"Quiero resolverme un par de ténis"* means "I'd really like a pair of tennis shoes," the implication being that one cannot simply go to a store and buy a pair. Rather, one has to trade one's radio or *resolver* a few meals for another family, who, in turn, may know of someone else who has a brother who can obtain a pair of Nike Air tennis shoes for an additional ten pounds of rice or coffee. In Havana, *resolver* implies not only obtaining a goal, but having to struggle to achieve it.

Resolver also implies relying on an informal network of people, both living and deceased, from all parts of one's life; the more people one knows, the more likely one's needs will be *resuelto,* resolved, efficiently. In its earthly context, *resolver* means surviving "on top" of the frequent wreckage and ruin of everyday life in Cuba. In its spiritual context, *resolver* means helping those who have passed on to the next world to rest peacefully, and persuading the dead to treat the living with care and respect rather than with malice and envy. Because the *muertos* "gave birth" to the *santos (los muertos parieron al santo),* the ancestors must be consulted first in all Santería ceremonies.

Practitioners of Santería believe that the dead can influence the living and must be treated with respect, awe, and kindness. All people carry a number of dead spirits with them, and these spirits can be beneficent, malicious, or any combination thereof. Through divination (usually with coconut shells or cowrie shells[2]), a Santero can determine the nature, number, and occasionally the specific identities of the dead spirits who accompany his godchildren. These spirit guides can also be summoned up by *misas espirituales* (spiritual masses), which are led by practiced *morteras* (lit., "deaders"; often women, those who can communicate easily with the dead). It is common practice for religious practitioners to place seven clear glasses of water on a white-covered table in honor of the dead. Some practitioners, in accordance with their knowledge of the tastes and preferences of the deceased relative(s), place a glass of strong liquor, a cup of espresso, a bottle of perfume, a cigar, *azucena* flowers (white, to evoke spiritual clarity), or some other strongly flavored or scented substance preferred by the deceased. These offerings serve to placate and please the dead, thus making them more likely to protect the living.

Although the dead are not considered as powerful as the *orichas,* they allow the divine potential of the *orichas* to manifest itself, and they are believed to be capable of intervening in the lives of humans to effect certain acts of good or evil, such as helping you find a parking place in San Francisco late on a Saturday night (good for you, evil for the person right behind you, who also wanted that space). For the living to allow the dead to communicate with them requires full relaxation and overwhelming concentration, as well as the suspension of fears and disbelief. In my apparently postmodern, outwardly secular, mostly urban life, I have only achieved such concentration infrequently. Talking with the dead takes time and practice, say the elders, but once you talk with them, you can see them, too. They always see you.

RESOLVER: IN THIS LIFE AND THE NEXT

I became very nervous as I waited for my *misa espiritual* to begin. It was to be held at Zoraida and Alberto's house just outside of Havana, the day before the *día del río* (day of the river), which would mark the beginning of my formal, seven-day initiation into the priesthood of Santería. I was nervous because I felt guilty about having ignored my *muertos* (dead relatives/ancestors) for years, despite repeated admonitions from Santeros and concerned friends to "tend to them, pay some attention to them." This mass, meant not only to honor and name my ancestors but also to receive their blessing for my initiation into Santería, could prove to be mortifying. What if they communicated their displeasure at having been ignored by witholding their blessings? What if they rebelled, acted out? (Vases and plates flying around the room, people—myself?—being thrown against the wall, the broken TV set exploding to life and shouting dire predictions. . . .) Or, worse, what if they abandoned me?

I had known of my ancestors' wish to be honored and attended to for the past six years, when my drum teacher (Alberto, from Havana) and a colleague in linguistics (Andrés, from Matanzas) both gave me a spiritual reading (an informal consultation) in which they determined that a strong, older, female presence was my main spirit guide and protector. Alberto and Andrés happened to drop by the house where I was staying on the same day in August 1992. Although neither knew the other, they got along immediately, and Andrés began to give Alberto an impromptu reading of his spiritual life. "You have strong *aché*,[3] and you are a son either of Eleguá or Ogún—one of the warriors. You have a Congo [Congo ancestral spirit] in your house, and an Indio [Amerindian ancestral spirit] by your bed. Both of them protect you. You don't talk much, but you get things done. Am I right?" Alberto nodded, half-smiling, and took his Eleguá *collar*, his sacred necklace, in this case made from alternating red and black beads, out of his shirt to show Andrés that he was correct in his assessment.

Andrés looked pleased with himself. "I'm a bit of a psychic. Really. OK, now tell me what you see when you look at me." Alberto protested at first, saying that he was not very good at readings. After some urging by Andrés, however, Alberto revealed that because the divination tablet of *Ifá* had told him that he was to be a diviner, he might as well start by giving Andrés an informal reading. "You're not happy in your marriage. Or—you weren't, but you've worked things out for now. You're a son of Changó. Your guardian spirit is a tall Lucumí [in this context, a Yoruba slave landed in Cuba], and you keep him busy. You've had a couple of close calls lately." Andrés smiled. "You're right. You'll make a good Babalawo."

They were silent for a moment, and then they looked at me. "You're a daughter of Ochún," said Alberto. "Or Changó," said Andrés. "And you have a very powerful spirit looking after you—she's older," said Alberto. "Is your grandmother still alive?" "No," I said, "both are dead." "Were you really close to one of them?" he asked. "Yes, to my maternal grandmother. I miss her. She was a lovely person." "She looks after you," said Alberto. "Was she big? Kind of fat?" "No," I said, "she was quite thin, especially toward the end of her life." "That's strange," he said, "I'm seeing a big, strong, grandmother looking after you. Don't worry, she loves you, and she takes good care of you. Fill the nicest clear glass you have with water and put it on a white cloth in your bedroom for her."[4]

Andrés, who had been silent for a while, suddenly spoke. "You have a very good relationship with the dead. You have large groups of dead people following you around. You attract them." "You mean spirits?" I asked. "Yes, the spirits of dead people, they follow you around." I was silent, not entirely comfortable with the image. "Just don't go to cemeteries by yourself," he added. "Why not?" I asked. "That's where the dead live, and if you walk by a broken tomb or an open grave, they could make you fall in." I laughed nervously. "Don't laugh; this is serious. Oyá owns the cemetery—she rules the dead, and the wind and the rain. Don't go there by yourself."

The next day I went to the cemetery, not heeding Andrés's warning, but not forgetting it, either. This was before the Cementerio Colón began charging admission, so I felt free to explore it at will, and my will that day was strong. It was a clear, sunny day, so I rode my bicycle there, intending to take some pictures of Ta' José's tombstone, as well as that of La Milagrosa. Ta' José was said to be a famous and powerful Santero,[5] long since dead, but so powerful that he was able to work miracles from the grave. His tombstone was said to be covered with cement thank-you plaques, flowers, and money from his satisfied *ahijados.* The tomb of La Milagrosa, marked by an angelic-looking, life-size marble mother and child, was famous for making barren women fertile, and it was said to be covered with flowers and articles of clothing. Both Ta' José and La Milagrosa are excellent examples of the belief that the dead can resolve things for the living.

When I first entered the cemetery, the sun was shining brightly, and I began taking pictures of La Milagrosa, whose tomb was located not far from the main entrance (see fig. 7.1). As I progressed toward the tomb of Ta' José, however, dark gray clouds began to gather overhead and the wind began whirling about bits of leaves and dirt. It started to rain hard immediately, and within minutes I was soaked through to the skin. I was closer to Ta' José's tomb than to the entrance where my bicycle was, so I decided to struggle on against the wind-slanted rain.

When the wind lifted the rain so that it fell in horizontal sheets and I could barely see, I ran for shelter. The closest shelter was an open marble shell over a tomb, just big enough for one person. I ran inside it and sat down, shivering. Once I was safely inside, the rain subsided and the sun came out again. As soon as I tried to go back outside, however, the rain started falling once more, and the wind howled. I tried to leave the shelter of the tomb three more times, and each time the rain began again. I finally decided to brave the rain and set off again for Ta' José's tomb. The rain and wind repeated their previous performances, and by the time I got to his tomb I was soaked, cold, and shivering once more—and afraid. I was in the middle of the cemetery, disoriented, next to the tomb of a deceased Santero with supernatural powers, and I could see no one else in the cemetery. I looked hard at the many cement thank-you plaques on Ta' José's grave, wanting to leave because I was scared, but also afraid to leave.

"*Estás mojándote*" (You're getting yourself all wet),[6] said a voice. I jumped and immediately looked around, but could see no one. "*Estás mojándote,*" it said again, louder this time. The voice came from the direction of a nearby concave tomb shelter, but because of the grayness and the rain I could not see inside it. I moved closer, and finally saw the vague outline of a man crouched in the corner. My stomach flipped, and I suppressed the urge to run. He got up and moved forward, and I could see that he was an elderly black man, small and thin, with only a few teeth in the front. "*Estás mojándote,*" he said for the third time. Feeling that his simple observation held another message that I couldn't quite grasp, I could only respond, "*Sí, yo sé*" (Yes, I know). He returned to his spot at the back of the open tomb, staring at me, and I felt a subtle pressure to place a few coins on top of Ta' José's grave. Calmer now, I made my way out of the cemetery, and looked back to see their dull metal sheens winking in the rising gray sky. As I got to the entrance, the rain gradually stopped and the sun came out again.

When I told Alberto about my experience in the cemetery, he looked at me with surprise. "You thought we were joking?" I fumbled around for an explanation, and eventually blurted out that because I was not a religious practitioner, not Afro-Cuban, and not even a white Cuban, I felt that perhaps the rules of the religion did not apply to me. Alberto's response was pointed: "So, you can study *batá* drums, and be a daughter of Ochún, and accept the religion for other people, but you won't accept it for yourself. This [the religion] isn't like the *diplo* [shopping]— you can't just pick out what you want and buy it. You have to take the whole thing." I felt ashamed and found out, a poseur, interested in the trappings of the religion but lacking the faith to integrate it into my practice of everyday life.

The next day, when I had regained my nerve and was able to describe to Al-

Figure 7.1. La Milagrosa, Cementerio Cristóbal Colón, Havana, 1992.

berto in detail the rest of the events at the cemetery, he told me that the old man who had correctly observed that I was getting wet in the cemetery was the *guardia* or caretaker of Ta' José's tomb, perhaps one of Ta' José's last *ahijados* or one of his blood descendants. Ta' José's tomb is never left unattended. Alberto also pointed out that I was able to leave the cemetery unharmed because I had reached Ta' José's tomb and showed him respect by leaving coins on top of it. Respecting one's elders and one's superiors is extremely important in Cuban culture, particularly in an Afro-Cuban religious context.[7] To lack respect *(faltar respeto)* in one's thoughts, words, or deeds is a serious thing, and is dealt with strictly not only by the living, but also by the dead. According to Alberto, I should not have gone to the cemetery by myself because this act showed disrespect for him, for the dead, and for my relationship with them. But by making the effort to visit Ta' José's grave and by leaving coins on his gravestone, I made up for this *falta de respeto,* and therefore Ta' José and his guardian then helped me find my way out. *"Tú te resolviste la salida"* (You found a way to get out). My means of *resolver* thus expanded to include the informal network of a deceased Santero and his living *guardia.*

LOS MUERTOS PARIERON AL SANTO

For the remaining month of my stay in Havana that year, and for the following year, I did keep a few glasses with water (sometimes seven) on a white-covered table in my apartment. But then I moved across the country, started a new job, finished my dissertation. . . . And the water evaporated from the glasses, leaving a whitish, sandy film along a ring in the middle, and the cats knocked over the glasses, and after a while I simply forgot about the dead. In 1996, I was told in a reading for the New Year that my main spiritual work for the year would be to make contact with my ancestors. Making contact with them meant filling the glasses with water again, lighting a candle, putting some flowers on my *bóveda* (an altar table covered with a white cloth in honor of the ancestors), and praying to them—and looking into the largest of the glasses and trying to "see" them. I thought about doing this for many months, but each time I came close, my childish fears of ghosts, goblins, zombies, vampires, and werewolves (no doubt fueled by too many episodes of the television show *Dark Shadows*) overwhelmed me. By the time I had gathered up my nerve to see dead people walking around my apartment in a glass of water, it was 1997, and I didn't have to do it anymore. I had successfully evaded my duty to the dead once more.

During the summer of 1997 I needed another *consulta* (divinatory reading, also called *registro*), this time just before I received Ochún, in which the dead were showing some irritation with me, although they still approved my Ochún ceremony. The act of receiving Ochún signaled my formal recognition that Ochún owns my head; that is, I am a child of Ochún, by divination and by reception. Several members of my *padrino's* Havana-based *familia de santo* presided over the quiet, one-day ceremony. Hens, doves, and a guinea hen were sacrificed for Ochún, and many songs were sung for her, after which a *rogación de cabeza* (literally, a prayer for the head, in this case a mixture of cooling white substances, including chalk, cocoa butter, coconut, water, and cotton) was placed on my head in the hope that Ochún would guide me in a more direct and benevolent way in the future.[8]

During this ceremony, the spiritual status of my ancestors with relation to me (loosely called "blessings," or *iré*), came out mostly through the *coco* divination (divination through coconut pieces, which are white on their concave meaty sides, and brown on their convex shelled sides). Rather than *alafia* (all whites—peace and health—good, though somewhat unstable)[9] or *eye ife* (two whites and two browns—good fortune—stable and solid; no need to throw again), the dead answered questions mostly with *etagua* (three whites and one brown—possible struggle, though still positive—potentially unstable; throw again just to be sure), or *ocana* (three browns and one white—one is surrounded by trouble—likely unstable; clarify with additional questions and throw again). I should note here that the dead did not give me the big bad "no" sign, which is *oyeku* (four browns—where the dead "come down"—bad news and very unstable; time to start sacrificing in a big way; throwing the *cocos* again might not make a difference), for which I am grateful.

By the time I became initiated into Santería as a priestess of Ochún in 1998, the dead had become very annoyed. In the many readings I received before, during, and after the ceremony, the dead kept asking to be noticed—flowers, water, *aguardiente* (strong sugar cane liquor), rum, wine, candles, fruit—these were only a few of the demands they made during my *asiento*. During the *misa espiritual,* however, they had not shown irritation, perhaps because the *misa* was specifically for them, a long-awaited formalization of my relationship with, and indebtedness to, my ancestors.

The main message from the three-hour *misa espiritual* was that my spirit guide was a female *familiar* (family spirit) from several generations back, as Alberto and Andrés had predicted, and that she was "evolved." Most of the people at the *misa* agreed that my guide was on my mother's side of the family, likely a great grandmother. The idea of evolved and unevolved spirits is important in the ancestral framework of Santería, because evolved spirits support their human carriers, and unevolved spirits wreak havoc in their carriers' lives, because they do not have the skill or the wisdom to assist their humans. If it is determined that one has unevolved spirits, one can help them evolve by praying for their evolution, leaving them offerings of water, flowers, and white candles, and by becoming more aware of who they are and were, and what they might want to accomplish during their new lifetime. Although it is not uncommon that one's main spirit guide is a family spirit, occasionally one's main spirit guide can be from one's *cuadro espiritual* (spiritual plane). That is, of the many spirits humans bring back with them when they are born, some are likely to attach themselves to the spirit of the newborn not for family reasons, but for reasons of affinity—such as a particular talent or way of being that the child may develop as she gets older. Ideally, the goals of one's spirits and oneself are aligned in reciprocity.

RESOLVER THROUGH *ACHÉ:* THE ESSENCE OF CUBAN SANTERÍA

Although the eminent scholar on Nigerian and Cuban *oricha* worship William Bascom wrote in 1950 that the focus of Cuban Santería is stones, herbs, and blood, I would argue that the focus of Santería is the efficacy and the flexibility of its belief system.[10] Through Santería (literally, the way of the saints), believers can resolve their problems, both spiritual and mundane, by appealing to the deities of this polytheistic, West African–based religion. Bascom's assertion that stones, herbs, and blood are important aspects of the process of spiritual *resolver* in Santería is certainly true in my experience. The *orichas* live within *otanes* (sing. *otán*), consecrated stones whose divine potential is determined previously by a Santero through *coco* divination. These *otanes* are both cooled and washed with the herbal mixture known as *osain,* and then are fed with the blood of sacrificed animals, so that they will have the strength to act on behalf of their mortal children. But the primary focus of the religion is serving the *orichas* so that these divine entities will respond to their adherents. In other words, these *orichas*-within-stones are washed and fed so that the *orichas* will remain amenable to resolving the problems of their children, so that their children will have the *aché* to prevail. In fact, the power of *resolver* can be understood as part of *aché,* or the power to make things happen.[11] It is through *aché* that all life occurs. *Aché* is neither good nor bad; rather, *aché* is motion. It is emotion, demotion, commotion, locomotion—all that moves us in and through the world.[12] *Aché* is divine, and is bestowed on humans by the *orichas.* It is through *aché* that the Santero and the *creyente* find the power to *resolver.*

One can look at all aspects of Cuban Santería through the lens of *resolver,* starting with the initiation process of a religious practitioner *(creyente)* into the religion, a rebirth, and ending with the death of the *creyente,* a transformation of the *creyente* (one who believes, and who honors the ancestors) into an ancestor (one in whom others believe, and whom others honor).[13] A central tenet of Cuban Santería is that all humans belong to an *oricha,* whether or not one chooses to formalize this relationship by becoming an *iyawó* or initiate. Another way of articulating this inevitable relationship between *orichas* and humans in Santería is to say that all humans are children of the *orichas,* or that the *orichas* own our heads and guide us.

Becoming initiated into Santería involves formalizing one's relationship with all the *orichas,* but especially with the *oricha* who owns one's head. If that *oricha* is clearly female, such as Yemayá (deity of the seas) or Ochún (deity of the rivers), that deity is said to be one's mother. If the *oricha* who owns one's head is clearly male, such as Changó (deity of thunder and lightning) or Ogún (deity of war and iron), that deity is said to be one's father. If one's head is owned by an *oricha* of somewhat ambiguous gender, such as Obatalá (deity of wisdom and the intellect), whether the deity is referred to as the mother or the father of the *iyawó* depends on the *camino* (avatar) of the *oricha.* The Santero or Santera who initiates the *iyawó* becomes the *iyawó's* godfather or godmother, respectively, and through this relationship, the *iyawó* takes on the entire ritual family of the initiating house. In this way, the *iyawó* gains numerous additional relatives and *ancestros*—both divine and human—thus strengthening the network of ritual kinship, and the ability to *resolver.*

The potential to negotiate with, and *resolver* through, the *orichas* is inherent in the philosophy of Santería. All of the *orichas* can be favorably influenced by offerings of water, flowers, candles, fruit, honey, candy, liquor, money, fish, birds, or, in serious situations, four-legged animals. Once the *creyente* has been initiated, during which process she finds out through divination the *camino* or road of the *oricha* that owns her head, she can continue to communicate with that *oricha* in accordance with the specific preferences and attributes of the deity. Santería is not only a polytheistic religion with many *orichas,*[14] but each *oricha* also has at least several (and sometimes several hundred) *caminos.*[15] Each *oricha* is generally associated with certain colors, foods, natural phenomena, and sacred attributes, and these associations and preferences become more specific with each *camino* or avatar of the particular *oricha.*

During the seven-day initiation process, the *iyawó* is ritually cleansed several times to get rid of the bad spirits that are believed to have accumulated in her "former" (that is, preinitiation) life. The ritual cleansing not only involves washing the *iyawó* with an herbal mixture, but usually requires shaving the *iyawó's* head, to make explicit the symbolism of cutting away / shaving off the physical reminders of the pain, injuries, and other toxic experiences the *iyawó* might have suffered previously. It is at this time that a mixture of herbs, water, and other secret ingredients that embody the head *oricha* is "installed" (rubbed onto) the *iyawó's* shaved head, after which the *iyawó* sits under a *trono* (throne) bearing the colors and attributes of her head *oricha.* It is from the images of the installation and throne that the initiation ceremony is called *asiento,* or "seating." The head *oricha* is "seated" in the *iyawó's* head, symbolizing the *iyawó's* sacred potential, and then the *iyawó* is seated on the throne, symbolizing the respect she is to be accorded as a result of this sacred potential.[16]

During the several days under the *trono,* the *iyawó* also learns about the preferences and attributes of the other important *orichas* who are related to her "head *oricha.*" For example, Yemayá is sometimes referred to as Ochún's mother or older sister. The two water deities are positively and intimately correlated; thus, Yemayá might be expected to play a caretaking role in the life of a child of Ochún. In this way, the *iyawó* learns about her new family, and is treated by the Santero as the most recent addition to the family, the most "newly born." The *iyawó* also assimilates important information about how to negotiate with the members of her new family, both human and divine. For example, if one's head *oricha* is Ochún, one learns that she especially loves honey and all things gold and brass. If one needs a favor of her, such as help with a lover or some extra money (Ochún is also the deity of romantic love and riches, so it makes ritual sense to ask her to *resolver* in those areas already in her domain), one knows that placing honey and a gold bracelet on her altar near her *sopera* will make her more willing to listen to the request and respond favorably.

The most important thing an *iyawó* learns during her initiation is her destiny, laid out by a professional diviner *(oríate* or *italero)* in an hours-long divination session, typically on the third day of the initiation. It is during this divination session, or *itá,* that the *iyawó* learns about her strengths, weaknesses, potential obstacles in life, beneficial (and malevolent) relationships, taboos she must observe, the best way to make a living given her attributes and defects, and the importance of good character. It is by following one's destiny (i.e., paying attention to and obeying the guidelines for behavior articulated in the *itá* by the *oríate*) that one is most likely to be successful in enlisting the help of one's head *oricha.* According to an American colleague and priest of Santería who was trained in Havana (see M. Mason 1997), the *orichas* need us to follow our destinies in order for them to be able to help us. When we follow our destinies, we strengthen ourselves, and by strengthening ourselves, we strengthen the *orichas,* thus opening the road for spiritual and mundane *resolver.*

DECONSTRUCTING THE SELF: REBIRTH ON SACRED GROUND

My own initiation into Santería was harrowing, which may be part of the point of being initiated. The significance of any religious initiation would be much more difficult to gauge without the physical markers that so often demarcate it (shaving the head, wearing particular clothes, eating specific foods, observing social taboos). Initiation into Cuban Santería is no different in this respect. In Santería these physical markers signify the beginning of a loss of personal agency, an erasure of one's previous self. Africanist Margaret Drewal refers to a similar initiation process among the Yoruba—the *Itefa,* or "establishment of the self"—as the "ritual construction of the self" (1992:64). Santería initiations have their roots in Yoruba initiations, yet I would contend that because the vast majority of people in Cuba and in the United States become initiated later in their lives rather than as small children (as in Drewal's Yoruba examples), their identities must be deconstructed before they can be reconstructed within a ritual context.

In Santería the *iyawó* becomes a "ritual object" during the initiation, with no rights, privileges, or control over the immediate future. Individuality, assertion of will, independence of thought—none of this has a place in the initiation process of Cuban Santería. One is tried, tested, taken to the edge, brought down, and then reborn before the *orichas.* Much of this breakdown and rebirth is accomplished through emotional and physical prostration: sleeping on the floor, eating on the floor, fully prostrating oneself before one's elders in the religion (which means everyone, because the *iyawó,* having just been "born," is the youngest), and doing what one is told to do at all times. The first two days were not so bad. Sleeping on the floor, surrounded by many live (and then suddenly dead) animals was unnerving, but ultimately did not challenge my will or my physical well-being. Spiritual rebirth requires physical sacrifice, and the animals were sacrificed as a strong material substitute for my prostrated self.

The physical discomfort began when the *omiero* (the herbal liquid meant to purify the *iyawó*) began to do its work, plowing through the days of tension and my well-fed past until most of my gustatory remnants, digested and not, had been flushed out several times over. But the *omiero* kept coming. Every morning, for breakfast: a half-cup of *omiero* served in a *jícara* (half of an empty calabash, or *güiro*), a piece of coconut, and a ritually correct number of guinea peppers on top (five, for five is Ochún's number).[17] The wretching and convulsing that characterized my afternoons and early evenings only evoked more of the same the next morning: *omiero* + coconut + pepper. I cried. I developed a fever, plus chills and night sweats. I whined. I asked for the stirred Canada Dry ginger ale and Saltines of my childhood—surely this magical mixture would calm my roiling stomach and tame my twitching intestines. My *padrino* obligingly set off on a challenging mission to find both products (or facsimiles thereof), as well as Pepto Bismol, in Havana. He returned with a bonanza bag, filled with the soothing elixirs of my past. I drank the ginger ale greedily and cautiously bit into a soda cracker. Within twenty minutes I had to rush to the bathroom again, dreams of a panacea shattered by the insistent rumblings of my lower abdomen.

This intense physical discomfort caused me to think differently. Zoraida, Alberto's wife and my *oyugbona* (ritual assistant), called this process *purificación del santo* (the purification of the *orichas*), which she said was meant to cleanse the *iyawó* physically, mentally, and spiritually. I was no longer in control of my destiny (certainly not immediately), and I had to offer myself up to Santeros and Santeras who, I hoped, were authentic and true representatives of divine (and benevolent?) will. As I quaffed the *omiero* during the difficult middle days of the week-long endeavor, I thought ruefully of part of the reading that had come out during my *itá:* "Take care of your health, especially your stomach. Your constitution is more delicate than you think." Like all children of Ochún, my stomach is both my weak point and message-giver: when stressed, I throw up or have diarrhea; when depressed, I become nauseated; when excited, my stomach does flip-flops.

During my *itá,* the divinatory revelation of my past, present, and future, all participants (except the *italero,* my *padrino,* and myself) were smoking furiously. Save those three, six people were puffing strong Cuban cigarettes (called *fuertes* because they are unfiltered and have a high nicotine content) for the duration of my *itá,* which lasted for about five hours. Twice I had silent heaving fits (though there was nothing left in my stomach to regurgitate) because I am allergic to smoke. But because I was an *iyawó,* I had no voice, no choice in whether people smoked in my presence. Each time I tried to speak, I was silenced by the *italero* with the question, "Do you know what it means to be *iyawó?* It means to be a baby. Babies don't talk. You were just born. Sit down and be quiet." Mostly I listened with a growing uneasiness; the *itá* tells one's past, present, and future, and focuses mostly on potentially dangerous trends in the hopes that they can be avoided or at least curbed in the future. Hearing one's character defects laid out in front of strangers and not being able to explain oneself is an exercise in humility and discipline.

I railed inwardly against most of these restrictions during my initiation. I did not act out publicly, as some *iyawóces* do, though I did allow disrespectful thoughts to permeate my consciousness. I began thinking of one of the older woman ritual assistants as *la bruja* (the witch), and softly mimicked certain people in the household (just out of earshot) in an attempt to resist their aggressive attempts to deconstruct my persona. This attitude, mostly made manifest by my occasionally sullen countenance, was no surprise to my ritual caretakers, for they had heard the *italero* say that I had a strong will, too strong, in fact, and that this steely determination was both my great asset and my potential downfall. The *italero* referred to me several times as "the whip of Ochún," suggesting a facet of the sweet Ochún not often dwelt upon by most practitioners and scholars of Santería. "You possess a hardness born of arrogance, and you must work to keep it in check." The battle of wills that occurred during my *asiento* was instructive to me, for it was precisely this hardness of character that the *italero* had warned against. I submitted to the restrictive and uncomfortable sleeping, eating, and washing arrangements, but not without a grudge.

Submission is especially difficult when one has been brought up to be independent, assertive, individualistic, and, eventually, in control. How does one give up one's "right" to know what is happening? My *padrino,* in the manner of many *padrinos* before him, noted that I had it easy in comparison to the *iyawóces* of times past, who were treated as servants in the *casa de santo,* even during the *asiento.* Although I had people telling me what to do all the time (and I could not talk back), at least I was not responsible for completing nauseating and difficult tasks (as were some of the older *iyawóces* and younger Santeras present at my initiation), such as scrubbing the floor clean of the blood and guts and feathers of the *matanzas.* I was simply told, "You can't leave the room," or "You can't talk to anyone," or "You can't go to the bathroom just yet," or "You can't read," or "You can't ask questions." Occasionally my *padrino* would come into the throne room and give me permission to read or write, which allowed me a welcome glimpse of my previous life. For the most part, however, I reflected on the experience of the initiation, my personal relationship with the *orichas* of Santería, and on my past, present, and future—which is, I would argue, the main purpose of the initiation. But enforced reflection does not come easily, particularly when one struggles against the authority that decrees it. Fortunately, the initiation experience is meant to last at least a lifetime, and, as such, merits a lifetime of reflection.

Part of the year-long experience of being an *iyawó* (the *iyaworaje,* or "journey" of the *iyawó*) is meant to evoke the experience being a slave. The very term *iyawó* is translated as both "slave of the *orichas*" and "bride of the *orichas*," which suggests a potentially misogynist equation. Other linguistic markers that support the slavery metaphor emerge in the proverbs, or *odus,* associated with the *itá.* For example, "It is better to be a slave to the *orichas* than a slave to your fellow man" refers to the fate of an *iyawó* should he decide to abandon the religion in favor of secular pleasures (that is, he will become a slave to his fellow man). Phrases that refer to appropriate conduct during the *iyaworaje* also evoke slavery: "You are your *padrino*'s slave until the end of your *iyaworaje.*" Being a slave in the religion serves several purposes, both historical and current. As a slave, one's expectations must be kept in line, but precisely because one's expectations are kept in line, one gains the promise of eventual control over one's life. (If one never expects too much, one will rarely be surprised, and lack of surprise can eventually evolve into resignation, which, in turn, signifies a limited control over a chaotic and unpredictable world.) In addition, being a slave to the *orichas* ensures a certain level of compliance within religious practice, which then serves to propagate religious practice, and thus the religion itself.

Among the most important of the religious practices propagated by this "slavery to the *orichas*" are those behavioral taboos practiced by *iyawóces*. The restrictions to which an *iyawó* must submit are manifold and are mostly dependent on the specific taboos and requirements laid out in her *itá*. But there are some general restrictions that apply to the vast majority of *iyawóces,* such as not getting a haircut for the first year after the initial shaving of one's head during the *asiento,* wearing white for the first year after the *asiento,* sleeping and eating on the floor for the first three months after the *asiento,* eating and drinking using only the white utensils (one cup, one plastic glass, one plate, one bowl, and one spoon) broken in during the *asiento,* abstaining from sexual intercourse for the first sixteen days after the *asiento,* never being outside at 12:00 noon for the first year, not staying out past 6:00 P.M. for the first three months, and not staying out after 12:00 midnight for the rest of the first year. These restrictions serve two main purposes: to maintain the spiritual and physical purity of the *iyawó,* the pinnacle of which was reached during the *asiento,* and to demonstrate the *iyawó's* purity and difference to the outside world—the shaved head, white clothing, and other behavioral restrictions are meant to act as a ritual flag alerting the rest of the community to the *iyawó's* special status.

I experienced these restrictions with immediate trepidation, temporary submission, subsequent rebellion, and ultimate negotiation. Wearing white all the time soon became too much for me. I attracted unwanted attention on the city streets of Los Angeles and San Francisco, and so searched for some flexibility within the prescriptions of my *itá.* I found this flexibility in a work dispensation, requested and granted to me by my *padrino* through *diloggún* divination, which allowed me to dress, eat, and behave like a non-*iyawó* in work situations. Eating on the floor greatly annoyed my husband, so we occasionally planned work activities that included eating out at a restaurant (although I used only a spoon and bowl during these meals). My family was alarmed by the uneven three-months' growth sprouting from my previously shaved head, so I asked and was granted permission to get a trim before I saw them again. (I explained my decision to get initiated into Santería to my parents the day before I left for Cuba. After several hours of discussion, they were more comfortable with the event than I was and seemed most disturbed not by its grander theological implications but by the ritual head shaving. As I left for the airport, my father, wishing me a good trip, and hoping to make light of this otherwise tense situation, said, "Have a nice haircut!") Eventually, I achieved a balance of *iyawó* and non-*iyawó* behavior acceptable to the *orichas,* my *padrino,* myself, my spouse, and my family.

RELIGIOUS TOURISM: SANTERÍA PAYS

As Cuba's political and economic difficulties deepen, one explanation for the recent increase in participation in African-based religions becomes clear. In contrast to Catholicism and Protestantism, Cuba's African-based religions are individualistic and anthropocentric (López Valdés 1985): their function is to resolve problems in the daily lives of mortals with help from the *orichas*.[18] The terms of exchange between the mundane and the divine are clear and efficacious: obey your *itá,* maintain good character (which helps the *orichas*), and you will be aided, directly or indirectly, by the *orichas*. In the context of the African-based religions, Catholicism provides the images (in the form of the *santos*) that help anthropomorphize the *orichas,* thus facilitating human contact with the divine and enabling a more efficient resolution of one's problems.

In a December 1991 interview, Rafael L. López Valdés addressed the individualistic and private nature of one of the most accessible and popular practices of Santería, the *consulta,* and how the "invisibility" of the practice contributes to the erroneous impression that more and more Cubans are becoming atheists.

> If you have a problem, you go see a *babalocha, iyalocha,* or *tata nganga,*[19] in a private consultation, and they use divination to tell you what to do to resolve your particular problem. And again, this *consulta* and this information is not public knowledge. You do what has been prescribed for you, and no one is informed of it. All of this has created the impression that atheism has grown in Cuba because the institutionalized religions in Cuba—Catholicism, Protestantism—have seen a diminution of their flocks. This has created the illusion among those who have formulated programs of scientific atheism that they have been achieving their goal of spreading atheism. However, such a religious vacuum does not exist. The only thing that has been accomplished by the "conditioning" of scientific atheism is an increase in the number of members and practitioners of African-based religions. . . .
>
> To be Catholic, a Baptist, or a Pentecostal requires a public and visible affirmation of one's faith by going to church regularly, becoming part of a religious community, participating in the sacramental processes of these religions. But in the African-based

religions, it's not that way. It is an individual phenomenon. One practices these religions because one believes in them, and one believes in them and practices them because it is in one's interest to do so. As a result, these practices don't have to be public, and in general they aren't public. In general, the great majority of practitioners of African-based religions don't make a public display of their beliefs. This practice is very simple: If you light a candle behind the door for Eleguá, no one sees it. If someone comes to see you, you put out the candle, and no one's the wiser, but you are a practitioner and a believer within a determined religious system.

Since the beginning of the *período especial económico* in 1990, daily life in Cuba has become a constant struggle because of the increasing shortages in food, gas, electricity, transportation, and all sorts of material goods. The *período especial económico* is the official euphemism for the severe economic tailspin caused by the economic and political withdrawal of the former Soviet Union, which had for decades subsidized Cuba's purchase of Soviet gas, oil, and machine parts, and had been paying roughly three times the world market price for Cuba's sugar in an attempt to prop up the island's failing economy. A chance to *resolver* (resolve) one's problems on a daily basis through the divine intervention of one's own personal *oricha* becomes more attractive in this atmosphere of increasing hardship.

The chance to *resolver* one's material problems is directly related to the swelling ranks of Santeros and Santeras in Cuba: the chance to make some *fula* (Cuban/KiKongo slang for hard currency). Cubans aren't the only ones who are becoming initiated into Santería in Cuba. Foreigners from Spain, Mexico, France, Canada, the United States, and other countries in Europe and South America arrive in Havana every month for the seven-day initiation ceremony. Cuba is fast becoming a primary destination for "religious tourism," as it is considered an authentic source for the practice of Santería, Palo Monte, Arará, and Abakwá. In fact, after his visit to Cuba in 1990, the Ooni of Ifé, spiritual head of the Yoruba people of Nigeria, proclaimed that the Cuban people had "nothing to learn" from the Nigerians regarding the practice of *oricha* worship.

Because an important idea behind the initiation process is an immediate and large sacrifice for the sake of improving one's future circumstances, initiation ceremonies are expensive, by both Cuban and American standards. An initiation ceremony in Cuba for a Cuban can cost the equivalent of a year's salary (several thousand pesos); an initiation ceremony in the United States can also cost the equivalent of a year's salary (US$15,000–$20,000). In this way, the costs seem comparable. But when a foreigner gets initiated in Cuba, the cost ratios change drastically. (The rate of exchange in Cuba is about twenty pesos to the dollar.) A foreigner may pay the equivalent of US$4,000 to become initiated into Santería in Cuba, including round-trip airfare, payment to all participants, animals, food, and so forth—a price much cheaper than a similar initiation in Spain, the United States, Canada, or even Mexico. But what happens in the case of "foreign" initiations in Cuba is that the Cuban participants may get paid the "flat" (rather than the "official") correspondence of dollars to pesos. For example, if a Santera is typically paid 100 pesos to be the *oyugbona* (ritual assistant) to a Cuban *iyawó* during the initiation ceremony, she would be paid US$100 to be the *oyugbona* to a foreign initiate. This means that the foreign *iyawó* may generate about twenty times the income as the Cuban *iyawó*, which results in a lot more enthusiasm on the part of Cuban ritual participants for a foreign initiate than a Cuban initiate.

Foreign initiates generate more than hard currency and consequent enthusiasm, however. They also inspire (or demand) ritual variation, as well as constant explanation. Most foreign initiates are less familiar with the ritual traditions and possibilities of Santería practice than their Cuban counterparts, and so they may be subject to uncommon or unorthodox variations. Or, just as likely, they are not accustomed to certain aspects of the initiation ceremony and do not wish to endure them. They request a change here or there, reminding certain members of the community of the fact that "they're paying for this"—and the seven-day ceremony suddenly becomes a five-day ceremony, the *omiero* is held back one morning, the floor suddenly has a mattress on it. . . . And although traditionally the *iyawó* is not supposed to ask questions, many foreigners cannot maintain such disciplined passive acceptance for longer than twenty minutes at a stretch. The questions, perfectly understandable in a European context, keep coming: "Why are you twisting off the head of that bird?" "What is that white thing in the middle of the goat's head?" "How long do I have to stay in this position?" "Why can't I have a pillow?" Eventually, a few get answered—not without several rebuffs. But with each answer, Europe has perhaps succeeded in recolonizing Cuba, just for a moment.

Such changes in the comfort and transparency of the initiation ceremony are encouraged by the Cuban government, which has also gotten into the business of religious tourism. For at least the past seven years, the Cuban government has been sponsoring religious tourism through what is ironically referred to as the Ochatur program. In 1992 I was not able to verify the official existence of the Ochatur program, but in 1994 I heard more about the program publicly. Two Santeros and one Santera whom I know actively participate in the program—one from Guanabacoa, one from Centro Habana, and one from Madruga. The Santero from Guanabacoa, nicknamed Enriquito, tells of his experiences in Tomás Fernández

Robaína's slim volume of interviews, *Hablen paleros y santeros* (1997). Enriquito first notes that his house is visited by "many tourists and foreign personalities who are interested in knowing more about the African roots of our culture" (1997:85). Later on in the interview, he allows that since 1959 Afro-Cuban religions have mostly been seen as something out of context, "folkloric," and "on the way to extinction" (1997:88), but that he was happy to see his religious traditions recognized at all, even if they were misrepresented. By the end of the interview, Enriquito asserts that he is helping his religion to be seen as *una fuerza viva* (a living force) by facilitating the initiations of not only black Cubans but also white Cubans, and not only Cubans but also Americans, Panamanians, Venezuelans, Dominicans, Mexicans, and "even Italians" (1997:89).

At this point in Cuba's evolution of itself, Ochatur and *santurismo* seem to benefit all involved. If a priest or priestess of Santería agrees to participate in Ochatur, he or she may be offered a nice house in an attractive beach location (in which to perform comfortable, picturesque initiations), relatively "free" travel within and without Cuba, and a cut of the profits. Estimates of Ochatur initiations range from US$6,000 to US$8,000, including round-trip airfare, hotel accommodations before and after the initiation, all food, all animals, and all fees to Ochatur and the religious officiants. (I estimate that roughly $1,000 goes to the presiding Santero, maybe $500 to the rest of the participants, $750 for airfare, and $250 for all hotel accommodations and food, and $500 for the animals, which leaves between $3,000 and $5,000 for Ochatur for each foreign initiation into Santería.)

This is potentially big business, although I have not been able to find out official Cuban estimates of how many people are initiated through the Ochatur program each year. The Santeros and Santeras whom I know who have participated in the Ochatur program also maintain their Cuban practices, although such priests and priestesses are occasionally dismissed by Cuban practitioners as "tourist Santeros," implying that they work the religion for money and not for faith. Santeros and Santeras who initiate foreigners on their own (not through Ochatur) are also accused of this, but to a lesser degree, presumably because they are not combining religious practice with working for the government.

LIVING IN A MATERIAL WORLD: SELLING THE SANTERÍA EXPERIENCE

At the end of every FolkCuba program, members of the Conjunto Folklórico and the new graduates of FolkCuba climb aboard a bus headed for Madruga, forty minutes inland from Havana. The bus pulls up in front of a well-kept house, and the door is opened by a large, friendly Santera dressed in royal blue. She welcomes the group to her *casa de santo* and shows them the various rooms, each dedicated to a different *oricha*. Her only request is that we do not touch anything. The altars for each of the *orichas* are brilliant with satins and velvets (blue for Yemayá, yellow for Ochún, red for Changó, and so forth), and the fine porcelain *soperas* gleam in the sunlight streaming through the high windows.

At the back of a large patio, there is a long buffet table heavy with food. Just to the right of the table, creating an arc with their *batá* drums, sit the drummers, ready to play. They play a quick and informal version of an *oru seco* (there is no *igbodu* [sacred throne room] and the *batá* drums are not consecrated, so the religious intent of this performance is contained), and then one of the singers of the Folklórico gets up and starts to call for Eleguá in a short, repetitive phrase. The drummers respond, and then yell to her to move on. They're hungry, and they want to finish this performance quickly so they can eat. The singer zips through Ogún and Ochosi, stays a while on Oyá, and then moves to Yemayá, Changó, and finally finishes with Ochún. During the songs to the last four *orichas,* a few of the dancers of the Conjunto Folklórico move halfheartedly, and a couple of the student dancers get up to join them. The drummers play one more time for Eleguá, and the performance is over. They walk to the buffet table, first in line for food.

This Santera is one of the participants in the Ochatur program, but even before she participated in that, she was inviting interested parties (from Cuba and abroad) to her house to learn more about Santería. Her house is featured in Gloria Rolando's film *Oggún,* and she is invited to most Afro-Cuban events in Havana—art openings, concerts, film previews, dinners honoring authors, receptions honoring poets, and so on. I am told that she and her husband ran a powerful *casa de santo* in Madruga in the 1960s and 1970s. Her husband died in the 1970s, and for about a decade it was difficult to make ends meet. But then she began to make the acquaintance of people who were interested in her house as a "typical *casa de santo,*" and those people knew other people who wanted to film it, or visit it, or hold performances there, and since the early 1980s, she has been comfortable. FolkCuba started in 1985, and graduates of the program started coming to Madruga in 1986.

On one level, it is difficult to see the harm in merging religion and tourism. After all, what about Lourdes, Mecca, Jerusalem, and other destinations of religious pilgrims? The pilgrims themselves might be classified as "tourists" of a sort; and then there are the people who come to see what the religious pilgrims are making such a fuss about, and what they look like while they're on the pilgrimage; and then there are the "closet pilgrims" who are intrigued by the religiosity of a place, but are not "out" enough to just get on their knees and become pilgrims (rather, they stand in awed attention as the pilgrims pass, and follow them into the chapel). (As Dean MacCannell (1990:9) writes, paraphrasing one of his students, "Let's face it. We are all tourists.") Many of the foreigners who come to Cuba to become initiated into Santería are in fact religious pilgrims who are also tourists. An Ochatur official might argue that it is the foreigners who have created this category of combining religion and tourism in the case of Santería, not he.

But the Cuban government has helped this convergence along in many ways, great and small. Ochatur would figure among the great ways, but there are other, smaller ways that are related specifically to the Conjunto Folklórico. The ritual objects used in African-based religions are also represented in each of the troupe's performances, in simplified and popularized performative frames. During every CFNC performance, artistic director Rogelio Martínez Furé or onetime dancer Alicia Santos gives a thumbnail sketch of the characters involved in each piece. The sketch for Ochún includes a reference to her *collar* (in this case, with amber, yellow, and red glass beads), her *abebé* (fan), her colors (gold, amber, and yellow), and her brass bracelets and earrings. The sketch for Eleguá includes a reference to his *garabato* (bifurcated cane), his *collar* (in this case, with red and black glass beads), and his colors (red and black). The symbolism of these objects is distilled during the performance, made accessible to the audience by the friendly and attractive dancers who portray these *orichas* week after week.

The Conjunto Folklórico is not responsible for marketing these objects, but the performances themselves are based on the anthropomorphizing of essentially abstract principles, which facilitates the commodification of ritual attributes. The marketing of Santería commodities in particular is accomplished most efficiently by the dollar stores in every tourist hotel in Havana. The many tourist shops of the Hotel Habana Libre provide perhaps the best and biggest example of the successful commodification and marketing of Santería objects and concepts. In a store that sells mostly souvenirs, rum, and tobacco, a tourist can buy T-shirts with an artist's rendition of Obatalá (the "sky-god" of both wisdom and insanity, and the creator of humankind), Ochún (*oricha* of the sweet waters and romantic love), and Ogún (a warrior *oricha*, "owner" of iron and of violent death).

The artist seems to have derived inspiration from the Peter Max paintings of the 1970s; the *orichas* appear to be both Nilotic and hallucinogenic, distorted and awesome. In an adjoining store that sells mostly perfume and cosmetics, one can buy an "authentic" (so says the tag) *garabato de Eleguá* (cane of Eleguá). Many of the people who buy these objects have been to at least one CFNC performance.[20] They are often in Cuba as part of a study group or package tour, and the Conjunto Folklórico is considered to be one of the highlights of being in Havana, along with catching a show at the Tropicana nightclub and eating at the Bodeguita del Medio (a restaurant Ernest Hemingway is said to have frequented when he lived in Cuba). The Conjunto Folklórico's performance is so simultaneously charming and powerful that there is an immediate impulse to buy something by which to remember it. There is nothing for sale at the Conjunto, but one can usually find something "ceremonial" at the hotel stores, says the Cubatur guide.

The brightly colored glass beads of Santería *collares* wink at customers from beneath the glass display case of the mini-post office in the Hotel Habana Libre. "What are those?" asks a young German-speaking tourist who is sending two postcards home. "*Collares,*" answers the clerk curtly. "How much are they?" "Ten dollars." The clerk turns his back to the woman and puts the postcards in a huge black plastic mail bin. "I would like to buy one," she says. "Which one?" asks the clerk, still with his back to her. "Oh, I don't know, you pick for me." She smiles. The clerk rummages through the tangled strands of beaded necklaces—Oyá, Ochún, Changó, Babalú-Ayé, and Orúnmila. He pulls up Babalú-Ayé (white beads, with dark blue and purple thin stripes) and gives it to her. "*Gracias,*" she says, putting on the necklace. "It looks good with my shirt." He nods once brusquely and takes her money. Babalú-Ayé is the *oricha* of poverty and disease, of illness and infirmity, purveyor of smallpox, he who absorbs (and dispenses) all the suffering in the world. It is true, however, that the beads look good with her shirt.

I enter the largest souvenir store in the hotel, and to my right I see a display of hundreds of Oyá dolls, a few Yemaya dolls, and about thirty generic "congo" dolls. They are all moderately dark-skinned, female, and in nineteenth-century puffy long dresses. In fact, they look like miniature versions of the dancers in the Conjunto Folklórico, down to the details of their dresses. The Oyás wear dresses of multicolored, swirling-patterned fabric and carry horsetail flywhisks. The Yemayás wear royal blue dresses with white trim and carry fans.[21] The "congo" dolls have their hands on their hips and wear gold hoop earrings. They are all smiling saucily, and are $12 each. All the prices here are in dollars, all the customers are *extranjeros,* and all the clerks are Cuban.

Beyond the army of dolls there are several sets of factory-made *batá* drums, roughly $500 for a set of three. The *batá* drums sit amid the cowbells, maracas, *claves, güiros,* bongos, and congas that are crammed into a corner. There are no explanatory labels on any of the instruments, but all of them have price tags. There is a new display of Cuban CDs behind the musical instruments, and the one that catches my eye features the late Merceditas Valdés and is called *Aché.* Merceditas

Valdés, who died in June 1996, was called "La Pequeña Aché" (little one who makes things happen) by Fernando Ortíz. Valdés was one of Ortíz's most celebrated informants and protégés because she knew many of the songs associated with Santería even as a teenager. She was born in the 1920s, and worked with Ortíz during the 1940s, 1950s, and 1960s.

There is a photograph of her on the cover, dressed all in white and wearing her *collares*. She is sitting across from a sculpture of a Babalawo that belongs to the Santería diorama of the museum of Guanabacoa, a part of Havana where Santería and other African-based religions are thriving. She looks animated and her hands are flipped up toward her shoulders, as if in surprise. An *ekeule* divining chain hangs from the Babalawo's fingers, and dried chicken claws rest at his feet. It is a strangely disturbing scene: a staged *consulta* in a museum in a part of town where Santería is an important part of everyday life. I buy an Oyá doll, a few small instruments (*claves*, cowbell, maracas), and the *Aché* CD. These items prove that I was here, and they add another link to the commodification chain.

Tourism reinforces the objectification and commodification of culture, but it is capitalism itself that instills this peculiar ethic of consumerism. I want to buy something simply because of how I was raised, because of my education. I am trained not to stop at the "real-time experience" itself, but to pursue it and "own" it by taking a little piece of it home—through the documentary processes of picture-taking and tape-recording, or through the more tangible means of postcards, hotel coasters, or the hundreds of souvenirs that are available in every dollar-store window. Communist Cuba has realized that the "shop-till-you-drop" mentality emerged with the growth of capitalist-style tourism, and Cuba is reaping the benefits of this well-targeted market, even in the midst of the decade-old *período especial*.

The uncertainties and daily traumas of the *período especial* have also created the need to buy among Cubans—an obsessive mentality born of years of material deprivation. Before 1993, when it became legal for Cubans to possess limited amounts of dollars, it was common for Cubans to give their illegal dollars (typically obtained on the black market or as a gift from friends and relatives) and a shopping list to *extranjeros* as they entered a *diplomercado* or *diplotienda*. In this way, coveted material goods could still be obtained without flagrantly violating the law. If at all possible, the goods would be bought in large volume (five pairs of tennis shoes, three skirts, seven bars of soap), the extras set aside to be used to *resolver* problems in the future. Now that it is legal for Cubans to possess dollars, the dollar has become even more valuable, and the mostly Cuban crowds jam themselves into ill-ventilated one-aisle dollar stores, hoping to buy an electric fan or a bottle of shampoo. For an increasing number of Cubans living in Havana in the post-Soviet era, the growing need to buy things—given the historical background of the revolution's centralized and often free distribution of commodities—translates into a newly heightened meaning of commodities. Life becomes measured in terms of things bought and sold; concepts and ways of life become commodified.

THE CONJUNTO FOLKLÓRICO ON TOUR: SOLD OUT

According to Alberto Villarreal and Ramiro Guerra, respectively the head percussionist and a former choreographer for the Conjunto Folklórico, during the past decade it has become apparent that many younger people are joining the CFNC not necessarily because they love to sing, dance, or play musical instruments, but because they want to travel.[22] Getting an exit visa out of Cuba under other circumstances is prohibitively expensive, and often unsuccessful. The ability to travel without incurring huge financial or political penalties becomes even more attractive when one realizes that travel allows a temporary escape from the growing inconveniences and indignities of everyday life in Cuba. Cuba's declining economy in the 1980s and 1990s has exerted pressure on the troupe, causing performance to be less important than the privileges that might accompany it. With each passing year, said Ramiro, the environment in the Conjunto Folklórico became less and less palatable:

> Traveling became like a cancer in the Conjunto Folklórico. People no longer wanted to join the troupe to perform, but rather to travel. Because, of course, travel means *divisa* [hard currency], which means things and more things. The Conjunto Folklórico has certainly become corrupted by that attitude. It's even worse today.

In essence, said Ramiro, travel is a means to escape from the little violences of everyday life in Cuba: "Each little violence here isn't so much, but taken all together they accumulate into something else. It's like each violent act is a bead on a necklace that becomes heavier and heavier with each bead."

According to Alberto, when the troupe goes on international tours, the members of the Conjunto Folklórico receive part of their salaries in hard currency (that is, currency that can be traded legally on the international market, such as francs, deutsche marks, or dollars). This hard currency provides myriad opportunities to *resolver* long-standing problems in a hurry. If one has been looking for a replacement headlight lamp for a '57 Chevy (vintage American car parts are difficult to find in Cuba), one has a moderate chance of finding it in Canada. Or if one has been looking for a nice compact stereo system, but the prices in the *diplo* stores are too high, one might find it in Mexico for a better price. Travel is now used by the troupe's administration as a bonus in the Conjunto Folklórico, and a performer's ability to *resolver* certain material aspects in his or her life can be seriously impeded by the punitive denial of a request to travel.

If one has performed well, has not caused problems (political or technical), and has enough family members in Cuba to ensure one's return, one will be allowed to go on a two-month international tour to France, Spain, and Algeria. If one has not performed well, or has created problems for the group's internal dynamics or for its relationship with outside organizations, or if one is a little too eager to travel and has no family ties, one will be denied permission to travel. The Conjunto Folklórico's international tours recently have become showcases of the few people who are favored at the moment by the group's directorship. The group is composed of 109 members, and anywhere between ten and fifty of them go on tour at any given time. The carrot (or stick) of travel has become the most effective means of controlling behavior within the group, because it offers (or withholds) material possibilities unavailable in Cuba.

During the last week of January 1996, the Conjunto Folklórico embarked on its first U.S. tour since 1980. Alberto and several other drummers and dancers with whom I had studied in Havana were among the lucky forty-plus members to go on this nationwide tour, and expectations among the performers were high that this would be an enjoyable and lucrative trip. By the end of the two-month tour, however, most members of the troupe were convinced that this was one of the worst foreign tours in the history of the group. Each member was paid roughly US$30 per day, which was supposed to cover expenses only, the result of a law initiated by the U.S. Treasury Department that prevented U.S. organizations from paying Cuban nationals anything resembling a salary. With this small per diem the performers were to purchase food, gifts, and all other "incidentals" (toothpaste, shampoo, cigarettes). Some members went without food for a day or two so they could buy gifts for family members. Some ate only at McDonald's because much of their per diem was spent on cigarettes, which, by Cuban standards, were outrageously expensive in the United States. Others asked for small gifts—a pen, a lighter, a lipstick—from staff members at sponsoring organizations (theaters, universities, community centers) so they could bring something back to their friends and families.

The performance schedule for the tour was grueling; there were very few rest or vacation days built into the trip. Sometimes the troupe would perform twice in one day; at other times it would give an evening performance, ride the bus all night to the next venue, and then start the sound check and staging for that day's show the next morning. When the troupe finally came to Pomona College for its Wednesday night performance on March 20, almost at the end of their tour, the members were exhausted. Although I was excited that my friends were finally coming to perform at my home institution, I, too, was exhausted. I had worked long hours for several months (in addition to my teaching job) with the tour manager in New York, the special events coordinator for the Claremont Colleges, the president and dean of Pomona College, the Music Department, and several close friends to arrange funding, publicity, food and lodging, ticketing, and a reception for the group during its stay in Los Angeles. Despite the difficult acoustics of the performance space and a half-full house (at the last minute, the UCLA Performing Arts Center had scheduled a show at the Wadsworth Theatre in Los Angeles the night before, drawing away a substantial percentage of nearby Pomona's audience), the show was successful and we managed to break even.

My carefully planned "welcome dinner" for the group (grilled chicken, beans, rice, salad, bread, chocolate cake, and an assortment of alcoholic and nonalcoholic beverages), though appreciated, was hardly touched, because the rehearsal and performance schedule did not allow sufficient time to eat. The members snuck bits of cake and wine in between costume changes during the show and wrapped up some of the chicken pieces in their flight bags for the bus trip to San Francisco the next day. At the reception after the show, few of the performers wanted to socialize with people they didn't know, so most of them grabbed glasses of wine in the lobby and went back to their dressing rooms to smoke. I invited the remaining members (about fifteen) of the troupe to my home, where we drank rum and beer and listened to music. We were in good spirits when we first arrived at my house, telling jokes and laughing and dancing. But after an hour or so, many of the performers looked haggard, and a few had fallen asleep on my couch, lit cigarettes drooping from their hands. Alberto pulled me aside and asked quietly whether he could take one of my compact discs home as a gift to Maykel, his older son, because he couldn't afford any of the compact discs in the record stores here. I looked at my collection of hundreds of compact discs and flushed with embarrassment. Yes, I said, take as many as you want.

At about 1:30 A.M. two friends and I drove the performers back to their hotel on a rundown section of Vermont Avenue in downtown Los Angeles, from which they were to leave by 7:00 A.M. for their next show. Our goodbyes were bittersweet; it had been wonderful to share my home with Alberto and the other drummers and dancers, and yet I was left with an almost tangible sense of disappointment. In one evening, I could not make up for the long hours of traveling and performing, the tasteless and greasy fast food, the lack of sleep, the cold weather, the cheap and noisy accommodations, and the conspicuous absence of family they had endured for the past two months. When they returned to Havana at the end of March, what would they have to show for this "historic" tour? What would they think of us? Many fans (including myself), knowing the financial restrictions under which the troupe labored, thrust $20s and $50s into the hands and pockets of performers we knew as they walked up the rickety metal stairs of the motel into their second-floor rooms. *¡Cuídate mucho! ¡Te abrazo, mi amor!* Tears temporarily obscured my vision as I drove back to Claremont along I-10 in the early hours of the morning, the freeway as empty and desolate as my helpless heart.

When I saw Alberto again in the summer of 1997, just before I received Ochún, we spoke again about the Folklórico's U.S. tour. He and his friends were convinced it was the worst tour they had ever experienced. When the troupe got back to Cuba, Cuban customs officials searched them for U.S. currency and expensive electronics, such as Sony Walkmans and Nikon cameras, gifts from friends and relatives in the United States meant for relatives and friends in Cuba. Some members of the troupe tried to hide money in their socks, but the customs officials searched there, too. Such treatment was typical after a foreign tour, Alberto said, but this time it was harder to handle, because the U.S. tour had been so difficult. I can see Alberto and his friends now, arms crossed, watching with resignation the uncertain and intermittent rain of U.S. dollars in the smoky Cuban customs lounge at José Martí International Airport, feeling the weight of their *collares* grow heavier around their necks.

NOTES

1. *Diloggún* is a form of divination common in Santería that employs the use of sixteen cowrie shells. The shells are thrown in the air, and a numerical ratio is assigned to their landing pattern based on whether they land "mouth up" or "mouth down" (cowrie shells have a ridged opening on one side of the shell that is said to represent the "mouth" of the *orichas*). The numerical ratio is used to determine the story or *pataki* that will be told to the person requesting the divination. There are said to be 256 possible landing patterns of the sixteen cowrie shells ($16 \times 16 = 256$), each of which is associated with specific *patakíes*. Some Havana-trained diviners claim that the numbers thirteen through sixteen cannot be divined by Santeros, leaving only 144 possibilities ($12 \times 12 = 144$). David Brown (2001, chap. 3) notes that all the cowries could fall mouth down (producing permutations based on 17, rather than 16), which would indi-

cate "extreme crisis," requiring immediate consultation with Ifá. (For more information on Yoruba-based divination practices, see Bascom 1980.)

2. Each of these methods of divination depends on the correlation between numerical results and Yoruba proverbs and/or states of being. Four pieces of coconut shells *(cocos)*, each with a light and a dark side, yield five broad divinatory possibilities. Sixteen cowrie shells *(caracoles)*, each with an "open" and a "closed" side, yield 256 (or 289, or 144; see the preceding note) divinatory possibilities.

3. *Aché* is life force, the power to make things happen. See again Drewal (1992) and J. Mason (1992).

4. Filling a clear glass with water and placing it on a white cloth away from altars for the *orichas* is a common way of showing reverence for the dead. The dead use water as their medium and are said to appreciate the coolness of white. They prefer to remain apart (that is, their altar space is separate) from the *orichas,* because they are ancestors, whereas the *orichas* are deities. The dead are also said to enjoy potent liquor, strong coffee, and big cigars.

5. Ta' is a truncation of Tata, which is a Congo term of both endearment and respect for an older male relative (by blood or ritual hierarchy), such as father, grandfather, or uncle. The fact that Ta' José is popularly known as a Santero (from the Yoruba-based Santería) rather than as a *tata nganga* (from the Congo-based Palo Monte) could be a result of the blending and mixing of Cuba's African-based religious traditions, or it could be proof of a general confusion about the differences among these religious traditions. In any case, Ta' José's name could be translated as Father Joe, with its priestly implications, or as Uncle Joe, with its avuncular familiarity.

6. In the context of Santería, getting rained on means more than simply getting wet. For many practitioners of Santería, getting rained on is dangerous, because unevolved spirits and negative energies in the air can become distilled by the rain, and thus can more easily enter the vulnerable head of a new or weakened initiate.

7. See D. Brown (2001, chap. 4) and Friedman (1982, chap. 6) for discussions of the importance of divine and mundane hierarchies, and concomitant respect, within Santería performance.

8. Ochún, though generally a sweet and supportive deity, does not treat those children who might be perceived as disobedient with equanimity. (Disobedience in this case often means not tending to Ochún's altar frequently or lavishly enough, or disregarding something Ochún has recommended in a divinatory reading.) If Ochún feels she has been offended by one of her children, she may severely punish the child by suddenly withdrawing Ochún-associated blessings (love, money, health), or by abandoning him or her. Asking for Ochún's benevolence is thus considered an extremely important part of "receiving" Ochún.

9. Some Santeros consider the all-white status of *alafia* to be highly unstable—"the quiet before the storm"—and so always throw the *cocos* again to determine what lies just beyond *alafia,* so as not to be unpleasantly surprised.

10. The information in this section comes from discussions over the past ten years with Cuban, Cuban-American, and Anglo-American Santeros, Santeras, and Babalawos, as well as my own experiences with Santería. There are many published sources on Santería, though the details of its practice vary widely from author to author. Bascom (1950 and 1952) and Duany (1982) provide fairly current and detailed "snapshot" English-language analyses of important aspects of the religion, such as divination and *soperas* (the ceramic receptacles for the baptized stones in which the *orichas* live). Murphy (1992), González-Wippler (1973), M. Mason (1997), and D. Brown (2001), also English-language sources, provide increasingly detailed pictures of how this Afro-Cuban religious practice exists between Cuba and the United States. Díaz Fabelo (1960), López Valdés (1985), and Cabrera (1980, 1986b), who relies on Ortíz, are reliable Spanish-language sources about the practice of Santería in Cuba.

11. Drewal (1992:201) defines *àse* (Yoruba spelling) as "performative power; the power of accomplishment; the power to get things done; the power to make things happen." See J. Mason (1992) and R. Thompson (1983) for additional definitions of this crucial concept in Santería and Yoruba cosmology.

12. It is perhaps no coincidence that the posh nightclub at the super-deluxe Hotel Meliá Cohíba is called Aché.

13. Typically, initiated practitioners of Cuban Santería provide one altar for their dead ancestors, complete with pictures of the deceased in youth, cups of coffee and strong liquor, and cigars; and another altar for the *orichas,* complete with *soperas* (ceramic receptacles) filled with the baptized *otanes* of the *orichas,* the *collares* of the *guerreros* or warriors (Eleguá, Ogún, Ochosi) and the five major *orichas* (Eleguá, Obatalá, Yemayá, Changó, Ochún), and other sacred attributes. Eleguá is both a *guerrero* and a major *oricha,* so he is listed twice, but he needs only one *collar* for both functions.

14. Murphy notes that "traditionally, the Yoruba recognize as many as 1,700 orishas, though only a few have achieved renown throughout the country. These great orishas are promulgated by organized priesthoods of men and women who have dedicated their lives to the service of a particular spirit." (1992:12) I would add that even fewer *orichas* survived the trip across the Atlantic to the New World; hence the groupings of the *orichas* into *guerreros* and the "major *orichas*" (those who survived the Middle Passage).

15. Obatalá, for example, has four female roads and eight male roads; according to Bolívar Aróstegui (1994:36–64), Echu has 236 *caminos,* although most Santeros recognize only twenty-one of them. As older practitioners of Santería die, however, the knowledge of *oricha caminos* specific to the turn-of-the-century practice of Santería dies with them. Most "major *orichas*" carry with them between seven and twenty-five well-known *caminos,* although two, Oyá and Changó, carry no roads at all.

16. See D. Brown (2001, chap. 4) for a discussion of the symbolic importance of the *asiento,* as manifested through the aesthetics and design of the throne room. In theory, the potential future respect gained in the *asiento* ceremony is to be directed toward the *iyawó's*

head *oricha*. In practice, Santeros and Santeras occasionally demand this additional respect for themselves, rather than for their head *orichas*.

17. In my anxious state, it sometimes seemed to me that the number of peppers corresponded to the respective day of my *asiento*. Perhaps some fell off the coconut en route from the kitchen to the *igbodu*. The number should have remained a constant five for each day of the *asiento*.

18. These *santos*, however, are not the typical saints of the Catholic church. Santa Barbara, for example, also known as Changó, was a fourth-century Christian martyr who chose to serve God rather than marry a man she did not love. She achieved martyrdom by committing suicide, which makes her inclusion in Catholic hagiology problematic at best.

19. The terms *babalocha* and *iyalocha* mean priest of Santería and priestess of Santería, respectively, and are contracted versions of *babaloricha* and *iyaloricha*. *Babaloricha* is a conjunction of the Yoruba term for father *(baba)* and deity *(oricha)*. *Iyaloricha* is a conjunction of the Yoruba term for mother *(iya)* and deity *(oricha)*. This transformation of *babaloricha* and *iyaloricha* into *babalocha* and *iyalocha* is the same type of contraction that allows *oricha* to become *ocha,* as in Regla de Ocha, which is another name for Santería. Cuban scholars write that *tata nganga* is a Bantu term meaning priest of Palo Monte. *Tata* means father, and *nganga* means deity. In all of these terms, the implication is that the priest or priestess is the responsible person or "parent" who takes care of the deities, and who teaches his or her godchildren to take care of the deities. The *babalocha, iyalocha,* and *tata nganga* serve as both mediators between the divine and the mundane.

20. I reached this conclusion after having attended many performances of the Conjunto Folklórico during the course of my fieldwork and after following the tour groups back to their tourist hotels, most of which have souvenir shops.

21. Fans are associated with both Yemaya and Ochún, who sometimes are said to be mother and daughter, and sometimes are said to be sisters. There are *patakíes* to support both relationships (see Cabrera 1986b; García Cortéz 1980; Bolívar Aróstegui 1990, and J. Mason 1992).

22. These observations follow various conversations with Alberto Villarreal during summer 1992 and an interview with Ramiro Guerra (August 6, 1992). See chapter 5 for a historical perspective of the privileges and responsibilities accorded to members of the Conjunto Folklórico.

CONCLUSION

When Ochún finally spoke on the day of my *itá,* she offered her blessings and wise counsel: The good day is known from dawn.... You are destined to have a long and successful
life.... Do not be in a hurry to succeed.... One who wants to learn fast will not value
knowing.... Step by step you will arrive from far away.... You are building a mountain....
The eternal stones of the *orichas* represent stability and patience.... Wisdom is the key to
your success, and wisdom will change your perspective.... Be humble but not stupid....
Surround yourself with your intellectual equals.... As you climb the mountain,
remember who has helped you build it.

STUDIES IN TRANSLATION

As I took my place among the other religious celebrants jostling in three loose
lines in a street-side room at the end of an alleyway, our loud singing energized
the close, humid air of the tiny Havana apartment. It was late July 1997, and even
though I didn't know the words to the praise songs the *akpwón* offered, I joined in
anyway, approximating the unfamiliar combination of consonant clusters and
nasal vowels. Sweaty bodies dressed in white bumped up against me as we danced
and sang. Some of us clapped our hands in time with the drumming. Finally the
akpwón began a song I knew for Ochún, "E lade Ochún," which means "You own
the crown, Ochún."[1] When the time came for the chorus to respond twice to the
akpwón's verse, we all sang "E lade Ochún" the first time, and "E lade Ochún"
the second time—or so I thought. I noticed after a few rounds that the second version of the chorus sounded different, and that some of the younger singers were

grinning broadly at each other. The chorus came around again, and its second incarnation, rather than "E lade Ochún," became "Helado Ochún," or "Ochún the Ice-Cream Girl." Some of the older practitioners looked back at the three who had started this mischief, and, still dancing, shook their heads and smiled slightly.

Ochún as Ice-Cream Girl catapults the translation and transformation of Yoruba texts into the sweetly ironic realm of contemporary Cuban life. Ice cream is an extra-cool commodity in contemporary Cuba, very much in demand, partially because there are occasional ice-cream shortages, just as there are shortages of almost everything else in Cuba. When Coppelia, a popular Havana ice-cream stand, has ice cream (especially chocolate ice cream), people stand in line for hours for a scoop of this frozen elixir. To associate Ochún with the much-awaited arrival of cool sweetness is perfectly in keeping with her divine persona: she is the coolness of the rivers and the sweetness of honey; she is the last of the *orichas,* like dessert, and the youngest of them; like many youngsters, she, too, loves ice cream.

For many practitioners, the liturgical language of Santería no longer signifies through the repetition and translation of discrete Yoruba phrases. The various languages of Afro-Cuban religions have been decontextualized and detextualized during the past two centuries. Because the practice of these religions was prohibited, or at the very least discouraged, until very recently, the source languages of religious performance began to decay and deform. Phrases from Afro-Cuban liturgical languages that were preserved through collective memory may have looked or sounded like Yoruba, a Bantu language, or Efik, but were not. Key aspects of these languages—such as palate formation, accenting, and rules of elision, which delineate not only spoken and written emphasis but also word difference—were lost or discarded.

Losing the ability to translate these praise-song texts immediately over time, and thus losing directly accessible lexical meaning, requires the simultaneous creation of new meanings "around" the text. Signification often occurs through a process of creative transliteration (*e lade* into *helado,* for example), as well as through a simultaneous series of performative events: song melodies, dance gestures, and rhythmic patterns associated with specific *orichas* and their praise songs.[2] These new meanings result in a less logocentric approach to the authentication of liturgical practice, suggesting instead an emphasis on the feel of linguistic gestures, combined with instrumental, melodic, and dance tropes.[3] *Creyentes* from Havana may not know they are singing for Ogún until the drums respond to the lead singer's chant with the characteristically strong 4/4 rhythmic patterns. Or, similarly, they may not know they are singing for Ochún until the lead singer performs one of her popular melodies, and a few of the older Santeras start doing Ochún's steps.

Lexical accuracy seems less relevant than religious efficacy. To sing the songs (or even an approximation of them) is very important for the successful completion of a religious ceremony (see chapter 3, n. 10); to know what the texts might have meant a hundred years ago (or what a translation is supposed to mean now) is less important. Ultimately, to understand the lexical meaning of these song texts for practitioners is a task worthy of a linguistics scholar, a theologian, and numerous practitioners. John Mason's *Orin Orisa* (1992), which compiles hundreds of variations of praise-song texts, often provides three or four variations in pronunciation and spelling for each phrase, each of which changes the meaning of the praise song drastically, if not absurdly.[4] Yet much of the early work of the Teatro Nacional and the Conjunto Folklórico focused on retrieving (or reconstructing) these "dying" languages—specific phrases, as well as their previous performative contexts. The act of retrieval, reconstruction, and revalidation implies confidence in maintaining control over the final product, the final resurrection. One reconstructs only something that has already been vanquished; the process assumes that the reconstruction cannot possibly wield the power of its predecessor. The feared and maligned traditions of prerevolutionary Afro-Cuban *brujería* were rehabilitated to become the positive folklore of the raceless, classless society of revolutionary Cuba: an Afro-[Cuban]-centrism disoriented, disempowered, shunted backward in order to be reborn in the present.

CAFÉ CON LECHE

Cuban intellectuals (both black and white) have spent much of the twentieth century revising their understanding of the black experience in Cuba (see Lourdes Casal 1989; C. Moore 1988a, 1988b). Their frequent comparisons of conditions before and after the revolution for Cuban blacks underscore the importance of the initial performances of the Conjunto Folklórico Nacional de Cuba: whites and blacks were working together, a venture publicly supported perhaps for the first time, in an educational and performative context. Many aspects of life in prerevolutionary Cuba had been segregated, such as private schools, clubs, restaurants, government jobs, and university posts (Domínguez 1976). Indeed, a primary focus of Castro's 1953 "History Will Absolve Me" speech was the eradication of racism.[5] After the revolution, within a few months of Fidel Castro's assumption of Cuba's leadership, so-called institutionalized racism (the racism that was supported and propagated through educational, leisure, and governmental institutions) was abolished. This change in Cuba's social and racial order, attributed to the revolution, was boldly embodied by the Teatro Nacional and the Conjunto Folklórico.

But racial hierarchy still towers above Cuba's supposedly "nonracial" society like a palm tree over hot pavement. The wind blows and the leaves flutter, leaving the shadowed pavement mottled and fluid ("A Cuban is simply someone who belongs to no race in particular!"[6]); the air settles again and the shadows come back, well defined and undeniable—Cubans are dark, light, and everything in between. For one who grew up amid the freckled whiteness and ruddy pinkness of a New Jersey suburb, and for whom the delicate olive skins of Jews and Italians often seemed exotic, the many shades and subtleties of skin colors of the Cuban population were initially overwhelming. Mostly, this variety of hues is a study in browns, and these browns stand out elegantly, defiantly against the pale, sun-washed walls of Havana. *La canela* (cinnamon), *café con leche* (coffee with milk), *chocolate* (chocolate), *café puro* ("pure" or black coffee), *tabaco* (tobacco), *miel* (honey)—the words used by Cubans to describe this small sample of colors are reminiscent of a breakfast buffet. It is the gentleness and playfulness of this referential (and at times reverential) language that seems to pervade current attitudes about race in Cuba.

Yet it is this same language that belies the complexity and endurance of long-standing, reciprocal prejudices and fears. At its best, this playful cascade of colors wraps the twins of slavery and miscegenation in a rainbow of redemption, offering up to the world its rich hues of survival. At its worst, the very playfulness of the metaphorical language can be distancing and alienating, masking the more serious problem of an implicit and static racial hierarchy, in which "white" is a powerful and unchallenged totality and "black" is a diffuse amalgam, each fragment continually negotiating its power through reconstructed fractions of racial heritage and exotic metaphoric codes.

What is striking is not that racial distinctions and prejudices persist after the revolution, but that many of Cuba's intellectuals (and Castro himself) seem to believe that verbal denials of their existence will make them disappear. Some statements, such as those implying a common African heritage for all Cubans, seem to conflate racism with race, or at least appear to overdetermine the causal relationship between constructs of race and racist attitudes. The logic resulting from this equation, then, is that by eradicating constructs of race one blurs perceptions of difference, and by blurring perceptions of difference, one erases racism. What is clear is not the success of the revolution's attempt to eradicate racism, but its noble intentions. Political theorist Jorge Domínguez maintains that the socioeco-

nomic situation of Cuban blacks improved not because of the revolution's attempts to eradicate racism, but because of the overall program to better the
plight of all downtrodden Cubans—of which blacks were the majority:

> Blacks benefited [from the Revolution] because they were poor, and not because they
> were Black. Apart from the modest steps required to dismantle what remained of
> legal race discrimination, the Cuban government has not had explicitly "pro-black" or
> "affirmative action" policies. And, at the top of the regime, those who rule are still
> white. This does not deny to the Cuban government the credit it deserves for improv-
> ing the lot of the poor, but it underlines yet again how difficult it is for this regime to
> be conscious of the problem of being Black in Cuba and of the legitimate and endur-
> ing question of the meaning of Afro-Cuban traditions in Cuba. (Domínguez in
> Moore 1988a:xii)

How does one evaluate the significance of Afro-Cuban traditions in a country
where being of African origin is in some contexts celebrated and in others implies
a diminished status? The majority of Cuban academics who study Cuba's African-
based religions still devalue these traditions. The persistent devaluing of these religions is most evident from the language used to analyze them. Santería, Palo
Monte, Arará, and Abakwá are characterized as "diffuse" by the sociologists of religion who work in the Cuban Academy of Sciences, meaning that these religious
traditions have no concrete belief system. They are either referred to as "syncretic
cults" (rather than "religions") or as "folklore"; both terms are a step closer to official disempowerment and secularization, and neither term approximates the
fullness of "religious tradition."[7]

DIVINE UTTERANCES

There is a thin line between sacred and secular, so thin that it occasionally seems
invisible. When Jesús Pérez, Aguedes Morales, and Pablo Roche played for Fernando Ortíz's conference on Afro-Cuban "folklore" in May 1936, in addition to
being made into popular and well-regarded spectacles, they were creating a safe
haven for themselves and for their progeny. This folkloric performance was a performance of emergence, a coming up from the deep space of the sacred to trans-
mit this just-surfacing knowledge to the unknowing, though appreciative, audiences of the secular sphere. The rules of engagement governing folkloric
performance were born on that day in May, as was the ability to convey sacred
memory through secular manifestation. The transgressive process of scholarship,

initiated by Fernando Ortíz, created the need for a permeable membrane between religious and folkloric performance, so that an appropriate context or sphere could be immediately understood and constructed by its participants. But this process of simultaneous translation helped blur the boundaries between sacred and secular, giving rise to such phenomena as "inappropriate possessions"— the hierophany of public performance. And this disorientation, this decentering of embodied memory has allowed the newer, shinier project of *oricha* tourism to emerge—a direct reference to the foreign exploitative commercial practices Cuba has avoided for so many decades, yet has now embraced.

As we continued dancing and singing to "Elade Ochún" in the hot Havana *solar,* the *akpwón* extended the praise song with the phrase, "O Feyisida" (the clever one becomes good).[8] We sang "O Feyisida" loudly, for we knew it well. And with each rendition of the chorus, the phrase moved imperceptibly closer to "O Felicidad" (O happiness), until we were all singing about happiness, smiling knowingly as we danced.

NOTES

1. "Ladé" is one of the terms for a child of Ochún, and refers to Ochún's crown (Cabrera 1986b:198); J. Mason (1992:350; see also pp. 349 and 364). I have heard people sing "E lade Ochún" and "A lade Ochún" to the same tune; during this *toque de santo,* people were singing "E lade Ochún."

2. See Palmié (1993) on the related subject of "ethnogenetic transfer," with specific reference to the transfer and continuation of rituals regarding the consecration of *batá* drums.

3. See chapter 4, part of which relies on Margaret Drewal's understanding of the correlation between the physical sensation produced by dancing for and performing the praise texts for a particular *oricha* (Ogún, in this case) and the characteristics of that *oricha.*

4. See chapter 4. What is interesting about John Mason's creative transliterations and translative variations is that each is appropriate for the *oricha* to which it refers. And despite the occasional ungainliness of Mason's word order, his versions of praise-song texts are deeply evocative.

5. This speech was Castro's defense of his attack on the Moncada Barracks in 1953. This spontaneous speech, later edited and distributed as a revolutionary pamphlet, is considered by most Cubans to be the beginning of the Cuban revolution.

6. Fidel Castro, quoted in *Revolución* (March 26, 1959), p. 2, cited in C. Moore 1988a:27. According to Moore, Castro's intent was to offend neither whites nor blacks, and thus maintain the support of both for the revolution.

7. Interview with Rafael L. López Valdés (December 3, 1991); see Argüelles Mederos and Hodge Limonta (1991).

8. J. Mason (1992:350) translates this phrase as "The clever person turns to good." I have also heard *akpwónes* in Los Angeles and Havana sing "O Feyikiya" (no translation available) to the melody of "O Feyisida." A possible translation for "O Feyikiya," relying on Ochún's *patakíes*, Cabrera (1986b), J. Mason (1992), and my understanding of linguistic elision, could be "Courageous mother [Ochún] emerges from the woods, fanning herself" (perhaps a reference to the *pataki* in which Ochún leads Ogún out of the forest). The variant "O Feyisida" eventually transforms itself into "O Felicidad," in my experience.

GLOSSARY

A = Amerindian
C = Carabalí
E = Ewe
F = Fon
K = KiKongo
L = Lucumí
S = Spanish

A

Abakwá: [C] (alt., *Abakuá*) Afro-Cuban elite male society derived from the secret male societies, such as the Leopard society, prevalent in the Calabar region (southeastern
Nigeria and western Cameroon) of West Africa; initially formed by Carabalí
slaves, but spread to *mulato* and white populations by the mid-nineteenth century;
see also *ñáñigo.*

abebé: [L] (alt., *abwé*) the fan Ochún uses to cool herself and to flirt with when she
dances.

aberíkula: [L] unconsecrated, as in *aberíkula batá,* drums played in secular contexts.

aché: [L] (alt., *ashé, asé*) ritual performative power; also, the power to make things happen; innate dynamic essence of all people and things.

achuchado: [S] enraged to the point of acting crazy.

actuación: [S] theatrical presentation.

adjogbo: [F] rhythm and dance performed by Fon communities in Togo and Benin.

aficionado/a: [S] a knowledgeable and accomplished fan of the arts.

agbeko: [E] rhythm and dance performed by Ewe communities in southeast Ghana.

agogo: [L] double-headed iron bell used in Afro-Cuban religious and popular music.

aguardiente: [S] strong, clear, fiery liquor made from sugar cane; said by practitioners of
Santería to be the preferred liquor of the ancestors and robust male *orichas* of Santería and Palo Monte.

ahijado/a: [S] godson or goddaughter of a priest or priestess of Santería

ajiaco: [S] stew; used as metaphor by Fernando Ortíz to describe Cuban expressive culture.

akpwón: [L] (alt., *akpón*) lead singer in a Santería ceremony.

alafia: [L] term from divination with four coconut pieces that refers to all four pieces
landed face up, on the white side; this means immediate stability and good energy,
although this divination result is not necessarily stable in the long run, as is *eye ife*
(two up and two down).

aleyo: [L] in general, a nonbeliever; in the context of Santería, someone who is not allowed to participate in certain ritual activities because he or she is not initiated
into Santería.

anaforuana: [C] sacred Abakwá pictographs typically drawn on walls, floors, and doors;
see also *firma;* see also *Abakwá.*

anciano/a: [S] old man/old woman.

añá: [L] (alt., *ayan, anya, anyé*) sacred inner substance of consecrated *batá* drums; also
refers to the *oricha* of the batá drums; often associated with Ochún; see also *tambor de fundamento.*

apagón(es): [S] blackout(s); prevalent during the special economic period in Cuba.

Arará: [F/L] Afro-Cuban name for people and their expressive culture originating from
Ewe-Fon territory of Ghana, Benin, and Togo; sometimes considered a subset of
Lucumí practices. The last remaining Arará *cabildo* is in Matanzas, Cuba.

asesor/a: [S] artistic advisor.

asiento: [S] term used to refer to the process of becoming initiated as a priest or priestess
of Santería.

atrevido/a: [S] bold, impudent, insolent, overbearing, pushy.

aura tiñosa: [S] vulture; one of the *caminos* (avatars) of Ochún.

auténtico/a: [S] authentic. Whether a theatrical presentation of Afro-Cuban performance
traditions was *auténtico* or not was a main concern of the founders of the Conjunto Folklórico.

ayé: [L] (alt., *aiyé*) earth, where the humans live; as opposed to *orún*, where the *orichas* live.

azucena: [S] a white, fragrant flower used to honor the ancestors; also known as Madonna
lily *(Lilium candidum).*

B

babalawo: [L] (alt., *babalao*) priest of Ifá divination; see also *Ifá.*

babaloricha: [L] (also *babalocha*) priestess of Santería; see also *santera.*

Babalú Ayé: [L] *oricha* of sickness and infirmity, closely associated with victims of smallpox and AIDS; of Arará origin.

baile: [S] dance, an important component of Santería religious and folkloric performance.

balsero: [S] popular name for person who fled from Cuba in the 1990s on the small wooden boats known as *balsas*.

Bantu: [S] language and culture of people from present-day Angola and surrounding area of equatorial and southern Africa; formed a significant plurality of landed slaves in Cuba; thought to be origin of Cuba's "Congo" performance traditions.

barrio: [S] neighborhood; community.

batá: [L] the three sacred double-headed drums used in Santería ceremonies.

batalero: [S / L] *batá* drummer.

bautizado: [S] baptized, as in baptized drums.

bembé: [L] drumming party for the *orichas,* although the drums are not *batá* drums and are not consecrated; name of staved-barrel peg drums used in *bembé* ceremony; name of rhythm used in *bembé* ceremony.

blanco: [S] white (person).

boca: [S] (also *enú*) lit., "mouth"; the larger head of the *batá* drum.

bongó: [C] two single-headed small drums connected together and played with hands.

Bosou: [F] three- (or two-) horned Haitian deity of the forest.

bóveda: [S] white-covered table that serves as an altar for the ancestors; usually includes at least a glass of water, a *cafecito,* a cigar, and some flowers.

bozal: [L] name of creolized language spoken by African slaves recently landed in Cuba; mostly eighteenth- and nineteenth-century usage

brujería: [S] witchcraft; the name given to Afro-Cuban religious traditions (such as Santería and Palo Monte) by nineteenth- and early twentieth-century observers in Cuba, including Fernando Ortíz.

brujo/a: [S] witch; the name given to priests and priestesses of Afro-Cuban religious traditions (such as Santería and Palo Monte) by nineteenth- and early twentieth-century observers in Cuba, including Fernando Ortíz.

C

cabildo: [S] fraternal mutual aid organizations for slaves in Cuba, first established in the 1500s under the auspices of the Catholic church. The religious and performative activities of *cabildos* were gradually curtailed throughout the 1880s by the civil government until they became mostly social clubs.

cafecito: [S] small cup of coffee, Cuban style; said to be a favorite drink of the ancestors.

camino: [S] road; in this context, refers to a particular avatar of an *oricha*.

canto: [S] song; an important component of Santería religious and folkloric performance.

Carabalí: [C] name of people from the Calabar region of West Africa, which includes southeastern Nigeria and western Cameroon, said to be the homeland of the Abakwá society.

caracol: [S] shell; in this context, usually refers to cowrie shells, the shells used in one of the divination practices of Santería; see also *diloggún*.

carnaval: [S] formerly a religious festival Cuba held in February or March, marked by
    street parades and boisterous festivities; in the years since the 1959 Cuban revolu-
    tion the festival has been celebrated more often on July 26, the day of the Mon-
    cada rebellion in 1953, during the early years of the struggle before the 1959 revolu-
    tion.

carné de identidad: [S] Cuban identity card/internal passport.

casa de santo: [S] (also *casa templo; casa de religión*) place of worship for practitioners of
    Santería, typically located in the home of a Santero or Santera.

casa templo: [S] see *casa de santo.*

casino: [S] popular Cuban group dance style.

chachá: [L] the smaller head of the *batá* drum.

chachalokofún: [L] syncopated rhythm in Santería *batá* drumming; can be inserted into
    toques for most *orichas* as a "break-out" dance section.

Changó: [L/S] (alt., Shangó, Sàngó) Afro-Cuban *oricha* of thunder and lightning; embodi-
    ment of virility; owner of *batá* drums; mythical king of Oyo.

chaworo: [L] (alt., *chaguoro*) leather straps of jingle bells affixed around both drum heads
    of Iyá, the largest and lead drum of the three *batá* drums.

clave: [S] wooden sticks played in pairs, as well as the various rhythms played by these in-
    struments; these rhythms provide the backbone of most Afro-Cuban religious,
    folkloric, and popular music.

coco: [S] coconut; four pieces of coconut are used in the Santería divination practice
    known as *obi;* see also *obi.*

collares: [S] (also *elekes*) consecrated, beaded necklaces that one receives on completing
    the first step of initiation into Santería; the colors of each necklace correspond to
    specific *orichas.*

columbia: [S] fast-paced solo male dance; type of *rumba;* see *rumba.*

Comité para la Defensa de la Revolución (CDR): [S] lit., "Committee for the Defense of the
    Revolution"; neighborhood committees, organized by block, responsible for re-
    porting counterrevolutionary activities and any extraordinary events to the Cuban
    authorities.

comparsa: [S] *carnaval* band, usually consisting of *congas, claves, cornetas chinas,* metal bells,
    shekeres, and other percussive instruments; it typically performs while
    marching/dancing down the street from the morning of *carnaval* to the early
    morning of the next day.

conga: [S] slim, single-headed, medium-pitched, barrel-shaped drum; usually played with
    the hands; typically played with two other drums *(quinto* and *tumbadora);* featured
    in *rumba* and in other Cuban popular music genres; see also *quinto, tumbadora.*

Congo: [S] name of group of people, language, and other forms of expressive culture in
    Cuba descended from Bantu-speaking people of equatorial southern Africa and
    central Africa; also refers to the spirits of slaves from this region who may appear
    in one's *cuadro espiritual;* see also Bantu; see also *espiritismo.*

consagrado: [S] consecrated, made sacred; see also *bautizado;* see also *tambor de fundamento.*

consulta: [S] consultation, usually involving divination; see also *registro.*

contradanza: [S] contradance; nineteenth-century salon dance genre in Cuba; also known as *habanera* (q.v.).

creyente: [S] lit., believer; religious adherent or practitioner of Santería or another Afro-Cuban religious tradition.

criollo: [S] a (white) person of European descent born in Cuba; a (black) person of African descent born in Cuba; mostly nineteenth-century usage.

cuadro espiritual: [S] spiritual plane; in the context of Santería and *espiritismo,* spirits who guide or care for one.

cubano: [S] Cuban.

culto: [S] cult, in the context of Cuban discourse on Afro-Cuban religious traditions.

D

dále: [S] lit., "do it! give it your all!"; encouraging exclamation offered by *batá* drummers when the drumming sounds good and makes people dance.

deje: [S] slang, from *dejado,* lit., careless, negligent; lit., "leave it off"; discouraging adjectival comment made by *batá* drummers when the rhythmic acuity of the drummers is off, or when people are not responding well to the drumming.

despacito: [S] slowly, delicately; often used to describe certain *batá* rhythms for Santería *orichas* Ochún and Obatalá.

día del río: [S] lit., "the day of the river"; the first step before one becomes initiated as a priest or priestess into Santería; going to the river involves cleansing oneself, making an offering to the river (Ochún), and cutting off one's clothing in the first of many symbolic sheddings of one's former life.

diablito: [S] (also *íreme*) lit., "little devil"; the main dancers in the public ceremonies of Abakwá; typically they are dressed in tall, pointed, raffia-enhanced cloth masks and colorful shirts and leggings.

diloggún: [L] Santería divination system using (sixteen) cowrie shells.

diplomercado: [S] lit., "diplo[mats'] market"; during the early years of privation of the special economic period in Cuba, this well-stocked supermarket was typically accessible only to foreign diplomats and other foreign nationals.

diplotienda: [S] lit., "diplo[mats'] store"; during the early years of the special economic period in Cuba, these were the only places where one could purchase clothing, toiletries, electronics, paper goods, jewelry, and other nonessential items; until late 1993, they were only open to foreign nationals.

dulce: [S] sweet; used to describe the songs, rhythms, and dance movements of Ochún.

E

ebbó: [L] (also *ebó*) ritual offering in Santería, the nature of which (animal sacrifice, fruit, ritual cleansing) is derived through divination.

Efik: [C] name of tribal group from the Calabar region (southeastern Nigeria and western Cameroon) of West Africa; known as the founding members of the Abakwá society in Cuba; see also *Ibibio*.

egun: [L] spirit of a deceased person; sometimes thought to be unevolved.

ekue: [C] sacred drum of the Abakwá; not used for public ceremonies.

Eleguá: [L] (alt., *Eshu-Eleguá, Elegguá, Elegbá, Elegbara*) Lucumí *oricha* of the crossroads; the first warrior *oricha;* unpredictable trickster and messenger of Olofi; must be saluted first and last in Santería ceremonies.

emancipado/a: [S] slave aboard a slave ship who was freed by governmental decree (1870s), but who had not yet bought his/her freedom, and thus was subject to exploitation by *criollo* plantation owners.

empresa: [S] business, firm, concern.

entrada: [S] lit., "entry"; in Santería, an *ebbó de entrada* prepares the way for the subsequent ceremony.

espectáculo: [S] spectacle, theatrical presentation.

espiritismo: [S] lit., "spiritualism"; the practice of communicating with the spirits of the deceased to help resolve the problems of the living; some aspects of *espiritismo* are included in Santería. Heavily influenced by the writings of controversial nineteenth-century figure Allan Kardec, *espiritismo* is widely practiced in eastern Cuba, as well as in other parts of the Caribbean, such as the Dominican Republic and Puerto Rico.

espíritu familiar: [S] family ancestor; in Santería, one's family ancestors are hoped to be evolved, inasmuch as they are likely to accompany one throughout life.

etagua: [L] term from divination with four coconut pieces *(obi);* refers to three pieces landing face up, and one piece landing face down (possible struggle, potentially unstable).

Ewe: [E] people, language, and expressive culture from southeastern Ghana.

extranjero/a: [S] foreigner, tourist.

eye ife: [L] term from divination with four coconut pieces *(obi);* refers to two pieces landing face up, and two pieces landing face down (enduring good fortune and stability).

F

faltar respeto: [S] lacking respect; a serious charge in the hierarchical relationships of Santería.

familia de santo: [S] one's family in *santo;* refers to ritual kinship in Santería.

fardela: [s] a brownish paste affixed to the larger head of the *iyá* to adjust the pitch.

fiesta de santo: [S] a celebration for the *santos.*

firma: [S] lit., "signature"; refers to the sacred pictographs used by practitioners of Santería, Palo Monte, Arará, and Abakwá (see also *anaforuana*).

folklore: [S] term used by Fernando Ortíz in the 1930s and his intellectual progeny from the 1940s through the 1990s to describe Afro-Cuban religious performance, as well as other rural and popular performance traditions in Cuba.

folklorización: [S] term used by several scholars, including C. Moore (1988a), to describe the devalorization of Afro-Cuban religious traditions in Cuba.

Fon: [F] people and expressive culture from Togo and Benin; constituted an important plurality of the slaves landed in Cuba in the nineteenth century; one of the sources of Arará performance traditions in Cuba.

fula: [K] gunpowder; in Cuban slang, money.

G

gankogui: [E] double-headed iron bell played in most E<u>w</u>e performance genres.

garabato: [S] cane; in the context of Santería, refers to Eleguá's bifurcated cane, with which he opens and closes the road.

gran mago: [S] lit., "great magician"; María Teresa Linares's (and others') term for the high priest *(tata nganga)* of Palo Monte.

grupo folklórico: [S] folkloric group; ensemble that specializes in theatrical presentations of Afro-Cuban religious performance.

guagua: [A] Cuban vernacular for bus.

guaguancó: [S] medium-paced couples' *rumba;* type of *rumba* (q.v.).

guardia: [S] guard, usually for embassies and government buildings; distinct from the police.

güemilere: [L] party for the *orichas;* see *bembé.*

guerreros: [S] warriors; in the context of Santería, the warriors refer to the *orichas* Eleguá, Ogún, Ochosi, and Osun—all of whom provide strength and protection to the initiate.

güiro: [S] musical instrument made from a beaded gourd, used in Santería ceremonies as well as in Cuban popular music; see also *shekere;* also refers to a party for the *orichas;* see also *bembé;* see also *güemilere.*

H

habanera: [S] nineteenth-century salon dance in Cuba; also considered a style of *contradanza;* its syncopated ostinato bass-line was evoked as a musical metaphor for Cuba's exoticism; see also *contradanza.*

héroe: [S] hero.

huelga: [S] labor strike.

huella: [S] scar, mark.

I

Ibibio: [C] one of the groups from the Calabar region of West Africa (southeastern Nigeria and western Cameroon); known as the founding members of the Abakwá society in Cuba; see also *Efik.*

idé: [L] beaded bracelet worn by practitioners of Santería; the color combinations of the beads of the *idé* correspond to particular *orichas.*

Ifá: [L] Yoruba religion (with other West African counterparts, such as Afá in Ghana and

Fa in Togo) and the Afro-Cuban divination system using palm nuts that stems from that religion.

igbodu: [L] (also *cuarto de santo*) the room where the *iyawó* stays during her initiation into the priesthood of Santería.

ìjinlèe: [Y/L] lit., "deep in the ground"; refers to linking human aspirations to the divine experience of the *orichas,* as manifested in their *patakíes,* or myths.

ilu batá: [L] set of three consecrated *batá* drums.

Indio: [S] Indian; in this context, refers to the aboriginal people who were settled in Cuba at the time of the Spanish invasion; also refers to the spirits of these Amerindian people who may appear in one's *cuadro espiritual;* see also *espiritismo.*

informante: [S] informant; in this context, refers to the religious practitioners who collaborated with the early endeavors of the Conjunto Folklórico Nacional de Cuba.

investigador/a: [S] researcher.

iré: [L] blessings; often communicated through coconut divination *(obi)* when two or more of the four pieces land face up, one touching or on top of the other.

íreme: [C] see *diablito* (Abakwá).

itá: [L] the long divination session that is a focal point of one's initiation into the priesthood of Santería, in which one hears about one's past, present, and future.

italero: [L] (also *oríate*) diviner in Santería who is trained to read and present the *itá.*

Itefa: [Y/L] the establishment of the self, in the context of initiation into Yoruba *oricha* worship.

itótele: [L] (also *segundo*) lit., "one who follows"; the middle and most responsive drum in the *batá* drumming ensemble; usually associated with Ochún.

iyá: [L] (also *caja*) lit., "mother"; the largest and lead drum in the *batá* drumming ensemble; usually associated with Yemayá.

iyaloricha: [L] (also *iyalocha*) lit., "mother [of the] *oricha*"; priestess of Santería; see also *santera.*

iyamba: [C] high priest of Abakwá who confirms new members into the society; also responsible for playing the *ekue* (sacred drum of the Abakwá).

iyawó(ces): [L] (alt., *yawó, yabó, yaguó*) new initiate(s) into the priesthood of Santería.

iyaworaje: [L] lit., "journey of the *iyawó*"; the yearlong period during which the *iyawó* observes certain restrictions related to the new status as a priest or priestess of Santería and begins to absorb and integrate the most important aspects of the *itá;* see also *iyawó, itá.*

Iyesa: [L] (also *Yesa*) people who lived near the Yoruba in southwestern Nigeria; also the name of a set of drums and the rhythms originally played on those drums said to come from that area; homeland of Ochún.

J

jícamo: [L] encouraging exclamation offered by *batá* drummers when the drumming sounds good and makes people dance; see also *dále, métele.*

jícara: [L] cup made out of half-gourd used in Santería rituals.

jinetero/a: [S] young Cuban who finds the loopholes in the dual economy and uses them to his/her best advantage by trading on the black market, engaging in prostitution, performing small acts of fraud or larceny, and the like.

juego: [S] in the context of Santería, refers to a set *(juego)* of *batá* drums; in the context of Abakwá, refers to a specific Abakwá society.

K

kariocha: [L] lit., "to make saint"; refers to the initiation process into the priesthood of Santería.

L

liberto: [S] freed slave (by governmental decree) living in Cuba; mostly nineteenth-century usage.

llamativo: [S] flashy, evocative; used in reference to the spectacles that portrayed the practices of Santería and other Afro-Cuban religious traditions.

lucha: [S] struggle; *"En la lucha"* was often the response to *"¿Cómo estás?"* during the decade-long "special economic period."

Lucumí: [L] name of language, people, religion, and all other aspects of Afro-Cuban expressive culture associated with the descendants of Yoruba slaves.

lwa: [F] (alt., *loa*) general name given to deities in Haitian Vodou (similar to *orichas*).

M

machete: [S] large knife; in the context of Santería, the machete is closely associated with Ogún, who uses it to cut his way out of the forest.

macho: [S] exhibiting stereotypically masculine behavior to the point of being boorish; often associated with Changó.

madrina: [S] godmother in Santería.

Manbo: [F] priestess of Haitian Vodou.

manifestación: [S] in the context of *grupos folklóricos,* a floor show; see also *grupo folklórico.*

maraca: [S] musical instrument made from a small gourd, with seeds inside that rattle when one shakes it; common in Cuban popular music.

matanza: [S] lit., "killing"; in the context of Santería, the ritual sacrifice of fowl and some four-legged animals; the *matanza* is an important *ebbó* for the initiation ceremony into the priesthood of Santería.

mestizo/a: [S] of mixed heritage; typically of white and Amerindian heritage; in nineteenth-century Cuba, *mestizo* could also mean of white and black heritage.

métele: [S] lit., "get into it!"; encouraging exclamation offered by *batá* drummers when the drumming sounds good and makes people dance; see also *dále, jícamo.*

misa espiritual: [S] spiritual mass; in the context of Santería, usually given for the ances-

tors of an initiate before the seven-day initiation process into the priesthood of
Santería.

moforibale: [L] lit., "I bow my head to the ground"; a gesture of submission and respect
performed by novitiates in Santería before their elders; performed by all practitioners before the *orichas.*

moreno: [S] a more refined term for *negro;* mostly nineteenth-century usage.

mortero/a: [S] lit., "deader"; someone (usually female) who has well-developed skills in
communicating with the ancestors.

muerte: [S] (also *iku*) death.

muerto: [S] (also *egun*) the spirit of a deceased person; an ancestor.

mulato/a: [S] a person of mixed black and white heritage.

música campesina: [S] rural folk music; music of the farming communities outside of the
big cities in Cuba.

N

narcotráfico: [S] drug trafficking.

negro: [S] black (person).

negros de nación: [S] ethnic Africans landed in Cuba as slaves; *nación* refers to the ethnic
group or tribe of origin.

nganga: [K] (also *nkisi, prenda*) refers to the spirit of the deceased person with whom the
priest of Palo Monte does his work; also refers to the large metal cauldron in
which the spirit of the deceased person lives and is fed.

normal: [S] OK, nothing special; in the context of a religious or folkloric performance of
Santería, *normal* means that the performance did not go as well as expected.

ñáñigo: [C] (adj. *ñañiguero*) popular name for members of the Abakwá secret society;
thanks in large part to the popular press, *ñáñigos* became synonymous with both
organized and random crime by the end of the nineteenth century and the beginning of the twentieth in Cuba; see also *Abakwá.*

ñañiguismo: [C/S] being a *ñáñigo* (member of the Abakwá secret society); the way of life
of the *ñáñigos;* see also *Abakwá.*

O

Obatalá: [L] Santería *oricha* of wisdom, insanity, purity, whiteness; the father of the
orichas; has both male and female avatars.

obi: [L] Santería divination practice using four pieces of coconut.

ocana: [L] term from divination with four coconut pieces *(obi);* refers to three pieces landing face down and one landing face up (surrounded by trouble and instability).

ocha: [L] (also *oricha*); another name for Santería is Regla de Ocha (the Law of the Oricha).

Ochatur: [L/S] conjunction of *ocha* and *turismo;* refers to the coupling of *oricha* worship
and tourism in contemporary Cuba.

Ochosi: [L] *oricha* of the hunt; brother of Eleguá and Ogún; warrior *oricha.*

Ochún: [L] *oricha* of rivers (sweet waters), romantic love, and money; youngest deity; said
   to be both sister and daughter of Yemayá, and lover or wife of most of the male
   orichas.

odu(s): [L] the many proverbs associated with the numerical results of *diloggún* divination;
   see *diloggún*.

Ogún: [L] *oricha* of iron and war; brother of Eleguá and Ochosi; warrior *oricha*; lives in
   the forest.

okónkolo: [L] (alt., *kónkolo*; also *omele*) smallest drum in the *batá* ensemble; usually associated with Changó.

olú batá: [L] (also *omo añá*) *batá* player initiated into *añá*, which means that the *batalero* can
   play consecrated *batá* drums in religious *toques de santo*; see also *añá*.

omiero: [L] (also *purificación del santo*) ritually purifying substance made of mostly herbs and
   water; ingested by the *iyawó* on each of the seven days of the *kariocha* ceremony.

opelé: [L] (alt., *ekuelé*) thin chain used in Ifá divination.

oríate: [L] Santero trained to divine with (sixteen) cowrie shells; see *italero*.

oricha: [L] (also *ocha, santo*) deity of Santería; see also *ocha*.

oru: [L] sequence of sacred songs or rhythms used to call the *orichas* in Santería.

oru cantado: [L/S] sequence of sacred songs accompanied by *batá* rhythms used to call
   the *orichas* in Santería; performed in public.

oru seco: [L/S] sequence of *batá* rhythms, without song, used to evoke the *orichas* "in their
   own language" at the beginning of a *toque de santo*; performed by *olú batá* players
   in front of the altar to the *orichas*, before the public part of the *toque de santo*.

orún: [L] heaven; in the context of Santería, where the *orichas* live, as opposed to *ayé*,
   where the humans live.

Orúnmila: [L] *oricha* of Ifá divination; to be initiated into Ifá means to be a priest of Orúnmila.

Osain: [L] *oricha* of healing herbs and plants; has only one eye, one leg, and one arm;
   practitioners of Santería must ask his permission before taking plants or herbs to
   make *omiero, osain*, or other herbal mixtures.

osain: [L] cleansing, cooling substance made mostly of water and herbs; used to clean
   Santería practitioners and initiates before a religious ceremony.

Osun: [L] Santería *oricha* who helps balance the head and life of an initiate; one of the
   warrior deities; must always be placed above the height of the initiate, and must
   not be disturbed; typically represented as a small metal rooster perched atop a
   pedestal, which is filled with a powder mixture unique to Osun.

otán: [L] sacred stone of Santería; these stones are said to both contain and represent the
   orichas.

Oyá: [L] Santería *oricha* of the cemetery and whirlwind; the only female warrior; wife of
   Changó.

oyeku: [L] term from divination with four coconut pieces *(obi)*; refers to four pieces landing face down ("the dead come down"; bad news; make sacrifice immediately).

oyugbona: [L] (alt., *ayugbona, yubbona, yubwona, yugbona*) ritual assistant to the primary godparent in Santería, especially during the *kariocha* ceremony, when the initiate "makes saint"; can also act as second godparent.

P

padrino: [S] godfather; godparent in Santería.

páginas rojas: [S] lit., "red pages"; pages in the Cuban newspaper where crimes and criminals were listed.

palenques: [S] secret encampments to which fugitive or runaway slaves fled during the eighteenth and nineteenth centuries in Cuba.

palero/a: [S] priest/priestess of Palo Monte (q.v.).

Palo Monte: [S] (also *Palo Mayombe, Palo Briyumba*) lit., "stick [and] forest"; Afro-Cuban religion originating from religious practices of Bantu-speaking people of equatorial and southern Africa ("Congo"), mainly focused on working with spirits of the deceased; see *nganga, Congo.*

pancito: [S] small bread roll allotted daily to each person with a ration book during the special economic period.

pardo: [S] a more refined term for *mulato;* a person of mixed (black and white) heritage; mostly nineteenth-century usage.

pataki(es): [L] (also *patakín, appatakí*) myth(s) or fable(s) about the *orichas* of Santería that establish and elaborate on their relationships to one another, as well as the specific characteristics of each one.

período especial económico: [S] special economic period; official euphemism for the severe economic difficulties caused beginning in 1990, when the Eastern bloc collapsed, causing the former Soviet Union to withdraw economic aid from Cuba.

peso: [S] Cuban unit of currency. As of 2000, the exchange rate was roughly 22 Cuban *pesos* to the dollar.

Petwo: [F] "hot" spirits in Haitian Vodou; see also *Rada.*

plante de Abakwá: [C/S] Abakwá ceremony; usually refers to Abakwá initiation ceremony.

potencia: [C] (also *juego, tierra, partido, sociedad*) specific subgroup of the Abakwá (q.v.) society.

presentación: [S] theatrical presentation; see also *espectáculo, manifestación.*

público: [S] public, as opposed to private or sacred.

Q

quinto: [S] highest-pitched drum of a set of three *conga* drums; solo improvisatory voice within the trio; see also *conga, tumbadora.*

R

Rada: [F] "cool" spirits in Haitian Vodou; see also *Petwo.*

refrán: [S] refrain; the sung *refrán* helps build the energy in Santería religious performance.

registro: [S] a divination session, typically using the *diloggún* (cowrie shell) technique, performed by a Santero or Santera; see also *consulta.*

Regla de Ocha: [S/L] lit., "law of the *orichas*"; a more formal name for the religious tradition popularly known as Santería.

religión: [S] religion; in Cuban discourse, it is rare to find Santería and other Afro-Cuban religious traditions referred to as "religions"; more often, they are referred to as *cultos* or *folklore.*

resolver: [S] lit., "to resolve"; in the context of contemporary Cuba, to struggle to obtain a goal by relying on an informal network of people.

respeto: [S] respect; an important aspect of social and ritual relations in the hierarchical socioreligious world of Santería.

responsable: [S] boss, leader, supervisor.

ritmo: [S] rhythm.

roncito: [S] a shot of rum, Cuban style; said to be a favorite drink of the ancestors; also said to be a favorite drink of *batá* drummers.

rumba: [S] Afro-Cuban dance, song, and rhythmic complex of Congo origins; said to be Cuba's national dance, originating in nineteenth-century slave barracks. There are three main types: *yambú,* a slow-paced and stately couples dance, imitating the gestures of older people; *guaguancó,* a medium-paced couples dance that pantomimes a man's effort to seduce a woman by using pelvic thrusts known as *vacunao;* and *columbia,* a fast-paced solo male dance, which emphasizes challenging feats of balance and style such as dancing around a bottle without knocking it over or breaking stride. All types of *rumba* rely on the *clave* to establish and articulate their rhythmic structure; see *clave.*

S

sagrado/a: [S] sacred, as opposed to profane or secular

salsa: [S] lit., "sauce"; in musical terms, the name of a popular Latin dance rhythm and musical genre with its origins in Afro-Cuban rhythms; first used by Ignacio Piñeiro in the 1920s *("Echale salsita")* and made popular in the 1960s and 1970s by various Cuban, Puerto Rican, Colombian, and U.S. bands.

sangre: [S] blood; in the discourse of postrevolutionary Cuba, leaders of the revolution have said that all Cubans possess *sangre negrita* (black blood), and have thus concluded that all Cubans are Afro-Cubans.

Santería: [S] the popular name for the Afro-Cuban polytheistic religious tradition that, during the almost four centuries of the slave trade in Cuba, gradually developed by the end of the nineteenth century into a series of religious practices born of mostly West African and some Spanish Catholic roots; more formally known as the Regla de Ocha (the law of the *orichas*); focuses on *oricha* worship; see also *oricha, Regla de Ocha.*

Santero/a: [S] priest/priestess of Santería; see also *babaloricha, iyaloricha.*

santo: [S] lit., "saint"; the popular Cuban name for *oricha.*

santurismo: [S] neologism coined by Rogelio Martínez Furé to refer to the ever more deeply entwined relationship between Santería and tourism.

shekere: [L] (alt., *chekere*) musical instrument made from a large beaded gourd; played in religious, folkloric, and popular Cuban music; see also *güiro.*

sindicato: [S] labor union; the *ñáñigos* were known for their strong labor unions *(sindicatos ñañigueros)* in Cuba.

socialismo: [S] socialism. In contemporary Cuba, billboards and posters proclaim "*¡Socialismo o muerte!*" (Socialism or death).

sociedad: [S] society; also refers to the specific subgroups of the Abakwá (also known as *juego, potencia, tierra, partido*); see also *juego, potencia.*

solar: [S] refers to a Cuban urban architectural style; usually a small structure which features a patio alongside or at the end of the main rooms; these patios are often the sites for *rumbas* or accommodate the spillover from a *toque de santo.*

son: [S] the most popular music and dance genre of the twentieth century in Cuba; forms the basis of *salsa* and other popular music and dance genres of Cuban origin.

sopera: [S] porcelain vessel (usually a soup tureen) that contains the sacred stones *(otanes)* and other sacred objects of the *orichas.*

suavecito: [S] softly, smoothly, gently; can refer to the way the *toques* for Ochún should be danced and played.

suplente: [S] substitute, replacement, understudy; often the second-in-command for a group of musicians or dancers in a folkloric ensemble.

T

tambor: [S] drum.

tambor aberíkula: [S/L] unconsecrated *(batá)* drum; typically used in folkloric ensembles that feature *batá* drums.

tambor de fundamento: [S/L] consecrated or baptized *(batá)* drum; *tambores de fundamento* must be used in the religious *toques de santo* of Santería.

tambor judío: [S] lit., "Jewish drum"; another name for an unconsecrated *(batá)* drum; see *tambor aberíkula.*

tamborero: [S] (alt., *tambolero*) drummer.

tata nganga: [K] priest of Palo Monte; see *Palo Monte, nganga.*

toque: [S] a specific rhythm for an Afro-Cuban *oricha;* any rhythm for an *oricha* of Santería; also refers to a *toque de santo* (q.v.).

toque de santo: [S] a religious celebration held by an initiate or practitioner of Santería, typically in honor of one particular *oricha;* features the performance of *batá de fundamento.*

trabajo: [S] lit., "work"; in the context of Afro-Cuban religious traditions, *trabajo* usually means a spell or a curse, the result of witchcraft.

tratado: [S] abstract musical structure of a *toque de santo.*

tres: [S] lit., "three"; musical instrument; from the guitar/lute family, smaller than a conventional guitar, with three double or triple courses of strings.

trigueño: [S] lit., "wheat-colored"; a nineteenth-century term of racial identification used mainly by whites to characterize people of African heritage in Cuba; synonymous with *moreno* (q.v.).

trono: [S] throne; in the context of Santería, refers to the colorful and well-appointed altar made for the *orichas* by religious practitioners.

tumbadora: [S] lowest-pitched drum of a set of three *conga* drums; maintains the bass rhythm within the trio; see also *conga, quinto.*

turista: [S] tourist.

V

viejo/a: [S] old man/woman.

vigilancia: [S] vigilance, especially as enacted by Committees for the Defense of the Revolution, and various types of guards; a hallmark of postrevolutionary Cuban society.

Vodou: [F] popular name of Haitian polytheistic religious tradition brought to Haiti by slaves from Togo and Benin; shares some formal similarities with Cuban Santería.

Y

yambú: [S] slow-paced couples' *rumba* (q.v.).

Yemayá: [L] *oricha* of the sea and motherhood; older *oricha;* said to be mother of Changó, and sister and mother of Ochún.

Yoruba: [L] name given in the early twentieth century to group of related tribes from southwestern Nigeria, including Iyesá, Oyo, Ijebu, and Egba; said to be the origins of the Lucumí religion, language, and other cultural practices.

Yuka: [K] drums, rhythms, and other cultural practices originating from Bantu-speaking people who were landed as slaves in Cuba from the sixteenth to the nineteenth century; see also *Bantu, Congo.*

Z

zafra: [S] sugar harvest.

SELECTED DISCOGRAPHY

Aguabella, Francisco. *Francisco Aguabella y Sus Tambores Batá: Oriki Ara Oko.* (1994.) OLM Records 10038.

Aguabella, Francisco, y Su Grupo, featuring Lázaro Galarraga. (1992.) *Oriza:Bembé y Afrocuban Music.* OLM Records 10037.

Aguabella, Francisco, y Sus Tambores Batá. *Santería: Oro Cantado Con Tambores Batá.* 3 cassettes. (1990?) Go Productions Stereo 10032.

Amira, John, Orlando Fiol, and Joe DeLeón. *Music of Santería: Oru del Igbodu.* (1994.) White Cliffs Media WCM 9346.

Barreto, Emilio. *Emilio Barreto Presents Santísimo.* (1996.) Luz Productions CD001.

Bunnett, Jane (with Merceditas Valdés, Gonzalo Rubalcaba, Grupo Yoruba Andabo). *Spirits of Havana.* (1993.) Messidor 15825-2.

Cardona, Miltón. *Bembé.* (1987.) American Clave AMCL 1004.

Conjunto Folklórico Nacional de Cuba. *Conjunto Folklórico Nacional.* (1989.) Areito/EGREM LD 3564.

Conjunto Folklórico Nacional de Cuba, featuring Lázaro Ros, Felipe Alfonso, Zenaida Armenteros, and others. *Música Yoruba.* (Reissue 1996.) Bembé Records CD 2010-2.

González, Celina. *Que Viva Changó.* (1990.) EGREM/ARTEX CD 012.

Grupo Afrocuba de Matanzas and others. *Cuba, 30.* (1995.) World Network WDR 58.392.

Grupo Afrocuba de Matanzas. *Raíces Africanas/African Roots.* (1998.) Shanachie Records CD 66009.

Grupo Afrocuba de Matanzas. *Rituales Afrocubanos.* (1993.) Areito/EGREM CD 0058 00.

Iluyenkori (Roger Fixy and ensemble). *Cuba: Tambours Batá: Hommage à Yemaya et Ochún.* (1995.) Playasound PS 65138.

Iluyenkori (Roger Fixy and ensemble). *Percussions Cubaines.* (Reissue 1992.) Playasound PS 65084.

Iroko (Lázaro Galarraga, Bill Summers, and others). *Ilu Orisha*. (1996.) Interworld Records CD 924.

Los Muñequitos de Matanzas. *Cantar Maravilloso*. (1990.) Ace Records CDORB 053.

Los Muñequitos de Matanzas. *Guaguancó, Columbia, Yambú*. (1989.) Vitral Records VCD 277.

Los Muñequitos de Matanzas. *Ito Iban Echu: Sacred Yoruba Music of Cuba*. (1996.) Qbadisc QB 9022.

Los Muñequitos de Matanzas. *Los Muñequitos de Matanzas: Vacunao*. (1995.) Qbadisc QB 9017.

Martín, Gina. *Santero: Cuban Cult Music, featuring Gina Martín, Vol. II*. (Reissue 1988.) T. H. Rodven CDD 159.

Orquesta Batachanga, with John Santos, Rebeca Mauleón, and Orestes Vilató. *Mañana Para Los Niños*. (Reissue 1995.) Earthbeat / Bembé Records 9 42513-2 (previously EBD 2557).

Orquesta Estrellas Cubanas. *Violin a Ochun*. (1997?) Bis Music CD 137.

Oviedo, Isaac, Andrés Sotolongo, Pedro Hernández, and members of the Oviedo family. *Routes of Rhythm, Vol. 3: Isaac Oviedo*. (1992.) Rounder Records CD 5055.

Pedroso, Amelia, Regino Jiménez, Librada Quesada, and others. *Ilu Aña: Sacred Rhythms*. (1995.) Fundamento Productions.

Ríos, Orlando "Puntilla," and Nueva Generación. *Spirit Rhythms: Sacred Drumming and Chants from Cuba*. (1996.) Latitudes LT 50603.

Ros, Lázaro. *Asoyi: Cantos Arará*. (1995.) Caribe Productions CD 9476.

Ros, Lázaro. *Olorún*. (1994.) Green Linnet GLCD 4022.

Ros, Lázaro, and Mezcla. *Cantos*. (1992.) Intuition Records INT 3080 2.

Ros, Lázaro, and Olorún. *Songs for Eleguá*. (1996.) Ashé Records CD 2001.

Síntesis. *Ancestros*. (1992.) Qbadisc QB 9001.

Síntesis. *Orishas*. (1997.) Milan Latino 73138 / 358330-2.

Spiro, Michael, Mark Lamson, and others. *Bata Ketu: A Musical Interplay of Cuba and Brazil*. (1996.) Bembé Records CD 2011.

Valdés, Chucho. *Briyumba Palo Congo: Religion of the Congo*. (1999.) Blue Note 7243 4 9891722.

Valdés, Merceditas. *Aché*. (1990?) EGREM / ARTEX CD 010.

Valdés, Merceditas, y los tambores batá de Jesús Pérez. *Cuba*. (1992?) ASPIC X 55512.

Various artists. *Abbilona: Tambor Yoruba—Aggayú*. (1999.) Caribe Productions CD9549.

Various artists. *Abbilona: Tambor Yoruba—Changó*. (1999.) Caribe Productions CD9550.

Various artists. *Abbilona: Tambor Yoruba—Elegguá, Oggún, y Ochosi*. (1999.) Caribe Productions CD9546.

Various artists. *Abbilona: Tambor Yoruba—Obatalá*. (1999.) Caribe Productions CD9545.

Various artists. *Abbilona: Tambor Yoruba—Ochún*. (1999.) Caribe Productions CD9547.

Various artists. *Abbilona: Tambor Yoruba—Oricha Oko, Oddúa, Ibeyis, Olokun, y otros*. (1999.) Caribe Productions CD9552.

Various artists. *Abbilona: Tambor Yoruba—Oyá.* (1999.) Caribe Productions CD9551.

Various artists. *Abbilona: Tambor Yoruba—Yemayá.* (1999.) Caribe Productions CD9548.

Various artists. *Afro-Cuba: A Musical Anthology.* (1994.) Rounder Records CD 1088.

Various artists. *Caliente = Hot: Puerto Rican and Cuban Musical Expression in New York.* (1977.) New World Records NW 244-2.

Various artists. *Cantos de Congos y Paleros.* (1994.) ARTEX CD 091.

Various artists. *Cantos de Santería.* (1994.) ARTEX CD 090.

Various artists. *Caribbean Revels: Haitian Rara and Dominican Gaga.* (Reissue 1991.) Smithsonian Folkways CD SF 40402.

Various artists. *Cuba: I Am Time.* 4 vols. (1997.) Blue Jackal Entertainment BJAC 5010-2.

Various artists. *Cuba: Les Danses des Dieux: Musique des cultes et fêtes afro-cubaines.* (1988.) Harmonia Mundi/Ocora HM 83/Ocora C 559051.

Various artists. *Official Retrospective of Cuban Music.* 4 vols. (1999.) Tonga Productions TNG4CD 9303.

Various artists. *Rhythms of Rapture: Sacred Musics of Haitian Vodou.* (1995.) Smithsonian Folkways SF CD 40464.

Various artists. *Routes of Rhythm, Vol. 1: A Carnival of Cuban Music.* (1990.) Rounder Records CD 5049.

Various artists. *Sacred Rhythms of Cuban Santería/Ritmos Sagrados de la Santería Cubana.* (1995.) Smithsonian Folkways SF CD 40419.

Various artists. *Yoruba/Dahomean Collection: Orishas across the Ocean.* (1998.) Library of Congress Endangered Music Project. Rykodisc RCD 10405.

Various artists. *Yoruba Drums from Benin, West Africa: The World's Musical Traditions, 8.* (1994.) Smithsonian Folkways CD SF 40440.

SELECTED FILMOGRAPHY

Blank, Les, dir.
>   1995   *Sworn to the Drum: A Tribute to Francisco Aguabella.* El Cerrito, Calif.:
>   Flower Films.

Butia, Lázaro, dir.
>   1991   *Los Dioses del Futuro: La Fiesta del Fuego.* La Habana: Instituto Cubano del
>   Arte e Industria Cinematográficos (ICAIC)/Videoamerica.

Castro, Leticia, dir.
>   1988   *Causas y Azares.* La Habana: Escuela Internacional de Cine y Televisión
>   (EICTV).

Conjunto Folklórico Nacional de Cuba.
>   n.d. (1988?)   Promotional video. La Habana: Mundo Latino.

Cutumba: Ballet Folklórico Afro-Cubano de Santiago de Cuba.
>   n.d. (1997?)   Promotional video. Santiago de Cuba.

Deren, Maya, dir.
>   1947–1951   *Divine Horsemen: The Living Gods of Haiti.* New York: Mystic Fire Video.

Dibb, Michael, dir.
>   1989–1990   *¿Qué Se Toca en Cuba?* BBC Television Production, in association with
>   Cuban Television.

Dratch, Howard, and Eugene Rosow, dirs.
>   1989   *Routes of Rhythm, Parts 1, 2, 3.* With Harry Belafonte. Los Angeles: Cul-
>   tural Research and Communication, Inc., in association with KCET Los
>   Angeles.

Espinosa, Julio G., Oscar Valdés, Héctor Veitía, and Constante Diego, dirs.
>   n.d. (1991?)   *Rumbas y Comparsas.* La Habana: Instituto Cubano del Arte e Industria
>   Cinematográficos (ICAIC).

259

Gleason, Judith, and Elisa Mereghetti, dir.

1992   *The King Does Not Lie: The Initiation of a Shangó Priest.* New York: Film-makers Library.

Gutiérrez Alea, Tomás, and Juan Carlos Tabio, dirs.

1994   *Strawberry and Chocolate.* La Habana: Instituto Cubano del Arte e Industria Cinematográficos (ICAIC). (also available through Miramax)

Iranzo, Irma, dir.

1988   *Yemayá.* La Habana: Escuela Internacional de Cine y Televisión (EICTV).

López, Rigoberto, dir.

1989   *Mensajero de los Dioses.* La Habana: Instituto Cubano del Arte e Industria Cinematográficos (ICAIC).

Octavio Gómez, Manuel, dir.

1983   *Patakín.* La Habana: Instituto Cubano del Arte e Industria Cinematográficos (ICAIC).

Quiñones, Tato, dir.

n.d. (1989?)   *Nganga Kiyangala.* La Habana: Instituto Cubano del Arte e Industria Cinematográficos (ICAIC).

n.d. (1990?)   *Aché Moyuba Orisha: Sobre La Santería Cubana.* La Habana: Instituto Cubano del Arte e Industria Cinematográficos (ICAIC), in cooperation with Television Latina.

Rolando, Gloria, dir.

1990   *Oggún.* La Habana: Instituto Cubano del Arte e Industria Cinematográficos (ICAIC). (Also available through afrocubaweb.com.)

Ruíz, Elio, dir.

1986   *En El País de los Orichas.* Conjunto Folklórico Nacional de Cuba. La Habana: Mundo Latino.

Ruíz, Elio, and Tato Quiñones, dirs.

1990   *¿Quién Baila Aquí?* La Habana: Mundo Latino.

Sanca, Domingos, dir.

1988   *Altares, Figuras, y Símbolos en Guanabacoa.* La Habana: Escuela Internacional de Cine y Televisión (EICTV).

Santana, Alfred, dir.

1986   *Voices of the Gods.* New York: Third World Newsreel.

REFERENCES

Abiodun, Rowland, Henry Drewal, and John Pemberton III, eds.

1994a   *The Yoruba Artist: New Theoretical Perspectives on African Arts.* Washington, D.C.: Smithsonian Institution Press.

Abrahams, Roger D.

1983   *The Man-of-Words in the West Indies: Performance and the Emergence of Creole Culture.* Austin: University of Texas Press.

Abrahams, Roger D., and Richard Bauman, eds.

1981   *And Other Neighborly Names: Social Process and Cultural Image in Texas Folklore.* Austin: University of Texas Press.

Abu-Lughod, Lila

1990   "Can There Be a Feminist Ethnography?" *Women and Performance: A Journal of Feminist Theory* 5 (1): 7–27.

1993   *Writing Women's Worlds: Bedouin Stories.* Berkeley: University of California Press.

Acosta, Leonardo

1982   *Música y descolonización.* La Habana: Editorial Arte y Literatura.

1983   *Del tambor al sintetizador.* La Habana: Editorial Letras Cubanas.

African Language Institute

1991   *Dictionary of the Yoruba Language.* Ibadan: Oxford University Press.

Alén, Olavo

n.d.   *Musical Genres of Cuba.* La Habana: CIDMUC.

1986   *La música de las sociedades de tumba francesa en Cuba.* La Habana: Casa de las Americas.

Allen, Ray, and Lois Wilcken, eds.

1998   *Island Sounds in the Global City.* New York: New York Folklore Society and Institute for Studies in American Music, Brooklyn College.

Amira, John, and Steven Cornelius

1992   *The Music of Santería: Traditional Rhythms of the Batá Drums.* Crown Point, Ind.: White Cliffs Media Company.

Anderson, Michelle

1982   "Authentic Voodoo Is Syncretic." *Drama Review* 26 (2): 89–110.

Angel Carreras, Julio

1985   *Esclavitud, abolición, y racismo.* La Habana: Editorial de Ciencias Sociales.

Apter, Andrew

1992   *Black Critics and Kings: The Hermeneutics of Power in Yoruba Society.* Chicago: University of Chicago Press.

Argüelles Mederos, Aníbal, and Ileana Hodge Limonta

1991   *Los llamados cultos sincreticos y el espiritismo.* La Habana: Editorial Academia.

Averill, Gage

1997   *A Day for the Hunter, a Day for the Prey: Popular Music and Power in Haiti.* Chicago: University of Chicago Press.

Babiracki, Carol

1997   "What's the Difference? Reflections on Gender and Research in Village India." In *Shadows in the Field: New Perspectives for Fieldwork in Ethnomusicology,* pp. 121–136. New York: Oxford University Press.

Barnes, Sandra, ed.

1997   *Africa's Ogun: Old World and New.* 2d ed. Bloomington: Indiana University Press.

Barnet, Miguel

1961   "La religión de los yoruba y sus dioses." *Actas del Folklore* 1 (1): 9–16.

Barz, Gregory F., and Timothy J. Cooley, eds.

1997   *Shadows in the Field: New Perspectives for Fieldwork in Ethnomusicology.* New York: Oxford University Press.

Bascom, William R.

1950   "The Focus of Cuban Santería." *Southwestern Journal of Anthropology* 6 (1): 64–68.

1952   "Two Forms of Afro-Cuban Divination." In Sol Tax, ed., *Acculturation in the Americas,* pp. 169–179. Chicago: University of Chicago Press.

1969a   *Ifa Divination.* Bloomington: Indiana University Press.

1969b   *The Yoruba of Southwestern Nigeria.* New York: Holt, Rinehart, and Winston.

1977   *Frontiers of Folklore.* Boulder, Colo.: Westview.

1980   *Sixteen Cowries.* Bloomington: Indiana University Press.

Bastide, Roger

1971   *African Civilizations in the New World.* New York: Harper & Row.

Baudrillard, Jean

1994   *Simulacra and Simulations.* Translated by Sheila Faria Glaser. Ann Arbor: University of Michigan Press.

Bauman, Richard, and Americo Paredes

1972   *Toward New Perspectives in Folklore.* Austin: University of Texas Press.

Béhague, Gerard

1984   "Patterns of *Candomblé* Music Performance: An Afro-Brazilian Religious Setting." In Gerard Béhague, ed., *Performance Practice: Ethnomusicological Perspectives,* pp. 222–254. Westport, Conn.: Greenwood.

1988   "The Effects of Tourism on Afro-Bahian Traditional Music in Salvador, Bahia (Brazil)." In International Council for Traditional Music, *Come Mek Me Hol' Yu Han': The Impact of Tourism on Traditional Music,* pp. 57–66. Kingston: Jamaica Memory Bank.

Beier, Ulli

1961a   "El Templo de Changó del Timi de Ede." *Actas del Folklore* 1 (2): 19–22.

1961b   "La actitud de los yorubas hacia los perros." *Actas del Folklore* 1 (8): 13–17.

1961c   "Comparación entre las artes ibo y yoruba." *Actas del Folklore* 1 (10–12): 21–24.

Bell, Diane, Pat Caplan, and Wazir Jahan Karim, eds.

1993   *Gendered Fields: Women, Men and Ethnography.* London: Routledge.

Ben-Amos, Dan, and Kenneth Goldstein, eds.

1975   *Folklore, Performance, and Communication.* The Hague: Mouton.

Benítez Rojo, Antonio

1988   "Fernando Ortíz and Cubanness: A Postmodern Perspective." *Cuban Studies* 18:125–132.

1996   *The Repeating Island.* 2d ed. Durham, N.C.: Duke University Press.

Betto, Frei

1988   *Fidel and Religion.* New York: Simon & Schuster.

Binder, Wolfgang, ed.

1993   *Slavery in the Americas.* Würzburg: Königshausen u. Neumann.

Blacking, John

1979   "Some Problems of Theory and Method in the Study of Musical Change." *Yearbook of the International Folk Music Council* 9 (1977): 1–26.

Blasier, Cole, and Carmelo Mesa-Lago, eds.

1979   *Cuba in the World.* Pittsburgh: University of Pittsburgh Press.

Blum, Joseph

1978   "Problems of Salsa Research." *Ethnomusicology* 22 (1): 137–149.

Blutstein, Howard I., et al.

1971   *Area Handbook for Cuba.* Washington, D.C.: U.S. Government Printing Office.

Bolívar Aróstegui, Natalia

1990   *Los orishas en Cuba.* La Habana: Ediciones Unión.

1994   *Los orishas en Cuba.* Edición revisada y ampliada por olochas y libretas de
        Ifá. La Habana: Ediciones PM.

1997   *Cuba: Imágenes y relatos de un mundo mágico.* La Habana: Ediciones Unión.

Booth, David

1976   "Cuba, Color, and the Revolution." *Science and Society* XI (2): 129–172.

Brandon, George

1993   *Santeria from Africa to the New World: The Dead Sell Memories.* Bloomington:
        Indiana University Press.

Brenner, Philip, William LeoGrande, Donna Rich, and Daniel Siegel, eds.

1989   *The Cuba Reader.* New York: Grove Press.

Brock, Lisa, and Digna Castañeda Fuertes, eds.

1998   *Between Race and Empire: African-Americans and Cubans before the Cuban Revo-*
        lution. Philadelphia: Temple University Press.

Brock, Lisa, and Otis Cunningham

1991   "Race and the Cuban Revolution: A Critique of Carlos Moore's *Castro, the*
        Blacks, and Africa." *Cuban Studies* 21:171–185.

Brown, David

1989   Garden in the Machine: Afro-Cuban Sacred Art and Performance in Urban
        New Jersey and New York. Ph.D. dissertation, Yale University.

1993   "Thrones of the Orichas: Afro-Cuban Festive Initiatory and Domestic Altars
        in African Diaspora Cultural History." *African Arts* 26 (4): 44–59, 85–87.

1996   "Toward an Ethnoaesthetics of Santería Ritual Arts: The Practice of Altar
        Making and Gift Exchange." In Arturo Lindsay, ed., *Santería Aesthetics in*
        Contemporary Latin American Art, pp. 77–146. Washington, D.C.: Smithson-
        ian Institution Press.

2001   *Thrones of the Orichas: Innovation and Change in an Afro-Cuban Religion.*
        Chicago: University of Chicago Press.

Brown, Karen McCarthy

1991   *Mama Lola: A Vodou Priestess in Brooklyn.* Berkeley: University of California
        Press.

Browning, Barbara

1995   *Samba: Resistance in Motion.* Bloomington: Indiana University Press.

1998   *Infectious Rhythm: Metaphors of Contagion and the Spread of African Culture.*
        New York and London: Routledge.

Bruner, Edward M., and Barbara Kirshenblatt-Gimblett

1994   "Maasai on the Lawn: Tourist Realism in East Africa." *Cultural Anthropology*
        9 (4): 435–470.

Buchanan, Donna

1995   "Metaphors of Power, Metaphors of Truth: The Politics of Music Profes-
        sionalism in Bulgarian Folk Orchestras." *Ethnomusicology* 39 (3): 381–416.

Bueno, Salvador
    1978   *Leyendas cubanas.* La Habana: Editorial Arte y Literatura.
Butler, Judith
    1990   *Gender Trouble: Feminism and the Subversion of Identity.* New York: Routledge.
    1993   *Bodies That Matter: On the Discursive Limits of "Sex."* New York: Routledge.
Cabrera, Lydia
    1970   *La sociedad secreta abakuá.* Miami: Ediciones C. R.
    1980   *Yemayá y Ochún: Kariocha, Iyalorichas y Olorichas.* New York: Ediciones C. R.
    1984   *Vocabulario congo (el bantu que se habla en Cuba).* Miami: Ediciones C. R.
    1986a   *Añagó: Vocabulario lucumí (el yoruba que se habla en Cuba).* Miami: Ediciones Universal.
    1986b   *El monte.* Miami: Colección del Chichereku.
Canizares, Raul
    1999   *Cuban Santería: Walking with the Night.* Rochester, Vt.: Destiny Books.
Cannon, Terence
    1983   *Revolutionary Cuba.* La Habana: Editorial José Martí.
Carbonell, Walterio
    1961   *Crítica: Como surgió la cultura nacional.* La Habana: Ediciones Yaka.
Carpentier, Alejo
    1988   *La música en Cuba.* La Habana: Editorial Letras Cubanas.
Carvalho, José Jorge de
    1993   "Aesthetics of Opacity and Transparence: Myth, Music, and Ritual in the Xango Cult and in the Western Art Tradition." *Latin American Music Review* 14 (2): 202–231.
Casal, Lourdes
    1979   Revolution and Race. Working Paper No. 39, Latin American Program, The Wilson Center, Washington, D.C.
    1989   "Race Relations in Cuba." In Philip Brenner et al., eds. *The Cuba Reader,* pp. 471–486. New York: Grove Press.
Casanova Oliva, Ana Victoria
    1988   *Problemática organológica cubana.* La Habana: Casa de las Americas.
Castellanos, Isabel
    1977   The Use of Language in Afro-Cuban Religion. Ph.D. dissertation, Georgetown University.
Castellanos, Israel
    1914a   "Etnología de la Hampa Cubana." *La Revista Semanario Ilustrado* I (9): 1–2.
    1914b   "El tipo brujo." *Revista Bimestre Cubana,* n.p.
    1916–1917   "Consideraciones sobre el ñañiguismo: El ñañiguismo es el 'duk—duk' del hampa cubana?" *La Reforma Social* 9:126–133.

Castellanos, Jorge, and Isabel Castellanos

1987 "The Geographic, Ethnologic, and Linguistic Roots of Cuban Blacks." *Cuban Studies* 17:95–110.

1988 *Cultura afrocubana: El negro en Cuba, 1492–1844.* Vol. 1. Miami: Ediciones Universal.

1990 *Cultura afrocubana: El negro en Cuba, 1845–1959.* Vol. 2. Miami: Ediciones Universal.

1992 *Cultura afrocubana: Las religiones y las lenguas.* Vol. 3. Miami: Ediciones Universal.

1994 *Cultural afrocubana: Letras, música, arte.* Vol. 4. Miami: Ediciones Universal.

Chao Carbonero, Graciela

1982 *Bailes yoruba de Cuba: Guía de estudio.* La Habana: Editorial Pueblo y Educación.

Chernoff, John Miller

1979 *African Rhythm and African Sensibility.* Chicago: University of Chicago Press.

Chomsky, Noam

1965 *Aspects of the Theory of Syntax.* Cambridge, Mass.: MIT Press.

Chopyak, James D.

1987 "The Role of Music in Mass Media, Public Education, and the Formation of a Malaysian National Culture." *Ethnomusicology* 31 (3): 431–454.

Clark, Linda L.

1984 *Social Darwinism in France.* University: University of Alabama Press.

Clifford, James

1988 *The Predicament of Culture.* Cambridge, Mass.: Harvard University Press.

1997 *Routes: Travel and Translation in the Late Twentieth Century.* Cambridge, Mass.: Harvard University Press.

Clifford, James, and George E. Marcus, eds.

1986 *Writing Culture: The Poetics and Politics of Ethnography.* Berkeley and Los Angeles: University of California Press.

Clytus, John

1970 *Black Man in Red Cuba.* Miami: University of Miami Press.

Code, Lorraine

1991 *What Can She Know? Feminist Theory and the Construction of Knowledge.* Ithaca, N.Y.: Cornell University Press.

Cornelius, Steven

1989 The Convergence of Power: An Investigation into the Music Liturgy of Santería in New York City. Ph.D. dissertation, University of California, Los Angeles.

Cosentino, Donald

1987 "Who Is That Fellow in the Many-Colored Cap? Transformations of Eshu in Old and New World Mythologies." *Journal of American Folklore* 100:261–275.

Courlander, Harold
  1963   *Negro Folk Music.* New York: Columbia University Press.
Crook, Larry
  1982   "A Musical Analysis of the Cuban Rumba." *Latin American Music Review* 3 (1): 92–123.
Cros Sandoval, Mercedes
  1979   "Santería as a Mental Health Care System: An Historical Overview." *Social Science and Medicine* 13B (2): 137–151.
Crowley, Daniel J., ed.
  1977   *African Folklore in the New World.* Austin: University of Texas Press.
Curtin, Philip
  1969   *The Atlantic Slave Trade: A Census.* Madison: University of Wisconsin Press.
Daniel, Yvonne Laverne Payne
  1995   *Rumba: Dance and Social Change in Contemporary Cuba.* Bloomington: Indiana University Press.
Davidson, Basil
  1980   *The African Slave Trade.* Rev. ed. Boston: Little, Brown.
del Aguila, Juan M.
  1984   *Cuba: Dilemmas of a Revolution.* Boulder, Colo.: Westview.
Deschamps Chapeaux, Pedro
  1967   "El lenguaje abakuá." *Etnología y Folklore* 4:39–47.
  1969   "Marcas tribales de los esclavos en Cuba." *Etnología y Folklore* 8:65–78.
Díaz Fabelo, Teodoro
  1960   *Olorún.* La Habana: Ediciones del Departamento de Folklore del Teatro Nacional de Cuba.
Díaz Ayala, Cristobal
  1981   *Música cubana: Del Areyto a la Nueva Trova.* San Juan: Editorial Cubanacan.
Domínguez, Jorge I.
  1976   "Racial and Ethnic Relations in the Cuban Armed Forces: A Non-Topic." *Armed Forces and Society* 2 (2): 273–290.
Dorson, Richard M., ed.
  1972   *Folklore and Folklife: An Introduction.* Chicago: University of Chicago Press.
Drewal, Henry John
  1988   "Performing the Other: Mami Wata Worship in West Africa." *The Drama Review* 32 (2): 160–185.
Drewal, Henry John, and Margaret Thompson Drewal
  1983   *Gelede: Art and Female Power among the Yoruba.* Bloomington: Indiana University Press.
Drewal, Margaret Thompson
  1986   "Art and Trance among Yoruba Shango Devotees." *African Arts* 20 (1): 60–67.
  1988   "Ritual Performance in Africa Today." *The Drama Review* 32 (2): 25–30.

1992   *Yoruba Ritual: Performers, Play, Agency.* Bloomington: Indiana University Press.

1997   "Dancing for Ogún in Yorubaland and in Brazil." In Sandra Barnes, ed., *Africa's Ogun: Old World and New,* pp. 199–234. Bloomington: Indiana University Press.

Duany, Jorge

1982   "Stones, Trees, and Blood: An Analysis of a Cuban Santero Ritual." *Cuban Studies* 12 (2): 101–115.

Dundes, Alan, ed.

1965   *The Study of Folklore.* Englewood Cliffs, N.J.: Prentice-Hall.

1973   *Mother Wit from the Laughing Barrel: Readings in the Interpretation of Afro-American Folklore.* Englewood Cliffs, N.J.: Prentice-Hall.

Dunstan, Elizabeth, ed.

1969   *Twelve Nigerian Languages.* New York: Africana.

Durkheim, Émile

1915   *The Elementary Forms of the Religious Life.* Translated by Joseph Ward Swain. London: George Allen and Unwin.

Dzidzienyo, Anani, and Lourdes Casal

1979   *The Position of Blacks in Brazilian and Cuban Society.* London: Minority Rights Group.

Eleburuibon, Ifayemi (Chief Priest)

1989   *The Adventures of Obatala, Ifá and Santería God of Creativity.* Oyo, Nigeria: A.P.I. Production.

Eliade, Mircea

1959   *The Sacred and the Profane: The Nature of Religion.* New York: Harper & Row.

Elliot, Jeffrey, and Mervyn M. Dymally

1986   *Fidel Castro: Nothing Can Stop the Course of History.* New York: Pathfinder Press.

Engerman, Stanley L., and Eugene Genovese, eds.

1975   *Race and Slavery in the Western Hemisphere: Quantitative Studies.* Princeton: Princeton University Press.

Epega, Afolabi A., and Philip John Neimark

1995   *The Sacred Ifa Oracle.* New York: HarperCollins.

Fattah, Ezzat A.

1997   *Criminology: Past, Present, and Future; A Critical Overview.* New York: St. Martin's.

Feijoo, Samuel

1986   *Mitología cubana.* La Habana: Editorial Letras Cubanas.

Feld, Steven

1990   *Sound and Sentiment: Birds, Weeping, Poetics, and Song in Kaluli Expression.* 2d ed. Philadelphia: University of Pennsylvania Press.

Fernández Robaina, Tomás

1997   *Hablen paleros y santeros.* La Habana: Editorial de Ciencias Sociales.

Ferri, Enrico

1967   *Criminal Sociology.* (Originally published 1917.) New York: Agathon.

Finkelstein, Sidney

1952   *How Music Expresses Ideas.* New York: International.

1989   *Composer and Nation: The Folk Heritage in Music.* 2d ed. New York: International.

Flores-Peña, Ysamur, and Roberta J. Evanchuk

1994   *Santería Garments and Altars: Speaking without a Voice.* Jackson: University Press of Mississippi.

Friedman, Robert

1982   Making an Abstract World Concrete: Knowledge, Confidence, and Structural Dimensions of Performance among Batá Drummers in Santería. Ph.D. dissertation, Indiana University.

Fuente, Alejandro de la

1999   "Myths of Racial Democracy: Cuba, 1900–1912." *Latin American Research Review* 34 (3): 39–73.

Fusco, Coco

1995   *English Is Broken Here: Notes on Cultural Fusion in the Americas.* New York: The New Press.

Galán, Natalio

1983   *Cuba y sus sones.* Valencia: Pre-Textos.

Galembo, Phyllis

1993   *Divine Inspiration: From Benin to Bahia.* Albuquerque: University of New Mexico Press.

Gallardo, Jorge Emilio

1986   *Presencia africana en la cultura de América Latina.* Buenos Aires: Fernando García Cambeiro.

García Canclini, Néstor

1993   *Transforming Modernity: Popular Culture in Mexico.* Translated by Lidia Lozano. Austin: University of Texas Press.

García-Carranza, Araceli, ed.

1970   *Bio-bibliografía de Don Fernando Ortíz.* La Habana: Instituto del Libro.

García Cortez, Julio

1980   *Pataki: Leyendas y misterios de orishas africanos.* Miami: Ediciones Universal.

Geertz, Clifford

1973   *The Interpretation of Cultures.* New York: Basic Books.

1983   *Local Knowledge: Further Essays in Interpretive Anthropology.* New York: Basic Books.

1988   *Works and Lives: The Anthropologist as Author.* Stanford: Stanford University Press.

Gerard, Charley, with Marty Sheller

1989   *Salsa! The Rhythm of Latin Music.* Crown Point, Ind.: White Cliffs Media Company.

Giddens, Anthony

1979   *Central Problems in Social Theory: Action, Structure, and Conflict in Social Analysis.* Berkeley: University of California Press.

Gleason, Judith

1975   *Santería Bronx.* New York: Atheneum.

1987   *Oyá: In Praise of the Goddess.* Boston: Shambhala.

Gobineau, Comte Joseph Arthur de

1970   *Selected Political Writings.* Edited by Michael Biddiss. London: Jonathan Cape.

González-Wippler, Migene

1973   *Santería.* New York: The Julian Press.

Goodsell, James Nelson, ed.

1975   *Fidel Castro's Personal Revolution in Cuba.* New York: Alfred A. Knopf.

Gould, Stephen Jay

1981   *The Mismeasure of Man.* New York: W. W. Norton.

Graburn, Nelson H. H.

1969   "Art and Acculturative Processes." *International Social Science Journal* 21 (3): 457–468.

1976   *Ethnic and Tourist Arts.* Berkeley: University of California Press.

Guanche, Jesus

1983   *Procesos etnoculturales de Cuba.* La Habana: Editorial Letras Cubanas.

Güerere, Tabaré

1995   *Las diosas negras: La santería en femenino.* Caracas: Alfadil Ediciones.

Guerra, Ramiro

1989   *Teatralización del folklore.* La Habana: Editorial Letras Cubanas.

Hagedorn, Katherine

1992   The Birth of the Conjunto Folklórico in Cuba. Unpublished paper.

1995   *Anatomía del Proceso Folklórico:* The "Folkloricization" of Afro-Cuban Religious Performance in Cuba. Ph.D. dissertation, Brown University.

1996   Review of Jocelyne Guilbault, comp., *Music Traditions of St. Lucia, West Indies: Dances and Songs from a Caribbean Island. Ethnomusicology* 40 (3): 530–532.

1998   Review of Les Blank, dir., *Sworn to the Drum: A Tribute to Francisco Aguabella. Ethnomusicology* 41 (2): 326–329.

1999a   Review of Peter Manuel, Kenneth Bilby, and Michael Largey, *Caribbean Currents: Caribbean Music from Rumba to Reggae. American Ethnologist* 26 (1): 256–257.

1999b   Review of Robin Moore, *Nationalizing Blackness: Afrocubanismo and Artistic Revolution in Havana, 1920–1940. Latin American Music Review* 20 (1): 145–148.

2000a   Review of María Teresa Vélez, *Drumming for the Gods: The Life and Times of Felipe García Villamil, Santero, Palero, Abakuá. Yearbook for Traditional Music* 32:192–193.

2000b   "Bringing down the Santo: An Analysis of Possession Performance in Afro-Cuban Santería." *World of Music* 3:99–113.

Halebsky, Sandor, and John M. Kirk, eds.

1992   *Cuba in Transition: Crisis and Transformation.* Boulder, Colo.: Westview.

Hall, Stuart, and Tony Jefferson, eds.

1976   *Resistance through Rituals.* London: Hutchinson.

Handelman, Don

1990   *Models and Mirrors: Towards an Anthropology of Public Events.* Cambridge: Cambridge University Press.

Hart Davalos, Armando

1983   *Cambiar las reglas del juego.* La Habana: Editorial Letras Cubanas.

Helg, Aline

1991   "Afro-Cuban Protest: The Partido Independiente de Color, 1908–1912." *Cuban Studies* 21:101–121.

1995   *Our Rightful Share: The Afro-Cuban Struggle for Equality, 1886–1912.* Chapel Hill: University of North Carolina Press.

Herskovits, Melville

1938   *Acculturation: The Study of Culture Contact.* New York: J. J. Augustin.

1958   *The Myth of the Negro Past.* (Originally published 1941.) Boston: Beacon Press.

Herzfeld, Michael

1982   *Ours Once More: Folklore, Ideology, and the Making of Modern Greece.* Austin: University of Texas Press.

Hobsbawm, Eric, and Terence Ranger, eds.

1983   *The Invention of Tradition.* Cambridge: Cambridge University Press.

Hopkins, Pandora

1986   *Aural Thinking in Norway.* New York: Human Sciences Press.

Horowitz, M. M.

1971   *Peoples and Cultures of the Caribbean.* New York: Natural History Press.

Hosking, Geoffrey

1985   *The First Socialist Society.* Cambridge, Mass.: Harvard University Press.

Howard, James H.

1983   "Pan-Indianism in Native American Music and Dance." *Ethnomusicology* 27 (1): 71–82.

International Council for Traditional Music

1988   *Come Mek Me Hol' Yu Han': The Impact of Tourism on Traditional Music.* Kingston: Jamaica Memory Bank.

Iznaga, Diana

   1989   *Transculturación en Fernando Ortíz.* La Habana: Editorial de Ciencias Sociales.

Jackson, Michael, ed.

   1996   *Things as They Are: New Directions in Phenomenological Anthropology.* Bloomington: Indiana University Press.

James, Joel, José Millet, and Alexis Alarcón

   1992   *El vodú en Cuba.* Santiago de Cuba: Ediciones CEDEE/Casa del Caribe.

Johnson, Samuel

   1969   *The History of the Yorubas: From Earliest Times to the Beginning of the British Protectorate.* (Originally published 1921.) London: Routledge & Kegan.

Jones, A. M.

   1959   *Studies in African Music.* London: Oxford University Press.

Jones, David A.

   1986   *History of Criminology: A Philosophical Perspective.* New York: Greenwood.

Journal of Decorative and Propaganda Arts

   1996   Cuba Theme Issue: 1875–1945. Vol. 22.

Kaplan, Amy

   1993   "Black and Blue on San Juan Hill." In Amy Kaplan and Donald Pease, eds., *The Cultures of United States Imperialism,* pp. 127–142. Durham, N.C.: Duke University Press.

Kaplan, Amy, and Donald Pease, eds.

   1993   *The Cultures of United States Imperialism.* Durham, N.C.: Duke University Press.

Kartomi, Margaret J.

   1981   "The Processes and Results of Musical Culture Contact: A Discussion of Terminology and Concepts." *Ethnomusicology* 25 (2): 227–249.

Keil, Charles, and Steven Field

   1994   *Music Grooves: Essays and Dialogues.* Chicago: University of Chicago Press.

Kertzer, David

   1991   *Ritual, Politics, and Power.* New Haven: Yale University Press.

Kirk, John

   1989   *Between God and Party: Religion and Politics in Revolutionary Cuba.* Tampa: University of South Florida Press.

Kirshenblatt-Gimblett, Barbara

   1995   "Theorizing Heritage." *Ethnomusicology* 39 (3): 367–380.

   1998   *Destination Culture: Tourism, Museums, and Heritage.* Berkeley: University of California Press.

Kisliuk, Michelle

   1997   "(Un)Doing Fieldwork: Sharing Songs, Sharing Lives." In Greg Barz and Tim Cooley, eds. *Shadows in the Field: New Perspectives for Fieldwork in Ethnomusicology,* pp. 23–44. New York: Oxford University Press.

1998   *Seize the Dance! BaAka Musical Life and the Ethnography of Performance.* New
        York: Oxford University Press.

Klein, Debra

2000   Yoruba Bàtá: Politics of Pop Tradition in Erin Osun and Overseas. Ph.D.
        dissertation, University of California, Santa Cruz.

Klein, Herbert S.

1986   *African Slavery in Latin America and the Caribbean.* Oxford: Oxford University
        Press.

Knauer, Lisa Maya

1999   Traveling Diasporic Cultures: Rumba, Community, and Identity in New
        York and Havana. Paper presented at the annual conference of the Society
        for Ethnomusicology, Austin, Texas.

Knight, Franklin W.

1970   *Slave Society in Cuba during the Nineteenth Century.* Madison: University of
        Wisconsin Press.

Koetting, James T.

1970   "Analysis and Notation of West African Drum Ensemble Music." *Selected
        Reports in Ethnomusicology* 1 (3): 116–146.

Koskoff, Ellen, ed.

1989   *Women and Music in Cross-Cultural Perspective.* Urbana: University of Illinois Press.

Labov, William

1972   *Sociolinguistic Patterns.* Philadelphia: University of Pennsylvania Press.

Lachatañeré, Rómulo

1939   "El sistema religioso de los lucumís y otras influencias africanas en Cuba
        (I)." *Estudios Afrocubanos* III:28–84.

1940   "El sistema religioso de los lucumís y otras influencias africanas en Cuba
        (II)." *Estudios Afrocubanos* IV:27–38.

1961a   "Nota histórica sobre los lucumís." *Actas del Folklore* 1 (2): 3–10.

1961b   "Tipos étnicos africanos que concurrieron en la amalgama cubana." *Actas
        del Folklore* 1 (3): 5–12.

1961c   "Nota sobre la formación de la población afrocubana." *Actas del Folklore* 1
        (4): 3–11.

1961d   "Las creencias religiosas de los afrocubanos y la falsa aplicación del tér-
        mino brujería." *Actas del Folklore* 1 (5): 11–15.

1961e   "La influencia bantu-yoruba en los cultos afrocubanos." *Actas del Folklore* 1
        (6): 3–8.

1961f   "El sistema religioso de los lucumís y otras influencias africanas en Cuba."
        Actas del Folklore 1 (7): 9–20.

1961g   "Rasgos bantus en la santería." *Actas del Folklore* 1 (8): 3–5.

1992   *¡¡Oh, Mío Yemayá!!* (Originally published 1938.) La Habana: Editorial de
        Ciencias Sociales.

1995   *Manual de santería (el sistema de cultos lucumís).* (Originally published 1942.) La Habana: Editorial de Ciencias Sociales.

Lamerán, Sara

1982   *El vestuario y su importancia en la danza.* La Habana: Editorial Pueblo y Educación.

Langness, Lewis

1981   *Lives.* Novato, Calif.: Chandler & Sharp.

Le Riverend, Julio

1973   "Fernando Ortíz y su obra cubana." In *Orbita de Fernando Ortíz,* n.p. La Habana: Instituto Cubano del Libro.

Leiner, Marvin

1989   "Cuba's Schools: Twenty-five Years Later." In Philip Brenner et al., eds., *The Cuba Reader,* pp. 445–456. New York: Grove Press.

León, Argeliers

1961a   "La expresión del pueblo en el TNC." *Actas del Folklore* 1 (1): 5–7.

1961b   "Las conmemoraciones mortuorias." *Actas del Folklore* 1 (5): 3–10.

1964   *Música folklórica cubana.* La Habana: Ediciones de la Biblioteca Nacional José Martí.

1969a   "Clausura del Seminario de Estudios Afroamericanos." *Etnología y Folklore* 7:95–106.

1969b   "Música popular de orígen africano en América Latina." *Etnología y Folklore* 8:33–64.

1984   *Del canto y el tiempo.* La Habana: Editorial Letras Cubanas.

1986   "De paleros y firmas se trata." *Unión* 1:70–106.

Levinson, Sandra, and Carol Brightman, eds.

1971   *Venceremos Brigade: Young Americans Sharing the Life and Work of Revolutionary Cuba.* New York: Simon & Schuster.

Lévy-Bruhl, Lucien

1985   *How Natives Think.* (Originally published 1926.) Translated by Lilian A. Clare. Princeton: Princeton University Press.

Lewis, Gordon, ed.

1983   *Main Currents in Caribbean Thought.* Baltimore: Johns Hopkins University Press.

Linares, María Teresa

1989   *La música y el pueblo.* (Originally published 1974.) La Habana: Editorial Pueblo y Educación.

Lindsay, Arturo, ed.

1996   *Santería Aesthetics in Contemporary Latin American Art.* Washington, D.C.: Smithsonian Institution Press.

Lindsay, Shawn

1996   "Hand Drumming: An Essay in Practical Knowledge." In Michael Jackson, ed., *Things as They Are: New Directions in Phenomenological Anthropology*, pp. 196–212. Bloomington: Indiana University Press.

Locke, David

1982   "Principles of Offbeat Timing and Cross-Rhythm in Southern E<u>w</u>e Dance Drumming." *Ethnomusicology* 26 (2): 217–246.

Lockwood, Lee

1969   *Castro's Cuba, Cuba's Fidel.* New York: Vintage.

Lofgren, Charles A.

1987   *The Plessy Case: A Legal-Historical Interpretation.* New York: Oxford University Press.

Lombroso, Cesare

1968   *Crime: Its Causes and Remedies.* (Originally published 1911.) Translated by Henry P. Horton. Montclair, N.J.: Patterson Smith.

Lombroso Ferrero, Gina

1911   *Criminal Man, According to the Classification of Cesare Lombroso.* New York: G. P. Putnam's Sons.

Loomis, Ormond H.

1983   *Cultural Conservation: The Protection of Cultural Heritage in the United States.* Washington, D.C.: Library of Congress.

López Valdés, Rafael L.

1961   "Las firmas de los santos." *Actas del Folklore* 1 (5): 17–24.

1966   "La Sociedad Secreta 'Abacuá' en un Grupo de Obreros Portuarios." *Etnología y Folklore* 2:5–26.

1971   *Racial Discrimination from Colonial Times to the Revolution.* La Habana: Instituto Cubano de Amistad con los Pueblos (ICAP).

1985   *Componentes africanos en el etnos cubano.* La Habana: Editorial de Ciencias Sociales.

1986   "Notas para el estudio etnohistórico de los esclavos Lucumí de Cuba." *Anales del Caribe* 6:55–74.

1989   African influence in Cuba. Lecture, Instituto Cubano de Amistad con los Pueblos (ICAP), Havana.

1991   African influence in Cuba. Lecture, Simposio de las Americas, Smithsonian Institution, Washington, D.C.

Luciano Franco, José

1980   *Comercio clandestino de esclavos.* La Habana: Editorial de Ciencias Sociales.

Macaloon, John J.

1984   *Rite, Drama, Festival, Spectacle: Rehearsals toward a Theory of Cultural Performance.* Philadelphia: Institute for the Study of Human Issues.

MacCannell, Dean

1999   *The Tourist: A New Theory of the Leisure Class.* 2d ed. Berkeley and Los Angeles: University of California Press.

Manuel, Peter

    1987   "Marxism, Nationalism, and Popular Music in Revolutionary Cuba." *Popular Music* 6 (2): 161–178.

Manuel, Peter, ed.

    1991   *Essays on Cuban Music: North American and Cuban Perspectives.* Lanham, Md.: University Press of America.

Manuel, Peter, with Kenneth Bilby and Michael Largey

    1995   *Caribbean Currents: Caribbean Music from Rumba to Reggae.* Philadelphia: Temple University Press.

Manzano, Juan Francisco

    1981   *The Life and Poems of a Cuban Slave, 1797–1854.* Edited by Edward J. Mullen. Hamden, Conn.: Archon.

Marcuzzi, Michael

    1996   Dancing with the Divine(r): Batá Drumming, Ifá Divination, and *Orisha* Worship in Cuba. Unpublished paper.

Marinello, Juan

    1989   *Cuba: Cultura.* La Habana: Editorial Letras Cubanas.

Marion, Jean-Luc

    1998   *Reduction and Givenness: Investigations of Husserl, Heidegger, and Phenomenology.* Evanston, Ill.: Northwestern University Press.

Marks, Morton

    1974   "Uncovering Ritual Structures in Afro-American Music." In Irving Zaretsky and Mark P. Leone, eds. *Religious Movements in Contemporary America,* pp. 60–134. Princeton: Princeton University Press.

Martínez Furé, Rogelio

    1961a   "Los collares." *Actas del Folklore* 1 (3): 23–24.

    1961b   "El bando azul." *Actas del Folklore* 1 (7): 21–23.

    1979   *Diálogos imaginarios.* La Habana: Editorial Arte y Literatura.

Mason, John

    1985   *Black Gods: Orisa Studies in the New World.* Brooklyn: Yoruba Theological Archministry.

    1992   *Orin Orisa: Songs for Selected Heads.* Brooklyn: Yoruba Theological Archministry.

    1993   *Four New World Yoruba Rituals.* 3d ed. Brooklyn: Yoruba Theological Archministry.

Mason, Michael

    1993   "'The Blood that Runs in the Veins': The Creation of Identity and a Client's Experience of Cuban-American *Santería Dilogún* Divination." *The Drama Review* 37 (2): 119–130.

    1994   "'I Bow My Head to the Ground': The Creation of Bodily Experience in a

Cuban-American *Santería* Initiation." *Journal of American Folklore* 107 (423): 23–39.

1997   Practicing *Santería,* Performing the Self: The Social Construction of Subjectivity in Humans and Gods in an Afro-Cuban Religion. Ph.D. dissertation, Indiana University.

Forthcoming   *Living Santería: Ritual and Experience in an Afro-Cuban Religion.*

McClary, Susan

1991   *Feminine Endings: Music, Gender, and Sexuality.* Minneapolis: University of Minnesota Press.

McManus, Jane

1989   *Getting to Know Cuba: A Travel Guide.* New York: St. Martin's.

Medin, Tzvi

1990   *Cuba: The Shaping of a Revolutionary Consciousness.* Translated by Martha Grenzback. Boulder, Colo.: Lynne Rienner Publishers.

Merriam, Alan P.

1955   "The Use of Music in the Study of a Problem of Acculturation." *American Anthropologist* 57:28–34.

Meyer, Leonard B.

1956   *Emotion and Meaning in Music.* Chicago: University of Chicago Press.

Millet, José, and Rafael Brea

1989   *Grupos folklóricos de Santiago de Cuba.* Santiago de Cuba: Editorial Oriente.

Ministerio de Cultura

1982   *La cultura en Cuba socialista.* La Habana: Editorial Letras Cubanas.

Miller, Tom

1992   *Trading with the Enemy: A Yankee Travels through Castro's Cuba.* New York: Atheneum.

Mitchell, M. Marion

1931   "Émile Durkheim and the Philosophy of Nationalism." *Political Science Quarterly* 46:87–106.

Montejo, Esteban

1980   *Biografía de un cimarrón.* Edited by Miguel Barnet. La Habana: Editorial Letras Cubanas.

Moore, Carlos

1988a   *Castro, the Blacks, and Africa.* Los Angeles: University of California Press.

1988b   "Race Relations in Socialist Cuba." In Sergio G. Roca, ed. *Socialist Cuba: Past Interpretations and Future Challenges,* pp. 175–206. Boulder: Westview.

Moore, Robin

1994   "Representations of Afrocuban Expressive Culture in the Writings of Fernando Ortíz." *Latin American Music Review* 15 (1): 32–54.

1997   *Nationalizing Blackness: Afrocubanismo and Artistic Revolution in Havana, 1920–1940.* Pittsburgh: University of Pittsburgh Press.

Moreno, Dennis

1988   *Un tambor arará.* La Habana: Editorial de Ciencias Sociales.

Moreno Fraginals, Manuel

1976   *The Sugarmill: The Socioeconomic Complex of Sugar in Cuba.* New York: Monthly Review Press.

1977   "Africa in Cuba: A Quantitative Analysis of the African Population in the Island of Cuba." In Vera Rubin and Arthur Tuden, eds., *Comparative Perspectives on Slavery in New World Plantation Societies,* pp. 187–201. New York: New York Academy of Sciences.

1978   *El ingenio: Complejo económico social cubano del azúcar.* La Habana: Editorial de Ciencias Sociales.

Mullen, Edward J.

1987   "'Los negros brujos': A Reexamination of the Text." *Cuban Studies* 17:111–129.

Murdock, George P.

1958   *African Cultural Summaries.* 10 vols. New Haven: Human Relations Area Files.

1959   *Africa: Its People and Their Cultural History.* New York: McGraw-Hill.

Murphy, Joseph M.

1992   *Santería: An African Religion in America.* Rev. ed. Boston: Beacon Press.

1994   *Working the Spirit: Ceremonies of the African Diaspora.* Boston: Beacon Press.

Murray, David R.

1980   *Odious Commerce: Britain, Spain, and the Abolition of the Cuban Slave Trade.* Cambridge: Cambridge University Press.

Nájera Ramírez, Olga

1989   "Social and Political Dimensions of Folklorico Dance: The Binational Dialectic of Residual and Emergent Culture." *Western Folklore* 48 (1): 15–32.

Nettl, Bruno

1978a   *Eight Urban Musical Cultures.* Urbana: University of Illinois Press.

1978b   "Some Aspects of the History of World Music in the Twentieth Century." *Ethnomusicology* 22 (1): 137–149.

Nettl, Bruno, and Melinda Russell, eds.

1998   *In the Course of Performance: Studies in the World of Musical Improvisation.* Chicago: University of Chicago Press.

Nettleford, Rex

1978   *Caribbean Cultural Identity: The Case of Jamaica.* Los Angeles: University of California Press.

1985   *Dance Jamaica: Cultural Definition and Artistic Discovery—The National Dance Theatre Company of Jamaica, 1962–1983.* New York: Grove Press.

Neumann, Peter
  1969   "Algunos aspectos nuevos acerca de la consolidación histórica y la vida
          económica de los negros de la selva de la Guayana Holandesa." *Etnología y
          Folklore* 7:85–93.
Oinas, Felix, ed.
  1978   *Folklore, Nationalism, and Politics.* Columbus, Ohio: Slavica.
Okely, Judith, and Helen Callaway, eds.
  1992   *Anthropology and Autobiography.* London and New York: Routledge.
Oppenheimer, Andres
  1992   *Castro's Final Hour: The Secret Story behind the Coming Downfall of Communist
          Cuba.* New York: Simon & Schuster.
Orovio, Helio
  1981   *Diccionario de la música cubana.* La Habana: Editorial Letras Cubanas.
Ortíz, Fernando
  1916   *Hampa Afro-Cubana: Los negros esclavos.* La Habana: Editorial Revista
          Bimestre Cubana.
  1920   "La fiesta cubana del día de reyes." *Revista Bimestre Cubana* XV:5–26.
  1921   "Los cabildos afrocubanos." *Revista Bimestre Cubana* XVI:5–39.
  1929   "Ni racismos ni xenofobias." *Revista Bimestre Cubana* XXIV:6–19.
  1937a   "La Sociedad de Estudios Afrocubanos contra los racismos: Advertencia,
          comprensión y designio." *Estudios Afrocubanos* I (1): 11–14.
  1937b   "La religión en la poesía mulata." *Estudios Afrocubanos* I (1): 15–62.
  1939   "Brujos o santeros." *Estudios Afrocubanos* III (3): 85–90.
  1940a   *Contrapunteo cubano del tabaco y el azúcar.* La Habana: Jesús Montero Editor.
  1940b   "Los factores humanos de la cubanidad." *Revista Bimestre Cubana* XLV (2):
          161–186.
  1951   *Los bailes y el teatro de los negros en el folklore de Cuba.* La Habana: Editorial
          Letras Cubanas.
1952–1955 *Los instrumentos de la música afrocubana.* 5 vols. La Habana: Publicaciones de
          la Dirección de Cultura del Ministerio de Educación.
  1965   *La africanía de la música folklórica de Cuba.* 2d ed. La Habana: Editora Uni-
          versitaria.
  1973a   *Hampa afro-cubana: Los negros brujos (apuntes para un estudio de etnología
          criminal).* (Originally published 1906.) Miami: Ediciones Universal.
  1973b   *La música afrocubana.* (Originally published 1906.) Madrid: Ediciones Jucar.
  1973c   *Orbita de Fernando Ortíz.* (Originally published 1921.) La Habana: Instituto
          Cubano del Libro.
  1976   *El engaño de las razas.* (Originally published 1946.) La Habana: Editorial de
          Ciencias Sociales.
  1985   *Nuevo cataura de cubanismos.* (Originally published 1923.) La Habana: Editor-
          ial de Ciencias Sociales.

1986   *Hampa afro-cubana: Los negros curros.* La Habana: Editorial de Ciencias Sociales.

Otero, Lisandro

1972   *Cultural Policy in Cuba.* Paris: UNESCO.

Pájares Santiesteban, Fidel

1993   *Ramiro Guerra y la danza en Cuba.* Quito: Editorial Casa de la Cultura Ecuatoriana.

Palmié, Stephan

1993   "Ethnogenetic Processes and Cultural Transfer in Afro-American Slave Populations." In Wolfgang Binder, ed., *Slavery in the Americas,* pp. 337–363. Würzburg: Königshausen u. Neumann.

Palmié, Stephan, ed.

1995   *Slave Cultures and the Cultures of Slavery.* Knoxville: University of Tennessee Press.

Paquette, Robert L.

1988   *Sugar Is Made with Blood.* Middletown: Wesleyan University Press.

Peacock, James L.

1990   "Ethnographic Notes on Sacred and Profane Performance." In Richard Schechner and Willa Appel, eds., *By Means of Performance,* pp. 208–220. Cambridge: Cambridge University Press.

Pérez, Cecilio (Obá Ecún)

1985   *Oricha: Metodología de la Religión Yoruba.* Miami: Editorial SIBI.

Perez, Louis A.

1983   *Cuba between Empires: 1878–1902.* Pittsburgh: University of Pittsburgh Press.

1988   *Cuba: Between Reform and Revolution.* Oxford: Oxford University Press.

Perez de la Riva, Juan

1961   "Cuadro sinóptico de la esclavitud en Cuba y de la cultura occidental." *Actas del Folklore* 1 (5): 1–25.

1975   *El barracón y otros ensayos.* La Habana: Editorial de Ciencias Sociales.

Perez Sarduy, Pedro, and Jean Stubbs, eds.

1993   *Afrocuba: An Anthology of Cuban Writing on Race, Politics, and Culture.* Melbourne: Ocean Press.

Perris, Arnold

1983   "Music as Propaganda: Art at the Command of Doctrine in the People's Republic of China." *Ethnomusicology* 27 (1): 1–28.

Pescatello, Ann, ed.

1975   *The African in Latin America.* New York: University Press of America.

Pichardo, Esteban

1985   *Diccionario provincial y casi razonado de vozes y frases cubanas.* (Originally published 1875.) La Habana: Editorial de Ciencias Sociales.

Pick, Daniel
    1996   *Faces of Degeneration: A European Disorder, c. 1848–c. 1918.* Cambridge: Cambridge University Press.

Plessy, Homer Adolph
    1968   *Plessy vs. Ferguson Records and Briefs (1893–1895).* Washington, D.C.: Judd and Detweiler.

Pozo Fernández, Alberto
    1993   *Cuba y el turismo: Actualidad y perspectivas de nuestra industria turística.* La Habana: Editora Política.

Pryor, Andrea
    1999   "The House of Añá: Women and Batá." *Center for Black Music Research Digest* 12 (2): 6–8.

Rawley, James A.
    1981   *The Trans-Atlantic Slave Trade.* New York: W. W. Norton.

Rex, John, and David Mason, eds.
    1986   *Theories of Race and Ethnic Relations.* Cambridge: Cambridge University Press.

Ridenour, Robert C.
    1981   *Nationalism, Modernism, and Personal Rivalry in Nineteenth-Century Russian Music.* Ann Arbor: UMI Research Press.

Robbins, James
    1989   "Toward a Practical and Abstract Taxonomy of Cuban Music." *Ethnomusicology* 33 (3): 379–389.

Roca, Sergio G., ed.
    1988   *Socialist Cuba: Past Interpretations and Future Challenges.* Boulder, Colo.: Westview.

Roche Monteagudo, Rafael
    1925   *La policía y sus misterios.* (Originally published 1908.) La Habana: n.p.

Rosaldo, Renato
    1989   *Culture and Truth: The Remaking of Social Analysis.* Boston: Beacon Press.

Roseman, Marina
    1991   *Healing Sounds from the Malaysian Rainforest: Temiar Music and Medicine.* Berkeley: University of California Press.

Rowe, William, and Vivan Schelling
    1991   *Memory and Modernity: Popular Culture in Latin America.* London and New York: Verso.

Rubin, Vera, ed.
    1960   *Social and Cultural Pluralism in the Caribbean.* New York: New York Academy of Sciences.

Rubin, Vera, and Arthur Tuden, eds.
    1977   *Comparative Perspectives on Slavery in the New World Plantation Societies.* New York: New York Academy of Sciences.

Ruby, Jay

  1982   *A Crack in the Mirror: Reflexive Perspectives in Anthropology.* Philadelphia: University of Pennsylvania Press.

Sartre, Jean-Paul

  1962   *Huracán sobre el azucar.* Lima: Editorial Prometeo, Prensa Latina—Peru.

  1974   *Sartre on Cuba.* Westport, Conn.: Greenwood.

Saussure, Ferdinand de

  1983   *Course in General Linguistics.* (Originally compiled and published in 1962, from Saussure's 1906–1911 lectures.) Edited by Charles Bally and Albert Sechehaye. Translated by Roy Harris. London: Duckworth.

Sayre, Elizabeth

  2000   "Cuban Batá Drumming and Women Musicians: An Open Question." *Center for Black Music Research Digest* 13 (1): 12–15.

Schechner, Richard

  1983   *Performative Circumstances from the Avant Garde to Ramlila.* Calcutta: Seagull Books.

  1985   *Between Theatre and Anthropology.* Philadelphia: University of Pennsylvania Press.

Schechner, Richard, and Willa Appel, eds.

  1990   *By Means of Performance: Intercultural Studies of Theatre and Ritual.* Cambridge: Cambridge University Press.

Schwartz, Boris

  1972   *Music and Musical Life in Soviet Russia, 1917–1970.* New York: W. W. Norton.

Schwartz, Rosalie

  1997   *Pleasure Island: Tourism and Temptation in Cuba.* Lincoln: University of Nebraska Press.

Scott, Rebecca

  1985   *Slave Emancipation in Cuba: The Transition to Free Labor, 1860–1899.* Princeton: Princeton University Press.

Segato, Rita

  1993   "Okarilé: Yemoja's Icon Tune." *Latin American Music Review* 14 (1): 1–19.

Serviat, Pedro

  1980   *El problema negro en Cuba y su solución definitiva.* La Habana: Editora Política.

Shiloah, Amnon, and Erik Cohen

  1983   "The Dynamics of Change in Jewish Oriental Ethnic Music in Israel." *Ethnomusicology* 27 (2): 227–252.

Singer, Milton

  1972   *When a Great Tradition Modernizes: An Anthropological Approach to Indian Civilization.* New York: Praeger.

Smith, M. G.

    1986   "Pluralism, Race, and Ethnicity in Selected African Countries." In John Rex and David Mason, eds., *Theories of Race and Ethnic Relations*, pp. 187–225. Cambridge: Cambridge University Press.

Smith, Robert

    1976   *Kingdoms of the Yoruba.* London: Methuen.

Smith, Wayne S.

    1987   *The Closest of Enemies.* New York: W. W. Norton.

    1988   *Subject to Solution.* Boulder, Colo.: Lynne Rienner Publishers.

Steiner, Wendy, ed.

    1981   *The Sign in Music and Literature.* Austin: University of Texas Press.

Stoller, Paul

    1989a   *Fusion of the Worlds: An Ethnography of Possession among the Songhay of Niger.* Chicago: University of Chicago Press.

    1989b   *The Taste of Ethnographic Things: The Senses in Anthropology.* Philadelphia: University of Pennsylvania Press.

    1994   "Ethnographies as Texts/Ethnographers as Griots." *American Ethnologist* 21 (2): 353–366.

Stoller, Paul, and Cheryl Olkes

    1987   *In Sorcery's Shadow: A Memoir of Apprenticeship among the Songhay of Niger.* Chicago: University of Chicago Press.

Stubbs, Jean

    1989   *Cuba: The Test of Time.* London: Latin America Bureau.

Suchoff, Benjamin, ed.

    1976   *Béla Bartók Essays.* New York: St. Martin's.

Sulsbruck, Birger

    1982   *Latin-American Percussion: Rhythms and Rhythm Instruments from Cuba and Brazil.* Copenhagen: Den Rytmiske Aftenskoles Forlag/Edition Wilhem Hansen.

Sweet, Jill Drayson

    1983   "Ritual and Theatre in Tewa Ceremonial Performances." *Ethnomusicology* 27 (2): 253–269.

Szulc, Tad

    1986   *Fidel: A Critical Portrait.* New York: William Morrow.

Taber, Michael, ed.

    1983   *Fidel Castro Speeches: Cuba's Internationalist Foreign Policy, 1975–80.* New York: Pathfinder.

Taussig, Michael

    1987   *Shamanism, Colonialism, and the Wild Man: A Study of Terror and Healing.* Chicago: University of Chicago Press.

1993   *Mimesis and Alterity: A Particular History of the Senses.* New York and London: Routledge.

Tax, Sol, ed.

1952   *Acculturation in the Americas.* Chicago: University of Chicago Press.

Tertz, Abram (Andrei Sinyavsky)

1960   *On Socialist Realism.* Berkeley: University of California Press.

Thomas, Brook, ed.

1997   *Plessy v. Ferguson: A Brief History with Documents.* Boston, Mass.: Bedford Books.

Thomas, Hugh

1971   *Cuba: The Pursuit of Freedom.* New York: Harper & Row.

Thompson, Robert Farris

1966   "An Aesthetic of the Cool: West African Dance." *African Forum* 2 (2): 85–101.

1983   *Flash of the Spirit.* New York: Random House.

Thompson, Robert Farris, and Joseph Cornet

1981   *The Four Moments of the Sun: Kongo Art in Two Worlds.* Washington, D.C.: National Gallery of Art.

Titon, Jeff Todd

1980   "The Life Story." *Journal of American Folklore* 93:276–292.

1988   *Powerhouse for God: Speech, Chant, and Song in an Appalachian Baptist Church.* Austin: University of Texas Press.

1997   "Knowing People Making Music: An Epistemology for Fieldwork in Ethnomusicology, or How Do We Know What We Know?" In *Shadows in the Field: New Perspectives for Fieldwork in Ethnomusicology,* pp. 87–100. New York: Oxford University Press.

1999   " 'The Real Thing': Tourism, Authenticity, and Pilgrimage among the Old Regular Baptists at the 1997 Smithsonian Folklife Festival." *World of Music* 41 (3): 115–139.

Toelken, Barre

1979   *The Dynamics of Folklore.* Boston: Houghton Mifflin.

Turner, Victor

1968   *The Drums of Affliction.* Oxford: Oxford University Press.

1969   *The Ritual Process.* Chicago: Aldine Publishing Company.

1982   *Celebration: Studies in Festivity and Ritual.* Washington, D.C.: Smithsonian Institution Press.

Turner, Victor, and Edward Bruner, eds.

1986   *The Anthropology of Experience.* Urbana: University of Illinois Press.

Urrutía y Blanco, Carlos, ed.

1882   *Los criminales de Cuba y D. José Trujillo.* Barcelona: Fidel Giró Press.

Valdés, Nelson P.

1989   "La Cachita y el Che: Patron Saints of Revolutionary Cuba." *Arete Magazine* (May–June): n.p.

Valdés Garriz, Yrmino (Oriate)

1991   *Ceremonias fúnebres de la santería afrocubana*. San Juan: Sociedad de Autores Libres.

1995   *Dilogún*. La Habana: Ediciones Unión.

Vaughan William, Ralph

1987   *National Music and Other Essays*. 2d ed. Oxford: Oxford University Press.

Vélez, María Teresa

2000   *Drumming for the Gods: The Life and Times of Felipe García Villamil, Santero, Palero, and Abakuá*. Philadelphia: Temple University Press.

Verger, Pierre Fatumbi

1982   *Orisha: Les dieux Yorouba en Afrique et au Nouveau Monde*. Paris: Editions A. M. Métailié.

Villalba Garrido, Evaristo

1988   *Cuba y el turismo*. La Habana: Editorial de Ciencias Sociales.

Vinueza, María Elena

1986   *Presencia arará en la música folklórica de Matanzas*. La Habana: Casa de las Americas.

Waterman, Christopher

1990   "Our Tradition Is a Very Modern Tradition: Popular Music and the Construction of a Pan-Yoruba Identity." *Ethnomusicology* 34 (3): 367–379.

Weber, Max

1963   *The Sociology of Religion*. Translated by Ephraim Fischoff. Boston: Beacon Press.

Welmers, William E.

1973   *African Language Structures*. Berkeley: University of California Press.

Wenger, Suzanne (Adunni Olorisa)

1977   *The Timeless Mind of the Sacred: Its New Manifestation in the Osun Groves*. Ibadan: Institute of African Studies.

Whitehead, Tony Larry, and Mary Ellen Conaway, eds.

1986   *Self, Sex, and Gender in Cross-Cultural Fieldwork*. Urbana: University of Illinois Press.

Whitten Jr., Norman E., and John F. Szwed, eds.

1970   *Afro-American Anthropology*. New York: Free Press.

Wilcken, Lois

1991   Music Folklore among Haitians in New York: Staged Representations and the Negotiation of Identity. Ph.D. dissertation, Columbia University.

1998   "The Changing Hats of Haitian Staged Folklore in New York City." In Ray

Allen and Lois Wilcken, eds., *Island Sounds in the Global City,* pp. 162–183. New York: New York Folklore Society and Institute for Studies in American Music, Brooklyn College.

Wilcken, Lois, and Frisner Augustin

1992   *The Drums of Vodou.* Tempe, Ariz.: White Cliffs Media Company.

Zaretsky, Irving, and Mark P. Leone, eds.

1974   *Religious Movements in Contemporary America.* Princeton: Princeton University Press.

INDEX